WITHDRAWN
UTSA Libraries

D1615887

RENEWALS 458-4574

DATE DUE			
NOV 1 0 MAR 21			
MAY 0 5 MAY 06 2008			
AUG 19 OCT 13 2008			
SEP 23			
OCT 17			
NOV 01			
DEC 15			
MAY 10			
FEB 01			
GAYLORD			PRINTED IN U.S.A.

ORIGINS OF PHOBIAS AND ANXIETY DISORDERS: WHY MORE WOMEN THAN MEN?

ORIGINS OF PHOBIAS AND ANXIETY DISORDERS: WHY MORE WOMEN THAN MEN?

MICHELLE G. CRASKE

Department of Psychology, University of California,
Los Angeles, California, USA

2003

ELSEVIER

Amsterdam – Boston – Heidelberg – London – New York – Oxford
Paris – San Diego – San Francisco – Singapore – Sydney – Tokyo

Library
University of Texas
at San Antonio

ELSEVIER Ltd
The Boulevard, Langford Lane
Kidlington, Oxford OX5 1GB, UK

© 2003 Elsevier Ltd. All rights reserved.

This work is protected under copyright by Elsevier, and the following terms and conditions apply to its use:

Photocopying
Single photocopies of single chapters may be made for personal use as allowed by national copyright laws. Permission of the Publisher and payment of a fee is required for all other photocopying, including multiple or systematic copying, copying for advertising or promotional purposes, resale, and all forms of document delivery. Special rates are available for educational institutions that wish to make photocopies for non-profit educational classroom use.

Permissions may be sought directly from Elsevier's Science & Technology Rights Department in Oxford, UK: phone: (+44) 1865 843830, fax: (+44) 1865 853333, e-mail: permissions@elsevier.com. You may also complete your request on-line via the Elsevier homepage (http://www.elsevier.com), by selecting 'Customer Support' and then 'Obtaining Permissions'.

In the USA, users may clear permissions and make payments through the Copyright Clearance Center, Inc., 222 Rosewood Drive, Danvers, MA 01923, USA; phone: (+1) (978) 7508400, fax: (+1) (978) 7504744, and in the UK through the Copyright Licensing Agency Rapid Clearance Service (CLARCS), 90 Tottenham Court Road, London W1P 0LP, UK; phone: (+44) 207 631 5555; fax: (+44) 207 631 5500. Other countries may have a local reprographic rights agency for payments.

Derivative Works
Tables of contents may be reproduced for internal circulation, but permission of Elsevier is required for external resale or distribution of such material.
Permission of the Publisher is required for all other derivative works, including compilations and translations.

Electronic Storage or Usage
Permission of the Publisher is required to store or use electronically any material contained in this work, including any chapter or part of a chapter.

Except as outlined above, no part of this work may be reproduced, stored in a retrieval system or transmitted in any form or by any means, electronic, mechanical, photocopying, recording or otherwise, without prior written permission of the Publisher.
Address permissions requests to: Elsevier's Science & Technology Rights Department, at the phone, fax and e-mail addresses noted above.

Notice
No responsibility is assumed by the Publisher for any injury and/or damage to persons or property as a matter of products liability, negligence or otherwise, or from any use or operation of any methods, products, instructions or ideas contained in the material herein. Because of rapid advances in the medical sciences, in particular, independent verification of diagnoses and drug dosages should be made.

First edition 2003

Library of Congress Cataloging in Publication Data
A catalog record from the Library of Congress has been applied for.

British Library Cataloguing in Publication Data
A catalogue record from the British Library has been applied for.

ISBN: 0 08 044032 0

♾ The paper used in this publication meets the requirements of ANSI/NISO Z39.48-1992 (Permanence of Paper). Printed in The Netherlands.

Library
University of Texas
at San Antonio

Contents

To Robert and Margeaux

Preface

I had two main goals when writing this book. The first was to provide a comprehensive review of the factors that contribute to excessive fear and anxiety disorders. This necessitated coverage of research from various domains of psychology, including psychopathology, cognitive psychology, experimental psychology, neuroscience, and developmental psychology, particularly given my aim of understanding the trajectory of fear and anxiety across the life span. By so doing, I hope to have achieved an up-to-date synthesis of temperament and experience in the formative months and years of life and later anxiousness, and to have highlighted the many complementary and converging theories and findings. In addition, the literature review provides a useful resource for inquiring minds (although clearly not every published finding of relevance is cited) as well as a treatise for understanding excessive fear and anxiety.

The second main goal was to delve into the factors responsible for why more women then men suffer from excessive fear and anxiety; again with a developmental perspective in mind. A comprehensive overview, let alone model, for understanding the gender differences in anxiety disorders was sorely needed. I evaluated whether the risk factors for anxiety disorders are moderated by sex-typed variables, and/or whether sex-typed variables mediate risk for anxiety disorders. From my synthesis of the available literature across the various domains of psychology, I reached the conclusion that many of the variables that place individuals at risk for anxiety disorders are more strongly associated with being female than male, and that the expression of anxiety itself is strongly female sex linked. The details of this model are outlined herewith.

Overall, I attempted to provide an objective viewpoint and give due consideration to controversial issues in the literature. I propose an interactive layer model in which broad vulnerability factors contribute to more specific pathways to excessive fear and anxiety, which in turn strengthen broad vulnerabilities. Hence, there is a continuous drawing together of issues raised in one chapter with what is presented in preceding chapters as well as in the chapters to follow.

For me, the most intriguing concepts discussed throughout the book are as follows: that early experiences from the first few days and months of life may be critical for the development of prediction and control; that prediction and control are intricately tied with attentional processes, which in turn are linked with the ability to clearly discriminate between what is threatening and what is not; that females are more sensitive than males to facial expressions, and hence more vulnerable to vicarious acquisition of fears and the communication of impending danger; that females may be less reliant on their own internal cues and more reliant on social interpersonal cues than are males for judging emotional state and thus their emotional experiences; and that females may be both biologically and socially driven to avoid threat, but by so doing become more vulnerable to persistent anxiousness. Conversely, males are more prone to face threat, and thus are more often traumatized but by the same token more likely to overcome fears and learn active means of coping that decrease their vulnerability to excessive fear and anxiety.

Chapter 1

Features of Fear and Anxiety

This chapter sets the scene by providing an overview of anxiety disorders and associated forms of distress, and their developmental trajectory. Themes and issues that are relevant to the discussion throughout the ensuing chapters are introduced. For example, the evidence that early expression of circumscribed fear confers very little risk upon later emotional development introduces the notions that "fear" is distinct from "disorder" and the latter is mediated and moderated by an array of factors other than fear itself. A similar conclusion is made from the evidence that occasional symptoms of distress in adulthood carry little predictive value for the development of anxiety disorders without the additional influence of other risk factors. Females are at greater risk than males for anxiousness and anxiety disorders across all ages. The epidemiology of sex differences is reviewed in this chapter before concluding with an overview of the principal factors believed to contribute to anxiety disorders, thus providing a structure for the chapters to follow.

Prevalence of Anxiety Disorders and Associated Forms of Emotional Distress

Diagnostic Criteria

The anxiety disorders refer to a cluster of fears and anxieties that persist at a level that interferes with normal functioning. The American Psychiatric Association (*Diagnostic and Statistical Manual of Mental Disorders*, 4th edition (DSM-IV)) provides a convenient way of categorizing the major types of anxiety disorders, but quickly evident are the commonalities among them. That is, the anxiety disorders all involve fear, anxiety, worry, and avoidant or corrective behaviors. They differ from each other in the primary object of threat. In brief, panic disorder refers to recurrent unexpected panic attacks accompanied by persistent apprehension over their recurrence or their consequences. Panic disorder may occur with or without agoraphobia, which refers to anxiety about places or situations from which escape might be difficult or help not available in the event of a panic attack. Agoraphobia without a history of panic disorder refers to the same situational anxiety but in the absence of full-blown panic attacks. Generalized anxiety disorder refers to excessive and uncontrollable worry about a number of different life events and accompanying symptoms of motor tension and vigilance.

Social phobia (or social anxiety disorder) represents excessive fear of social or performance situations in which embarrassment might occur. Obsessive–compulsive disorder refers to recurrent intrusive thoughts, images or impulses (obsessions) and/or repetitive behaviors designed to prevent or lessen distress (compulsions) that are time-consuming or cause distress or impairment. Posttraumatic stress disorder refers to a set of symptoms following exposure to a traumatic event at which time intense fear, helplessness, or horror is experienced; the symptoms include re-experiencing of the trauma, avoidance of associated stimuli, and increased arousal. Specific phobia refers to marked and persistent fear of clearly discernible and circumscribed objects or situations. Other anxiety disorders include acute stress disorder, and anxiety disorders due to medical conditions or substance abuse.

Prevalence

Epidemiological studies of adult community samples indicate that anxiety disorders are one of the most commonly occurring forms of psychological disturbance. The National Comorbidity Survey (NCS; Kessler, Davis, & Kendler, 1997) is the most recent large-scale epidemiological study of mental health in the United States, superceding the earlier Epidemiological Catchment Area Study (ECA) published in 1984 (Myers *et al.*, 1984). NCS findings of diagnostic prevalence are based on an earlier version of DSM (third edition — revised (DSM-III-R); American Psychiatric Association, 1987) and slightly different diagnostic criteria for some of the anxiety disorders in comparison with DSM-IV. Nonetheless, from the NCS community sample of 8098, aged 15–54 years, approximately 29 percent reportedly met criteria for a lifetime history of at least one anxiety disorder, and that was without diagnosing obsessive–compulsive disorder. Although this rate is derived from a fully structured instrument (the Composite International Diagnostic Interview) that was administered by lay interviewers, and therefore is susceptible to error, the figure is comparable to the rate for substance-use-related disorders (27 percent) and higher than the rate for lifetime history of mood disorders (20 percent) obtained from the same diagnostic instrument. Weissman *et al.* (1994) examined prevalence of obsessive–compulsive disorder across seven different countries, to find a lifetime range of 1.9–2.5 percent. Thus, the NCS figure of 29 percent may well be an underestimate of the actual rate of anxiety disorders in total given the likelihood of at least some non-overlapping cases of obsessive–compulsive disorder. Moreover, the upper age limit of 54 years in the NCS sample may lead to a further underestimate of the prevalence of anxiety disorders in the adult population.

Co-occurring Distress

Anxiety disorders cluster with various forms of emotional distress. They tend to co-occur not only with other anxiety disorders, but also with mood disorders, substance-use-related disorders, somatoform disorders and personality disorders. From the NCS community sample, 74 percent of those who met criteria for an anxiety disorder also met criteria for at least one lifetime co-occurring mental disorder (Kessler, 1997). Similar rates are apparent in patient samples, where from 50 to 80 percent of adults with a principal diagnosis of an anxiety disorder meet criteria for at least one other concurrent mental disorder diagnosis (e.g., Brown & Barlow, 1992; Brown, Chorpita, & Barlow, 1998; Flick, Roy-Byrne, Cowley, Shores, & Dunner, 1993; Kessler, Nelson, McGonagle, Liu, Swartz, & Blazer, 1996; Kessler, 1997; Rief, Hiller, Geissner, & Fichter, 1995; Westermeyer, Tucker, & Nugent, 1995). In the most recent report of 1127 adults seeking help for anxiety or mood disorders, Brown, Campbell, Lehman, Grisham, and Mancill (2001) reported current and lifetime rates of co-occurrence with other Axis I disorders as 57 and 81 percent, respectively. As with previous data sets, other anxiety or mood disorders accounted for most of the co-occurring distress. Differential patterns of clustering existed among the disorders. For example, high rates of co-occurrence existed for posttraumatic stress disorder, major depression/ dysthymia, and generalized anxiety disorder (Brown *et al.*, 2001). Particularly strong associations occurred between panic disorder/agoraphobia and posttraumatic stress disorder, between social phobia and mood disorders, and between posttraumatic stress disorder and mood disorders (Brown *et al.*, 2001).

The study of clustering amongst anxiety disorders and mood disorders may provide important insights into etiological factors and common pathways for emotional distress. However, the specific relationships among disorders are dependent on the sample studied, the diagnoses assessed, and the method of diagnostic assessment. For instance, the NCS community sample analyzed by Kessler (1997) and the patient sample analyzed by Brown *et al.* (2001) yielded significantly different patterns of co-occurrence. The most likely reason for this discrepancy is that the former included a considerably larger subset with posttraumatic stress disorder than the Brown *et al.* (2001) study, excluded obsessive–compulsive disorder that was included in the Brown *et al.* (2001) study, and was based on a fully structured lay-administered interview, compared with the semi-structured clinician-administered interview in the Brown *et al.* (2001) study.

Nonetheless, regardless of specific clustering weights, the overall high rate of co-occurrence among anxiety and mood disorders raises the possibility of shared etiological factors. Indeed, common vulnerability factors may explain why family transmission studies show increased risks for depression and substance abuse in relatives of probands with anxiety disorders who themselves do not suffer from anxiety (e.g., Biederman *et al.*, 2001; Chassin, Pitts, DeLucia, & Todd, 1999).

Anxiety Disorders in Youths

Diagnostic Issues

Although certain anxiety disorders do not become full fledged until adulthood, some youths are afflicted with excessive anxiety, and some anxiety disorders typically emerge during childhood years (e.g., separation anxiety disorder, and specific phobias of animals and blood, injury, and injection). Systematic diagnostic criteria for anxiety disorders in youths did not emerge until DSM-III (American Psychiatric Association, 1980). Significant changes have since been made, such that the only remaining childhood anxiety disorder in the current nosology (DSM-IV; American Psychiatric Association, 1994) is separation anxiety disorder. Other youth anxiety disorders are subsumed under adult disorders, for which diagnostic criteria have been revised to include descriptors for children and adolescents. This change represents an emphasis upon continuity of anxiety disorders in children and adults (Allen, Leonard, & Swedo, 1995), a point re-emphasized below. Unlike adults, children are not required to acknowledge that their fears are unreasonable or excessive, and persistence of symptoms is required for at least 6 months for specific and social phobias in order to minimize the overdiagnosis of transitory, normal developmental fears.

Separation anxiety disorder is characterized by excessive anxiety and fear concerning separation from home or from significant attachment figures, to a degree that is beyond normal developmental expectations (i.e., 7 months to 6 years old; Bernstein & Borchardt, 1991). Overanxious disorder of childhood/adolescence, which is now subsumed under the diagnosis of generalized anxiety disorder, is characterized by excessive and uncontrollable worry and symptoms of motor tension and vigilance (although children are required to report only one symptom, in comparison with three symptoms for adults). Mean ages of onset for youths range from 5 to 10 years, although estimates for adult samples average the early 20s (Öst & Treffers, 2001). Thus, as with other anxiety disorders, the modal ages of onset differ between youth and adult samples. This discrepancy may be due to a number of factors, including reporting errors, given that much age of onset data is gathered from retrospective recall. Alternatively, as reviewed below, clusters of anxiety symptoms tend to shift throughout childhood and early adolescence, and stabilize in later adolescence and adulthood, such that ages of onset for a given anxiety disorder may well vary across different age cohorts. Avoidant disorder of childhood/adolescence is now subsumed under social phobia, and because it was conceptualized as excessive withdrawal from unfamiliar people, the diagnostic criteria for social phobia have been expanded to include fears of unfamiliar people as well as fears of social evaluation. The modal age of onset for social phobia in youths varies from 8 to 12 years of age (Weiss & Last, 2001), compared with the late teens in adult samples (Öst & Treffers, 2001). Symptoms of obsessive–compulsive disorder in youths are similar to adult symptoms, although children tend to experience fewer obsessions and more compulsions (e.g., Rapoport, Swedo, & Leonard, 1992). The mean age of onset in youth samples is 10 years (Albano, Chorpita, & Barlow, 1996), compared with the late teens in adult samples (Öst & Treffers, 2001). Several descriptors are altered for childhood posttraumatic stress disorder. For example, children may demonstrate their anxiety through repetitive play in which themes of the trauma are expressed. Naturally, posttraumatic stress disorder has no average age of onset. Common specific phobias include fear of heights, darkness, loud noises, injections, insects, dogs and other small animals, and school (Silverman & Rabian, 1994). Many of these begin before the age of 7 years, and elevations occur between the ages of 10 and 13 years (Strauss & Last, 1993). In adult samples, animal, blood, injury, and injection phobias are cited as developing around 8 years of age, whereas situational phobias develop during the 20s (Öst & Treffers, 2001).

Several investigators have studied panic attacks in youths. Hayward *et al.* (1992) examined 754 sixth- and seventh-grade girls, to find that 5.3 percent of the sample reported at least one panic attack. Interestingly, the incidence increased with sexual maturity, regardless of age. King, Gullone, Tonge, and Ollendick (1993) also examined the incidence of panic attacks in a group of 534 adolescents aged 13–18 years. Almost 43 percent reported having a panic attack at some stage in their lives. However, as with adult samples in the general population, the vast majority was not perturbed by these experiences, and only 6.8 percent indicated that the panics created "quite a bit or very much" interference in their lives. What proportion of these panic attacks were "out of the blue" is not clear. Nelles and Barlow (1988) argued that without the cognitive capacity for attributions of losing control or going crazy about bodily sensations, children are unlikely to have unexpected panic attacks. Indeed, youths referred to an anxiety disorders clinic did not endorse fears of bodily sensations if under the age of 12 years (Chorpita, Albano, & Brown, 1996a). Thus, panic symptoms that occur prior to adolescence are most often an associated feature of another anxiety disorder, such as separation anxiety, rather than unexpected panic attacks that are characteristic of panic disorder (Last, Perrin, Hersen, & Kazdin, 1992).

Prevalence and Co-occurring Distress

Unfortunately, our knowledge of the prevalence of anxiety disorders among youths is hampered by a lack of well-conducted research, differing criteria, and inconsistencies in reliance upon parental report in the absence of confirmatory child report or vice versa. Thus, estimates of prevalence for anxiety disorders in youths vary greatly. In community samples, they range from 10.7 percent (McGee, Fehan, Williams, Partridge, Silva, & Kelly, 1990) to 17.3 percent (Kashani & Orvaschel, 1990). In the most recent study of 1200 Canadian adolescents, the prevalence was estimated at 14 percent (Romano, Tremblay, Vitaro, Zoccolillo, & Pagani, 2001). Estimates for separation anxiety disorder alone similarly vary, ranging from 2 to 12 percent in community youth samples (e.g., Bowen, Offord, & Boyle, 1990; Kashani & Orvaschel, 1990). Notably, the overall prevalence for anxiety disorders appears to be less in youths than in adults: rates for anxiety and depression increase from 11 to 21 years of age (e.g., Newman *et al.*, 1996). For example, in their prospective database of an unselected birth cohort of approximately 1000 from Dunedin, New Zealand (referred to herein as the Dunedin Multidisciplinary Study), McGee, Feehan, Williams, and Anderson (1992) reported prevalence rates for anxiety disorders (excluding obsessive–compulsive disorder) of 5.3 percent at the age of 11 years and 8.7 percent at the age of 15 years. Closer examination reveals different profiles of prevalence for different anxiety disorders. Separation anxiety disorder, for example, generally declines in prevalence from 11 to 15 years of age (McGee, Feehan, Williams, & Anderson, 1992), although rates may resurge in later adolescence (Kashani & Orvaschel, 1990). In contrast, the prevalence for specific phobia increased from 1.7 to 3.1 percent from 11 to 15 years of age (McGee *et al.*, 1992). The same was true for overanxious disorder (2.5–5.2 percent) (McGee *et al.*, 1992), although this may decline again in a slightly older age range as another study reported rates of 19 percent in 9–12-year-olds compared with 12.7 percent in 13–18-year-olds (Velez, Johnson, & Cohen, 1989). The replicability of these exact figures is questionable, but the general trends for separation anxiety disorder to decline and other anxiety disorders to increase over adolescence appear robust.

As with adults, high rates of co-occurrence exist among the anxiety and mood disorders in youth samples. For example, co-occurring anxiety disorders are found for up to 39 percent of children with an anxiety disorder in community samples (Anderson, Williams, McGee, & Silva, 1987; Kashani & Orvaschel, 1990; Newman *et al.*, 1996), and youths with depression are likely to meet criteria for anxiety as well (Last, Strauss, & Francis, 1987).

Continuity of Anxiety Disorders

Assessment of the course of anxiety from childhood throughout adolescence and into adulthood is complicated by methodological inconsistencies and the effects of treatment. That is, to study an untreated youth sample over long periods of time is an almost impossible if not unethical task, and thus many studies of the course of anxiety derive from clinic-based treated samples. Several prospective longitudinal studies of community samples exist, but treatment effects are rarely reported let alone factored into the variance for explaining the course of anxiety in such studies. That being said, extrapolation from extant data suggests that specific anxiety symptom clusters tend to shift and even remit throughout childhood and early adolescence. For example, from the Dunedin Multidisciplinary Study, nearly two-thirds of those reporting clinically significant fears at the age of 13 years did not report those same fears at the age of 15 years (Poulton *et al.*, 1997). In addition, only one-quarter of 4–12-year-olds with an "emotional disorder", defined as elements of overanxious disorder, obsessive–compulsive disorder and affective disorder, were similarly categorized 4 years later in the Ontario Child Health Study (Offord *et al.*, 1992).

On the other hand, several other pieces of evidence indicate that although symptoms may shift, the syndrome of anxiety is retained in one form or another for a substantial proportion of youths as they mature. Beidel, Fink, and Turner (1996) monitored a group of 7–12-year-olds ($n = 150$) over a period of 6 months. Initially, 21 percent met criteria for an anxiety disorder diagnosis. Although shifting in symptom status was very common even within this short interval of time, anxious children tended to exhibit continuing anxiety. For example, of 12 children initially diagnosed with social phobia, only 8 percent had no diagnostic features 6 months later: 33 percent still met criteria for social phobia, 41 percent continued to endorse social fears but did not meet diagnostic criteria (i.e., subthreshold), and 16 percent were newly diagnosed with overanxious disorder. Of 12 children initially diagnosed with overanxious disorder, 25 percent had no diagnostic features; 50 percent still met criteria, and 25 percent were newly diagnosed with social phobia 6 months later. Notably, 39 percent of the group that initially did not meet criteria for any disorder exhibited subthreshold features of either social phobia or overanxious disorder 6 months later, indicative of the commonality of anxious *symptoms* throughout childhood. Often these symptoms are transient, but symptoms that persist over a sufficiently long period of time may develop into an anxiety disorder. For example, prodromal symptoms among unselected youths, especially when exhibiting an "increasing" pattern over a 4 year period, predict onset of internalizing disorders at 15 or 16 years of age (Rueter, Scaramella, Wallace, & Conger, 1999).

The emergence of different types of anxiety and mood disorders over time is also seen in samples of treated youths. For example, in their re-examination of clinic-referred children after a 3 year interval, Cantwell and Baker (1989) found that whereas 71 percent of young children initially diagnosed with avoidant disorder, 89 percent with separation anxiety disorder, and 75 percent with overanxious disorder no longer met diagnostic criteria for their entrance disorder, the majority met criteria for a different disorder. Berg *et al.* (1989) also found that whereas only 31 percent of 16 adolescents with obsessive–compulsive disorder still met criteria for that diagnosis 2 years later, 56 percent had additional mood and anxiety disorders. In another study of 54 children treated for obsessive–compulsive disorder who were assessed on average 3.4 years later, 43 percent continued to meet criteria for obsessive–compulsive disorder, and 96 percent had developed additional diagnoses (Leonard *et al.*, 1993). Last, Perrin, Hersen, and Kazdin (1996) found that 3–4 years following initial diagnosis of clinic-referred children and adolescents, the majority of whom were treated, 82 percent no longer met criteria for their initial anxiety disorder: separation anxiety disorder had the highest recovery rate (96 percent), and specific phobia the lowest (69 percent). However, as with the prior studies, albeit not as pronounced, a proportion (30 percent) developed new psychiatric disorders, and half of these developed new anxiety disorders. Together, these data suggest that although instability in the severity and specific type of anxiety disorder exists, anxious children and adolescents often retain some form of emotional distress over time.

Durability of anxiety disorders may increase with the age of the sample. For example, in the Canadian sample of 8–16-year-olds, only 33.1 percent with an "emotional disorder" had a history of either emotional, conduct, or hyperactivity disorder 4 years earlier (Offord *et al.*, 1992). Similarly, only 42 percent of 15-year-olds retained their anxiety disorder that was diagnosed when they were 11 years old in the Dunedin Multidisciplinary Study (McGee *et al.*, 1992). In fact, 81 percent of those with an anxiety disorder at the age of 15 years did not have an anxiety disorder at the age of 11 years. In contrast with these youth samples, only 38.5 percent of 21-year-olds from the same Dunedin sample did not meet diagnostic criteria for an anxiety disorder during adolescence (11, 13, 15, or 18-year-olds). In addition, the percentage of incident anxiety disorder cases at the age of 21 years that emerged in the *absence* of any type of emotional distress throughout adolescence was only 19.5 percent, lower than the rate for mood disorders (27.9 percent). Other follow-up studies similarly lead to the conclusion that anxiety disorders during adolescence result in a high risk of anxiety disorders during adulthood (e.g., Pine, Cohen, Gurley, Brook, & Ma, 1998), including obsessive–compulsive disorder (Berg *et al.*, 1989). In comparison with the childhood samples, these data suggest a pattern of stabilization with age. More direct evidence was reported by Agras, Chapin, and Oliveau (1972), who found that 100 percent of phobic children and adolescents had improved (60 percent) or recovered (40 percent) by 5 years later, whereas only 43 percent of those aged 20 years or more had improved (37 percent) or recovered (6 percent) over the same interval of time, and 37 percent worsened. Unfortunately, this study was hampered by small cell sizes (10 youths, 20 adults), and closer examination of the data indicates that many of the improved youths continued to have significant phobic problems (Ollendick, 1979). Nonetheless, prospective evaluation of older adult samples indicates that anxiety disorders are enduring, despite waxing and waning of symptoms in relation to ongoing stressors (Mackinnon, Henderson, & Andrews, 1990). For example, remission from anxiety disorders ($n = 77$) was estimated at only 17–30 percent from the Munich Follow-up Study of a large community sample followed from 1974 to 1981 (Wittchen, 1988), and from their review of community studies Angst and Vollrath (1991) concluded that recovery rates ranged from 12 to 25 percent only for generalized anxiety disorder and panic disorder. Interestingly, phobic symptoms are more stable than other symptoms of anxiety (Tyrer, Alexander, Remington, & Riley, 1987), perhaps due to the self-perpetuating effects of phobic avoidance, described in more detail in Chapter 5. The fact that many of the adult anxiety disorders begin in childhood and adolescence (especially specific phobias, social phobia, obsessive–compulsive disorder, and panic disorder) in and of itself represents their longevity. The general consensus is that, without treatment, anxiety disorders in adult populations tend to be chronic or recurrent (Angst & Vollrath, 1991; Wittchen, 1988; Yonkers, Dyck, & Keller, 2001). Still, the notion of progressive continuity with age is mostly extrapolated from various sources, and direct comparisons of age-dependent remission rates throughout childhood, adolescence, and adulthood are yet to be conducted. Furthermore, whereas these findings suggest that much of adult anxiety originates in childhood and adolescence, it is equally important to remember that youth anxiety disorders neither guarantee the development of adult anxiety nor are necessary for adult anxiety. The imperfect relation between childhood and adult anxiety epitomizes the complex and interactive array of factors that contribute to anxious psychopathology.

The Impact of Anxiety

Several cross-sectional studies of diagnostic history indicate that anxiety disorders often predate co-occurring conditions. In 62 percent of cases of lifetime major depression in the NCS community database, depression was secondary to other disorders, most of which were anxiety disorders (68 percent) (Kessler *et al.*, 1996). Even in selected samples of anxious and depressed youths aged 8–13 years, anxiety preceded major depression two-thirds of the time (Kovacs, Gatsonis, Paulauskas, & Richards, 1989). (In contrast to major depression, dysthymia was more likely to predate than follow anxiety disorders. Conceivably, dysthymia is closely tied to a broad-based negative affect that represents vulnerability for both anxiety and depression.) Similarly, co-occurring anxiety disorders predate the onset of eating disorders in most cases (anorexia 75 percent, bulimia 88 percent) (Godart, Flament, Lecrubier, & Jeammet, 2000), and are more likely to precede than follow substance disorders (Burke, Burke,

& Rae, 1994; Merikangas, Dierker, & Szatmari, 1998). Phobic disorders, in particular, tend to predate alcohol abuse/dependence (Swendsen *et al.*, 1998).

Not only do anxiety disorders precede other disorders but their developmentally earlier manifestation *predicts* later forms of distress. Specifically, anxiety symptoms predict later development of depressive symptoms in school-aged children (Cole, Peeke, Martin, Truglio, & Seroczynski, 1998), panic attacks predict the onset of depression in adolescents (Hayward, Killen, Kraemer & Taylor, 2000), anxiety disorders in adolescence predict depression in early adulthood (Pine *et al.*, 1998), and panic and anxiety disorders predict later depression in adult community samples (Kessler *et al.*, 1998; Stein *et al.*, 2001). Finally, anxiety and depression may even contribute to substance-use-related disorders, given that, along with other peer factors, they predict initiation of smoking in adolescents (Patton *et al.*, 1998).

In summary, anxiety disorders are common in youth and adult populations. Although the symptom clusters of anxiety disorders tend to shift throughout childhood, anxious youths often remain vulnerable to anxiety or other forms of emotional distress, and the majority of young adults with anxiety disorders exhibit anxiety disorders throughout adolescence. Childhood anxiety disorders neither are necessary nor guarantee adult anxiety disorders, but, nevertheless, they appear to increase the risk of later distress, and this risk may increase the older the individual or the longer the anxiety disorders have persisted. The finding that anxiety disorders co-occur with other forms of emotional distress, particularly depressed mood, raises the possibility of shared vulnerability factors. Moreover, the fact that anxiety disorders precede and even predict later depressed mood suggests that anxiety disorders may be an earlier developmental manifestation of a shared vulnerability. The distress of early anxiousness may even strengthen shared predisposing temperamental features and thereby increase the likelihood of other later manifestations of the same broad vulnerability. In general, this is referred to as a complication or scar hypothesis (see Clark, Watson, & Mineka, 1994). In this model, early anxiety may not only signify but also directly increase the risk for later depression.

Normal versus Abnormal Fear and Anxiety

Fears in Childhood

Anxiety disorders clearly are different from fears of circumscribed objects or situations. Such fears are very common in youths, even at very young ages. In their sample of 4–12-year-olds, Muris, Merckelbach, Gadet, and Moulaert (2000) found that 75.8 percent reported such fears. General fearfulness tended to peak around 7–9 years of age and then decrease (Muris *et al.*, 2000). The content of fears varies with age, shifting from tangible, immediate fears to less tangible, anticipatory fears (Scherer & Nakamura, 1968). Ollendick, Yule, and Ollier (1991) attribute such changes to developing cognitive abilities to recognize and understand dangers in different situations. Thus, during infancy, children fear stimuli within their immediate environment, such as loud noises, objects, and strangers, with fear of separation from caretakers, animals, and the dark emerging during toddler years (Miller, Barrett, & Hampe, 1974). By 5–6 years of age, fears shift to robbers, supernatural creatures, and being left alone (Bowlby, 1973). With further development, fears shift to anticipatory events and abstract stimuli (Field & Davey, 2001). Using the Fear Survey Schedule for Children, Ollendick and King (1991) found that 8–11-year-olds feared items in the following order: not being able to breathe, being hit by a car, bombing attacks, burning in a fire, falling from a high place, burglary, earthquake, death, illness, and snakes. Using a free option method of assessment instead of a checklist, Muris, Merckelbach, and Collaris (1997) obtained somewhat different and perhaps more generalizable results for 9–13-year-olds. Specifically, fears of animals were the most common, followed by fears of the unknown, danger and death, medical fears, and fear of failure and criticism. In general, social fears begin to predominate over the course of adolescence (Gullone & King, 1993, 1997).

By virtue of being so common, fears of circumscribed objects or situations are considered developmentally appropriate and even innate. Moreover, Ollendick *et al.* (1991) view such fears as adaptive because they constitute protective responses to stimuli that are neither comprehensible nor controllable. That is, fears develop as the child is increasingly able to perceive potential dangers in different situations but has not yet advanced to the point of understanding the situation fully, nor being able to exercise control over the situation. Although developmentally appropriate and adaptive, these fears are not necessarily without associated distress or interference with daily activities. Hence, significant proportions of unselected youth samples report avoidance behaviors and functional interference related to their fears (McCathie & Spence, 1991; Ollendick & King, 1994). Muris *et al.* (2000) examined to what extent fears of 290 unselected children aged 8–13 years were related to clinically significant anxiety disorders by using a semi-structured diagnostic interview. They found that the reported fears represented subclinical anxiety disorders in 49 percent of children, and significant anxiety disorders in 23 percent of children. These data beg the question of what accounts for the shift from transient, developmentally appropriate fears to persistent and impairing fears and anxiety — or anxiety disorders.

The number and/or intensity of childhood fears correlate with general anxiety in children (Scherer & Nakamura, 1968), and high levels of toddler fearfulness of novelty and strangers are associated with increased rates of anxiety disorders in later childhood (e.g., Hirshfeld *et al.*, 1992). Such excessive fearfulness is conceptualized as a behaviorally inhibited temperament, the evidence for which is reviewed in detail in Chapter 3. Similarly, shyness has been associated with subsequent anxious behaviors (Stemberger, Turner, Beidel, & Calhoun, 1995). Caspi, Henry, McGee, Moffitt and Silva (1995) found that boys who were confident and eager to explore novel situations at 5 years of age were less likely to manifest anxiety in childhood and adolescence, whereas passive, shy, fearful and avoidant girls from the ages of 3 to 5 years were likely to exhibit anxiety at later stages. Thus, *excessiveness* of developmentally appropriate fears (i.e., fears of strangers and novelty) represented in traits such as behavioral inhibition and shyness is a likely risk factor, but the vulnerability to anxiety disorders encompasses additional factors, and, as reviewed in the chapters to follow, involves a complex dynamic between temperament and environmental influences.

Symptoms in Adulthood

Just as most youths experience circumscribed fears, much of the adult population reports occasional or mild symptoms of fear and anxiety. Anywhere from 25 to 85 percent of the adult population experiences occasional intrusive thoughts (e.g., Rachman & de Silva, 1978; Salkovskis & Harrison, 1984), compulsive behaviors (e.g., Muris, Merckelbach, & Clavan, 1997), panic attacks (e.g., Norton, Cox, & Malan, 1992; Telch, Lucas, & Nelson, 1989), public speaking anxiety and other social fears (Caspi, Elder, & Bem, 1988; Stein, Walker & Forde, 1996), worry (e.g., Roemer, Molina, & Borkovec, 1997), as well as specific fears of circumscribed objects (Agras & Jacob, 1981). Adults with occasional ("non-clinical") symptoms appear to be somewhat more likely to develop anxiety disorders than those who do not endorse such symptoms. For example, individuals who occasionally panic (including those with a specific phobia or no anxiety disorders) are more likely to develop panic disorder over the course of a year than control participants who never panic (15 versus 2 percent, respectively) (Ehlers, 1995). Similarly, in our sample of college students, 13.6 percent of those with occasional panic attacks and moderately high anxiety sensitivity (i.e., the tendency to believe that symptoms of anxiety are harmful) developed panic disorder over a 6 month interval (Gardenswartz & Craske, 2001). This rate is considerably higher than incidence rates for panic disorder in unselected community samples. Others have shown that subclinical symptoms are associated with increased risk of obsessive–compulsive disorder (Berg *et al.*, 1989), albeit with a very small sample, and not replicated in a younger sample (Valleni-Basile *et al.*, 1996).

Moreover, the presence of internalizing symptoms in general predicts later disorders of anxiety and depression. As mentioned already, persistent anxiety symptoms predict the onset of internalizing disorders during middle adolescence (Rueter *et al.*, 1999). Murphy *et al.* (1989) examined subclinical features in an adult sample in 1952 and incident "cases" of anxiety and depression in the same sample 16 years later. The percentage who met the criteria for an incident anxiety disorder (excluding anxiety comorbid with depression) increased from 3 percent among those having no internalizing symptoms 16 years earlier to 9.3 percent among those with "conceivable" internalizing disorder, to 16.9 percent among those with a "borderline" internalizing disorder. No doubt these incident rates would be higher if co-occurring depression were included. In addition, Eaton, Badawi, and Melton (1995) reported evidence for a prodromal build up of symptoms spanning months and years before the onset of anxiety disorders. Even sleep disturbance is associated with the later development of anxiety, depression, and substance abuse (Gillin, 1998).

Nonetheless, it is equally important to note that just as the majority of developmentally appropriate fears in childhood remit, the majority of subclinical manifestations of fear and anxiety in adulthood remain subclinical or remit. For example, in the 16 year follow-up study by Murphy *et al.* (1989), 54 percent of those classified initially as "borderline" cases for either anxiety or depression improved, and an additional 18 percent remained "borderline"; only 28 percent shifted to the "disorder" category. Similarly, 43 percent of those classified initially as "conceivable" improved and 30 percent remained "conceivable"; only 26 percent shifted to a more severe category. Also telling in this regard is that almost 85 percent of those with occasional panic attacks do *not* progress to panic disorder, at least within a year's interval (Ehlers, 1995; Gardenswartz & Craske, 2001). Thus, occasional anxious symptoms are quite common throughout adulthood, but in and of themselves pose a relatively small risk for the later development of anxiety disorders.

Just as with the transition from normal fears to anxiety disorders in childhood, the transition from occasional symptoms to excessive and impairing fear and anxiety in adulthood presumably is influenced by a myriad of vulnerability, maturational, and life experience factors. Moreover, such risk factors may strengthen over time in an unfolding dynamic, thereby accounting for the insidious course of development of many anxiety disorders as exemplified in the studies of prodromal symptoms. These factors are the topics of the chapters to follow. Of particular interest is the contribution of each of these factors to sex differences in fear and anxiety. The epidemiological data on sex differences are presented next, but the pathways through which females acquire greater risk are addressed in Chapter 8.

Sex and Anxiety Disorders

Sex Differences in Adults

Epidemiological research has established that females are more at risk than males for fear and anxiety (Bourdon *et al.*, 1988). For example, women score higher than men on scales such as the Fear Survey Schedule (e.g., Kaloupek, Peterson, & Levis, 1981; Kirkpatrick, 1984). An interesting exception is fears of public speaking or social-evaluative situations, where men report just as many fears as women (e.g., Klorman, Hastings, Weerts, Melamed, & Lang, 1974). In addition, women are more at risk than men for most anxiety disorders (Weissman & Merikangas, 1986). The sex ratio for anxiety disorders was at least 2:1 (female:male) in the Zurich study (Angst & Dobler-Mikola, 1985). From the NCS study (Kessler *et al.*, 1994), lifetime prevalence rates for any anxiety disorder, excluding obsessive–compulsive and posttraumatic stress disorders, were 30.5 percent for females and 19.2 percent for males. As found in the earlier ECA study, and mirroring results from self-report scales, female-to-male discrepancies were least apparent for social phobia. One year prevalence rates from the Ontario Health Study, which excluded obsessive–compulsive disorder and posttraumatic stress disorder, were 15.5 percent for females and 8.9 percent for males (Offord *et al.*, 1996). Obsessive–compulsive disorder is somewhat more evenly distributed between the sexes (e.g., Breslau, Chilcoat, Peterson, & Schultz, 2000; Karno & Golding, 1991), but there are large sex differences in the case of posttraumatic stress disorder. Results from the NCS data set indicated lifetime prevalence rates for posttraumatic stress disorder of 10.4 percent for women and 5.0 percent for men (Kessler *et al.*, 1995), again replicating findings from the earlier ECA study where the prevalence was approximately twofold higher in women than men (Helzer, Robins, & McEvoy, 1987).

Females are more likely than males to suffer depression in combination with anxiety disorders. For example, in their examination of a large series of 1051 patients, Ochoa, Beck, and Steer (1992) found that the rates for pure anxiety disorders were almost equivalent among female and male patients (9.1 and 7 percent, respectively), whereas the rates for anxiety disorders co-occurring with secondary mood disorders were proportionately higher among female patients (14.9 percent) than male patients (9.3 percent). Greater co-occurrence between anxiety and depression for females has been reported by others as well (Chambless & Mason, 1986; Scheibe & Albus, 1992), although it was not found in a sample of socially phobic individuals (Yonkers *et al.*, 2001). Whether the elevated depression in general results from greater anxiety in females (as suggested in a retrospective study by Breslau *et al.*, 2000) represents a heightened vulnerability to all forms of negative affect is unknown.

Sex differences are not attributable to females being more likely than males to seek help for their anxiety, given that the prevalence data are derived from non-treatment-seeking community samples. In addition, Pollard, Pollard, and Corn (1989) found the same ratio of females to males among anxiety-disordered individuals who did not seek help versus those who did seek help (although, as addressed later, the same is not true for youth samples). For these reasons, epidemiologists note that once a phobia has become established, males seem no different from females in seeking professional help (Bourdon *et al.*, 1988). On the other hand, clinicians may be biased toward viewing females as more anxious than males, in line with social stereotypes and expectations. For example, Oei, Wanstall, and Evans (1990) found sex differences in clinician-rated scales of symptomatology for agoraphobia despite the absence of differences between males and females in self-reported symptomatology. These social influences are revisited in the discussion of emotion regulation and gender role socialization in Chapter 8.

Sex Differences in Youths

Sex differences in fear ratings are apparent as early as 9–12 years of age, when the average number of fears endorsed (of at least mild intensity) is close to 50 for girls and 40 for boys (Ollendick, 1983; Scherer & Nakamura, 1968). In a slightly older group (8–16-year-olds), the average number of at least moderate fears was 18 for girls and 10 for boys (King *et al.*, 1989). In addition, girls report more distress after natural disasters (e.g., Vogel & Vernberg, 1993), such as following earthquakes (Pynoos *et al.*, 1993) and vehicle accidents (Curle & Williams, 1996). In addition, girls report more general anxiety on scales such as the Children's Manifest Anxiety Scale (Reynolds & Richmond, 1978). In their study of 560 children, aged 6–16 years, Campbell and Rapee (1994) found that girls reported more worries than boys overall. Interestingly, the difference was explained mostly by items pertaining to negative social outcomes; boys and girls did not differ in terms of worries about physical outcomes. The social outcome variable contrasts with other reports of greater equivalency between males and females on measures and diagnoses of social anxiety.

Some of the differences between boys and girls may be attributable to physical maturity. For example, Hayward *et al.* (1992) found that after controlling for age, panic frequency in girls related to pre-pubertal stage, with more physically mature girls reporting more panic attacks. Similarly, early maturing girls experienced more symptoms of anxiety and depression that were more stable over a 4 year period than did normally maturing girls (Ge, Conger, & Elder, 1996). Also, Abe and Masui (1981) reported that fears of blushing and being looked at peaked at an earlier age in girls than in boys. Hence, the fact that girls mature at an earlier age than boys may result in higher levels of anxiety in age-matched male and female youths. However, maturity is unlikely to account for all of the sex differences in anxiety disorders.

Overall, girls predominate in the assignment of anxiety disorder diagnoses (e.g., Anderson *et al.*, 1987), although fewer sex differences may occur with respect to separation anxiety disorder than the other anxiety disorders (Velez *et al.*, 1989). Despite methodological inconsistencies, there is reason to believe that sex differences enhance with age. For example, we found no sex differences in the rates of separation anxiety at 3 years of age but more females than males with separation anxiety at 11–18 years of age from the Dunedin Multidisciplinary Study data set (Poulton, Milne, Craske, & Menzies, 2001), and even stronger sex differences were found for adolescents in the Ontario Child Health Study (female:male ratio of 6:1) (Bowen *et al.*, 1990). Similarly, whereas no sex differences were reported for overanxious disorder at the age of 11 years, the ratio of females to males was estimated at 6:1 for adolescents in the Dunedin study (McGee *et al.*, 1990), similar to the estimate of 4:1 among adolescents in the Ontario Child Health Study (Bowen *et al.*, 1990). In their prospective evaluation of 1–10-year-olds who were studied 8 and 10 years later, Velez *et al.* (1989) found no sex differences in overanxious disorder at 9–12 years of age, but more females than males by 13–18 years of age, due to the prevalence rates declining in boys and remaining stable in girls. Others have similarly noted more remission in boys than girls (Werry, 1991). In addition, three times as many more pre-pubertal boys than girls are diagnosed with obsessive–compulsive disorder (Karno, Golding, Sorenson, & Burman, 1988; Weissman *et al.*, 1994), yet the incidence increases in females and surpasses that of males after puberty (Pigott, 1994). In a reverse profile, more girls than boys met criteria for social phobia at 11 years of age (Anderson *et al.*, 1987) whereas slightly more boys than girls from the same sample were socially phobic at the age of 15 years (McGee *et al.*, 1990). These data are consistent with adult samples where sex differences are not as apparent for social phobia as for other anxiety disorders. From a diagnostic survey of 14–17-year-old adolescents (*n* = 1201) in Quebec, Canada, the following rates were obtained for anxiety disorders associated with impairment in functioning: based on adolescent interview, 13.5 percent of females and 4.3 percent of males; based on mother interview, 8.5 percent of females and 4.6 percent of males; and based on adolescent and/or mother interview, 19.4 percent of females and 8.8 percent of male adolescents (Romano *et al.*, 2001). Overall, the 2:1 ratio of females:males in adolescents parallels the ratio in adult samples.

Hence, adolescence is considered a critical time for the female propensity for internalizing disorders in general to become magnified (Offord *et al.*, 1987). This becomes even more evident when examining the developmental progression of anxiety disorders across the sexes. As reviewed earlier, anxiety disorders in childhood tend to shift, and although many anxious children remain anxious in one form or another, the majority do not retain their anxiety disorders as they develop into adolescence. However, anxiety and depression in childhood predict anxiety and depression in adolescence more for girls than for boys (Costello & Angold, 1995; McGee *et al.*, 1992). Moreover, the tendency for anxiety disorders to stabilize with age may be stronger for females than for males, given the evidence that internalizing symptoms are more stable from adolescence (13–16 years) to adulthood (21–24 years) for females than males (correlation coefficient of 0.38 versus 0.15) (Ferdinand & Verhulst, 1995).

The divergence between male and female risk for anxiety disorders may continue to expand throughout adulthood. From the Ontario Health Survey, Offord *et al.* (1996) compared 1 year prevalence rates for males and females across different age groups. Although they did not assess for obsessive–compulsive disorder or posttraumatic stress disorder, and although diagnoses were established using a fully structured lay-administered interview (Composite International Diagnostic Interview or CIDI), the relative shifts across age ranges remains a valuable comparison. The female-to-male ratios were as follows: aged 15–24 years, 1:1.74; aged 25–44 years, 1:1.56; and aged 45–64 years, 1:2.38. Hence, these data suggest that the 45–64 year age range may be another critical time for female propensity for anxiety to be magnified. Perhaps relevant here is the evidence for certain anxiety disorders such as panic disorder (Hollifield *et al.*, 1997; Yonkers *et al.*, 1998) and posttraumatic stress disorder (Breslau & Davis, 1992) to follow a more chronic course for women than men. However, this has not been found for social phobia (Yonkers *et al.*, 2001) or generalized anxiety disorder (Yonkers, Warshaw, Massion, & Keller, 1996). In general, sex and chronicity is in need of more systematic investigation, and the notion of progressive female/male divergence in anxiety is not without debate. Breslau *et al.* (2000) found that whereas the cumulative percentage curves for major depression began to diverge between males and females at about 12 years of age, the cumulative percentage curves for anxiety disorders were divergent across all ages. That is, the sex discrepancies for anxiety did not increase with age. Moreover, higher rates for major depression in females were largely attributable to their higher rates of earlier anxiety disorders; once anxious, males and females were equally likely to become depressed. Unfortunately, Breslau *et al.* (2000) collected data from lifetime interviewing and retrospective recall, and thus it is difficult to place much confidence in their accuracy. More prospective evaluation is clearly needed.

In contrast to patterns for internalizing disorders, more boys than girls show physically aggressive behaviors that increase or stay stable from kindergarten through seventh grade (Keenan & Shaw, 1997), and more males develop externalizing disorders such as conduct disorder and attention deficit/hyperactivity disorder (Offord *et al.*, 1992; Romano *et al.*, 2001). For example, rates of conduct disorder were 10.4 percent for males and 4.0 percent for female adolescents in the Ontario Child Health Study; rates for hyperactivity were 7.3 and 3.3 percent, respectively (Boyle & Offord, 1991).

As was apparent from the study by Romano *et al.* (2001), parents tend to report less anxiety symptoms in their offspring than do youths themselves (Edelbrock, Costello, Dulcan, Conover, & Kala, 1986; Weissman *et al.*, 1987). Moreover, the results suggest that mothers are less likely to view their anxious female offspring as suffering from anxiety whereas they are more concordant with their male offspring's judgments of the presence of significant anxiety (see Romano *et al.*, 2001). In a related vein, Last *et al.* (1992) found relatively comparable proportions of males and females in their consecutive sample of 188 anxiety-disordered children and adolescents, aged 5–18 years, who attended an anxiety disorders clinic, despite the evidence reviewed earlier for generally higher levels of anxiety disorders in female youths. Conceivably, their clinic distribution was due to caregivers perceiving anxious behaviors as less warranting of therapeutic intervention in girls. Shyness and withdrawal may be considered more normative for girls than boys, resulting in anxious behaviors being dismissed or minimized more so in girls, and possibly leading to fewer efforts to encourage girls to overcome their anxiety. Alongside caregivers' perceptions, shyness in boys may have a greater negative impact on life achievement than is the case for girls. Caspi *et al.* (1988) examined the adult outcomes 30 years later of children who were judged to be shy and reserved in late childhood. Although shyness did not relate to extreme pathology in adulthood, males who were shy as children showed delayed marriage, fatherhood, and entrance into stable careers relative to males who were not shy. The fact that childhood shyness did not impact adult development of females was attributed to the compatibility of shy behavior with female sex role expectations.

Avoidance Behavior

Sex differences are particularly pronounced with respect to avoidance behavior. For example, the proportion of females increases as the level of agoraphobia intensifies (Cameron & Hill, 1989; Reich, Noyes, & Troughton, 1987; Thyer, Himle, Curtis, Cameron, & Nesse, 1985), even though, after controlling for level of agoraphobia, few sex differences emerge in self-reported panic disorder symptomatology (e.g., Chambless & Mason, 1986; Cox, Swinson, Shulman, Kuch, & Reichman, 1993; Oei *et al.*, 1990). In an experimental study, Speltz and Bernstein (1976) compared male and female college students who were fearful of snakes. Participants were assigned to high- or low-demand conditions of approach to a live snake. Overall, highly fearful males achieved closer proximity to the snake than highly fearful females. However, according to behavioral observations of overt motor fear, such as extraneous hand and arm movements, hand tremors, emotional verbalizations, and accelerated breathing, males and females experienced the same degree of distress. Furthermore, highly demanding conditions increased the proximity with which females approached the snake. These data suggest that overt behavior under fearful conditions is in part a function of incentives and expectations, and that stronger expectations for approach may account for the greater willingness on the part of fearful males to approach phobic objects. However, females will also approach feared stimuli given sufficiently strong expectations.

Very pertinent in this regard is the finding that although anxiety disorders are far more common among female offspring than male offspring of anxious parents, patterns of familial aggregation for anxiety disorders were found to be similar for male and female offspring aged 7–17 years when the criteria of impairment and avoidance were excluded (Mcrikangas, Avenevoli, Dierker, & Grillon, 1999). These findings suggest that male and female differences in propensity for anxiety disorders may stem more from the reaction to distress (avoidance behavior) than the distress itself. As argued in later chapters, avoidance behavior is perhaps central to the onset of fully fledged anxiety disorders, and thus may be critical to the elevated risk for females. Also relevant is the finding that when adjusted for effects of past or current depression, adolescent females were no more likely than males to report panic attacks (Hayward *et al.*, 2000). Similarly, other studies of adolescents and young adults indicate relatively equal rates of panic attacks across males and females (Essau, Conradt, & Petermann, 1999; Telch *et al.*, 1989), although there may be more females in the subgroup with more severe panic attacks (Hayward, Killen, & Taylor, 1989). This raises the possibility that females and males are equally vulnerable to true fear (i.e., panic) and that eventual sex differences in the rates of panic disorder reside in the reaction to fear. If so, then females who panic occasionally would be expected to be more likely to develop panic disorder than males who panic occasionally. Unfortunately, only one study to date has evaluated this question: there were no sex differences in the subsample of non-clinical panickers who developed panic disorder over the course of 12 months (Ehlers, 1995). Replication with larger sample sizes is warranted.

Avoidance behavior is viewed as one way of coping with the anticipation of distress and fear (see Chapter 5). Another way is reliance on substances, a method that appears to be used more commonly by males than females. For example, males with panic disorder and agoraphobia report significantly greater use of alcohol and more reliance upon alcohol than females (e.g., Cox *et al.*, 1993). Similarly, males with social phobia have a higher rate of substance use disorders than females with social phobia (Yonkers *et al.*, 2001). The fact that male relatives of individuals with panic disorder and agoraphobia, who themselves do not suffer from anxiety, are more likely to suffer from alcoholism than female relatives (Harris, Noyes, Crowe, & Chaudhry, 1983) suggests that sex differences in substance use may involve more than preferred coping style with anxiety. The same conclusion can be drawn from the large overlap between substance-use-related disorders and conduct disorders/antisocial behavior (Boyle & Offord, 1991), another highly male dominant syndrome. Nonetheless, despite the multitude of other problems that it brings, substance abuse may not directly contribute to the onset of anxiety disorders in the same way as avoidance behavior.

Summary

Anxiety disorders are common in youths and adults. Symptoms of anxiety disorders tend to shift during childhood, but children often remain anxious or depressed in one form or another when adults. In addition, anxiousness possibly becomes more stable with age, particularly from adolescence to adulthood. The co-occurrence among anxiety disorders and mood disorders may be indicative of common vulnerability factors, of which anxiety is a developmentally earlier manifestation. In addition, the evidence that anxiety symptoms and disorders predict later anxiety and depression could reflect a scarring impact of anxiety once it is manifest, increasing the risk for other manifestations of the same vulnerability. Given the developmental appropriateness and commonality of circumscribed fears in childhood, the risk for anxiety disorders in youths appears unlikely to reside in the expression of fear *per se*. Also, although adolescents and adults with occasional symptoms of fear and anxiety are at increased risk of developing anxiety disorders later on, the risk is relatively small, and other factors appear to moderate or mediate the shift from occasional symptom expression to persistent and disabling anxiety.

Overall, females are at considerably greater risk for anxiety and anxiety disorders than males. The sex discrepancy is evident in youths as well and appears to progressively diverge from childhood through adolescence and early adulthood. Middle age, 45–64 years, may be another critical time for female propensity for anxiety. However, more prospective evaluation of rates of remission and progression for females versus males is needed. Females also are more likely than males to become depressed, although whether this is fully explained by their higher rate of anxiety is unclear. A very pronounced feature for anxious females is to exhibit more avoidant behavior than anxious males. Interestingly, female and male differences in extreme fear (i.e., panic attacks) subside when differences in depressed mood are taken into account. Furthermore, familial aggregation patterns for severe and persistent fear and anxiety are similar across males and females; the risk for female offspring only exceeds the risk for male offspring when the criteria of impairment and avoidance are added. Therefore, the heightened risk of anxiety disorders among females appears due to factors other than fear itself, thereby mirroring the conclusion with regard to factors responsible for the progression from circumscribed fears to anxiety disorders in the first place.

The Origins Model and the Structure of this Book

As alluded to in the preceding discussion, a distinction can be made between the expression of circumscribed fear and the state of anxiety. The nature and functions of fear and anxiety, when considered in isolation from psychological disorders, are discussed in Chapter 2. An appreciation of their distinctiveness is considered necessary before developing a model of the origins of phobias and anxiety disorders in the ensuing chapters.

Each major factor believed to contribute to pathological anxiety is presented in Chapters 3 through 7. The chapters represent separate but interactive layers of a model that build upon each other, with upward as well as downward directions of influence across the layers. The model has two main tiers, with the base representing broad, non-specific factors of vulnerability for all anxiety disorders as well as other forms of emotional distress, and the upper layer representing unique factors relevant to specific anxiety disorders.

Chapters 3 and 4 present the broad-based vulnerabilities, and their genetic and environmental contributions, that increase the risk for all forms of anxiety, depression, and emotional distress. The broad vulnerabilities are viewed as contributory but not necessary to the eventual expression of persistent and impairing anxiety. They are

Stimulus salience and threat value

Learning history   *Differentiates anxiety disorders*
Maturational factors   *(Chapter 7)*
Biological propensities
(Chapter 6)

Anxious processes

Vigilance and associated physiology   *Expression of anxiety*
Threat-laden beliefs
Avoidant behavior
(Chapter 5)

Broad-based vulnerabilities

Threat-based style of emotion regulation: *Vulnerability to anxiety disorders*
threat value of negative affect
(Chapter 4)

Negative affectivity: salience of negative   *Vulnerability to emotional disorders*
affect
(Chapter 3)

Figure 1.1: The origins model.

divided into negative affectivity (Chapter 3) and a threat-based style of emotion regulation (Chapter 4). Negative affectivity primarily influences the intensity and frequency — or the salience — of negative affect, whereas emotion regulation primarily influences the reactions to — or the meaning of — negative affect. The differentiation between anxiety and depression as well as other forms of emotional distress is believed to derive in part from different styles of reacting to negative affect: reactions in the form of danger-laden expectations and avoidant behavior are particularly relevant to the development of anxiety as they serve to maintain the threat value of negative affect and associated stimuli. The processes of vigilance and supportive physiology, threat-laden beliefs, and avoidant behavior that serve to detect, define, and protect from danger are described in Chapter 5. These anxious processes are non-specific and relevant to all anxiety disorders. They are modulated by ongoing stressors and underlying vulnerabilities, and in a progressive scarring cycle also influence reactivity to future stressors and vulnerability to further anxiety. Anxious tendencies become synthesized around stimuli, be it people, objects, situations, or internal states, that possess elevated salience and threat value. As described in Chapter 6, learning history, maturational factors, and, in some cases, biological propensities together render certain stimuli more salient and threatening at specific points in development. Differentiation among the anxiety disorders is believed to occur mainly at the level of stimulus salience and threat value, although the contribution of broad-based vulnerability factors is likely to vary across the anxiety disorders as well. The specific types of learning experiences and biological propensities relevant to each anxiety disorder are discussed in Chapter 7. A summary of the origins model is depicted in Figure 1.1. The various origins factors in which females acquire more risk for anxiety disorders than males, and the biological, evolutionary, and socialization underpinnings of these differences are described in Chapter 8 before a final summary is presented in Chapter 9.

Chapter 2

Functions of Fear versus Anxiety

It is generally agreed upon that fear and anxiety are protective states that serve the function of detecting and avoiding threat. In certain people, fear and anxiety become excessive due to the various influences described throughout the remainder of this book. Before delving into factors responsible for the shift from normal to excessive fear and anxiety, an ethological perspective of the nature and functions of fear and anxiety is presented to understand what it is that becomes disordered.

Threat Imminence

The model of species-specific defense reactions (SSDRs) proposed by Fanselow and Lester (1988) in their extension of the work of Bolles (1970) provides an ethological perspective that differentiates fear from anxiety. SSDRs are responses elicited by natural environmental threats, of which there are several to choose from. Fanselow and Lester (1988) propose that response selection is determined by predatory imminence, as judged by spatial distance from threat, temporal likelihood of contact with threat, and other factors of psychological and physical distance. The continuum of imminence spreads from "no predatory potential" to "predator makes the kill" (Figure 2.1). At the point of no predatory potential, organisms engage in their preferred mode of activity, which is also the state to which organisms return after any disruption. Three stages of imminence are outlined: pre-encounter defenses emerge when there is predatory potential; post-encounter defenses emerge when the predator is detected and behavior is designed to avoid contact with it; and circa-strike defenses emerge when the predator makes contact and behavior is designed to allow the prey to escape from contact with the predator. The defensive behaviors are qualitatively different at different points on the imminence continuum, and are designed to prevent the development of further imminence. For example, freezing (a post-encounter defensive reaction) results in less likelihood of being detected by the predator. Also, release of natural analgesics (a post-encounter and circa-strike defensive behavior) is adaptive because it reduces nociception and thereby eliminates disruption of defensive behavior due to pain. Fighting and escape behavior obviously occur when contact with a predator is occurring or inevitable. Finally, if not killed by the predator, the prey enters a recuperation phase and eventually returns to the preferred activity. Fanselow (1994) outlined a neural organization for the three main levels of predatory imminence that represents different activation pathways for qualitatively different responses.

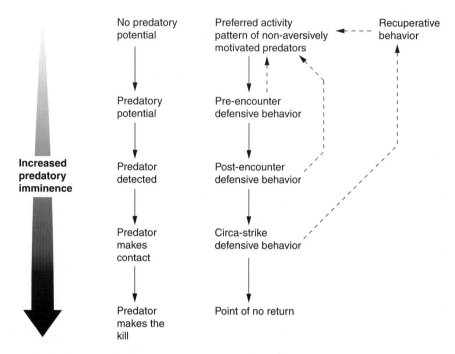

Figure 2.1: The predatory continuum. (Redrawn by permission of Lawrence Erlbaum Associates from Faneslow & Lester (1988).)

Obviously, this model is anchored to predatory types of threat for non-primates. Nonetheless, the principle of qualitatively different response profiles being dictated by proximity to threat may hold true across different types of threat for humans, even though the actual response characteristics may differ from those of non-primates under attack. Thus, whereas escape behavior may be the most appropriate response at the point of contact with a physical threat (e.g., pain) it may not be the most appropriate response at the point of contact with social threat (e.g., ridicule) where instead the physical portrayal of defeat (e.g., lowering of eye gaze) may be more fitting. Moreover, whether it be social threat or physical threat, the response that is driven by imminent threat is likely to differ from the response that is driven by distal threat: at close proximity, escape is appropriate whereas at a distance avoidance is the preferred option. Threat imminence for humans is probably based on physical characteristics of the stimulus (e.g., temporal and physical distance, size) as well as psychological perceptions of threat (e.g., appraisal of danger, coping resources). In humans, the source of threat may be external (people, places or objects) or internal (thoughts, images or sensations), and, as with non-primates, the source of threat may be unconditioned or conditioned due to learning experiences (Craske, 1999).

By extrapolation from the SSDR model, fear and anxious worry may lie on the same continuum but at positions that differ dependent on proximity to threat. Theoretically, undetected but uncertain threat (akin to predatory potential) elicits anxious worry and alertness, whereas detected threat (akin to post-encounter defenses) elicits fear directed at a particular stimulus, with varying reactivities based on the degree of imminence of threat, extending all the way up to a panic attack (akin to circa-strike defenses). Although not listed because of lack of information to date, a final step of predatory attack may elicit immobility and autonomic shut down, as might occur during severe abuse (Barlow, 1988). In this model, fear and anxious worry are likely to involve response characteristics that are uniquely tailored to their different functions; so much so that the response characteristics may even be incompatible with each other. In other words, fear (and panic) is viewed as qualitatively different from anxious worry because differing levels of threat imminence warrant different response systems for most effective manafgement of threat. However, this model is superfluous unless the available evidence indicates separability of fear from anxiety. Three arguments exist in support of this separation.

First, structural equation modeling and factor analyses of symptom scales in anxious samples indicate two distinct factors. One is characterized by a sense of extreme fear or impending doom, strong autonomic arousal, and fight or flight behavioral tendencies, and is referred to as "fear". The other is characterized by apprehension, worry, and tension (Brown *et al.*, 1998; Joiner *et al.*, 1999; Mineka, Watson, & Clark, 1998), and is referred to as "anxiety". Similarly, among unselected youth samples, items on fear scales are relatively homogeneous, and load on factors that are distinct from those shared by anxiety and depression scales (Ollendick *et al.*, 1991).

Second, specific heritabilities may exist for panic/fear that are independent of heritability for anxiety. Kendler, Heath, Martin, and Eaves (1986) found that whereas many symptoms of anxiety were attributable to shared genetic effects (see Chapter 3 for a more detailed discussion), symptoms of panic were somewhat attributable to unique sources of genetic variance. In a more detailed evaluation, Martin, Jardine, Andrews, and Heath (1988) analyzed data from 2903 same-sex twin pairs using multivariate genetic analysis, to find genetic factors that were specific to panic and independent of those that affected the more general trait of neuroticism. For example, the symptom of a pounding heart was attributable to environmental experiences unique to the individual (67 percent), and heritability (33 percent), of which one-third reflected additive genetic variance and 22 percent reflected non-additive genetic variance. One half of the additive and non-additive variation was attributed to genes that influence neuroticism, but the remainder of the variation was attributed to genes that specifically influence the symptom of a pounding heart. Caution in interpretation is necessary, however, given that the symptom of a pounding heart is far from being synonymous with fear and panic.

Third, emotion theorists have argued that fear represents one of several basic emotions that are distinct from mood states such as anxiety. Given the universality and specificity of facial expression for emotions of fear versus anger for example (e.g., Ekman, 1973; Ekman, Levenson, & Friesen, 1983), albeit with some cultural constraints (Elfenbein & Ambady, 2002), theorists such as Izard (1992) suggest that fear and emotions in general are non-cognitive, involving primitive brain mechanisms, whereas anxiety and other mood states involve more highly developed brain mechanisms and cognition. Interestingly, empirical evidence accrued over the last decade, reviewed in this chapter, is consistent for the most part with this perspective.

Anxiety and Worry: Responses and Function

Within the threat imminence model, anxious worry is elicited by a sense of potential danger in the absence of detection of a specific threat. Thus, conditions of uncertainty about threat and expectation for adversity would be most likely to elicit anxiety and worry. In turn, worry becomes a preparatory state designed to alert the system to potential danger. For example, Barlow (1988) views worry as the attentional vigilance and distortion in information processing (e.g., attention, encoding, etc.) component of anxiety that represents a functional state of preparation for future threat. Similarly, Mathews (1990) notes that worry acts as a preparator, lessening surprise and increasing readiness for coping should anticipated events actually occur. In Eysenck's (1992) hypervigilance theory, worry serves to alarm the system about new incoming threatening information, prompting retrieval of threat-related images and thoughts into consciousness, and preparation for a future situation. Wells and Morrison (1994) suggest that worry is a processing strategy for dealing with threat. In effect, by creating conditions of expectancy (e.g., Gray, 1982a), worry serves an adaptive preparatory function because unexpected aversive events are potentially more compromising and dangerous than expected aversive events (Weiss, 1970). Consistent with its preparatory function, worry is associated with a number of problem-focused coping strategies (Davey, 1993; Davey, Hampton, Farrell, & Davidson, 1992), and individuals report perceiving the function of worry to be that of problem solving (Borkovec, 1994; Tallis, Davey, & Capuzzo, 1994). Being elicited by uncertain threat, worry becomes a means for gaining certainty.

The process of worry appears to be one of covert, primarily verbal or semantic, activity (i.e., thinking) that includes proportionately less visualization, or imaginal activity, than baseline mental activity. For example, clinically anxious individuals and normal controls report having more thoughts than images when instructed to worry (Borkovec & Inz, 1990; East & Watts, 1994). Also, when asked about worry episodes, non-clinical community and student samples report a significant predominance of thought over imagery (Borkovec, 1994; Borkovec & Lyonfields, 1993; Freeston, Dugas, & Ladouceur, 1996a; Tallis *et al.*, 1994). Normal subjects, who kept records of the content and nature of their worries, rated worry as involving primarily verbal content (Wells & Morrison, 1994), and the act of worrying for unselected groups was associated with proportionate increases in the amount of verbalizing (e.g., Stober, Tepperwien, & Staak, 2000). In addition, a group of public-speaking anxious worriers who were given no instruction about how to think in advance of a public-speaking task significantly decreased the proportion of time they spent visualizing as they shifted from thinking about a neutral scene to the feared public-speaking scene, at least according to retrospective reports (Bergman & Craske, 2000).

More objective indices of mental activity were measured by Rapee (1993), who, drawing from Baddeley's (1990) model of working memory, instructed participants to worry while also continually engaging in tasks that utilized only part of working memory, either the phonological loop (storage and manipulation of verbal information) or the visuo-spatial sketchpad (storage and manipulation of visual and spatial information). Only the phonological activity interfered with ability to worry, suggesting that worry is a verbal process that competed for resources with the phonological loop. Other objective indices include patterns of brain activation. Generally speaking, verbal processing is localized in the left hemisphere, and Carter, Johnson, and Borkovec (1986) found that episodes of worry were associated with left frontal cortex EEG activation specifically as opposed to elevated cortical arousal in general. Also, Heller, Nitschke, Etienne, and Miller (1997) found that highly trait-anxious students had relatively less right hemisphere activation and an asymmetry favoring left hemisphere activation at rest, in comparison with non-anxious students.

Given that the right hemisphere is involved in the generation of autonomic responses to emotional material (Spence, 1992), and given that worry or high trait anxiousness is linked with more left hemisphere than right hemisphere activation, it is understandable why worry would correlate with reduced autonomic reactivity. For example, autonomic symptoms were among the lowest ranked physical symptoms in association with worry (Freeston *et al.*, 1996b). The specific connection between worry as a verbal state and autonomic symptoms was addressed by Freeston *et al.* (1996a), who found that stronger endorsement of thoughts versus images correlated with reduced autonomic hyperactivity among non-clinical worriers. Also, high scorers on a worry questionnaire exhibited less cardiac reactivity to personally fearful imagery than low scorers (Szollos, Eshelman, & Keffer, 1990), and we found immunological suppression in high worriers when exposed to a snake they had previously rated as fearful, in comparison with equally fearful low worriers (Segerstrom, Glover, Craske, & Fahey, 1999). Borkovec and Hu (1990) found that physiological reactions to imagined scenarios of public speaking in public-speaking-anxious individuals were lessened after an interval of worry in contrast to an interval of imagery. Similar results were obtained by Borkovec, Lyonfields, Wiser, and Diehl (1993). Furthermore, chronic worriers (i.e., generalized anxiety disorder patients) show decreased autonomic reactivity relative to non-anxious controls (Hoehn-Saric & Masek, 1981; Hoehn-Saric & McLeod, 1988; Hoehn-Saric, Mcleod, & Zimmerli, 1989; Lyonfields, 1991; Lyonfields, Borkovec, & Thayer, 1995; Thayer, Friedman, & Borkovec, 1996). In particular, chronic worriers show reduced *variability* in heart rate and skin conductance during psychological stress challenges. Autonomic rigidity of this kind is interpreted as evidence for diminished cardiac vagal tone because even though heart rate variability is controlled by sympathetic and parasympathetic inputs, the findings extend to particular measures that index parasympathetic influences only (Thayer *et al.*, 1996; Yeragani *et al.*, 1990). Similar autonomic inflexibility has been observed in other anxiety disorders including panic disorder (Hoehn-Saric, McLoed & Zimmerli, 1991; Yeragani *et al.*, 1990), although possibly less so than in generalized anxiety disorder (Bruce & Lader, 1991), and obsessive–compulsive disorder (Hoehn-Saric, McLeod, & Hipsley, 1995). Decreased autonomic variability may thus reflect high levels of worry across all anxiety disorders, although the fact that it is sometimes low in depression as well (e.g., Rechlin, Weis, Spitzer, & Kaschka, 1994) suggests a broader relationship to ruminative states in general. (Inconsistencies do exist in the depression literature, however (e.g., Moser *et al.*, 1998).) As described in Chapter 4, restricted autonomic reactivity is closely intertwined with attentional processes.

Thus, it appears that worry is characterized by elevated verbal processing and may be linked with an inhibition of autonomic response to threat. These response characteristics could be conceived as being consistent with the proposed function of worry — to prepare and plan effectively for potential threat. Excessive autonomic arousal may impede complex cognitive processing; ongoing autonomic suppression commensurate with active verbal problem solving may represent the most adaptive response profile under conditions of *potential* threat.

Fear: Responses and Function

In contrast to worry about undetected but uncertain or potential threat conditions, fear is induced when threat is detected, at which time response systems shift to more active coping for self-preservation. Detection of threat implies some degree of certainty in comparison with the uncertain threat conditions that elicit worry. Hence, with detection, autonomic activation becomes more prominent, as demonstrated in various studies of exposure to phobic stimuli (e.g., Kozak, Foa, & Steketee, 1988; see Chapter 7), and most clearly shown in studies of an approaching threat stimulus (whether conditioned or not) in unselected individuals. For example, Katkin and Hoffman (1976) observed an anticipatory rise in skin conductance over 10 minutes preceding the introduction of a spider. Similarly, individuals performing in public (whether reporting significant anxiety or not about the situation) demonstrate significant elevations in heart rate prior to performances (e.g., public speaking — Hofman, Newman, Ehlers, & Roth, 1995; musical performance — Craske & Craig, 1984), suggesting an arousal response to meet a challenge. Perhaps the strongest evidence derives from studies of autonomic arousal (e.g., Deane, 1969) and startle potentiation (e.g., Grillon, Ameli, Merikangas, Woods, & Davis, 1993; Grillon, Amelia, Woods, Merikangas, & Davis, 1991) in anticipation of shock. In fact, with sufficient durations, an inverted U-shaped function has been found, with an initial acceleration of heart rate and startle potentiation when first informed about upcoming shock, followed by deceleration, and gradual acceleration as the shock approaches (Grillon *et al.*, 1993). This is depicted in Figure 2.2. Conceivably, the decelerative component reflects engagement in preparation and worry. A more linear association is found with shorter anticipatory intervals, suggesting insufficient time for preparatory coping.

Lang (1979, 1985) proposed that imagery and autonomic arousal are central to fear — that imagery is the mental process through which perceptual-motor memories are activated and that the physiological responses observed in imagery are a regeneration of the action pattern displayed in the original context (Hebb, 1968; Lang, 1985). The association between imagery and arousal is supported by several studies showing a strong positive correlation between vividness of imagery and level of

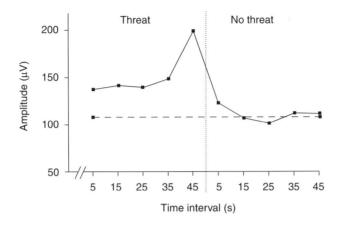

Figure 2.2: Eye blink amplitude in reaction to startle as threat of shock approaches and after threat of shock is removed (at the point of intersection with the dotted line). The dashed line represents eye blink amplitude at the interval of 55 seconds in the condition with no threat. (Redrawn by permission of Blackwell Publishing from Grillon et al. (1993).)

autonomic arousal (e.g., Borkovec & Sides, 1979; Levin, Cook, & Lang, 1982). Also, Vrana, Cuthbert, and Lang (1989) demonstrated that imaginal representation of a feared situation produced significantly greater cardiovascular response than verbal articulation of the same content.

The state of heightened autonomic arousal and fear may place a limit on depth of cognitive processing. That is, effortful cognitive processing of information may be impeded at the height of intense fear (e.g., Watts, Trezise, & Sharrock, 1986). Others have similarly noted that cognitions associated with emotions (e.g., fear) are relatively elementary or automatic, in contrast to the more complex cognitive processing of mood states (e.g., anxiety) (Goldsmith, 1994). It may be for this reason that ongoing monitoring of thought content during exposure to most feared situations is almost devoid of appraisals of danger (Williams, Kinney, Harap, & Liebman, 1997). Instead, the stated thought content mostly represents escape and behavioral responding. When one step removed from imminent threat, however, danger appraisals in respect to feared situations are strongly endorsed (e.g., Menzies & Clarke, 1995a).

Consistent with the notion of limited cognitive processing, several studies indicate reduced activation of the frontal cortex during fear induction. For example, phobic fear has been associated with relative increases in regional cerebral blood flow (rCBF) in the secondary or associative visual cortex, and relative reductions in rCBF in the hippocampus, prefrontal, orbitofrontal, temporopolar, and posterior cingulate cortex (Fredrikson, Wik, Annas, Ericson, & Stone-Elander, 1995; Fredrikson *et al.*, 1993). The authors suggest that activation of the associative visual cortex is consistent with increased vigilance and perceptual acuity associated with execution of the fight/ flight response, whereas reduced activity in the paralimbic and limbic cortex is possibly reflective of reduced conscious cognitive processing. Similarly, data from rhesus monkeys indicate stressor-induced impairment to working memory and the prefrontal cortex, as if the control of behavior is relinquished to subcortical circuits (Arnsten & Goldman-Rakic, 1998). The subcortical units are believed to involve the brain stem periacqueductual gray region (PAG) that mobilizes immediate fear reactions and is mostly responsive to visceral and somatosensory input (Luu, Tucker, & Derryberry, 1998).

To summarize, fear induced by a certain or a detected threat involves response characteristics of autonomic activation and inhibition of complex cognitive processing that could be viewed as supporting the proposed function of fear — engaging in fight or flight action in order to survive imminent danger. Under these conditions, complex cognitive processing may slow the organism to dangerous levels, whereas high autonomic activation propels immediate action. Once a threat is detected, the level of imminence ranges from actual attack or confrontation with innately aversive stimuli, to explicit stimuli that have been associated with aversive events, to surrounding conditions closely associated with aversive events or explicit threat stimuli. Responding to stimuli and contexts associated with aversive events includes conditioned responding, whereas responding to true aversives represents unconditioned responding. Some have argued that the neuroanatomy of conditioned responding differs from that of unconditioned fear: that in contrast to the more primitive state of fear and the PAG, conditioned anxiety is more directly linked with the limbic system and cortex (Luu *et al.*, 1998). Conceivably, the limbic system organizes more directed forms of escape for more distal threats than in the case of unconditioned fear responding, and in accord the limbic system has more access to information from the external environment than is true of the PAG (Luu *et al.*, 1998).

An accruing body of research supports the role of the amygdala (part of the limbic system) in aversive conditioning. Non-primate studies have established that various nuclei in the amygdala are responsible for the acquisition and expression of conditioning to explicit aversive stimuli (Davis, 1998; LeDoux, 1998) and startle potentiation by presentation of explicit threat stimuli is mediated by the amygdala (see Grillon, 2002a). Two functional magnetic resonance imaging (fMRI) studies demonstrated bilateral amygdala activation during the early stages of conditioning (Buchel, Morris, Dolan, & Friston, 1998; LaBar & Le Doux, 1998). Also, a series of studies have measured elevated amygdala activation in response to images of conditioned angry and fearful faces even when masked (i.e., presented in a way that cannot be consciously perceived) (e.g., Morris, Öhman, & Dolan, 1998, 1999; Whalen *et al.*, 1998). In fact, in one study the intensity of the fear displayed in the faces systematically related to the increases in blood flow to the amygdala, whereas disgust faces failed to elicit amygdala activation (Phillips *et al.*, 1997).

Various studies have examined neuroanatomical pathways in anxiety-disordered samples. Although these studies do not validate etiological factors, they help to elucidate the neuroanatomy of fear and anxiety. Results from these studies are generally consistent with those from unselected samples. For example, using positron emission tomography measures of blood flow, Rauch, van der Kolk, Fisler, and Alpert (1996) exposed patients with posttraumatic stress disorder to imagery scripts designed to activate traumatic memories, and Breiter *et al.* (1996) used fMRI to examine patients with obsessive–compulsive disorder as they were exposed to stimuli designed to provoke their anxiety. In each study, bilateral activation of the amygdala was observed in comparison with control stimuli. Also, Birbaumer *et al*. (1998) observed bilateral amygdala activation in response to neutral facial expressions, compared with resting baselines in a group of males with social phobia, and the activation was comparable in magnitude to that elicited by an aversive odor. In their controls, they observed amygdala activation to the aversive odor but not to the faces.

Whereas the amygdala is central to conditioned fear to discrete objects, some propose that the hippocampus is central to conditioning to environmental contexts, especially given the role of the hippocampus in memory for spacial, contextual, and relational information (Luu *et al*., 1998). In accord, panic disorder patients as well as controls showed activation in the hippocampus when imagining highly anxious relative to neutral situations (Bystritsky *et al*., 2001). The dorsal portion of the hippocampus in particular may be responsible for contextual conditioning (Kim & Fanselow, 1992) although there is ongoing debate on hippocampal involvement (see Grillon, 2002a). Overall, the differentiation between cue explicit and contextual conditioning may be very important as there is a growing body of evidence to suggest that anxiousness and the anxiety disorders are characterized mostly by overgeneralized contextual conditioning. Such overgeneralization implies that following an unpleasant experience many things associated with that experience become defined as threatening. The evidence for cue explicit and contextual conditioning is reviewed in chapters to follow.

As an aside, it is notable that the PAG (linked with unconditioned fear), amygdala (linked with conditioned anxiety to discrete objects), and hippocampus (linked with conditioned anxiety to contexts) each have projections to the cortex, perhaps less extensively in the first case. Luu *et al*. (1998) raise the very intriguing notion that influence from the cortex may occur *before* most responses are elicited. For example, "such cortical modulation can serve an anticipatory function in the sense that relevant pathways, such as those related to threat and safety, can be facilitated before overt orienting movements (e.g., eye movements) are made, and even before the sensory information becomes physically available" (Luu *et al*., 1998, p. 582). This would explain why conditioned and unconditioned responding to threat is influenced by shifts in appraisal systems, a topic discussed in more detail in Chapter 6.

Summary

Various data sets converge on the notion that fear and anxious worry are qualitatively different states. The threat imminence model in particular suggests that fear and anxiety are functionally different states elicited by different levels of proximity to threat. Events that are in the future and as yet undetected or are very distally associated with aversive stimuli and raise uncertainty elicit worry; as threat is detected and more certain, anxious worry shifts to fear. The fear response itself varies in direct proportion to proximity to the detected threat, extending from anticipatory arousal to contexts closely associated with threat, to anxious and fearful responding to explicit stimuli associated with threat, to panic or intense fear experienced at the point of actual threat or confrontation (as depicted in Figure 2.3). The exact responses at each stage of

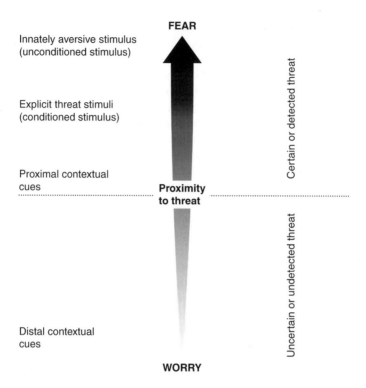

Figure 2.3: Worry, fear, and threat cues.

imminence may differ across different types of threat (e.g., social versus physical), but each stage is associated with a different response profile that is most adaptive for that particular level of imminence for that particular type of threat. Thus, the state of worry is proposed to constitute a primarily cognitive–verbal state, involving left frontal cortical activation and ongoing inhibition of autonomic activation to facilitate elaborate cognitive processing and planning in preparation for threat. As threat-related stimuli are detected, a state of autonomic arousal is activated in preparation for fight/flight mobilization, which is intensified as imminence increases. At the same time, depth of cognitive processing may be progressively limited as fearfulness intensifies. The amygdala and hippocampus are implicated in anticipatory, conditioned anxiety to explicit threat stimuli and contextual stimuli, respectively. More primitive neuroanatomical pathways involving the brain stem PAG are implicated in unconditioned fear.

The threat imminence model represents an ethological perspective of the basic nature and functions of fear and anxiety. It provides a framework for explaining response profiles at any given point in time — for explaining a shift from a state of worry to a state of panic. The relevance of the threat imminence model to the anxiety disorders can be best addressed through a number of questions. First, are the anxiety disorders as a group fueled by elevated threat imminence relative to non-anxious groups? Is threat judged to be more imminent across a broader array of stimuli for some anxiety disorders versus other anxiety disorders — for example, is generalized anxiety disorder associated with more pervasive perceived threat than is specific phobia? Second, do the anxiety disorders represent heightened manifestation of worry as well as fear, and evaluated responding to contextual as well as explicit threat cues? As reviewed in chapters to follow, overgeneralization of responding to contextual stimuli may be the most characteristic feature of anxiety disorders. Also, does the relative importance of each defensive response system vary for each anxiety disorder? Does generalized anxiety disorder load more heavily on worry responses whereas posttraumatic stress disorder load more heavily on conditioned anxiety and fear responses? Finally, does over-activation of one defensive response increase the propensity for other defensive responses — for example, does heightened worry increase the propensity for fear responding? These are the types of questions to which attention is now turned.

Chapter 3

Disposition to Fear and Anxiety: Negative Affectivity

This chapter reviews the theory and data pertaining to negative affectivity as a vulnerability factor that places individuals at risk for anxiety as well as other emotional disorders. After presenting the evidence for a link between negative affectivity and later emotional distress, the biological and environmental factors that influence negative affectivity are reviewed.

Numerous theories of the etiology of anxiety disorders hypothesize an underlying trait or temperament that predisposes certain individuals to later experience a full anxiety disorder. Variability in temperament, at least in adults, is mostly explained by five broad factors — surgency/extraversion, agreeableness, conscientiousness, emotional stability/neuroticism, and openness to experience (i.e., the "big five" model of personality) (McCrae & Costa, 1987). There are four ways in which temperament can influence the development of psychopathology. First, temperament may serve as a predisposition, playing a direct causal role in psychopathology, as is reflected in the diathesis–stress model whereby a relevant stressor in combination with a temperament disposition triggers the onset of a disorder. By example, the unexpected loss of a parent through heart attack may trigger panic attacks and anxiety but only in someone with an emotionally vulnerable temperament. Second, temperament may moderate the expression or course of the disorder without having a direct causal role. This is referred to as pathoplasticity, and it encompasses the notion that temperament influences the shaping of the environment for the individual. For example, interpersonal reactions from others may be partly influenced by temperamental variables, and the resultant social interactions may in turn contribute to anxious processes in the long term. Third, temperament may be altered by the experience of the disorder — known as the complication or scarring model mentioned in Chapter 1. For example, once a conditioning event has established an anxious response, temperament may be negatively affected such that the manifestation of anxiety strengthens the vulnerability to anxiety. Fourth is the continuity model, in which both temperament and disorder are seen as reflecting the same underlying process (Lonigan & Phillips, 2001). It is unlikely that a continuity model accounts for the majority of anxiety disorders given that about only one-third of children considered to be temperamentally predisposed to develop anxiety disorders (reviewed below) actually do so. These models are not mutually exclusive and support exists for almost all possibilities (Mineka *et al.*, 1998).

Temperament for Anxiety

The temperament most associated with anxiety disorders is neuroticism/emotional stability, or, as it is more recently termed, "negative affectivity" (Watson & Clark, 1984; Zinbarg & Barlow, 1996). The concept of negative affectivity draws heavily from the work of Eysenck (1967) and his model of neuroticism. In addition, the concept overlaps with theories that link states of motivation (largely appetitive versus aversive) to neuroanatomical pathways. These theories propose that individual differences in anxiety reflect heightened levels of activation of the defensive motivational system and its associated structures (e.g., Cloninger, 1986; Fowles, 1993; Gray, 1982a).

Eysenck (1967) originally proposed extraversion and neuroticism as primary dimensions of personality that were orthogonal to each other and equally contributory to anxiety and depression. A profile of high neuroticism and low extraversion was posited to contribute specifically to anxiety. Neuroticism was assumed to reflect individual differences in reactivity to negative environmental stimuli, with high scorers being more negatively reactive or prone to negative experiences. The neural substrate was thought to involve the septum, hippocampus, amygdala, and hypothalamus. Individual differences in extraversion, on the other hand, were assumed to reflect levels of cortical arousal, resulting from differences in reactivity of the ascending reticular activating system to environmental stimuli. In support, compared with extraverts, introverts show elevated cortical arousal at rest as indexed by regional cerebral blood flow (Mathew, Weinman, & Barr, 1984), higher tonic levels of autonomic activity, and larger responses to stimuli of low to moderate stimulation (Wigglesworth & Smith, 1976), larger changes in pupil size to stimulation (Stelmack & Mandelzys, 1975), greater increases in heart rate to mental arithmetic tests (Hinton & Craske, 1977), and greater dishabituation of electrodermal responding to stimulus changes (Smith & Wigglesworth, 1978). However, the results are not always positive. For example, Hare (1972) found no relationship between extraversion and heart rate responses to aversive stimuli.

Gray (1982a, 1987) proposed "anxiety" and "impulsivity" as the major dimensions of personality. These dimensions were rotated in relation to Eysenck's concepts of neuroticism and extraversion. Specifically, anxiety positively associates with neuroticism and negatively associates with extraversion, whereas impulsivity positively associates with extraversion and with neuroticism. Anxiety is thought to reflect individual differences in the behavioral inhibition system (BIS), a defensive motivational system to which high neuroticism and, to a lesser degree, low extraversion contribute as activators. The BIS is hypothesized to be mediated by noradrenergic and serotonergic pathways through the septohippocampal system and related structures, consistent with that area of the brain most associated with anticipatory, conditioned anxiety to contextual stimuli (see Chapter 2). Notably, Gray separates fear from panic, with fear being elicited by activation of the BIS and panic attacks attributed to the "fight–flight" system that mediates responses to unconditioned aversive stimuli and involves the central gray, medial hypothalamus, and amygdala (Gray & McNaughton, 1996). As such, Gray's model contrasts with notions presented in the Chapter 2 for the amygdala to be more central to conditioned anxiety than to primitive, unconditioned fear. Obviously, debates regarding the neuroanatomical substrates of different aspects of fear and anxiety continue.

In Gray's model, impulsivity reflects individual differences in the behavioral approach system (BAS), an appetitive motivational system, regulated by dopaminergic pathways. The BIS and BAS are linked theoretically to different types of reinforcements. Thus, the BIS is purported to be sensitive to signals of punishment, frustrative non-reward (i.e., omission of expected reward), extreme novelty, high intensity stimuli, and innate fear stimuli such as blood and snakes. The principal task of the BIS is to compare actual environment cues to expected stimuli; if a mismatch occurs, the BIS is activated, execution of other ongoing motor programs is inhibited, and a series of precautional consequences occur such as tagging of the discordant stimuli for further review, increased attention to the environment and increased arousal. The short-term outputs of the BIS are narrowing of attention, inhibition of gross motor behavior, increased stimulus analysis (i.e., vigilance), increased central nervous system arousal (e.g., alertness), and priming of hypothalamic motor systems for possible rapid action. The BAS, on the other hand, is thought to be sensitive to signals of reward and non-punishment, and its activation increases approach behavior toward these stimuli and is associated with positive mood.

In support of Gray's theory, Gomez, Cooper, and Gomez (2000) found that the level of positive mood induction via monetary reward was predicted by students' extraversion scores whereas level of negative mood induction via withdrawal of money during the same type of task was predicted by their neuroticism scores, alone and in interaction with extraversion scores. In another study of procedural as opposed to declarative learning, a positive relationship was observed between anxiety and performance under conditions of punishment (Corr, Pickering, & Gray, 1997). Thus, individual differences in anxiety appeared to moderate the degree to which threatening conditions motivated learning. By enhancing learning for anxious individuals, aversive situations may contribute to associative learning with surrounding contexts and thereby enhance generalizability of responding. The relationship between anxious temperament and conditioning is reviewed in Chapter 6. Finally, because the appetitive and aversive motivational systems are considered distinct, conditionability in one does not necessarily predict conditionability in the other. By implication, individual differences in emotional expression are not necessarily stable across positive and negative emotional states. Zinbarg and Mohlman (1998) in fact demonstrated that aversive conditioning was not matched by appetitive conditioning. Therefore, anxiety is linked with heightened negative activity of the BIS but not with heightened emotional reactivity overall.

At least two other models converge on similar or overlapping constructs. Cloninger (1987) proposed three dimensions of personality, of which the first — novelty seeking — is similar to Gray's behavioral activation system — and characterized by a tendency toward frequent exploratory activity and intense excitement in response to novel stimuli. A second dimension is harm avoidance, similar to Gray's behavioral inhibition system, characterized by intense responding to aversive stimuli. Activity is manifested as high anticipatory anxiety. The third dimension is dependency, characterized by intense response to reward and relief. Finally, Davidson (1992,

1998) outlined a model similar to Gray's, but emphasizing somewhat different neuroanatomical substrates. The approach system in his model facilitates appetitive behavior and positive affect generated in the context of moving toward a desired goal (i.e., pre-goal attainment positive affect, not to be confused with post-goal attainment positive affect which reflects a different system and refers more to contentment). Davidson (1998) links this system to the prefrontal cortex, and, in particular, a profile of asymmetry favoring the left over the right prefrontal cortex. However, asymmetry favoring the right prefrontal cortex does not correlate with BIS, and excessive anxiety is not well explained by these profiles of asymmetry (Coan, Allen, & Harmon-Jones, 2001). Instead, the amygdala is believed to be central to the system that is involved in withdrawal from sources of aversive stimulation and generates negative affect of fear and disgust.

Thus, various theoreticians propose that differences in aversive or defensive motivational systems underlie the predisposition to anxiety. Converging with these neuroanatomical models of motivation are models of personality that are derived largely from factor analyses of symptom scales of anxiety and depressed mood. From this work has arisen the construct of "negative affectivity", or a tendency to experience a variety of negative emotions, including fear, sadness, guilt, and hostility, across a variety of situations, even in the absence of an objective stressor (Watson & Clark, 1984). From their comprehensive analyses, Clark and Watson established that heightened negative affect is common to anxiety and depression whereas low positive affect or anhedonia is relatively specific to depression (e.g., Watson, Clark, & Tellegen, 1988; Watson & Tellegen, 1985). Others, too (e.g., Fowles, 1993), hypothesize low positive affectivity to be a trait vulnerability marker for depression.

In Clark and Watsons' (1991) tripartite model, the counterpart to low positive affectivity that is specific to anxiety is physiological hyperarousal. Hence, three primary traits are proposed: negative affectivity, positive affectivity, and hyperarousal. However, the evidence for physiological hyperarousal as a higher order trait is mixed. A structural analysis of a large sample of patients and controls established one higher-order factor of negative affect that distinguished each anxiety disorder as well as depression from a no-mental-disorder control group (Zinbarg & Barlow, 1996). However, the notion of physiological hyperarousal as another higher-order factor that was common to all of the anxiety disorders was not corroborated. Instead, there was a series of other lower-order factors that were more specific and discriminated among the anxiety disorders. These were labeled fear of fear, social anxiety, generalized dysphoria, obsessions and compulsions, agoraphobia, and simple fears. Brown, Chorpita, and Barlow (1998) reached a similar conclusion, with evidence for physiological hyperarousal being more specific to panic disorder and the higher-order factors being restricted to negative affectivity and positive affectivity. An important caveat, however, is that these structural models are developed from symptom reporting, and reports of physiological arousal are not synonymous with objective indices of hyperarousal (Pennebaker, 1982). With more objective indices, evidence for "hyperarousal" as a higher-order factor may yet emerge.

The notion of common higher-order factors has been extended beyond the emotional disorders to psychological disturbance in general. Krueger, Caspi, Moffitt, and Silva (1998) established two core factors from a latent structure of 10 common mental disorders among an unselected birth cohort (Dunedin Multidisciplinary Study) at the ages of 18 and 21 years. The first factor encompassed internalizing disorders — major depressive episode, dysthymia, generalized anxiety disorder, agoraphobia, social phobia, simple phobia, and obsessive–compulsive disorder. The second factor encompassed externalizing disorders of antisocial personality and substance dependence. Krueger *et al.* (1998) suggest that psychiatric disorders are best viewed as stemming from core psychopathology factors, with internalizing and externalizing disorders associated with high negative affectivity/neuroticism, and externalizing disorders also uniquely associated with low conscientiousness/constraint (i.e., impulsivity). Others have proposed similar overarching models of psychopathology (e.g., Clark *et al.*, 1994; Fowles, 1993).

In summary, neuroanatomical models of motivational states, and structural models of personality and symptom reporting converge on negative affectivity (or proneness to engage in defensive reactions) as a common factor underlying all anxiety disorders. In reference to the threat imminence model outlined in Chapter 2, proneness to defensive response styles of worry as well as fear seems to be enhanced by an underlying temperament of negative affectivity. Importantly, however, Gray's model of the behavioral inhibition system emphasizes the centrality of anxious rather than fearful responding for the anxiety disorders. For the sake of simplicity, the term "negative affectivity" is used throughout the remainder of the discussion even when the original source term was "neuroticism".

Empirical Evidence for Temperament as a Vulnerability Factor

Negative Affectivity

As would be hypothesized from a predispositional model, measures of negative affectivity at one point in time predict negative affect and symptoms of emotional distress at later points in time (Costa & McCrae, 1980; Levenson, Aldwin, Bosse, & Spiro, 1988). Lonigan, Kistner, Hooe, and David (1997) found that scores on the negative affect subscale of the Positive and Negative Affect Scale (Watson, Clark, & Carey, 1988) predicted changes in fourth to 11th graders ($n = 300$) self-reported anxiety over a period of 7 months. Negative affectivity predicted later emotional and behavioral problems in adolescents (Ge & Conger, 1999) and college students, even after controlling for initial symptom levels, albeit only in interaction with low extraversion (Gershuny & Scher, 1998). Negative affectivity (even without low extraversion) predicted later anxiety and depression in a sample of elderly people (Jorm *et al.*, 2000).

Negative affectivity also predicts later anxiety disorders. From the Dunedin Multidisciplinary Study, we found that "emotional reactivity" at 3 years of age was a significant variable in the classification of panic disorder in males at the age of 18 or 21 years (Craske, Poulton, Tsao, & Plotkin, 2001). However, emotional reactivity was based on observed lability of emotions during a series of cognitive and motoric tasks, and thus was not a direct measure of negative affectivity. In another, albeit small, study, high levels of the trait labeled "emotionality" from Buss and Plomins' (1984) EAS questionnaire (completed by parents) predicted whether siblings ($n = 31$) of probands with depression or anxiety disorders met criteria for a disorder (Kelvin, Goodyer, & Altham, 1996). However, theirs was a cross-sectional rather than a longitudinal design, and suffers from the limitations of parental report. More direct evidence comes from negative affectivity predicting panic attacks as well as major depression in a 4 year prospective study of adolescents (Hayward *et al.*, 2000). In addition, negative affectivity measured with the stress reaction subscale of the Multidimensional Personality Questionnaire (Tellegen, 1982) at 18 years of age in the Dunedin Multidisciplinary Study predicted internalizing symptoms at the age of 21 years (Krueger, Caspi, Moffitt, Silva, & McGee, 1996). Stress reaction was elevated across those with anxiety as well as affective disorders, and was especially elevated in individuals with co-occurring forms of distress. Others report that negative affectivity predicts subsequent diagnoses and chronicity of major depression (e.g., Roberts & Kendler, 1999) as well.

Behavioral Inhibition

Negative affectivity/neuroticism is closely linked with another construct operationalized by Kagan, Reznick, Clarke, Snidman, and Garci-Coll (1984) as behavioral inhibition. In the first few months of life, the observable forms of behavioral inhibition are described as high reactivity in the form of crying, irritability, high levels of motoric activity in response to stimuli, and emotionality. At the toddler age, behavioral inhibition manifests as withdrawal, seeking comfort from a familiar person, and suppression of ongoing behavior when confronted with unfamiliar people or novelty, as opposed to vocalizing, smiling, and interacting with the unfamiliar object or setting. If consistently inhibited, the shy and fearful toddler transforms into a cautious, quiet, and introverted child upon reaching school age.

The construct of behaviorally inhibited temperament clearly resembles in name the behavioral inhibition system posited by Gray (1982a). Conceptually they overlap, and, in fact, it is difficult to fully distinguish them from each other or from the construct of negative affectivity. In general, negative affectivity/neuroticism is defined by emotional responding whereas the behavioral inhibition system and behaviorally inhibited temperament are defined by emotional as well as behavioral responding. Also, whereas negative affectivity indicates a proneness to all kinds of negative affect, the two behavioral inhibition models pertain mostly to anxious and fearful affect. Whereas the behavioral inhibition system represents a broad motivation system that is activated by environmental mismatches with expectations, behaviorally inhibited temperament is more tightly defined as reactivity to unfamiliarity and particularly social unfamiliarity. Hence, negative affectivity represents a broader construct followed next by the behavioral inhibition system, which in turn is followed by the more narrowly focused construct of behaviorally inhibited temperament, and it is probably for this reason that some construe behaviorally inhibited temperament as a behavioral manifestation of the more comprehensive disposition represented in concepts such as neuroticism or negative affectivity (Turner, Beidel, & Wolff, 1996).

Kagan, Reznick, and Snidman (1987) reported that approximately 10–15 percent of US white children show signs of a behaviorally inhibited temperament, although others judge this to be an overestimate due to sample selection biases (Turner *et al.*, 1996). Also, they claim that this is one of the most stable personality traits, found to be relatively enduring for approximately three-quarters of children originally assessed at 21 or 31 months of age who were reassessed at 4, 5, or 7½ years of age (Kagan, 1989; Kagan, Reznick, Clark, Snidman, & Garcia-Coll, 1984; Reznick *et al.*, 1986). However, Turner *et al.* (1996) note that closer examination of the data shows that as many as 40 percent of behaviorally inhibited children at 21 months of age become less inhibited over time, suggesting that the trait is not quite as stable as initially thought.

Physiological corollaries of behavioral inhibition, including increased salivary cortisol levels, increased laryngeal muscle tension, pupillary dilation, high and stable heart rates, and elevated urinary catecholamine levels, are suggestive of heightened sympathetic and possibly parasympathetic activation. Turner *et al.* (1996) conclude from their review that high and stable heart rate may be the strongest predictor of behavioral inhibition that persists over years. The physiology associated with anxious-prone temperaments is described in more detail in Chapter 5, but in light of such physiological corollaries, Kagan (1997) views behavioral inhibition as a category of behavior that is qualitatively different from uninhibited behavior and which results from lowered thresholds of limbic system arousal, particularly in the amygdala and hippocampus (Kagan *et al.*, 1987). Notably, these are the areas of the central nervous system linked with conditioned anxiety responding rather than unconditioned fear. Although Kagan and others describe behaviorally inhibited features as a largely inherited response disposition, inhibited behavior may be influenced by environmental stressors, including prenatal as well as postnatal events, a point to which a large section of the next chapter is devoted.

The predisposing influence of behavioral inhibition upon the development of anxiety disorders has been investigated in a number of ways. One approach is to evaluate rates of behavioral inhibition in the offspring of parents who suffer from anxiety disorders, given that such offspring are themselves at heightened risk of developing anxiety (as described in Chapter 4). In 1988, Rosenbaum *et al.* reported that children (2–7-year-olds) of parents with panic disorder and agoraphobia, with or without accompanying depression, were more likely to be behaviorally inhibited to the unfamiliar than children of control parents. Children of depressed parents were at an increased risk for behavioral inhibition relative to controls also. The rates were 85 percent in children of panic disorder parents, 70 percent in children of parents with panic and major depression, 50 percent in children of parents with major depression, and 15 percent in children of control parents (healthy or other psychiatric disorders). As with the data regarding negative affectivity, these findings suggest that behavioral inhibition is a vulnerability factor for both anxiety and depression. In contrast, offspring of parents with anxiety disorders were no different from offspring of control parents (Merikangas *et al.*, 1999). However, some of those data were recalled retrospectively, and all of the data consisted of parent ratings. As noted earlier, parental ratings do not necessarily concur with children's internalizing symptoms, and thus behavioral observations are generally preferred.

A second approach is the family study design. Rosenbaum *et al.* (1991) found that relatives of children who were behaviorally inhibited were more likely to have multiple anxiety disorders (two or more), and a higher percentage of childhood anxiety disorders, than relatives of uninhibited and control children. The parents were most likely to be diagnosed with social phobia and avoidant disorder rather than panic disorder and agoraphobia, which some interpret as evidence for specificity of behavioral inhibition for social phobia. However, generally higher base rates for social anxiety may explain these findings, and Rosenbaum *et al.* (1991) argue for the more parsimonious model in which behavioral inhibition is a vulnerability factor for all anxiety disorders.

The third and most direct methodological approach is the longitudinal study of behaviorally inhibited children. Biederman *et al.* (1990) found that behaviorally inhibited children were at higher risk for two or more anxiety disorders (18–22 percent) than uninhibited children (0 percent). Hirshfeld *et al.* (1992) classified children as stably or unstably inhibited or uninhibited across four assessment occasions (21 months, 4 years, 5½ years, and 7½ years), and then evaluated their clinical status at 7½ years old. The stably inhibited group had more anxiety disorders than the other groups. Finally, Biederman *et al.* (1993) found that behaviorally inhibited children were more likely to have two or more anxiety disorders than non-inhibited children, although sample limitations restrict the validity of these results. Unfortunately, the overlap in samples across these three studies is not well delineated, and independent studies are few and far between. One independently conducted prospective study showed that behaviorally inhibited children, as measured by a variety of behavioral observations, were at greater risk for major depression in early adulthood but, surprisingly, not for anxiety disorders (Caspi, Moffitt, Newman, & Silva, 1997). In another independent study, retrospective self-reported behavioral inhibition predicted social phobia and depression in adolescence (Hayward, Killen, Kraemer, & Taylor, 1998), although the retrospective nature of the data is a significant limitation.

Nonetheless, Turner *et al.* (1996) conclude from their review that although the research is beleaguered by methodological limitations, particularly differing criteria for behavioral inhibition, inhibited children are more likely to have a significant anxiety syndrome and are more likely to have phobias than uninhibited children; and that this result is particularly so for stably inhibited children. Also, inhibited children are more prone to fears that have a social-evaluative basis, such as crowds, strangers, and public speaking. At the same time, it is important to remember that close to 70 percent of inhibited children remain free of any anxiety disorder (Biederman *et al.*, 1990). Consequently, rather than functioning as a trait that culminates in the development of anxiety, as would occur in a continuity model (Akiskal, 1983), behavioral inhibition may lead to a proneness to respond intensely to anxiety-producing events, perhaps due to physiological and behavioral regulatory systems, as would occur in a predisposition model such as described for negative affectivity.

Genetic Influences on Negative Affectivity

The evidence for genetic contributions to negative affectivity and its corollaries is reviewed in this section. The review extends to genetic influences on anxiety disorders because such influences are presumably mediated by temperamental factors. Strong genetic contributions are found for traits in animals that appear similar to the trait of negative affectivity in humans. For example, Suomi, Kraemer, Baysinger, and DeLizio (1981) and Suomi (1987) found a trait of "high reactivity" that influences anxiety-like behavior in rhesus monkeys. Highly reactive monkeys tend to react to repeated stressors (such as forced separations) with retreat, diminished exploration, and increased physiological arousal, in the same way as behaviorally inhibited children respond to unfamiliarity. Similar to behavioral inhibition in children, heart rate reactivity during conditioning trials at 1 month of age in these monkeys was correlated with later anxious behaviors at 12–30 months of age (Suomi *et al.*, 1981). Importantly for the current discussion, the factors most predictive of the development of such reactivity in monkeys are genetically determined (Suomi, 1987). Similarly, emotional reactivity of this type can be bred in rats and mice (Broadhurst, 1975; Gray, 1987), and selectively bred strains of reactive mice react differently to inescapable shock, even though raised in identical environments (Wieland, Boren, Consroe, & Martin, 1986). Thus, the phenotype of emotionality (aroused and reduced activity in novel environments) in mice is considered to be under strong genetic control (Trullas & Skolnick, 1993).

Until the human genome map for anxiety and depression is more fully developed, the evaluation of genetic factors in humans is mostly dependent on multivariate genetic analyses that typically compare dizygotic and monozygotic twin pairs to examine how much variation in symptoms is attributable to genetic versus environmental factors. This approach is limited in several ways, such as the frequent confounding of error variance with variance attributable to unique environmental experience, and a bias toward viewing different outcomes for monozygotic versus dizygotic twin pairs as primarily genetically versus environmentally controlled. Nevertheless, the available studies tend to yield consistent patterns of results, which are summarized below.

To facilitate the review of multivariate genetic analyses, some definitions are first provided. Additive genetic influences represent alleles from different loci adding up to influence liability for a trait or disorder. Non-additive genetic influences refer to alleles at a single locus (dominance) or at different loci (epistasis) that interact to influence a trait or a disorder. Shared environment influences refer to influences that distinguish the general environment of one family from that of another family and impact all of the children within the family to the same degree (e.g., socioeconomic status). Non-shared environmental influences include factors that have differential effects on individual family members (e.g., illness, differential child rearing) and extend to extra-familial networks such as differences in peer groups or teachers. Non-shared environment represents the residual variance after the influences of additive and non-additive genetic factors and shared environment have been removed. Thus, non-shared environmental influences usually include measurement error as well as random and non-systematic effects, although more recent analyses have attempted to extract unique environmental variance from error in measurement.

A major study was reported in 1984 by Jardine, Martin, and Henderson, who in their sample of 3180 twin adults found that approximately one-half of the variation in negative affectivity (termed neuroticism in their study) was explained by additive genetic effects. In a much smaller study, Stein, Jang, and Livesley (1999) evaluated 179 monozygotic and 158 dizygotic twins pairs to find a moderate heritability for anxiety sensitivity (the tendency to believe that anxiety is harmful), which some have suggested is a lower-order trait of neuroticism (Zinbarg, 1998). In particular, 45 percent of the variance was attributable to additive genetic influences, and 55 percent of the variance attributable to non-shared environmental influences/error. Another very comprehensive study of heritability of negative affectivity was reported by Lake, Eaves, Maes, Heath, and Martin (2000), who criticized traditional twin and adoption studies for various reasons, such as environmental similarity in monozygotic twin studies inflating non-additive genetic effects, and the skewness of the environmental situation in adoptee families. They extended from the study of twin pairs to their parents, siblings, spouses and children from Australia (21 222 respondents) and the United States (24 905 respondents) using mailed questionnaires. They found that the majority of family resemblance for neuroticism was explained by genetic influences. However, large portions of the variance were attributed to environmental influences as well. Specifically, when estimates of some of the error were taken into account, the amount of variance attributable to non-shared environmental factors was 37 percent in females and 43 percent in males; none of the variance was attributable to shared environmental factors.

Consistent with the findings pertaining to negative affectivity, several studies suggest a genetic contribution to behavioral inhibition. Matheny (1989) found that monozygotic twin pairs showed greater concordance for behavioral inhibition (measured as fearfulness, emotional tone, and approach/withdrawal behaviors) than dizygotic twins at 18–30 months of age. Also, DiLalla, Kagan, and Reznick (1994) found that monozygotic twins were more similar in their inhibited behaviors than dizygotic twins, as did Robinson, Kagan, Reznick, and Corley (1992) at 14, 20, and 24 months. However, concordance between twin pairs could be influenced by environmental factors as well and is not as telling of genetic influences as the results from multivariate genetic analyses.

Importantly, the genetic influence for negative affectivity is shared with both anxiety and depression. That is, the observed phenotypic covariation among anxious symptoms, depression symptoms and negative affectivity is due largely to a single common genetic factor (Jardine *et al.*, 1984; Kendler, Heath, Martin, & Eaves, 1987). For this reason, Mackinnon *et al.* (1990) concluded that anxiety and depression appear to be variable expressions of the heritable tendency toward negative affectivity. More recently, Kendler, Karkowski, and Prescott (1999) found a common genetic diathesis for various phobias that was strongly linked to negative affectivity as well. As alluded to in Chapter 2, symptoms of fear (i.e., breathlessness or heart pounding, feelings of panic) may be additionally explained by a unique source of genetic variance that differentiates them from symptoms of depression and anxiety (Kendler *et al.*, 1987) and from negative affectivity (Martin *et al.*, 1988). Mineka *et al.* (1998) interpret this genetic data to mean that the cognitive/affective symptoms of anxiety and depression are more closely linked with negative affectivity than are the somatic symptoms of arousal. This interpretation harkens back to the distinction made in Chapter 2 between fear (i.e., panic) and anxious worry. Thus, together with the predictive evidence presented before, these findings suggest a strong link between negative affectivity and the vulnerability to anxiety and depression, and one with which fear *per se* may not be as closely associated.

If emotional disorders represent the extreme end of the vulnerability continuum, then evaluation of genetic influences upon anxiety disorders may be a valuable endeavor. Many such studies exist but unfortunately suffer from severe methodological problems. One such problem pertains to issues of diagnostic reliability and validity. In particular, most studies of genetic variance in anxiety disorders rely on the Diagnostic Interview Schedule (DIS), which has been heavily criticized in terms of diagnostic validity. Consequently, the conclusions drawn from these studies that major depression and generalized anxiety disorder are genetically indistinguishable, reflecting a common genetic diathesis that is somewhat separate from the genetic diathesis common to panic and phobias (Kendler, 1996; Kendler, Neale, Kessler, Heath, & Eaves, 1993; Roy, Neale, Pedersen, Mathe, & Kendler, 1995), may be severely confounded by diagnostic error. Generalized anxiety disorder and major depression possess considerable symptomatic overlap and rates of diagnostic agreement for generalized anxiety disorder are lower than for most other anxiety disorders (e.g., DiNardo *et al.*, 1993) even when using diagnostic instruments more valid than the DIS. Moreover, the fact that generalized anxiety disorder is defined by 1 month instead of the usual 6 months in these studies raises the likelihood of diagnostic error even higher. As another example of the limitations of the DIS, agoraphobia is defined as unreasonable fear of going out of the house alone, being in crowds and being in open spaces, without being tied to the experience of panic or panic-like sensations. Thus, what may actually be a fear of social situations or fear of harm from others is labeled as agoraphobia. Moreover, a lifetime history approach was used for at least some if not all diagnoses. This too raises serious concerns about validity and reliability, especially given the likely inflation of historical reporting by current levels of distress. In fact, this was one of the sources of error targeted by Kendler *et al.* (1999), who established poor reliability for phobias when assessed over time.

With these limitations in mind, it is difficult to know how much value to place in the following results. First, as already mentioned, generalized anxiety disorder and depression are believed to share full genetic diathesis. Other anxiety disorders share less in common with the genetic diathesis for depression, although major depression still shares a moderate amount of genetic influence with agoraphobia, social phobia, and animal phobias (Kendler *et al.*, 1993). Originally, heritabilities for agoraphobia, social phobia, and animal phobia were estimated at between 30 and 40 percent, whereas situational phobias and blood, injury, and injection phobias showed less genetic heritability with more variance attributed to shared family environmental factors, at least in females (Kendler, Neale, Kessler, & Heath, 1992; Neale, Walters, Eaves, Kessler, Heath, & Kendler, 1994). More recently, Kendler *et al.* (1999) reassessed the role of genetic and environmental risk factors for phobias by controlling for error in reliability of diagnosis. When measurement error was taken into account, heritability estimates for these phobias increased. For example, total heritability increased for any phobia from 32 to 55 percent, for agoraphobia from 39 to 61 percent, and for social phobia from 30 to 50 percent. In addition, in this corrected analysis, the role of shared environmental factors was no longer significant for situational phobias or blood, injury, and injection phobias.

Overall, results from multivariate genetic analyses for disorders suggest two broad but distinct genetic factors. One factor is primarily defined by high loadings for major depression and generalized anxiety disorder, with moderate loadings for panic disorder. The second factor is defined primarily by panic disorder and phobias. Thus, panic disorder is viewed as being genetically distinguishable from generalized anxiety disorder and depression (Kendler, 1996; Kendler *et al.*, 1995). This separation was recently demonstrated by Scherrer *et al.* (2000), who analyzed the Vietnam Era Twin Registry of 36–55-year-old twin pairs (*n* = 6724). In this sample, 37.9 percent of the variance in risk for generalized anxiety disorder was due to additive genetic factors, with the remainder of the variance due to environmental factors. For panic disorder, 22.6 percent of the variation in risk was due to additive genetic factors in common with generalized anxiety disorder; 21.2 percent of the variance was attributed to non-additive genetic contributions specific to panic disorder, and the remainder was attributable to environmental influences.

While keeping issues of questionable diagnostic reliability and validity in mind, the findings nonetheless concur with findings based on measures of temperament and symptomatology presented earlier. That is, broadly speaking, the first of the two main genetic factors for anxiety and mood disorders (most relevant to generalized anxiety and depression, and less so but still relevant to panic disorder) may represent the genetic influences shared among negative affectivity and symptoms of anxiety and depressed mood. This possibility is made more probable given that genetic influences for symptoms of anxiety appear to be of the same ilk as genetic influences for anxiety disorders. Specifically, Kendler and colleagues (Kendler *et al.*, 1993) found that "possible" cases of panic disorder were on the same continuum of genetic liability as those diagnosed with greater certainty. The second of the two main genetic factors for anxiety and mood disorders (mostly relevant to panic disorder and phobias) may represent separable, additional genetic influences that pertain to fear and panic. Again, this possibility is made more probable by the evidence that fears of milder manifestation are on the same genetic liability dimension associated with fears of clinical severity, at least in men (Kendler, Myers, Prescott, & Neale, 2001).

Whereas most of the genetic influences are broad, most of the environmental influences are specific to either anxiety or depression (Kendler *et al.*, 1987). Another robust finding is that environmental factors are mostly composed of non-shared, individually unique influences rather than shared environmental influences, at least in adult samples. That is, experiences specific to the individual within a family appear more prominent for adult anxiety than the experiences shared by the family. Consequently, after controlling for measurement error in the assessment of risk factors for phobias, Kendler *et al.* (1999) concluded that individually specific environmental factors play a significant etiological role, with the amount of variance ranging from 40 to 60 percent for an array of phobias. Thus, a combination of broad genetic factors and individually specific environmental factors are presumed to explain most of anxious and phobic responding.

Mineka *et al.* (1998) proposed a hierarchical model that posits a higher-order variable of negative affectivity that influences all emotional disorders and thereby accounts for their co-occurrence. However, each separate disorder has its own unique component of variance that leads to different manifestations among the disorders. Presumably, environmental factors contribute to the unique components of variance for each disorder. Recently, a similar model structure has been proposed for externalizing disorders. Specifically, from their analysis of 1048 male and female 17-year-old twins, Krueger *et al.* (2002) concluded that co-occurrence among alcohol dependence, drug dependence, conduct disorder, and antisocial behavior could be traced to a highly heritable externalizing factor, and significant variance that remained unique to each syndrome was attributed to non-shared environmental factors.

What is Genetically Transmitted?

Research on what it is that is genetically transmitted has only just begun. Findings to date point to the role of serotonin. Serotonin is important because the limbic regions, particularly the amygdala, are modulated by this neurotransmitter and, therefore, are important in the regulation of anxiety (Rosen & Schulkin, 1998). The first reported human anxiety phenotype associated with a specific genetic locus was neuroticism. Lesch *et al.* (1996) found that a polymorphism in the promoter region of the serotonin transporter gene was associated with higher scores on measures of neuroticism and trait anxiety. (The transporter regulates the magnitude and duration of serotonergic responses and is partly responsible for fine tuning serotonergic neurotransmission.) Schmidt *et al.* (2000) evaluated whether genotypes of the same serotonin transporter gene predicted response to carbon dioxide challenge, an anxiogenic procedure. They also evaluated the extent to which genetic factors interacted with a psychological risk factor, that being Anxiety Sensitivity Index scores. In their community sample, genetic factors predicted level of fearfulness, and accounted for more of the variance than anxiety sensitivity. They also found a genotype × anxiety sensitivity interaction but only for heart rate variability, the reasons for which are not fully clear. Clearly, these types of studies will become more prominent in the future and provide much more direct evidence for the role of genetic factors in current psychological functioning than is provided by multivariate genetic analyses.

Genetic Influences and Age

Eley (2001) provides an excellent review of the data regarding heritability in youths. Directly parallel to adult samples, genetic influences appear to be shared between anxiety and depression in youths. Eley and Stevenson (1999) found that all genetic variance was shared across measures of anxiety and depressive symptomatology in 490 twin pairs aged 8–16 years, and this genetic factor accounted for 80 percent of the phenotypic correlation between the measures. Also as with adult samples, environmental influences were almost entirely specific to anxious or depressive symptoms. Notably, and replicating findings with adult samples yet again, the genetic and environmental influences followed the same patterns for severe fears as they did for mild fears.

In direct contrast to adult samples, however, the evidence points to a strong component of shared family environment variance in youths. For example, Eley reports a study by Stevenson, Batten, and Cherner (1992) of 319 twin pairs aged 8–18 years, where 23–59 percent of the variance for fears and phobias was attributed to shared family environment. Also, in their more recent study, Eley and Stevenson (1999) found that the amount of variance in anxiety attributed to genetic factors was 10 percent, whereas 39 percent was attributed to shared environment influences. The reasons for the more prominent role of shared family environment in youths are not fully clear. Conceivably, shared family environment influences become progressively diluted over the course of development by environmental experiences outside of the family and unique to the individual, such that non-shared environmental experiences account for more of the variance in anxiety and fearfulness by adulthood.

Several studies have examined genetic influences across different ages. Eley (2001) concludes that heritability of anxiety appears to *increase* with age from childhood to adolescence (Feigon, Waldman, Levey, & Hay, 2001), perhaps particularly for females (Eley & Stevenson, 1999; Topolski *et al.*, 1997). However, age differences were not replicated in other studies (e.g., Eaves *et al.*, 1997). That heritability for anxiety would increase with age raises the interesting possibility that genetic influences exert more influence as one is exposed to more and more life events, perhaps due to the impact of genetically predisposed temperament upon reactivity to events. The latter is described in more detail in the sections to follow.

Summary of Genetic Influences

In summary, the temperament of negative affectivity appears to be approximately 50 percent heritable in humans and under strong genetic influence in other primates and non-primates as well. Genetic influences for negative affectivity appear to be in common with genetic influences upon symptoms of anxiety and depression. Moreover, genetic influences for negative affectivity and internalizing symptoms appear to represent some of the same genetic influences found for anxiety disorders (with methodological caveats in mind). Conceivably, then, the genetic contributions to anxiety disorders are mediated by negative affectivity. Alongside a non-specific genetic influence upon negative affect, symptoms of anxiety and depression, and generalized anxiety and mood disorders, there may be a separate but still broad genetic influence upon symptoms of fear and panic, and panic disorder and phobias. The remaining variance in symptom reporting is attributable to unique environmental experiences that are different for anxiety versus depression, although shared environmental influences may be more potent in explaining variations in symptoms among youths.

Environmental Influences on Negative Affectivity

Life stressors impact proneness to negative affect, and intertwine with negative affect in such a way that life stressors are more likely and more potent in individuals with more negatively prone temperaments. Thus, sufficiently intense and chronic levels of stress may generate negative affectivity in someone who possesses no other heritable characteristics for such a temperament. In addition, it is likely that stress is more "damaging" in those with already negatively prone temperaments.

The effect of stress upon negative affectivity is well shown in the work on stress sensitization, wherein prior adversity generates heightened stress reactivity to future stressors. The fact that significant childhood adversity increases the risk for anxiety disorders as well as other disorders (Brown, Harris, & Eales, 1993; Faravelli, Webb, Ambonetti, Fonnesu, & Scarpato, 1985; Kessler *et al.*, 1997) is attributed at least in part to this type of progressively intensifying cycle of stress reactivity. For example, early trauma, especially multiple incidents of violence in childhood, increases the likelihood of posttraumatic stress disorder in reaction to later traumas (Breslau, Chilcoat, Kessler, & Davis, 1999), as well as other anxiety disorders. Hence, high rates of childhood adversity are found in Vietnam veterans who develop posttraumatic stress disorder (Bremner, Southwick, Johnson, Yehuda, & Charney, 1993; Davidson, Hughes, Blazer, & George,1991). Results from the National Comorbidity Survey indicated that the effects of childhood adversity were non-specific to particular disorders (Kessler *et al.*, 1997). In fact, early life adversities are common to depressed mood (e.g., Oakley-Browne, Joyce, Wells, Bushell, & Hornblow, 1995; Sadowski, Ugate, Kolvin, Kaplan, & Barnes, 1999) as well as to anxiousness. This non-specificity is consistent with the notion that the effects of traumas are mediated by broad factors such as negative affectivity.

Stress sensitization effects are not limited to childhood traumas. In perhaps the most comprehensive analysis of trauma sensitization to date, Breslau *et al.* (1999; Detroit Area Survey of Trauma) studied over 2000 individuals to assess the posttraumatic stress disorder effects of a randomly chosen trauma for each person (index trauma). They found that people who reported any previous trauma were more likely to experience posttraumatic stress disorder from the index trauma, and repeated traumas increased the risk in comparison with one earlier trauma. This was particularly so for a history of assaultive violence. Interestingly, there was no evidence that trauma in childhood was associated with any greater risk for posttraumatic stress disorder after an index trauma than traumas that occurred later in life. That is, the age at which exposure to trauma occurred did not relate to risk for posttraumatic stress disorder. Although this study was limited by reliance on retrospective estimates of lifetime traumatic experiences, the results are consistent with a sensitization hypothesis.

Experimentally, the effects of stress sensitization have been examined through the physiological impact of maternal separation on non-primates. Although brief maternal separations for rat pups in the first few weeks of life appear to buffer the later expression of fear and anxiety in novel environments, prolonged separations result in increased activation of the hypothalamic–pituitary–adrenal axis as seen in circulating adrenocorticotropic hormone and corticosterone, increased corticotropin-releasing hormone receptor binding at extra-hypothalamic sites, and increased hypothalamic corticotropic-releasing hormone mRNA expression in response to stressors (McIntosh, Anisman, & Merali, 1999; Meaney *et al.*, 1996). In primates too there is evidence for stress sensitization. Rosenblum and Paully (1984) subjected nursing mothers of infant monkeys to unpredictable demands when foraging for food, as opposed to predictable low-demand and predictable high-demand control environments. Unpredictable demands led to adversely altered behavior toward the infant. As a result, the infant monkeys had heightened anxiety-like behavior throughout development, including increased behavioral inhibition in response to separation, to fear stimuli, and to new social groups and environments (Coplan, Rosenblum, & Gorman, 1995). When challenged with yohimbine, these monkeys were hyperresponsive, and their corticotropin-releasing factor levels were persistently elevated (Coplan *et al.*, 1998).

Uncontrollable stressors over protracted periods of time appear to yield effects similar to prolonged maternal separation and disrupted maternal relations. Rosen and Schulkin (1998) attribute the effects of chronic and severe stress in part to non-associative neurobiological processes involving the amygdala that creates a hyperexcitability or "easier to trigger" state. Others have proposed similar models. Heim and Nemeroff (1999) speculate permanent effects on brain function of early traumas, specifically on the developing hypothalamic–pituitary axis, causing an increase in response to psychologically stressful events as adults. In addition, Sullivan, Coplan, Kent, and Gorman (1999) suggest that early adversity interacts with genetic predispositions to set general thresholds for stress activation. After such thresholds have been set, stressful life events continue to elicit stress responses that cumulatively add to stress responsivity. In turn, such stress reactivity is likely to enhance negative affectivity and increase the vulnerability to anxiety disorders.

Not only does life stress enhance negative affectivity but negative affectivity increases the likelihood and impact of life stressors. For example, Fergusson and Horwood (1987) found that negative affectivity predicted more life changes for women over a 6 year period. Headey and Wearing (1989) found that individuals who reported high extraversion scores reported more favorable life events whereas high neuroticism scores were related to the report of more negative life events. Magnus, Diener, Fujita, and Payot (1993), who followed college-age students for 4 years, found the same result. In another study, negative affectivity was a predictor of exposure to traumatic events as well as their impact (Breslau, Davis, Andreski, & Peterson, 1991). In the most recent study on this topic, Os and Jones (1999) conducted a 43 year follow-up of a general population cohort of 5362 individuals to examine the relationship between temperament at 16 years of age and adult life events and depression. Neuroticism, but not extraversion, independently increased the impact of stressful life events measured at the ages of 36 and 43 years, as well as the probability of reported stressful life events, independent of mental health. Coping behavior such as turning to others and problem solving, which buffers the effects of stressful life events, itself is influenced by genetic factors that explained 30–31 percent of the variance (Kendler, Kessler, Heath, Neale, & Eaves, 1991). Various indices of social support were similarly predicted by genetic factors in another study (Kessler, Kendler, Heath, & Neale, 1992). These data could be interpreted as heritable temperamental characteristics influencing interactions with the environment in a way that moderates the effect of stressors. Unfortunately, much of this research is tainted by self-report measurement of life events, which is likely to be highly colored by negative affect and mood state. Still, for this very reason, perceived stress may be equally important as objectively defined stress for gauging vulnerability to later distress.

Whereas the effects of stress and trauma in general appear to be non-specific and probably so because of their mediation through negative affectivity, there is some differentiation between anxiety and depression in *types* of stressors. Such differentiation would be consistent with the evidence presented earlier for most of the differentiation between anxiety and depression to be attributable to environmental influences. For example, Smith and Allred (1989) conceptualize anxiety as a response to threat of future loss, whereas depression is a reaction to past loss, and some supportive evidence was provided by Monroe, Imhoff, Wise, and Harris (1983) and Finlay-Jones and Brown (1981). Although the concept of danger was defined vaguely, significantly more anxious individuals reported a severe danger in the 3 months before onset than did depressed individuals in the study by Finlay-Jones and Brown (1981). Moreover, they argue that their results do not reflect a personality variable such as neuroticism, because the same associations were found when analyses were limited to events that were considered independent, or not provoked by the behavior of the respondent. In addition, several studies indicate that medical illnesses increase the risk for anxiety disorders in particular (Allen, Lewinsohn & Seeley, 1998; Craske *et al.*, 2001; Kagan *et al.*, 1984). Furthermore, in a review of various forms of psychopathology in adolescence and early adulthood, it was found that anxiety disorders were associated specifically with illness during the first year of life, particularly high fevers (Allen *et al.*, 1998), and in a longitudinal study of youths, Cohen, Velez, Brook, and Smith (1989) found that early somatic problems, illnesses, and injuries were associated with anxiety in adolescence but not with depression. In addition, Merikangas *et al.* (1999) found that offspring of parents with anxiety disorders were more likely to have childhood illnesses of allergies, eczema and high fever than offspring of control parents, although they did not differ from offspring of parents with substance abuse. Early illness experience has been associated with temperament as well. For example, Kagan *et al.* (1984) reported an association between allergic symptoms, particularly hay fever, and inhibited temperament in young children. Thus, medical illness may both influence and/or be influenced by negatively prone temperament, but in addition appears to have a unique relationship with anxiety disorders. Aside from biological factors (such as suppressed immune system functioning with elevated hypothalamic pituitary axis activation), medical distress at a young age is likely to increase attentional threat bias, and/or overprotectiveness of parenting style, and thus serve to magnify other known risk factors for anxiety disorders that are outlined in the chapters to follow.

Summary

Neuroticism or negative affectivity, the proneness to experience an array of negative emotional states, and to activate defensive motivational systems, predicts the later development of symptoms of anxiety and depression as well as disorders. Behavioral inhibition, or uncertainty in the face of unfamiliarity, is closely tied to negative affectivity, and predicts the development of anxiety disorders among youths as well.

Genetic as well as environmental factors appear to influence negative affectivity. Non-specific genetic influences explain approximately half of the variance in negative affectivity, and these genetic influences are in common with the genetic influences upon symptoms of anxiety and depression. There may be an additional genetic factor separate from negative affectivity that influences symptoms of intense fear or panic. Although confounded methodologically, studies of the genetic contribution to emotional disorders parallel the symptom data by converging on two broad genetic factors, one defined by high loadings for generalized anxiety disorder and depression and the other by high loadings for panic disorder and phobias. Also, genetic influences at the level of disorder appear indistinguishable from genetic influences at the level of symptomatology. Thus, the combined results suggest non-specific genetic influences upon the vulnerability to anxiety and depression, possibly mediated by negative affectivity, and additional genetic influences upon the vulnerability to fear and panic. In contrast to the mostly non-specific nature of genetic influences, environmental influences appear to be more specific to either anxiety or depression. In addition, environmental influences are mostly from shared family sources of variance in youths but are mostly unique to the individual's environment in adulthood.

Data from trauma histories in humans and experimental stress induction in animal studies indicate that life adversity lowers thresholds for stress activation and thus contributes to negative affectivity. In studies of primates and non-primates, critical stressors have included disrupted parent–offspring relationships as well as uncontrollable adverse events. Moreover, negative affect appears to enhance the likelihood as well as the impact of life stressors, thus generating a self-perpetuating cycle of stress and distress. Conceivably, sufficiently severe and prolonged stressors may generate high negative affectivity even in the absence of heritable features, although the combination of heritability and stressors no doubt generates even more negative affectivity. The effects of being stressed and suffering adversity appear to be non-specific and therefore potentially signify the mediating role of negative affectivity. However, differentiation between anxiety and depression occurs at the level of type of stressor, with the potential for a particular relationship between "danger" events and medical illness and the development of anxiety disorders. This differentiation is consistent with the evidence from multivariate genetic analyses that suggest most differentiation among emotional disorders is attributable to environmental influences.

In addition to increasing stress reactivity in a non-associative stress sensitization model, negative affectivity is presumed to enhance vigilance as proposed by Gray's (1982a) model of the behavioral inhibition system. In addition, processes of associative learning are likely to be facilitated by negative affectivity, especially in terms of overgeneralization of threat associations. Finally, processes of habituation may be impeded so that reactivity to aversive stimuli is maintained over time. These processes are outlined in the chapters to follow as the pathways through which excessive and persistent anxiety becomes manifested.

Chapter 4

Threat-based Style of Reacting to Negative Affect: Influences upon Emotion Regulation

Not only do genetic factors and major life adversities influence the proneness to negative affect but the expression of negative affect is greatly moderated by the manner in which negative emotions are managed. Indeed, management of negative affect may be as important as negative affectivity itself in the manifestation of excessive and persistent anxiety, and maladaptive reactions to negative affect may be sufficient for the emergence of anxiety disorders. Also, reactions to negative affect provide another pathway through which distinctions arise between anxiety and depression. That is, whereas negative affectivity is common to anxiety and depression, the style with which negative affect is regulated is likely to differ between them.

Emotion Regulation Defined

Power, Brewin, Stuessy, and Mahony (1991) suggest that a range of verbal and situational stimuli can lead to the automatic expression of basic emotions, and importantly in normal individuals these emotions become rapidly inhibited. For example, after presentation of a negative self-reference piece of information, normal controls are less likely to endorse negative adjectives about themselves than they were before such a presentation, if given enough time. Power *et al.* (1991) attribute this to self-regulatory processes, or "negative affect repair" processes. This is what is meant by emotion regulation — the ability to rebalance upon experiencing negative affect. The means by which such repair takes place is likely to differ at different stages of development. For a youngster, emotion regulation may take the form of diversion of attention away from aversive or overly stimulating events, whereas for a school-aged child emotion regulation may take the form of coping self-talk or problem solving.

Normal inhibitory processes seem vulnerable to breaking down in individuals with emotional disorders. Poor emotion regulation may come about in part from experiencing high levels of distress and therefore be a result from anxiety disorders. However, a certain style of emotion regulation is likely to contribute to the vulnerability to high levels of anxiety as well. In fact, some would argue that it is a necessary factor, and that negative affectivity alone is insufficient for the development of excessive fear and anxiety (Lonigan & Phillips, 2001).

Various definitions of emotion regulation exist. From the perspective of developmental psychology, Thompson (2001, p. 162) defines emotion regulation as "extrinsic and intrinsic processes responsible for monitoring, evaluating, and modifying emotional reactions". Parents promote effective management of children's emotions, presumably through modeling of their own emotion regulation as well as by actively teaching children ways of coping, such as to redirect their attention to more positive circumstances or to develop more benign construals of emotionally arousing stimuli. Hence, parent–child interactions are considered essential to emotion regulation, as reviewed later in this chapter.

From a psychobiological developmental perspective, Rothbart (1989) describes ease of arousal to stimulation — reactivity — and ability to modulate that arousal — self-regulation — as two fundamental temperaments of the first year of life. More specifically, reactivity is the ease with which motor activity, crying, vocalization, smiling, and autonomic and endocrine responses are provoked by stimulation. Rothbart's operationalization of reactivity overlaps with what was described in the last chapter as the earliest forms of negative affectivity and behavioral inhibition. One difference is that Rothbart's (1989) description of emotional reactivity incorporates positive as well as negative affectivity, whereas the models of motivational state (e.g., Davidson, 1992; Fowles, 1993; Gray, 1982a) and negative affectivity described in Chapter 3 emphasize an asymmetry toward aversive states. Self-regulation, in Rothbart's model, refers to the processes that modulate reactivity, such as attention, approach, withdrawal, attack, and self-soothing. Also noteworthy is Rothbart's description of self-regulation as a component of temperament, suggesting that it is a stable trait that influences proneness to later distress. This notion is re-emphasized in the more recent elaboration of the model by Derryberry and Rothbart (1997), who describe temperament as a self-organizing system comprising two sets of processes — reactive as well as effortful. Reactive processes are the motivational influences involving both activation and inhibitory systems, very similar to Gray's (1982, 1987) model of the behavioral activation and behavioral inhibition systems. In contrast, effortful processes involve executive functions such as intentional allocation of attention that serve to modulate the effects of reactive motivational systems. This includes features of attention that regulate the extent to which an organism can be distracted from potentially aversive stimuli (Derryberry & Reed, 1996) and the capacity for self-generated imagery to replace emotions that are unwanted with more desirable imagery scripts. Both reactive and effortful processes are believed to be central to the development of excessive anxiety.

In summary, emotion regulation is viewed as the reaction to emotional reactivity, with an emphasis on the ability to shift attention (such as from something unpleasant) and to focus attention in a sustained way, and the ability to activate or inhibit behavior. Some would argue that the style of coping with negative affect is more essential to the development of anxiety than is negative affectivity, although undoubtedly both play a role. Negative affectivity can be viewed as the propensity to activate defensive motivational states and experience negative emotions — it translates to the frequency and intensity of fearful and anxious responding (among other emotions), which is important to the *salience* of negative affect and associated stimuli. Emotion regulation

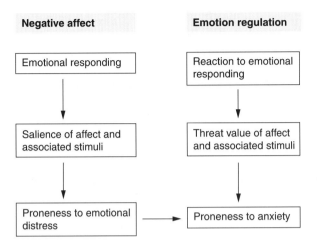

Figure 4.1: Negative affect, emotion regulation and anxiety.

is the propensity to sooth emotional reactivity — it translates to the reaction to negative affect. Certain styles of reacting are presumed to be more likely to contribute to excessive anxiety than other styles, just as other styles may be more likely to contribute to depressed mood or conduct disordered behavior. Reactions that enhance the *threat value* of negative affect are presumed to be most relevant to excessive anxiety (Figure 4.1).

Factors that contribute to style of responding to negative affect are reviewed in this chapter. As will be seen, emotion regulation both contributes to anxiety *and* represents the manifestation of anxiety: "rarely does an emotion get generated in the absence of recruiting associated regulatory processes. For this reason, it is often conceptually difficult to distinguish sharply between where an emotion ends and regulation begins" (Davidson, 1998, p. 308). The intertwining becomes very evident as the discussion proceeds through this chapter and the next, where processes of anxiousness are described.

Biological Influences upon Emotion Regulation

Emotion regulation is developmentally determined in part by neurophysiological maturation. For example, throughout the first year of life, excitatory processes of emotional arousal begin to stabilize due to changes in neuroendocrine and parasympathetic systems (Porges, Doussard-Roosevelt, & Maiti, 1994) that enable the infant to become more effective at self-soothing and soothable. Indeed, the parasympathetic branch of the autonomic nervous system, and in particular the vagus nerve, is considered critical to this self-regulatory process, because it imposes a very potent dampening on the output of sympathetic activation and is central to attentional processing. In contrast to phasic, reactive, and reflexive orienting to a stimulus, sustained attention involves more voluntary processes of vigilance that is facilitated by suppression of heart rate variability. As noted in Chapter 2, the state of worry and possibly depressive rumination is associated with lowered heart rate variability, consistent with the sustained vigilance that is invoked. More important, however, is tonic level of heart rate variability that is presumed to "index the ability to organize physiological resources and respond adaptively" (Thayer, Friedman, Borkovec, Johnsen, & Molina, 2000, p. 362). Specifically, individuals with chronically low vagal tone (i.e., attenuated heart rate variability due to respiratory sinus arrhythmia) are presumed to lack flexibility whereas those with higher physiological variability have more self-regulatory capacity to adjust to stressful events (Porges, 1990). Hence, tonic heart rate variability correlates positively with the strength of phasic reflexive orienting responses (Thayer *et al.*, 2000). In other words, higher tonic vagal tone facilitates orienting to discrete environmental stimuli that is needed for a style of responsive engagement with the environment. By contrast, lower tonic cardiac vagal tone is indicative of non-responsiveness characterized by poorer attention to and poorer discrimination among environmental cues (Friedman & Thayer, 1998b). (How well this relates to the more effortful attentional control as described by Derryberry and colleagues (i.e., shifting attention away from unpleasant stimuli and focusing attention on given tasks) is not clear but conceivably orienting and discrimination enable more effortul attentional control.)

Poor discrimination among external stimuli and inflexible responding to variations in the environment may contribute to indiscriminant responding and over-generalizability of anxiousness. For example, explicit recognition of triggers for emotional responses as well as the relations among external stimuli is likely to be impaired, and thereby contribute to a sense of unpredictability. Moreover, contingency awareness of the relationship between a neutral and an aversive stimulus may have a profound impact upon the generalizability of conditioning. Evidence for this derives from studies in which the predictability of an aversive stimulus is manipulated. Specifically, predictable or signaled shocks lead to conditioned fear responding to a discrete stimulus whereas unsignaled shocks lead to more conditioned fear responding to surrounding contextual stimuli (Grillon, 2002a). Similarly, pairings of shock with the offset of a conditioned stimulus led to potentiated startle during presentation of the conditioned stimulus whereas random shocks that were not presented in association with a conditioned stimulus resulted in greater startle potentiation in the anticipatory baseline phase of a second recording session (Grillon & Davis, 1997) as if to imply greater anxiety in response to the laboratory context in which shocks had previously been administered. In another study, awareness or verbalization of the contingency between a shock and a conditioned stimulus was associated with better conditioning to explicit conditioned stimuli whereas failure to recognize that the conditioned stimulus predicted shock led to enhanced reactivity across the board, including to a neutral stimulus that was never paired with shock (Grillon, 2002b). Grillon (2002a) viewed the unaware group as being in a more generalized state of anxiety throughout conditioning, consistent with other evidence for contingency awareness to relate negatively to trait anxiety (Chan & Lovibond, 1996). Although there is some debate over the importance of *verbal recognition* of the conditioned–unconditioned stimulus contingency for all forms of conditioning (Öhman & Mineka, 2001 versus Lovibond & Shanks, 2002), the profile of responding that is seen with unpredictable aversive stimuli as well as "unaware" participants who presumably experience aversive stimuli in an unpredictable manner is consistent with enhanced anticipatory reactivity in highly anxious individuals (see Chapters 5 and 6).

Grillon (2002a, p. 970) suggests that "if the OR [orienting response] is related to the organism's ability to perceive environmental changes, to discriminate among stimuli, and to learn appropriate conditioned responses, deficits in OR could be a risk factor for anxiety or could contribute to the maintenance of anxiety symptoms". Thus, a robust orienting response to discrete environmental cues, which appears to be vagally mediated, may be necessary for flexible and adaptive responding: chronically low vagal tone may contribute to unpredictability and lack of awareness of contingencies by mitigating the orienting response and impairing the ability to discern relations among events in the environment, that in turn contributes to overgeneralized responding to environmental threats.

If all of this is true, then vagal tone should correlate with and predict levels of emotion regulation and emotional distress. Fox (1989) found that compared with infants with low vagal tone, 5-month-old infants with high vagal tone were more likely to use effective emotion regulation strategies, such as vocalizing when distressed. During later toddler and early childhood years, vagal tone associates positively with uninhibited and assertive behavior, sociability in boys, expressiveness, the ability to deal with new situations and sustained attention (see Eisenberg *et al.*, 1996). Low vagal tone is associated with negative emotionality and exaggerated fear responses to novel stimuli (Quas, Hong, Alkon, & Boyce, 2000). Cole, Zahn-Waxler, Fox, Usher, and Welsh (1996) found poor emotion regulation (defined by emotional expressiveness) to be associated with low vagal tone in elementary school-aged children. Even though inconsistencies occur, leading Quas *et al.* (2000) to conclude that psychobiological indices should not be considered in isolation as determinants of emotional state, low vagal tone correlates with high trait anxiety (Yeragani *et al.*, 1998) and lower levels of tonic cardiac vagal tone are observed in adults with anxiety disorders, including generalized anxiety disorder (e.g., Thayer *et al.*, 1996), obsessive–compulsive disorder (e.g., Hoehn-Saric *et al.*, 1995), and panic disorder (e.g., Aikins & Craske, 2003 in press; Hoehn-Saric *et al.*, 1991; Yeragani *et al.*, 1990). Of course, these data may just as easily reflect the effect of high levels of emotional distress upon vagal tone, especially since vagal tone is positively affected by treatments for anxiety and depression (e.g., Craske, Lang, Aikins, & Mystkowski, 2003 in press; Middleton & Ashby, 1995;). Evidence for a *contributory* role of low vagal tone in the development of psychopathology is sparse, although Katz and Gottman (1995) found that the level of vagal tone at 5 years of age predicted behavior problems (broadly defined) 3 years later. In addition, indirect evidence comes from the study of behaviorally inhibited children (see Chapter 3), who themselves are at heightened risk for anxiety disorders, and who possess high and stable heart rates (e.g., Turner *et al.*, 1996), indicative of low cardiac vagal tone.

Vagal tone itself is not completely biologically determined, and other influential factors include parent–child relations. In fact, Schore (2001) speculates that the primary caregivers' behavior toward the infant has a significant impact on the maturing limbic system and the resultant flexibility and adaptablity of emotional responding. Such parental influences are described next.

Parental Influences on Emotion Regulation

Parent–infant Interactions: Prediction and Control

The effects of parenting style are relevant even in the first few months of life. As reviewed by Papousek and Papousek (2001), infants are capable of processing informational input, such as maternal voice, in the later months of intrauterine life, of simple forms of learning and intentional and instrumental acts in the earliest postpartum months, and of detecting rules in environmental events and adjusting behaviors accordingly by 3–4 months. Human crying in its earliest postpartum forms is a part of self-regulation, but it very soon becomes intentional due to operant conditioning when it repeatedly elicits a contingent response from the caregiver. As already mentioned in reference to orienting responses, contingency is central to emotion regulation, and contingency awareness is influenced by reciprocal interactions between caregiver and infant.

Papousek and Papousek (2001) describe "intuitive parenting", or responding to infant signals at a latency that is below that necessary for conscious perception. In particular, parents sometimes respond within 200–400 ms to infant signals even though a minimum of 500 ms is necessary for conscious perception. Papousek and Papousek argue that this type of intuitive parenting is best activated by stress-free play with the infant so that the first signs of attention and responsivity from the infant can prime intuitive predispositions in the parent for further interchanges. While the majority of parental behaviors toward offspring is not intuitive, a certain minimal level may be critical because intuitive parenting facilitates "coordination" in the way mothers and infants respond to each other's affective and behavioral displays. Tronick (1989) defines coordination as the caregiver's behavior being guided by the infant's expressive displays — gaze, facial expressions, gestures, vocalizations — and in turn the infant states being affected by the expressive displays of the caregiver.

A relative amount of coordination between parent and infant may be critical to the development of a sense of prediction and control; two factors that are central to emotional distress and the management of such distress. By observing their caregivers' responses to their own cues, infants learn associations between response and outcome, how to influence their carer's behavior, and the principle of instrumental learning (Papousek & Papousek, 1997). That is, reciprocal reactions to the infant's own state teaches an awareness of contingency. Also, through coordination infants learn to develop expectations of the behavior of others (Rochat & Striano, 1999). A body of evidence shows that when the parent's responses are not synchronized with the child's behavior, learning is reduced and performance in subsequent learning tasks is adversely affected (Dunham & Dunham, 1990). For example, contingent parent–child interaction predicts infant persistence in habituation tasks (Ruddy & Bornstein, 1982) and in mastery motivation tasks (Yarrow *et al.*, 1984). Some of these effects are attributable to attentional processing, given that contingent or coordinated interactions with the parent facilitate the development of sustained attention (e.g., Papousek & Papousek, 1997; Ruff & Rothbart, 1996), orienting and attentional control (e.g., Kochanska, Murray, & Harlan, 2000). As just reviewed, orienting and attentional involvement in the environment appear to be vagally mediated, and hence parent–infant synchronicity may impact tonic levels of cardiac vagal tone that in turn influences proneness to overgeneralized anxiety. The end of the first year of life is a critical time for the infant's behavior and attention to be affected by the caregiver's responses events because that is when infants themselves become more aware of the focus of caregiver's attention (as seen by following the direction of an adult's gaze) (e.g, Reddy, Hay, Murray, & Trevarten, 1997). Finally, by carefully monitoring the infant's state and using calming and soothing, parents regulate infant's arousal (Ruff & Rothbart, 1996) and enable the child to develop greater tolerance for higher arousal states (Roggman, 1991), which together promote early self-regulation.

In summary, parental monitoring and reactivity to infant signals enables the infant to orient and learn contingency between response and outcome, and awareness of such contingencies is the foundation of a sense of predictability. Initially, the predictability is between the infant's cues and the caregiver's response; eventually it transfers to a contingency between the infant's own attention/behaviors and emotional state (i.e., self-regulation). Such self-regulation soothes current distress and facilitates effective management of future stressors because predictability is inherently calming for the most part and it offsets the stressfulness of aversive experiences. The degree to which unpredictability fuels over generalizability of conditioned responding to aversive contexts was already reviewed. Other effects have been experimentally investigated in both primates and non-primates, and although the results are complex (Abbott, Schoen, & Badia, 1984; Mineka & Henderson, 1985; Minor, Dess, & Overmeir, 1991) they can be summarized as follows. We possess a general preference for being able to predict aversive events, by knowing their intensity or duration or by a warning signal (e.g., Weinberg & Levine, 1980). Unpredictable aversive events generally elicit more physiological disturbance than do predictable events (e.g., Miller, Greco, Vigorito, & Marlin, 1983; Weiss, 1970) and prolonged exposure to aversive unpredictable events sometimes leads to chronic anxiety, depressive mood, lowered motivation, lowered sexual interest, and cognitive deficits (e.g., DeCola & Rosellini, 1990; Weiss, 1970). There are also positive effects of having prediction over aversive events. For example, negative effects of uncontrollable stressors are minimized by predictability of the stressors (e.g., DeCola, Rosellini, & Warren, 1988; Jackson & Minor, 1988; Minor, Trauner, Lee, & Dess, 1990; Overmier & Murison, 1989), and prediction of aversive events lowers catecholamine levels and anticipatory anxiety (e.g., Frankenhauser, 1986; Geer & Maisel, 1972). Very importantly, negative effects can develop in animals when unpredictability is experienced over *positive* events such as food or even environmental stimulation (Mineka & Hendersen, 1985; Tazi, Dantzer, & Moal, 1987).

Notably, much of the experimental research refers to prediction of one stimulus by another stimulus, whereas the concept of emotion regulation refers to prediction of outcome by response. It is for this reason that emotion regulation is intricately tied to controllability as well as predictability. Tronick and Cohn (1989) propose that coordination serves an important developmental function because, when successful, it leads to a sense of control and effectance in the infant, the promotion of interaction skills, and self-regulation of emotion (Tronick, 1989). By example (Chorpita & Barlow, 1998, p. 11),

> healthy infants who become overstimulated during interaction with the mother can signal the mother to de-escalate the interaction using subtle cues (e.g., head turning). Mothers who respond to these cues appropriately allow the child to return to a state of less arousal, and hence prevent crying or other disorganized affect in the child. At some point, this ability to negotiate the intensity of the interaction is thought to become internalized in the infant.

Thus, infants learn to control their own emotional responses.

Very relevant in this regard is the evidence for early experience with control to buffer the later expression of fear and anxiety. In a study by Mineka, Gunnar, and Champoux (1986), infant rhesus monkeys were either allowed control over appetitive events (toys and food) or were yoked with the master group and thus matched on exposure to appetitive events but without personal control over when such exposure would occur. Several months later, the master group of monkeys was observed to habituate more quickly to a mechanical toy robot, demonstrate more exploratory behavior in a novel play room setting, and show enhanced active coping responses during selected trials of separation from peers. In another study, administrations of a benzodiazepine agonist for a group of monkeys that had previously been given, experiences of control and mastery resulted in the display of more aggression whereas the group without such prior experiences exhibited more distress and avoidance (Insel, Champoux, Scanlan, & Suomi, 1988). Hence, Mineka and Cook (1986) concluded that mastery and control immunize the effects of stressful experiences. Parenting styles that enhance the infant's sense of control therefore may buffer the child against future negative stressors.

In summary, the buffering effect of early control and prediction on subsequent reactivity to stressors is potentially critical to the proneness to anxiety. In the context of infants and emotion regulation, prediction refers to attention to and prediction of stimuli by other events in the environment, as well as prediction of outcomes by virtue of one's own responding. Thus, an *awareness of contingent relationships* is formed, and such contingency awareness is tied to attentional processes and cardiac vagal tone that may be critical to generalizability of anxious responding. Control, in this case, refers mainly to control over outcomes and emotions by virtue of one's own attention and behaviors — or the *personal exertion of contingency.* (Hence, some have argued that the effects of control are explained by prediction, because it is the predictability inherent in making a control response that accounts for the positive effects of having control (Averill, 1973; Mineka & Hendersen, 1985).) In either case, the immediate effects of lack of prediction and lack of control for the infant are increased emotional distress, and the long-term effects are impedance of effective self-regulation of negative affect and increased negative impact of future stressors. Conversely, early control and prediction presumably facilitates more effective self-regulation skills and buffers the impact of later stressors.

Parent–child synchronicity is likely to be moderated by both the parent's as well as the child's temperament. Anxious or otherwise distressed parents perhaps possess poorer intuitive parenting due to rumination and worry that diverts them from responding to infant signals. The research to date is limited to depressed mothers who do indeed show impaired responsiveness to their children who in turn become distressed and more avoidant of contact (Field, 1984). The link with anxiety and intuitive parenting skills is yet to be empirically investigated. Moreover, parenting is not independent of the child's responding. Lowinger (1999) assessed 56 male infants 3 days postpartum, in terms of irritability to aversive stimuli, general irritability and consolability, and orientation to animate and inanimate stimuli. Mother–infant interactions and irritability were monitored again behaviorally at 10 weeks postpartum. Reciprocity of mother–infant interactions was coded in terms of the mother and infant showing the same mode of social behavior (gaze, vocal, smile behaviors) and reciprocal hold (holding and being held). Lowinger (1999) found that irritability to aversive stimuli at 3 days old correlated positively with reciprocal social interaction 10 weeks later, and did not correlate with hold behaviors. General irritability correlated positively with reciprocal social interaction but negatively with reciprocal hold behaviors 10 weeks later. The measure of general irritability included "consolability by the mother", and thus it makes sense that less consolability at 3 days correlated with less holding reciprocity at 10 weeks. Lowinger proposed that crying that is not in relation to the mother's attempts to console but instead represents irritability to aversive stimuli has no adverse bearing on the baby's interactions with the mother and in fact correlates positively with later social reciprocity. If the irritability extends beyond specific aversives and crying occurs in relation to the mother's attempts to console, then reciprocity in the form of touch and hold may be dampened. These findings highlight the interaction between offspring temperament and parenting behavior. They raise the possibility that negative affectivity in the infant, evident in general irritability and lack of consolability, may elicit less synchronous parenting for certain behaviors. In turn, such desynchrony may contribute to a sense of lack of control and negatively impact emotion regulation in the child. Again, however, more research is needed on this topic and its relation to anxiety disorders.

Parent–child Interactions

Over the course of development, poor parental responsiveness to infant signals may be replaced with a parental style guided by rigid rules or biases. Bowlby (1969, 1980) was a major pioneer in the study of parent–child relationships and attachments. He proposed that caregivers serve an evolutionary and biological function of a protective and secure base from which the child operates. Critical is a secure and predictable relationship with the caregiver so that when the child encounters novelty or threat he/she can retreat safely to the caregiver. According to Bowlby, a disrupted relationship may lead to anxious attachment in which the child is chronically dependent or apprehensive. Attachment research has been fraught with methodological difficulties, but recent studies have been informative about characteristics of parenting style of parents of anxious children and of anxious parents.

The first, albeit weakest, line of research is the study of anxious individuals' recollections of their parents' behavior. Parker, Tulping, and Brown (1979) designed the Parental Bonding Instrument, which incorporated two principal variables that they believed influenced parental bonding — care (i.e., communication and expression of affection and promotion of closeness) and overprotection/control (inability to allow personal growth, independence, and respect of child's autonomy). They found that agoraphobic patients scored their mothers and fathers as less caring and more overprotective than did controls. The same was found for patients with panic disorder and generalized anxiety disorder (Silove, Parker, Hadzi-Pavlovic, Manicavasagar, & Blasvysnski, 1991). Unfortunately, these types of studies are severely confounded by retrospective biases and the influence of current mood state on judgment.

Other studies evaluate children's current perceptions of their parent's behavior. In general, children of anxious parents view their families as less cohesive, more conflictual, less independent, and more controlling than children in normal control families (see Whaley, Pinto, & Sigman, 1999). In addition, anxiety-disordered children describe their family environments as promoting less independence than do control children (Messer & Beidel, 1994). Bennet and Stirling (1998) compared families with low-trait-anxious children, high-trait-anxious children, and anxiety-disordered children, using the Parental Bonding Instrument. The anxiety-disordered group rated their mothers as less caring than the other two groups, and the high-trait-anxious group rated their mothers as less caring than the low-trait-anxious group. Also, anxiety-disordered children rated their mothers as more overprotective than each of the other two groups. Again, however, these studies are limited by reliance on self-report and the effects of current distress on perceptions of family functioning.

Observational studies are the least contaminated by bias and fortunately they yield results that converge with the subjective data. Dumas, LaFreniere, and Serketich (1995) coded interactions of parents with anxious children, parents with aggressive children and parents with controls (averaging around 4 years of age) as the dyad planned an efficient route through a miniature grocery store laid out as a three-dimensional board game. In the aggressive dyad, children made relatively high use of coercive control, and mothers responded indiscriminately or failed to oppose their children's more extreme form of coercion. In anxious dyads, mothers were more controlling and more likely to be aversive in their behavior or affect. The differences between anxious and aggressive dyads suggest that certain types of parenting may guide an anxious-prone style of reacting whereas other parenting behaviors guide more of an aggressive prone style of reacting. Siqueland, Kendall, and Steinberg (1996) analyzed observer ratings and self-ratings of parental psychological autonomy and warmth/acceptance in discussions with children with anxiety disorders and control children. Each family participated in four 6-minute discussions of topics rated as very prevalent and contentious. Psychological autonomy granting was defined as "the degree to which the parent constrains or encourages the child's individuality through the use of inductive disciplinary techniques. This is in contrast to psychologically coercive forms of control such as guilt induction, love withdrawal, and power assertion" (Siqueland *et al.*, 1996, p. 229). Warmth was defined as "the affective or emotional qualities of the parent–child relationship" (Siqueland *et al.*, 1996, p. 230), extending from cold, distant, and lacking expressions of warmth to frequent and consistent expressions of warmth. Parents of children with anxiety were coded as less granting of psychological autonomy than parents of control children. There were no differences in terms of observer ratings of warmth, although anxious children rated their parents as less accepting than did control children. Thus, the authors concluded that the combination of the child's experience of lack of acceptance or tolerance of his/ her own views or feelings and discrepancies between the child's and parent's views and feelings may contribute to anxiety disorders. Furthermore, Siqueland *et al.* (1996) suggested that due to over-involvement and overprotection, children with anxiety may form a working model of themselves as incompetent and fragile.

Other studies confirm these findings. In interactions with their children, mothers of anxious children agreed less with their child than did mothers of control children, and were less likely to point out positive consequences (Barrett, Rapee, Dadds, & Ryan, 1996; Dadds, Barrett, Rapee, & Ryan, 1996). Hudson and Rapee (2001) evaluated mothers and their 7–15-year-old children engaged in two difficult cognitive tasks (anagrams and Scrabble), comparing anxious children ($n = 43$) with oppositional children ($n = 20$) and controls ($n = 32$). As with previous research, mothers of anxious children were more involved and more intrusive than mothers of control children, and were more negative during the interactions than with control children. In addition, despite an overall reduction in parental involvement with age, the differences between anxious child interactions and control child interactions remained the same over different ages. However, in contrast to the findings of Dumas *et al.* (1995), there were no differences in the interactions between mothers and anxious children versus oppositional children. The authors provide several explanations for this finding. First, "overinvolvement may be a parenting style general to pathology, in that whenever a child develops a problem, a parent responds by becoming more involved" (Hudson & Rapee, 2001, p. 1422). Second, overinvolvement may derive from the fact that parents attempt to prevent their children — whether anxious or oppositional — from becoming distressed. Comparison with the type of involvement expressed by the same mother toward non-distressed children in the family may help clarify these issues. A third possibility, that overinvolvement of mothers represents their own pathology, was not supported by their finding that mothers of oppositional and anxious children reported as much anxiety and depression as mothers of control children. However, this is not to suggest that parental distress is unimportant to parenting style.

Whaley *et al.* (1999) studied anxious mothers in an attempt to disentangle the effect of the mother's pathology from the child's. In comparison with control mothers, anxious mothers were observed to catastrophize and criticize more, be less granting of autonomy, and display less warmth (Whaley *et al.* 1999). Whaley *et al.* (1999) also found that parenting behaviors predicted offspring anxiety levels, and, conversely, the child's anxiety level predicted maternal granting of autonomy, although not other parenting features. Also, when child anxiety was covaried, the relationship between maternal anxiety and these parenting behaviors remained for the most part, with the exception of criticism. In other words, not all of the parental behaviors were solely attributable to offspring anxiety. However, there is clearly a magnifying relation between parenting behaviors and offspring anxiety. As Rapee (1997) acknowledges, anxious mothers are likely to have low perceived control in the caregiver role, resulting in a tendency to react poorly to temperamentally difficult children. For example, unconfident parents may be more likely to use more intrusive and controlling behaviors with temperamental children. Thus, mothers with psychopathology and/or low perceived control may exhibit poorer parenting behaviors in general, and these behaviors become exacerbated by "problem" children of any type. Noteworthy here are the previously mentioned results from Lowinger (1999): an irritable unconsolable infant may contribute to parental lack of confidence, and perhaps especially so in already anxious parents. Conversely, responsive parenting may offset negative affectivity in the child. For example, Gunnar, Larson, Hertsgaard, Harris, and Broderson (1992) found that 9-month-old infants showed an elevated stress reaction (as measured by cortisol) to separation from their mother but that this effect was eliminated when the infant was with a highly responsive versus a less responsive caretaker.

Adding to the effects of excessively desynchronous and uncoordinated parenting, intrusive or overprotective parenting may detract from a child's sense of control that in turn increases proneness to anxiety. In support, although derived from self-report instead of behavioral observations, locus of control was found to mediate between perceived family control and symptoms of anxiety and depression in a mixed group of non-clinical and clinical youths (Chorpita, Brown, & Barlow, 1998). Instrumental effects of lack of control are also damaging. That is, by being protected from experiencing distress or from independence of thought and action, children are prevented from learning effective ways of problem solving and managing distress. Thus, the overcontrolled child's history of successful coping, mastery, or resolution of difficult situations and emotions may be quite restricted, rendering the child less prone to future mastery and coping. Similarly, in their comprehensive review of environmental influences on anxiety, Chorpita and Barlow (1998) concluded that early experiences with diminished control, particularly as a result of parenting, lead to perceptions of low control when encountering new situations, or a generalized tendency to perceive events as not within one's control, that in turn creates distress. Thus, control is both a mediator and a moderator of ongoing anxiety. Related is the notion of self-efficacy, or "the conviction that one can successfully execute the behavior required to produce an outcome" (Bandura, 1977, p. 193). Self-efficacy expectations are presumed to influence the choice of activities and settings, and determine the degree of effort expended and persistence in the face of obstacles or aversive experiences. In other words, self-efficacy is believed to influence coping in threatening situations. Self-efficacy not only predicts performance but is elevated by performance accomplishments, and yet such competencies may be limited due to overprotective or controlling parenting. Cole and colleagues (e.g., Cole, 1991; Cole, Jacquez, & Maschman, 2001; Cole, Peeke, Dolezal, Murray & Canzoniero, 1999) found that children's judgments of self-competency in areas such as athletics, academics, social acceptance, physical appearance and behavioral conduct related negatively to depression and anxiety. Their self-competency judgments were not solely biased self-appraisals because they were strongly related to ratings of their competency by parents, teachers, and peers. Importantly, prospective longitudinal evaluation indicated that changes in certain competency judgments predicted changes in negative affect and changes in negative affect predicted changes in other competency judgments (Cole *et al.*, 1999). Thus, developing competency in various domains of functioning may buffer against over-anxiousness. It seems reasonable to assume that self-efficacy and perceived self-competency are intricately tied with a parenting style that encourages independence.

Another result of intrusive or overprotective parenting is limited breadth of experience in different activities and situations. A wide range of experience may offset the impact of subsequent negative experiences. That is, the principle of latent inhibition (Rescorla, 1974) presupposes that non-fearful experiences with specific stimuli lessen subsequent acquisition of conditioned aversive associations with those stimuli. For example, prior history of athleticism may decrease the likelihood of becoming fearful of unexpected autonomic sensations in much the same way that prior history of air travel may decrease the likelihood of becoming fearful of flying after a turbulent flight. Thus, exposure to a number of different activities (e.g., physical activities, traveling, social activities, caring for animals) may not only serve to increase self-efficacy and self-competency but decrease the vulnerability to phobic responding following negative experiences. Furthermore, exposure to a wide array of situations and activities may facilitate habituation of fears, especially fears that are developmentally appropriate (see Chapter 1) and could develop into clinically significant phobias if they do not habituate (Menzies & Clark, 1995c: see Chapter 6).

In summary, relative lack of synchronicity with an infant's signals may represent the developmentally earlier manifestation of the same process as intrusive, overcontrolling and rejecting parenting during childhood. Such a style of parenting may be common to a variety of emotional disorders, and more research is needed of parenting style in anxious versus depressed versus otherwise distressed parents with anxious versus depressed versus otherwise distressed children, within and across families. Moreover, the degree to which an intrusive and negative parenting style is primed by the child's own temperament warrants further research evaluation. Finally, and most importantly, is the need for prospective evaluation of parenting style and the development of offspring anxiety.

Parental Expectations

Maturation of cortical processes that inhibit emotion, especially in the prefrontal cortex, begins in infancy but continues throughout childhood. Cortical forms of emotion regulation include interpretations, and these are particularly likely to be influenced by learning from parental figures. According to Thompson (2001), children often alter their constructions of reality for the purpose of managing their emotions — "its just a story", or "my friend didn't really mean to hurt me". Adults attempt the same reconstruction to help manage their children's emotions. Parents with fixed and biased interpretations of the world as a dangerous place are likely to model and/or teach more threatening interpretations that leave the child at greater risk of poor management of their own emotions (Thompson, 2001). Similarly, parents' expectations of their own children's distress may have dramatic effects on the children's ability to manage their emotions effectively.

Parents of anxious children tend to selectively focus on future negative outcomes for their children's current activities in comparison with parents of non-anxious children, and such expectations may increase childrens' anxiety. For example, Chorpita *et al.* (1996b) found that parental discussion with their child about ambiguous scenarios resulted in changes in the child's interpretation and plan for coping in a way that correlated with the level of anxiety expressed by the parents. They suggested that threat biases in the child were primed by anxious ideas from the parents. Unfortunately, their study was limited by a small sample of only four anxious children and eight non-anxious controls. With larger sample sizes and a comparison group, Barrett *et al.* (1996) replicated their basic findings; parents of socially anxious children expected their children to avoid as a way of coping with socially threatening situations, and parents of children with specific phobias expected more avoidance in response to physically threatening situations. In addition, after a family discussion, avoidant responses as a way of coping with potentially threatening situations increased in anxious children but remained unchanged in oppositional children. These findings highlight the reinforcing role of parental expectations and behaviors upon anxious children, and indicate a kind of specificity in the method of coping for anxiety (i.e., avoidance) versus conduct problems. Further analyses of the family discussion revealed that parents of anxious children indeed encouraged avoidant responding (Dadds, Barrett, Rapee, & Ryan, 1996). These results strongly suggest that certain types of parental reactions may contribute specifically to the development of fear and anxiety. Thus, "children might be learning to interpret and respond to certain situations within their family contexts. The children's dysfunctional response patterns (avoidant–anxious, aggressive–oppositional) might be maintained and fueled by parental reinforcing expectations and modeling of negative behaviors (reassurance, overprotection with anxious children; aggression, hostility with oppositional children)" (Barrett *et al.*, 1996, p. 201). Note, again, the interactions between the child's temperament and parental expectations and behaviors.

Parental Informational Transmission and Modeling

Another parental influence pertains to the pathways through which specific types of fears are acquired in children and adolescents. As reviewed in Chapter 6, research with adults has shown that specific fears often are acquired via conditioning (e.g., being attacked by a dog), vicarious observation (e.g., observing a friend show intense distress during public speaking), or informational transmission (e.g., being warned about the dangers of thunder and lightning) (Rachman, 1978). Parental influences may be particularly prominent in the vicarious modeling and informational transmission of fears to children, and represents an aspect of parental influence that is specific to anxiety relative to other forms of distress in their children.

Surveys of adults whose current fears developed during childhood confirm these three pathways of fear acquisition (e.g., Öst, 1985), although these data are heavily biased by retrospective reconstructions. In youth samples, Ollendick and King (1991) reported that the majority of 9–14-year-olds attributed the onset of their fears to modeling (56 percent) and informational (89 percent) processes. In addition, parents indicated that 26 percent of their 5-year-old children developed fears of water due to modeling (Menzies & Clark, 1993). Of course, verbal report of fear onset, particularly by a third party (the parent) who is not privy to every childhood experience is a weak method for assessing the role of modeling and informational transmission.

Instead of verbal report of the onset of their child's fears, Muris, Steerneman, Merckelbach, and Meesters (1996a, 1996b) asked parents to rate the degree to which they generally expressed their own fears in the presence of their children. Children of mothers who often expressed their fears exhibited the highest fear levels, while children of mothers who reported never expressing their fears showed the lowest fear (and mother's and children's fears were related). Their results are consistent with an earlier finding by Silverman *et al.* (1988) that children of parents who were most avoidant (i.e., most overtly fearful) showed the most anxiety problems. Again, however, the credence that can be given to parents self-reports of their own behavior is obviously limited. More convincing is the observation of children's reactions to their parent's distress. For example, 1-year-olds placed on a visual cliff were more fearful and did not cross the cliff when mothers on the other side displayed fearfulness, while 74 percent crossed the cliff when mothers showed joy and interest (Sorce, Emde, Campos, & Klinnert, 1985). Also, toddlers exhibit fear of novel stimuli after observing their mothers express a fearful facial expression toward the stimulus (e.g., Mumme & Fernald, 1996). For example, Gerull and Rapee (2002) evaluated 15–20-month-old toddlers' (*n* = 30) reactions to their mother's facial expression toward a toy rubber snake or spider. In the negative condition, mothers indicated by facial expression how "horrible, scary, and yucky" the toy was, and in the positive condition they indicated how "fun, cute, and nice" the toy was. The infants' responses were coded in terms of approach–avoidance and affect. All toddlers were more fearful and avoidant of the toy after the negative condition. These findings were attributed to social referencing, whereby children actively search for emotional information from their caregiver and use this to appraise uncertain and unknown situations. An alternative explanation involves principles of conditioning, whereby the display of fearful behavior in an affiliated other is an unconditioned stimulus that generates conditioned fear in the observer (Mineka & Cook, 1993), and has been offered as an explanation for monkeys developing persistent fears from observing other monkeys display fearful behavior (Mineka & Cook, 1993; Mineka, Davidson, Cook, & Keir, 1984). Furthermore, Mineka has shown that prior exposure to others (monkeys) behaving non-fearfully in the presence of a particular stimulus can immunize against the development of fears upon exposure to others behaving fearfully (Mineka & Cook, 1986). This may potentially explain why exposure to fearful parents does not inevitably result in the same fears in their offspring; presumably fear development is buffered in part by exposure to additional significant others who display non-fearful behavior. Recent data from Rapee and Egliston (2003) confirm the buffering effects for toddlers of prior exposure to non-fearful expressions before being exposed to fearful expressions. Also, the absence of such a buffer may explain the increased risk for anxiety in offspring when both parents are anxious compared with only one parent (Dierker, Merikangas, & Szatmari, 1999). Of course, such learning would be moderated by predispositional variables, so that more negatively affective prone children, for example, are more susceptible to developing fears from a modeling experience than less anxious children given the same modeling experience. Whether parental display of overt fearful behavior of a particular stimulus in the presence of their child is influenced by the child's own temperament is yet to be determined. Parents may be more likely to express distress for a child they believe more prone to emotional distress in order to encourage the child's avoidance.

Familial Aggregation for Anxiety

The preceding discussion outlined features of parenting that may contribute to anxiety in their offspring, with intrusive and negative parenting being more non-specific to a variety of forms of emotional distress whereas parental expectations and modeling and informational transmission of fears being more specific to anxiety. As noted, these features may be enhanced in anxious parents, as well as in parents of anxious children. In addition, they may account for some of the elevated rates of transmission of anxiety disorders from parents to children. That is, all major types of anxiety disorders aggregate in families, and with a degree of specificity that is typically stronger than is true for depression.

The risk for anxiety disorders among offspring of parents with anxiety disorders averages 3.5 (range 1.3–13.3) times greater than the risk for controls (Merikangas *et al.*, 1999). Paternal anxiety appears equally likely as maternal anxiety to increase risk for anxiety in offspring (Connell & Goodman, 2002; Dierker *et al.*, 1999) although research with fathers is sparse. Studies of specific disorders show that children of parents with agoraphobia or obsessive–compulsive disorder are seven times more likely than control offspring to have anxiety diagnoses (Turner, Beidel, & Costello, 1987). In terms of social phobia, 49 percent of 47 offspring (4–18 years old) of parents with social phobia met criteria for at least one anxiety disorder (Mancini, Van Ameringan, Szatmari, Fugere, & Boyle, 1996), and parental social anxiety and avoidant personality disorder predicted a threefold increase in risk for social anxiety in relatives, including offspring (Tillfors, Furmark, Ekselivs, & Fredrikson, 2001). One study reported an earlier age of onset for anxiety disorders in offspring than in their parents (Ohara, Suzuki, Ochiai, Yoshida, & Ohara, 1999). Although these findings were based on retrospective recall by a relatively small sample of patients with anxiety disorders, they are suggestive of "anticipation" wherein "disease" severity increases and/or age of onset decreases in successive generations.

Other forms of parental psychopathology also increase the risk for offspring anxiety. For example, Warner, Mufson, and Weissman (1995) found heightened anxiety in offspring of parents with depression. Biederman *et al.* (2001) found that parental depression increased the risk for offspring separation anxiety, social phobia, and multiple anxiety disorders. Others find increased risk for anxiety in the offspring of parents with alcohol abuse/dependence, especially maternal alcoholism (Chassin *et al.*

1999), although the results are not always consistent (Merikangas *et al.*, 1998), and the risk is much weaker than for offspring of anxiety disordered parents (Merikangas *et al.*, 1998). In fact, some studies show specificity of familial anxiety transmission, such that offspring are at risk only for the anxiety disorder exhibited by the parents, as was found in the case of parental panic disorder (Beiderman *et al.* 2001), and parental specific phobia, social phobia, and agoraphobia (Fyer, Mannuzza, Chapman, Liebowitz, & Klein, 1993; Fyer, Mannuzza, Chapman, Martin, & Klein, 1995; Fyer, Mannuzza, Gallops, & Martin, 1990). Unfortunately, some of these studies are confounded by exclusion of parents with co-occurring disorders, resulting in less severe samples who possibly possess lower loadings on predisposing traits; higher parental loadings on these traits may enhance offspring vulnerability for all anxiety disorders (Craske, 1999). Assuming, nonetheless, that a certain level of specificity does exist, it is unlikely to be due to specific genetic transmission given the evidence presented earlier for mostly broad and non-specific genetic influences upon anxiety. Instead, the familial aggregation may be explainable by an interaction between general anxiety proneness (negative affectivity) and the specific learning environment in which the child is raised. For example, parental modeling of one particular type of anxiety disorder may lead a child prone to negative affect to be more likely to develop that particular anxiety disorder than other types of anxiety disorders, given the evidence presented already for modeling and informational transmission.

In contrast to anxiety disorders, affective disorders in offspring appear to be associated indiscriminately with any type of parental disorder — anxiety, depression or substance abuse (Merikangas *et al.*, 1998) — although one report indicated that offspring depression was more strongly related to parental depression than parental anxiety (Merikangas *et al.*, 1999). The greater specificity in familial transmission of anxiety compared with depression may derive from the added potency of modeling and information regarding threat. That is, negative affectivity in the parent, whether manifested primarily as anxiety or depression, may contribute to negative affectivity in the offspring, via genetic influences and overcontrolling and negative parenting styles; additionally, the observation of fearful and anxious parental behaviors in relation to specific stimuli may convey information that is pertinent to survival and therefore motivates learning to respond in a manner similar to the parent. In contrast, the observation of depressive behaviors does not communicate information valuable for self-protection and survival and therefore may carry less learning potential. Instead of a behavioral reaction to specific stimuli, children of depressed parents may learn an attributional style that is depressionogenic in general. In other words, observers may be less prone to acquiring depressive behaviors through observation of a depressive model than they are to acquiring anxious behaviors by observing an anxious model. When such modeling is combined with direct parental encouragement of avoidant behavior due to the parents' own negative expectations, then the specificity of familial aggregation for anxiety becomes even more understandable.

Children of parents who both suffer from psychopathology may be at incremental risk for anxiety disorders (Dierker *et al.*, 1999; Merikangas *et al.*, 1999). For example, Merikangas *et al.* (1999) found that offspring have an additional threefold increased risk for over-anxious disorder when both parents are affected compared with one parent. A similar finding occurred with respect to social phobia. Merikangas *et al.* (1999) interpret this as evidence for increased genetic propensity for anxiety. However, the findings regarding incremental risk are not consistent (Biederman *et al.*, 2001), and even if they were, they may be equally well explained by stronger reinforcement of learned anxious behaviors in the absence of a non-anxious parental buffer.

Thus, alongside heritability influences, at least some of the variance in patterns of familial aggregation is attributable to environmental influences. The latter may include broad contextual variables such as socioeconomic stressors and religious contexts, but the research has focused on parenting factors. To summarize, these parenting factors include an intrusive and negative parenting style, parental expectations and encouragement of avoidance, and informational transmission and modeling of anxious behaviors (Field & Davey, 2001; King, Gullone, & Ollendick, 1998). Notably, the latter features of parenting specifically raise expectations of threat and avoidant responding in the offspring — the very elements that define anxious ways of responding.

Summary

Emotion regulation refers to the ability to modulate arousal and distress, and is viewed by some as an essential aspect of an anxious-prone temperament. Construal of emotion regulation as a *temperament* is most congruent with the evidence for a biological contribution to self-soothing and other regulatory behaviors during infancy. Low vagal tone in particular is connected with poorer self-regulation, perhaps due to impaired orienting to and discrimination among external stimuli and the resultant unpredictability of emotional responding and of relations among events. Unpredictability and lack of contingency awareness contribute to generalizability of conditioning to aversive contexts, and thus may be a critical pathway to the development of over-anxiousness. Attentional control is additionally influenced by the degree of coordination between caregiver and infant. That is, excessive or continuous desynchrony between parent and infant is believed to detract from learning contingency awareness between one's own behavior and outcomes where outcomes encompass events external to the self (e.g., parental behavior) as well as one's own emotional state. Consequences of such unpredictability include poorer sustained attention and poor orienting to discrete stimuli, and, as such, parent–infant coordination may impact cardiac vagal tone. In addition, excessive desynchrony is also presumed to detract from a sense of controllability — or the personal exertion of contingencies — that is important for buffering the effects of later stressful experiences. Predictability and controllability are both central to anxiousness and ability to cope with future stressors; however, the link between intuitive parenting and subsequent offspring anxiousness is yet to be directly evaluated.

The more cortical form of emotion regulation — ways of attending, interpreting, and behaviorally reacting to negative affect — that develops throughout childhood and beyond is also influenced by parent–child interactions. Of course, other life experience factors are likely to be relevant to emotion regulation as well, especially cultural factors and peer and romantic relations, but these have received very little direct empirical investigation. Parenting styles that are overcontrolling and negative are definitely characteristic of parents of anxious children and of anxious parents too. Such a style is hypothesized to limit the child's history of success in managing negative emotional experiences as well as to restrict their breadth of experience and performance success in general. By detracting from a sense of control, these types of parenting may also contribute directly to negative affect as well as to persistence or lack thereof in managing negative affect. Overcontrolling and negative parenting styles are not restricted to anxious children but are observed in parents of children with conduct disorders as well. An overcontrolling and negative parenting style may therefore be best viewed as a non-specific factor in offspring distress, and only in combination with other parenting features that emphasize threat expectations and avoidant coping is a specific influence upon anxiety exerted. Very compelling in this regard is the evidence from discussions between parents and children about ways of coping with potentially threatening situations, with parents of anxious children reinforcing avoidant solutions. Also, parents who hold negative expectations of their child, and who display more fearful and avoidant behaviors in response to specific classes of stimuli, are likely to model and transmit a sense of threat and avoidant coping. Some of the differentiation between anxiety and depression may stem from these particular parental influences. That is, the evidence reviewed thus far suggests that depression and anxiety share in common negative affectivity along with certain parenting influences. The divergences appear to occur in terms of positive affectivity and specific familial transmission in the modeling of fearful and avoidant behaviors around specific stimuli.

As mentioned, negative parenting styles are likely to be more pronounced in anxious or otherwise distressed parents, who in turn are influenced by their own myriad of inherited and environmental influences. Also, the child is likely to play a critical role in eliciting parenting behaviors. A shy and timid child, for example, is more likely to elicit protective parenting behaviors and expectations than is an outgoing and confident child. In addition, the child's response to parenting behaviors (in turn influenced by their own temperament) is a potentially stronger mediator of familial transmission than the parenting behaviors *per se*. In other words, a dynamic model of reciprocating influences occurs between the child and the parent, and the child's temperament could influence not only parenting style but also their response to parenting.

In essence, parenting influences the child's ability to moderate threatening interpretations and to approach rather than avoid potential problems. Thus, whereas negative affectivity is hypothesized to intensify the *salience* of negative affect and related stimuli, the style of emotion regulation that contributes to anxiousness is hypothesized to be one that elevates the *threat value* of negative affect and related stimuli. Theoretically, adequate emotion regulation could offset the development of excessive anxiety in someone who was prone to negative affect, and excessive anxiety could emerge in the absence of negative affectivity but with a sufficiently threat-based style of emotion regulation.

Chapter 5

Anxious Processes

Negative affectivity and style of emotion regulation each contribute to anxious processes that are described in this chapter as hypervigilance toward threat and supportive physiology, threat-related judgments about the self and the environment, and avoidance behaviors. These processes represent a threat-based style of responding, and they both define anxiety (i.e., constitute the symptoms) and, by generating distress, contribute to the risk for further anxiety. The pervasiveness with which anxious processes are manifested — or the overall level of anxiousness — is considered to be dependent on the strength of the predisposing vulnerability factors described thus far.

Attention and Hypervigilance

As described in Chapter 4, attentional processes are regarded as central to emotion regulation, modulating temperament, and negative affect (Derryberry & Reed, 1996; Wilson & Gottman, 1996). Rapid detection of threat is one part of an overall system biased toward threat. Other biases in the system include prioritized encoding of threat (Mathews, 1990; Mogg & Bradley, 1998), measured via allocation of attentional resources. Research has consistently demonstrated attentional bias for threat-related information in anxious populations.

Selectivity of Attention

One method for measuring selectivity of attention is the dot probe detection task. In this paradigm, neutral and positively valenced words are presented and, at intervals unknown to participants, one of the words is replaced with a target "dot" requiring a response. Individuals with anxiety disorders respond faster than non-anxious controls when the target dot follows a threat word of personal relevance (e.g., Broadbent & Broadbent, 1988; MacLeod & Mathews, 1988; Mogg, Mathews, & Eysenck, 1992; Tata, Leibowitz, Prunty, Cameron, & Pickering, 1996). The same has been observed for children and adolescents with diagnosed anxiety disorders (Dalgleish, Moradi, Taghavi, Neshat-Doost, & Yule, 2001; Taghavi *et al.*, 1999; Vasey, Daleiden, Williams, & Brown, 1995). Also, the effects persist when using subliminal presentations of threatening stimuli or conditions that otherwise restrict awareness (e.g., Macleod, Mathews, &

Tata, 1986; Mogg & Bradley, 2002; Mogg, Bradley, & Williams, 1995). For this reason, a preattentive type of processing is implied in which biases operate at a very initial stage of attention to stimuli that are threatening. Also, recent evidence suggests a slower disengagement from threat. That is, using a spatial orienting task, Derryberry and Reed (2002) demonstrated attentional bias in trait-anxious participants only when a negative cue was followed by a target in a different location and not when the target occurred in the same location. However, further testing is required. Generally speaking, attentional selectivity is less reliably observed in less severely anxious individuals, such as high-trait-anxious but non-disordered youths (Vasey, El-Hag, & Daleiden, 1996) and adults (e.g., Mogg, Bradley, Williams, & Mathews, 1993; Yovel & Mineka, 2000).

Interference

Interference effects are measured using the dichotic listening paradigm in which participants wearing headphones are required to verbally repeat ("shadow") non-threatening information being relayed to one ear while threat and non-threat words are presented to the other ear. Anxious groups exhibit more disruptions of their shadowing task when threat words are presented to the non-shadow ear (e.g., Foa & McNally, 1986; Mathews & MacLeod, 1985; Mogg, Mathews, & Weinman, 1989), as if to imply that threat words possess more meaning for them and therefore interfere with ongoing tasks. Another measure of interference is the modified Stroop paradigm, in which individuals are shown threat-related words and control words printed in different-colored inks. The task is to name the color of each word. Significant delays in color naming are thought to measure disproportionate allocation of attentional resources to the word stimuli. Research has shown a substantial delay in naming the colors of threat-related words (modified Stroop task), and this delay is pronounced in individuals diagnosed with anxiety disorders (e.g., Chen, Lewin, & Craske, 1996; Mathews & MacLeod, 1985) and non-clinical participants with high levels of trait anxiety (MacLeod & Hagan, 1992; MacLeod & Rutherford, 1992; Mogg *et al.*, 1993a). As with the dot probe task, these effects extend to subliminal presentations (Bradley, Mogg, Millar, & White, 1995; Mogg *et al.*, 1993a).

   Results with youths are more mixed. Martin and Jones (1995) reported an attentional interference in anxious children as young as 4–5 years old using the modified Stroop task. Kindt, Brosschot, and Everaerd (1997a) were unable to replicate this effect, and again failed to replicate with slightly different stimuli (Kindt, Bierman, & Brosschot, 1997b). Instead, all children appeared to show a bias toward threat, although this bias decreased with age. In a more recent study, older spider-fearful children again showed more bias than younger spider-fearful children who did not differ from controls (Kindt, van den Hout, de Jong, & Hoekzema, 2000). Consequently, Kindt and colleagues propose that with age, non-anxious children learn to inhibit the processing of threatening information (i.e., they learn emotion regulation) whereas anxious children do not. In accord, Kindt *et al.* (1997a) found a negative association between age and threat bias in control children but not in anxious children. The notion of inhibiting processing of threatening information was addressed from a different perspective by Waters, Lipp, and Spence (2003 in press), who again found that anxious and control youths, aged 9–12 years, were equally effected by threat pictures in dot probe and modified Stroop tasks. However, retention times (dot probe) slowed and performance interference (modified Stroop) lessened for positive and negative stimuli across trials in the control group. In contrast, anxious children did not shift their performance over time, as if they remained vigilant to both positive and negative emotional stimuli. In other words, their responding did not become inhibited over time.

Inhibition and Disengagement

Under the same conditions in which anxious individuals overly attend to threat, non-anxious adults have been observed to direct their attention away from threat (Macleod & Mathews, 1988; Macleod *et al.*, 1986). Vasey *et al.* (1996) similarly observed an attentional bias away from threat words in low-trait-anxious children, at least boys. Also, high-trait-anxious groups are less likely to show attentional bias with supraliminal presentations than clinically anxious groups who retain selectivity of attention to conscious as well as preconscious threat stimuli (e.g., Mathews & MacLeod, 1985). The less distressed group appears more able to override selective processing of threat stimuli of which they are consciously aware (e.g., Chan & Lovibond, 1996; MacLeod & Hagan, 1992) presumably by being more capable of engaging in regulatory efforts than the more severely anxious group. Thus, the combined evidence implies that non-anxious individuals divert their attention away from threatening stimuli (albeit in degraded form) because of greater inhibitory control than occurs for high-trait-anxious individuals, who in turn exhibit greater inhibitory control than severely distressed samples.

Attentional vigilance for the very anxious individual enables early detection of threat, even if not well discriminated (see Chapter 4) and avoidance of anxiety-producing situations. However, although preventing immediate distress, such vigilance is likely to contribute to ongoing distress by interfering with the development of coping or with reappraisal of the threat value of stimuli. After an initial attentional bias toward threat, anxious individuals show an attentional shift away from threat cues if given sufficient time, a profile of responding termed "vigilance avoidance" (Mogg, Mathews, & Weinman, 1987). Vasey *et al.* (1996) propose that avoidance away from threat serves different functions depending on level of anxiety. For the low-trait-anxious person, avoidance represents a means of regulating anxiety and enabling behavioral organization to continue in ongoing tasks, which is presumably adaptive as long as avoidance does not interfere with the processing of true threat. For the high-trait-anxious person, the avoidance response that comes after initial vigilance is motivated by subjective distress, and is a maladaptive means of "not coping".

Posner and Rothbart (1998) distinguished between processes of attention that are involuntary (the posterior attentional system responsible for engagement and disengagement from one spotlight to another spotlight) and voluntary (the anterior attentional system that exerts executive control). Moreover, the anterior system can influence the posterior system, such that expectations and motives can guide the allocation of attention in space. The influence of the executive system upon involuntary mechanisms may explain two major moderators of attentional bias, the first being that pre-attentive biases are specific to areas of personal relevance. In other words, the meaning that is given to stimuli influences involuntary attentional biases toward them. For example, Mogg *et al.* (1989) found the greatest interference effects for threat words relevant to predominant worries of generally anxious individuals. Also, Logan and Goetsch (1993) found that high-trait-anxious individuals demonstrated greater Stroop interference for threatening information related to current worries. Finally, Rieman and McNally (1995) showed that both normal and anxious participants demonstrated a bias for positive and negative stimuli that were concordant with current concerns. Second, the role of the anterior executive system explains why explicit forms of attention control can influence the vigilance stage of attentional biases. In accord, Derryberry and Reed (2002) found that individual differences in attentional control moderated attentional bias effects. Hence, their work illustrates the importance of emotion regulation in the form of attentional control upon vigilance toward threat.

Together, the data suggest that the most anxious individual is overly attentive to and perhaps delayed in disengaging from threat (as seen in the various tasks of attentional bias) but eventually diverts attention away from threat as a means of avoiding subjective distress. The least anxious individual is faster to disengage from threat and therefore engages in more immediate diversion as a means of continuing ongoing tasks and activities. Moreover, executive control may moderate these effects. As mentioned, executive control includes beliefs and motives that influence the judgment of threat or personal relevance of stimuli, as well as strategies for shifting attention. Consequently, the more threatening the stimulus, the greater should be the vigilant attentional bias. In accord, Mogg and Bradley (1998) proposed that even low-trait-anxious individuals would exhibit a bias for threat stimuli under conditions of objectively high threat value. In their cognitive-motivational model, stimuli are first evaluated in terms of valence via a rapid automatic analysis of the stimulus characteristics, along with information about current state of anxiety and anxiety vulnerability. Output from this valence evaluation is used to evaluate goal engagement, which determines the allocation of resources for cognitive processing and action. If a stimulus is evaluated with high threat value, then ongoing activities are interrupted, and processing resources are allocated to the threatening stimulus. The difference between low and high anxiety, in their model, is in valence evaluation: a high-trait-anxious individual is likely to appraise a mild stimulus as having a high subjective threat value whereas a low-trait-anxious individual is less likely to do so. But, under conditions of high threat value, even low-trait-anxious individuals will show an allocation of resources toward threat. Mogg *et al.* (2000b) found support for this hypothesis in a series of studies using the dot probe task in high- and low-trait-anxious adults; both groups were more vigilant for higher threat scenes versus mild threat scenes (from the International Affective Picture System, IAPS;

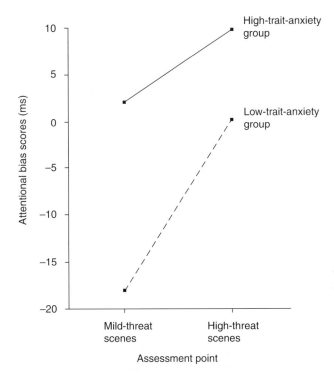

Figure 5.1: Mean attentional bias scores for mild- and high-threat scenarios. (Redrawn by permission of Psychology Press from Mogg *et al.* (2000b).)

Lang, Bradley & Cuthbert, 1998), and although the low-trait-anxious group avoided the milder scenes, their avoidance lessened as the threat value increased (Figure 5.1). Clearly, factors described in the previous chapter would contribute to the tendency to view stimuli as threatening.

   In addition to individual differences in the perceived threat value of a given stimulus, certain stimuli may innately possess elevated threat value and hence be given more attentional resources. In particular, Öhman (1993, 1996) proposed that certain stimuli possess such meaning because of an evolutionary representation of threat to survival of the species. These "prepared" stimuli include reptiles, heights, and the dark. Öhman, Flykt, and Esteves (2001) evaluated the attentional value of such stimuli using stimulus arrays. In accordance with the "pop out" effect (Treisman & Souther, 1985), stimuli whose rate of detection occurs independently of the number of distractors or location within the array are processed automatically rather than strategically or consciously. Öhman *et al.* (2001) found that participants were consistently faster in detecting fear-relevant stimuli against backgrounds of fear-irrelevant stimuli than vice versa, and did so in a way that implied automaticity of detection. Thus, they concluded that there exists a broad default setting of preference for evolutionarily fear-relevant stimuli, reflecting a genuine pre-attentive automaticity to orient toward these innate threats. Notably, most phobias are of evolutionary fear-relevant stimuli (see Chapter 6). The effects were enhanced in spider- and snake-fearful individuals, leading Öhman *et al.* (2001) to conclude that emotion drives attention and fearful participants are sensitized specifically to have their attention automatically captured by the feared stimulus. Others have replicated the faster speed of detection for fear-relevant stimuli, but have not confirmed the automaticity of such detection (e.g., Lipp, Waters, Logies, & Derakshan, 2003 in press). As an aside, the stimulus array design for measuring attentional biases differs from the tasks presented to date (e.g., modified Stroop, dot probe, and spatial orientation tasks) in that there is no competing cognitive task. In other words, faster detection was observed even without the effort of simultaneous task requirement. Moreover, since there is no competing task, these types of designs illustrate that the vigilance portion of attentional bias is not all explained by slowed disengagement.

Another type of fear-relevant stimulus is the angry or fearful face (Öhman, 1993). In fact, recent evidence suggests that populations of cortical neurons respond specifically to facial expression (see Fox *et al.*, 2000). In humans, the basic emotions are associated with very specific facial expressions that are recognized across different cultures (Ekman, 1973) despite some cultural constraints (Elfenbein & Ambady, 2002). Even infants as young as 5–6 months of age can distinguish between facial expressions of fear, anger, sadness, and anger (Fox *et al.*, 2000). For example, Balaban (1995) found that 5-month-old infants had a stronger startle response to an acoustic probe in the presence of angry faces compared with happy faces. Thus, we seem to be biologically prepared for expression recognition.

Angry and fearful faces represent evolutionarily primed fear-relevant stimuli because social rejection can lead to ostracization that is fatal for humans, and because the expression of fear serves an important communication function about threats in the environment (Öhman, 1986). Adults seem able to detect an angry face in a crowd much faster than a happy face (Hansen & Hansen, 1988), although, as with other fear-relevant stimuli, there is debate over whether such detection is automatic (i.e., preconscious) or "serially" (i.e., strategic) based. Given that search times for an angry face did not increase substantially with increasing numbers of distractors, whereas search times for happy faces did, Hansen and Hansen (1988) concluded that angry faces were detected automatically in a "pop out" effect whereas detection of happy faces requires a serial and linear search. However, after some criticism of their methodology and some failures to replicate (e.g., White, 1995), Hansen and Hansen (1994) retracted their original interpretation. Fox *et al.* (2000) replicated the basic design with improvements to methodology. In a series of five experiments, they reliably demonstrated the "face in the crowd" effect, with angry faces being found more efficiently than happy faces (holding visual attention for longer when in a display of similar faces, and faster detection when in a display of neutral or happy faces). However, Fox *et al.* (2000) did not find evidence for parallel and pre-attentive processing of angry faces. In other words, angry faces seem to be detected more efficiently but not automatically. White (1995) reached a similar conclusion. In contrast, Öhman *et al.* (2001) argue for automaticity for detection of facial stimuli in the same way as they demonstrated for other evolutionarily significant stimuli.

Regardless of whether the process is automatic or not, anxious and depressed individuals direct their attention to angry or fearful faces even more quickly than controls (e.g., Bradley, Mogg, & Millar, 2000; Bradley *et al.*, 1997; Bradley, Mogg, White, Groom, & de Bono, 1999). Also, preferential attentional allocation to threatening faces has been measured without participants being consciously aware, using masked dot probe detection tasks. Specifically, Mogg and Bradley (1999) found a preferential allocation of attention to masked facial expressions of threat, especially in high-trait-anxious individuals, although interestingly the effect was not found under conditions of marginal threshold in which the facial stimuli may have been consciously perceived. Similarly, generalized anxiety disorder patients more quickly moved their eyes toward threatening faces than neutral faces relative to controls and depressives (Mogg *et al.*, 2000a), as did non-clinical individuals with high social anxiety (Mogg & Bradley, 2002).

Impact of temperament upon attentional biases

The research presented thus far fairly reliably indicates an initial attention bias toward or slowed disengagment from threat, at least before subsequent attentional avoidance ensues in individuals who have anxiety disorders. In addition, the work of Mogg and colleagues suggests that attentional biases are influenced by threat valuations, and, as noted in Chapter 4, expectations and interpretations of stimuli as threatening in general is believed to contribute to the vulnerability to anxiety disorders. Thus, individuals who are highly trait-anxious and children at risk for anxiety disorders would be expected to exhibit attentional biases. However, as already reviewed, the findings regarding high-trait anxiety are not reliable, and the same is true for "at-risk" youths. For example, Moradi, Neshat-Doost, Taghavi, Yule, and Dalgleish (1999) compared children who had a parent suffering from posttraumatic stress disorder with those with parents who had no anxiety disorders. They found evidence for more selective attention to threat-relevant words (combining general threat and trauma-related threat) in the former group using the modified Stroop task despite the fact that the two groups of children did not differ in terms of anxiety. On the other hand, they did not establish this finding in an earlier study (Neshat-Doost, Taghavi, Moradi, Yule & Dalgleish, 1997) in which trauma words and general threat words were analyzed separately.

In more direct evaluations of temperament and attential bias, "neurotic introverts" exhibited delayed disengagement from negative stimuli using the spatial orienting task (Derryberry & Reed, 1994). Also, Fulcher, Mathews, Mackintosh, and Law (2001) associated neutral picture stimuli with other positive or negative images and then assessed attentional bias to the neutral pictures. They observed greater attentional interference for pictures previously associated with negative images in individuals who scored high on neuroticism relative to those who scored low. The latter group showed more interference for pictures previously paired with positive images. In other words, stimuli with acquired negative evaluations appeared to capture attentional resources more readily in individuals prone to negative affect. In this case, establishment of the personal relevance of the stimuli via conditioning trials may have contributed to attentional bias, given that attentional biases are most apparent for stimuli judged to be most threatening. In contrast, attentional biases may have been mitigated in the studies of high risk children due to the absence of personally relevant stimuli. It would be particularly interesting to assess whether temperament influences attention to fear-relevant stimuli as well.

Impact of Attentional Biases on Anxiety

It is assumed that an attentional bias toward threat contributes to ongoing anxiety. For example, MacLeod and Mathews (1988) proposed a self-perpetuating model in which highly anxious individuals respond to state anxiety with increased tendencies to selectively encode threatening information that intensifies anxiety, biasing attention further, and so on. However, the attempts to separate trait and state effects, mostly done using the modified Stroop task, have yielded confusing results. In direct support of the MacLeod and Mathews (1988) proposal, Stroop interference effects were amplified by the addition of an acute stressor in high-trait-anxious individuals in a study by Richards, French, Johnson, Naparstek, and Williams (1992). However, others have not replicated this finding (e.g., McNally, Riemann, Louro, Lukach, & Kim, 1992; Mogg, Kentish, & Bradley, 1993). In studies of spider-fearful individuals, we found that state anxiety increased interference effects (Chen *et al.*, 1996) whereas Mathews and Sebastian (1993) did not.

More promising than attempting to disentangle state from trait anxiety is the research showing that pre-existing biases in attention predict reactivity to stressors. MacLeod and Hagan (1992) administered the emotional Stroop task to women undergoing a test for cervical cancer, and followed those receiving a diagnosis of cervical pathology. Among these women the subliminal threat interference index from the original Stroop was the best predictor of later anxious and dysphoric reactions to the diagnosis ($r = -0.54, p < 0.05$). Moreover, two other studies using students found similar results. MacLeod and Ng (cited in MacLeod, 1999) found that measures of subliminal threat interference on the Stroop was the best predictor of the amount of state anxiety experienced by Singaporean students after arrival in Australia to attend university. Also, Pury (2002) replicated these results using students who were given the subliminal Stroop during a period of low academic stress. Threat interference was positively associated with anxiety symptoms during the final exam week ($r = 0.42$) when stress levels were high. Together, these findings imply that cognitive biases contribute to distress.

The strongest evidence for a contributory role of attentional biases comes from experimental induction. MacLeod, Rutherford, Campbell, Ebsworthy, and Holker (2002) demonstrated that by training attentional bias in a negative direction, subsequent reactivity to a stressor was more negative. Specifically, a randomized group of mid-range trait-anxious college students underwent a series of dot probe detection task trials in which the probes in the training trials always appeared in the vicinity of a negative word. The aim was to induce a negative bias away from the neutral word and toward the negative word. Other participants were exposed to probes always in the vicinity of neutral words. Following the training phase, all participants were

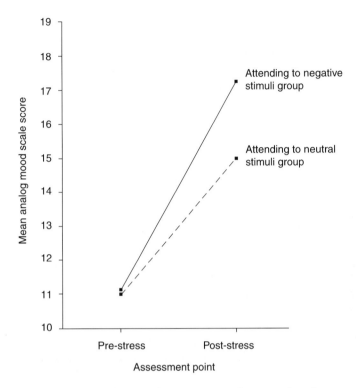

Figure 5.2: Effect of anagram stress task on mean analog mood scale score after attentional training. (Redrawn by permission of the American Psychological Association from MacLeod *et al.* (2002).)

exposed to an anagram-based stress task while being videotaped for ostensible class demonstration purposes. Even though the training manipulation had no direct effect on state distress, those who were trained via attending to negative stimuli subsequently showed more negative mood state in response to the final stress task than those who were initially trained to attend to neutral stimuli (Figure 5.2). This finding was replicated in a second study, and similar sets of findings are summarized by Mathews and MacLeod (2002). These findings confirm the anxiety-inducing effects of attentional biases. Very importantly, they also indicate that high negative affectivity is not necessary for the manifestation of anxiousness — a threat-based style of emotion regulation alone in the form of attention to threat may be sufficient for anxiety. Whether it is sufficient for an anxiety disorder remains to be seen.

Judgments

Threatening beliefs about both the self and the environment are often reflected in "anxious self-talk" (Kendall & Hollon, 1989), and are characterized by expectations of heightened risk, negative valence, and perceived inability to cope with potentially dangerous stimuli and events. Judgments such as these serve to enhance the threatening meanings of potentially dangerous stimuli so that greater precaution is taken when such stimuli are detected. The content of judgments can be studied in terms of risk estimates, judgments of association, and interpretations or meanings given to ambiguous stimuli.

Judgment of Risk

Butler and Mathews (1983) presented negative (or unpleasant) and positive (or pleasant) statements of events to high-trait-anxious individuals and control participants. All participants were asked to subjectively rate the statements on a 0–8 scale of future probability where 0 = "not at all likely" and 8 = "extremely likely". Trait-anxious individuals significantly overestimated subjective personal risk for negative events when compared with controls, especially when those events were self-referent. The two groups did not differ, however, on estimates of future positive events. Subsequently, Butler and Mathews (1987) demonstrated particularly heightened probability of risk among highly trait-anxious subjects as a stressor became more proximal, illustrating that estimations of risk not only fuel anxiety but are exacerbated by anxiety. We similarly found increased risk estimation as anxiety increased in relation to a college exam (Chen & Craske, 1998). Current mood state influences risk estimates probably not through a process of logical calculation but because of the ease with which instances or similar events are brought to mind (availability heuristic: Tversky & Kahneman, 1974) or because mood is used as a source of information for formulating risk (Gasper & Clore, 1998). In a replication of the study by Butler and Mathews (1987), Constans (2001) asked students to complete a subjective risk questionnaire 6 weeks before and immediately before an examination. As was found by Butler and Mathews (1987), proximity to the exam was associated with increased state anxiety and increased perceived risk of performing poorly, although the risk inflation did not extend to non-exam areas. In other words, risk estimates tend to be most inflated in relation to personally relevant concerns. The same kinds of personally relevant risk estimates are observed in anxiety disorder groups as well. Socially anxious individuals judge negative social events to be more likely and positive social events to be less likely than do controls (e.g., Foa, Franklin, Perry, & Herbert, 1996), and acrophobic individuals overestimate the danger inherent in heights relative to controls (Menzies & Clark, 1995a). Similarly, anxious children tend to expect a high number of negative outcomes (Chorpita *et al.*, 1996b). In their study of 277 fifth-and sixth-grade students, aged 10–11 years, Suarez and Bell Dolan (2001) found that high worriers rated threatening events as more likely to occur to them than did low worriers (2.8 versus 1.7, 0–5-point scale). Also, children with social phobia significantly underestimated the likelihood of positive social events in comparison with control children (Spence, Donovan, & Brechman-Toussaint, 1999).

On the other hand, Dalgleish, Taghavi, Neshat-Doost, Moradi, and Yule (1997) found no differences in probability estimates among clinically anxiou s and depressed youths versus controls. The same null result was obtained in a second study with children and adolescents suffering from posttraumatic stress disorder (Dalgleish *et al.*, 2000). A positive correlation existed between anxiety and probability estimates in their control youths, but the correlation decreased with age. As with the downward shift in attentional biases over age (see Kindt *et al.*, 1997), the authors attributed the age effects to the development of inhibitory regulation. The absence of a correlation between anxiety and probability estimation in their sample with posttraumatic stress disorder was also attributed to inhibitory processes but inhibition in order to avoid negative affect, especially because of that group's bias to judge greater risk for others in relation to trauma-matched events. Obviously, inhibition of judgment biases in anxious youths contrasts with explicit judgment biases in anxious adults. To explain this discrepancy, Dalgleish *et al.* (2000) speculate that over long periods of time, anxiety and worry about negative possibilities eventually augment availability effects and outstrip inhibition. Of course, these possibilities remain to be empirically tested.

Judgment of Association

Biased perceived risk extends to judgments of negative associations. For example, Chan and Lovibond (1996) presented a series of trials in which one stimulus was reliably paired with shock and the other stimulus was never paired with shock. Participants rated their expectancy for shock delivery. High-anxious college students had higher expectancies for future shock trials for stimulus configurations that were never paired with shock, in contrast to controls. This finding was consistent with their previous evidence for consistent overestimations of aversive occurrences in trait-anxious populations (Lovibond & Chan, 1990). As mentioned in Chapter 4, tendencies to over-judge the association between specific stimuli and negative events mimic the effects of unpredictability, and may reflect an individual difference variable in ability to attend to and discriminate among external stimuli, and awareness of contingencies, all of which contribute to overgeneralized anxiety (see Grillon, 2002a).

As with measures of attentional selectivity, judgment of association appears to be influenced by stimulus relevance as well as individual differences in anxiousness. Tomarken, Mineka, and Cook (1989) exposed high- and low-fear participants to slides of snakes, spiders, mushrooms, or flowers, which were followed by electric shock, a tone, or nothing. The association between the slides and shocks was random. Yet, individuals with high fear overestimated the relationship between the fear slides and shock, even though they were relatively accurate with respect to other covariation estimates. These findings have been replicated with other fear stimuli (Pury & Mineka, 1997), especially evolutionarily prepared fears (e.g., Davey & Craigie, 1997). Inflated estimates occur for the likelihood of outcomes following encounters with stimuli judged to be safe as well as threatening (Cavanagh & Davey, 2000b), in line with the notion that by being the converse of "threat", "safety" is evaluated on the same valence dimension.

Judgment of Meaning

Judgment bias is additionally observable in interpretations of ambiguous verbal stimuli, such as interpretations of ambiguous information (Amir, Foa, & Coles, 1998; Clark *et al.*, 1997), spelling of homophones (i.e., words with different spellings but the same phonetics, such as "die" and "dye") (Mathews, Richards, & Eysenck, 1989), word selection following ambiguous sentence tasks (Eysenck, Mogg, May, Richards, & Mathews, 1991), primed lexical decision tasks (Calvo & Castillo, 1997; Richards & French, 1992), reading times for sentences that matched or mismatched threatening interpretations of prior ambiguous sentences (MacLeod & Cohen, 1993), and lexical decisions for words matching benign or threatening interpretations of an ongoing ambiguous scenario (Hirsch & Mathews, 1997). In each case, anxious adults (high trait anxiety and anxiety disorders) exhibit signs of more threatening interpretations than do healthy controls. Anxious children similarly show biases toward interpreting ambiguous hypothetical situations as threatening (Barrett, Rapee, Dadds, & Ryan, 1996; Bell-Dolan, 1995; Chorpita *et al.*, 1996b). In addition, levels of trait anxiety in 7–9-year-olds correlated with the number of threatening interpretations given in a pictorial homophone task (Hadwin, Frost, French, & Richards, 1997). In that study, children were asked to point to the picture that went with the word they had heard. In another study, they were asked to create a sentence using the homophone, and again clinically anxious children 9–16 years of age were more likely to produce threatening related sentences than normal controls (Taghavi, Moradi, Neshat-Doost, Yule, & Dalgleish, 2000).

Impact of Temperament on Judgments

We know that judgment biases are correlated with the level of trait anxiety (Macleod & Cohen, 1993; Mathews *et al.*, 1989b), and to the degree that trait anxiety is a facet of negative affectivity, then these data support the influential role of temperament upon judgments. According to Teasedale's (1993) differential activation hypothesis, negative affectivity increases the activation of negative thinking, which in turn enhances negative affect. In accord, dysphoric mood induction was found to elicit more negative self-descriptors in a high- versus low-emotionality group, albeit based on a small sample size (Kelvin, Goodyer, Teasedale, & Brechin, 1999). Assuming this result is replicable, it seems reasonable to suspect that acute stressors may be more likely to prime danger-laden interpretations in individuals with high negative affectivity, and this was indeed demonstrated in the studies of risk estimation reviewed earlier. On the other hand, we found that interpretations of ambiguous information and risk perception at three times surrounding a college exam were predicted by state changes in anxiety but not by trait anxiety (Chen & Craske, 1998). Moreover, induction of physiological arousal (i.e., state anxiety) in high-trait-anxious participants did not affect their tendency to impose threatening interpretations on ambiguous sentences (MacLeod & Cohen, 1993), perhaps because physiological arousal was an irrelevant stressor. Thus, the role of trait anxiety in relation to state anxiety is not fully clear.

Impact of Judgment Biases on Anxiety

Unfortunately, there has been relatively little prospective evaluation of the impact of judgments upon ongoing levels of distress. In our small-scale study just mentioned, we found that pre-exam tendencies to overestimate risk and judge ambiguous scenarios negatively predicted levels of anxiety immediately after an exam and before the grades were posted, at least for college students who judged the exam to be relatively easy (Chen & Craske, 1998). This predictive relationship did not exist for those who judged the exam to be difficult, which we interpreted as the intensity of the stressor overriding the influence of pre-existing judgmental biases.

Much more telling is the series of studies by Mathews and Mackintosh (2000), who demonstrated that interpretive bias could be trained by providing continuous feedback on the correctness of answers provided to interpretations of ambiguous sentences. The evidence for such bias included memory recognition for threatening versus benign interpretations of a set of ambiguous sentences, with those first trained in a threatening bias showing better recognition for threatening interpretations of the ambiguous stimuli. In addition, anxiety increased after encouragement of negative interpretations and decreased after encouragement of positive interpretations, although this was not the case when subjects simply were exposed to negative versus positive interpretations: their active generation of the interpretations was critical to the shifts in anxiety. These findings demonstrate the contribution of a judgment bias to ongoing anxiety.

Memory

Current research suggests that anxiety and depression have differential effects on processing of emotional information. As just reviewed, anxiety disorders are characterized by attentional biases for threatening stimuli. However, depression does not seem to be characterized by a similar attentional bias toward depression-relevant stimuli; effects occasionally seen often can be attributed to elevated anxiety in depressed participants (see Mathews & MacLeod, 1994; Williams *et al.*, 1997). By contrast, depression is characterized by memory biases, whereas anxiety is less so.

Bower's (1981) hallmark paper on mood and memory defined mood-dependent memory as facilitated retrieval when mood at retrieval is consistent with mood during encoding, and mood-congruent recall as facilitated retrieval when the target material is mood-congruent, regardless of mood at encoding. Investigations of memory biases in depression have consistently revealed a robust interaction between mood and memory, especially for stimuli that are self-referential (for a review, see MacLeod & Mathews, 1991). That is, depressed individuals recall more negative self-referential material than neutral or positive material (Matt, Vazquez, & Campbell, 1992; Mineka & Nugent, 1995; Williams *et al.*, 1997). Depressed individuals also show biased memory on autobiographical memory tasks (i.e., slower to recall positive memories than controls, and sometimes faster to recall negative memories). Another feature is for depressed subjects to be more likely to recall overgeneral memories (vague features rather than specific details) (Healy & Williams, 1999), or summaries of repeated memories rather than specific autobiographic events (Watkins & Teasedale, 2001).

In contrast, findings regarding memory biases in anxiety are inconsistent and weak. Mogg *et al.* (1987) reported that anxious patients recalled *fewer* anxiety words than did normal controls, as did phobic individuals in a study by Watts and Dagleish (1991). Foa, McNally, and Murdock (1989) found no evidence for mood-dependent memory, mood-congruent recall, or mood-congruent encoding in anxious individuals. Mogg and Mathews (1990) did find a free-recall mood-congruent memory bias in individuals with high state anxiety compared with controls, but studies of clinically anxious populations most often indicate no recognition memory bias favoring threat (Mathews & MacLeod, 1985; Mogg, Gardiner, Stavrou, & Golombok, 1992). Very few memory studies exist using youth samples. Daleiden (1998) found evidence for favoring of negative information in memory among high-trait-anxious children in grades 6–8. However, this effect was dependent on the specific nature of the memory task, and replication is warranted. In general, more positive results may require stimuli that are more potent than degraded stimulus inputs (i.e., word lists). For example, we found evidence for enhanced recognition memory for pictures of phobic material (Echiverri, Mystkowski, Shirinyan, Hazlett-Stevens, & Craske, 2003). However, there was no such enhancement in an earlier study (Watts *et al.*, 1986).

Lang (1985) suggested that similarity between physiological arousal occurring at encoding and retrieval mediates mood dependency and mood congruency. Yet, in a test of mood congruency, McNally, Foa, and Donnell (1989) found that even though panic disorder patients recalled more anxiety than non-anxiety words, this effect was *not* significantly greater in panic disorder patients whose physiological arousal had been increased. Eich (1995) suggested that for mood-dependent memory effects to occur, mood at encoding and retrieval must be similar in valence (positive versus negative) as well as arousal (high versus low). In addition, he stressed the importance of a strong, stable mood, and internally generated retrieval processes, in order to evoke mood-dependent effects (i.e., free recall as opposed to recognition). Using these conditions, we were able to demonstrate mood-dependent memory in relation to states of fear and relaxation in college students fearful of spiders or snakes (Lang, Craske, Brown, & Ghaneian, 2001). Fear was induced via *in vivo* exposure to a spider or a snake whereas relaxation was induced via music. Although replication is necessary, and especially with clinical populations, our findings suggest that mood-dependent memory effects may exist in anxiety disorders under very specific conditions. Overall, however, the evidence remains weak in comparison with the evidence for memory biases in depressed mood.

The studies presented above refer to explicit memory, or the conscious retrieval of information, assessed through use of free recall, cued recall, or recognition tasks. Implicit memory, or priming, is defined as a performance change, without reliance on conscious awareness, as a result of prior exposure. Implicit memory paradigms typically involve presentation of word stimuli ostensibly for a task ulterior to learning, such as reading words aloud or making judgments of words. Later, the previously seen words, along with new words, are presented in a word task, such as word-stem completion or a perceptual identification task. The degree to which the previously seen words impact performance on the word task is considered a measure of implicit memory (Graf & Masson, 1993). Enhanced implicit memory for threatening information has been observed in non-clinical trait-anxious populations (Eysenck & Byrne, 1994; Richards & French, 1991, 1992), but negative findings exist as well (e.g., Lundh, Czyzykow, & Öst, 1997; Rapee, McCallum, Melville, Ravenscroft, & Rodney, 1994). In samples of anxiety disorder patients, the evidence is more consistent for implicit memory than for explicit memory biases, but it is still variable (e.g., Becker, Roth, Andrich, & Margraf, 1999; Macleod & McLaughlin, 1995; Mathews, Mogg, May, & Eysenck, 1989).

Implicit memory biases are viewed as consonant with attentional biases, and as involving different memory processes than explicit memory biases. Specifically, distinctions are drawn between processes required to activate a mental representation of a word and processes required to further elaborate the meaning of a word (Graf & Mandler, 1984). Activation is described as an automatic process in which exposure to a word facilitates previously associated words. Activation requires attentional resources, and is sufficient for encoding into implicit memory. Williams *et al.* (1988) proposed that when anxious individuals are exposed to threatening stimuli, additional fear-related associations become automatically activated, and further attentional resources are allocated. Priming or implicit memory arises from these same automatic processes. In contrast, elaboration is described as a strategic process in which exposure to a word facilitates new associations with additional words. Elaboration is considered necessary for encoding into explicit memory. In light of the sparse evidence for explicit memory biases, Williams *et al.* (1988) and others suggested that further processing in the elaboration stage is avoided. In other words, anxious individuals may be biased to attend to threat-related material but then to avoid further encoding into memory (Mogg *et al.*, 1987). This model is consistent with teleological formulations of the purpose of anxiety as one of identifying potentially threatening stimuli rapidly rather than reflecting upon past events (Mineka & Sutton, 1992).

However, the notion of enhanced activation and inhibited elaboration is not well established. For example, Williams *et al.* (1988) did not specify how processing during the automatic activation stage could discriminate threat- from non-threat related information in order to determine whether the later elaboration stage is to be avoided. Furthermore, a test of attentional and memory processing in which the elaboration hypothesis was directly tested failed to support the model (Bradley, Mogg, & Williams, 1994), and directed forgetting paradigms have failed to show evidence for heightened avoidance of encoding of threatening information (McNally, Metzger, Lasko, Clancy, & Pitman, 1998; McNally, Otto, Yap, Pollack, & Hornig, 1999).

Physiology

"Physiological arousal" refers to a variety of hyperarousal tendencies, ranging from increased central nervous system activity (such as alertness, restlessness, and muscle tension) to increased autonomic nervous system activity and startle reactivity, needed to support the mode of heightened vigilance and attention to threat. A large amount of research has addressed the central and peripheral physiology of patients with different anxiety disorders in an attempt to understand the underlying causes of these disorders. In general, this is a misguided attempt for two main reasons. First, what is observed is very likely attributable to the effects of being anxious as opposed to etiologically significant variables. Second, this kind of research severely confounds salience of cues with etiological factors. For example, the fact that panic disorder patients respond more dramatically than other anxiety disorder groups to carbon dioxide inhalations or yohimbine infusions is easily attributable to their learned fear reactions to bodily sensations that these experimental procedures resemble. This is not to say that psychophysiological research is valueless. To the contrary, it is highly important for understanding processes of anxiety and other emotional states, and may help explain factors that maintain pathological levels of anxiety. For example, psychophysiological research connected with the process of worry has helped elucidate a self-perpetuating model for excessive worry (see Chapter 7). Measurement of physiological responding across various states (worry, fear, etc.) provides important information about information/emotion interactions, whereas comparing different anxiety disorders in response to a "challenge" tells mostly about what cues are relevant to the individuals who meet criteria for that disorder. More critical for etiological models is the assessment of psychophysiology in those at risk for anxiety disorders, such as the study of startle reactivity and autonomic tone in at-risk youths by the Yale Family Study group (Merikangas *et al.*, 1999), or elevated reactivity to carbon dioxide inhalations in relatives of patients with panic disorder (Perna, Bertani, Caldirola, & Bellodi, 1996). That being said, the main findings from the abundance of research with clinically anxious groups are summarized briefly because they highlight a particular feature of responding that differentiates anxiety disorder samples from controls, that being anticipatory arousal; a feature that resonates with the evidence presented in Chapter 4 pertaining to unpredictability, lack of contingency awareness, and enhanced reactivity to contexts associated with aversive events.

First, physiological differences between anxious and non-anxious groups in response to acute stressors usually disappear after taking baseline differences into account (Margraf *et al.*, 1989; Roth *et al.*, 1992). Even with strongly anxiogenic procedures such as carbon dioxide inhalations, investigations do not yield reliable psychophysiological differences between patient groups and healthy controls (Roth *et al.*, 1986, 1992) once baseline differences are taken into account. (One exception may be circumscribed phobias, where there is less generalized anxiety overall and more exaggerated responding to phobia-relevant stimuli (Barlow, 1988; Grillon, 2002a; Lader, 1967).) In fact, sometimes *non-anxious* individuals have stronger autonomic responses to acute stressors (Hoehn-Saric *et al.*, 1989, 1991, 1995; Kelly, 1980; Lader & Wing, 1966; Thayer *et al.*, 1996; Yeragani *et al.*, 1990), albeit with a faster return to baseline (Forsman, 1980; Lader & Wing, 1966) and a faster rate of habituation with repeated stressors (Lader & Wing, 1964). That is, as reviewed in Chapter 2, excessive anxiety may be associated with autonomic restriction in response to acute stressors (e.g., Hoehn-Saric & McLeod, 1988; Hoehn-Saric *et al.*, 1989, 1995; Lyonfields, 1991; Lyonfields *et al.*, 1995; Thayer *et al.*, 1996; Yeragani *et al.*, 1990).

The most robust finding in anxiety disorder samples is elevation in sympathetic adrenal as well as hypothalamic–pituitary axis activation at the *baseline*, indicative of a physiologically prepared set, again with the exception being circumscribed phobias. For example, Nesse, Cameron, Curtis, McCann, and Huber-Smith (1984) reported that in addition to elevated heart rate, panic disorder patients showed elevated plasma norepinephrine and elevated cortisol levels relative to control subjects, *prior* to an acute laboratory stressor. Similar baseline elevations have been recorded multiple times (e.g., Craske, Lang, Tsao, Mystkowksi, & Rowe, 2001; Grillon & Morgan, 1999; Margraf, Ehlers, & Roth, 1986; Orr *et al.*, 2000; Roth *et al.*, 1992). In a very elegant study, Grillon, Ameli, Goddard, Woods, and Davis (1994) evaluated the time course of startle responding after a threat cue indicated that a 50 second count down had begun, toward the end of which a shock would be delivered. Baseline startle was enhanced in panic disorder subjects relative to controls, but the groups showed otherwise equivalent patterns of responding to the approaching shock.

Elevated baseline measurement in the laboratory setting is recorded in advance of a specific task or stressor. Under these conditions, the "baseline" actually represents a state of anticipatory anxiety about upcoming experimental procedures, and is representative of the vulnerability to respond to a wide variety of situations with elevated anxiety. In other words, anxious individuals show sensitivity to stressful conditions but not an exaggerated fear response to explicit cues. This mode of responding does not necessarily extend to 24-hour recordings of physiology. Ambulatory studies of peripheral autonomic functioning have been mostly limited to samples of panic disorder. Some find no differences from normal controls, suggesting that panic disorder patients do not have generally elevated arousal (e.g., Freedman, Ianni, Ettedgui, & Puthezhath, 1985; Shear *et al.*, 1992). In another study, Anastasiades *et al.* (1990) found higher average heart rates in panic disorder patients relative to controls, and we found higher diastolic blood pressure relative to matched controls (Bystritsky, Craske, Maidenberg, Vapnik, & Shapiro, 1995). In another study we found that panic disorder patients have a higher average heart rate, lower cardiac variability, and more leg movement during sleep in comparison with age–and sex-matched controls (Aikins & Craske, 2003 in press). The lowered cardiac variability points to the possible role of chronically lowered vagal tone described in Chapter 4. Results regarding epinephrine and norepinephrine collected over 24-hour periods are mixed also. For example, Nesse *et al.* (1984) found higher levels of epinephrine and norepinephrine among anxious patients, whereas Mathew, Ho, Francis, Taylor, and Weinman (1982) did not. Contradictory findings are apparent for stress hormones as well, such as cortisol, growth hormone, and prolactin (Cameron & Nesse, 1988). However, results with posttraumatic stress disorder are more consistent and illustrative of elevated epinephrine, norepinephrine and overactivation of the hypothalamic–pituitary axis (as indexed by lower cortisol secretion but upregulation of glucocorticoid receptors (see Yehuda, 2001, and details in Chapter 7)).

If elevated baseline arousal is evident outside of the laboratory setting, what does it reflect? One possibility is pervasive anticipation of danger or threat, generated by relatively continuous stimulation via external stimuli, internal images, or thoughts. An expectation of danger or threat may even pervade sleep (Craske & Rowe, 1997; Craske *et al.* 2001). Alternatively, it may represent a sensitized state perhaps due to highly aversive fear experiences that resets arousal at a higher level (Groves & Thompson, 1970; Rosen & Schulkin, 1998; Sullivan *et al.*, 1999), consistent with the evidence for stress sensitization following severe traumas described in Chapter 3. However, except in cases of severe stress, Grillon (2002a) argues for anticipatory arousal rather than non-cue-dependent sensitization, especially given his demonstration that anticipatory baselines did not differ between patients and controls when participants knew that the laboratory session would not include aversive stimulus presentations (Grillon, Morgan, Davis, & Southwick, 1998). If so, then differences observed during 24-hour recordings outside of the laboratory setting would disappear once patients were convinced that there was no threat potential, and, indeed, we have recently found evidence for lowered leg movement and heart rate during sleep after panic disorder patients taught to lessen their threat appraisals through cognitive behavioral therapy (Craske *et al.*, 2003 in press). Similarly, as posttraumatic stress disorder symptomatology improves, so does cortisol responding collected over 24-hour measurements normalize (Kellner, Yehuda, Artl, & Wiedermann, 2002).

In summary, the evidence suggests that anxiety disorders are characterized by elevated baseline activation, which appears to represent anticipatory states or heightened vigilance to potential threats. This state of anticipatory arousal may be less evident for specific phobias in comparison with other anxiety disorders (Lader, 1967). Anxious individuals do not appear to react more strongly to stressors (after taking baseline differences into account), and may even react less strongly. Notably, the notion that the anxiety disorders are characterized mostly by elevated anticipatory contextual anxiety versus elevated acute fear responding concurs with the previous discussion of vulnerability factors and their connection with amygdala and hippocampal pathways as opposed to more primitive brain stem fear activation (see Chapter 3). Moreover, it converges with the emotion regulation literature on unpredictability and poor attention to and discrimination among external stimuli that in turn contributes to generalized anxious responding to contextual cues associated with threat (see Chapter 4).

Despite the evidence for sympathetic adrenal medullary activation, more attention has been recently given to hypothalamic–pituitary axis activation and cortisol secretion as the physiological substrate of anticipatory or contextually based reactivity. For example, corticotropin-releasing hormone has been implicated in sustained startle responding during baseline recordings (Grillon, 2002a), and Dienstbier (1989) related the effects of unpredictability and uncontrollability to excessive hypothalamic–pituitary axis activity. Also, male baboons who were better able to discriminate actual rival threat cues from mild threat cues or neutral cues showed normal basal cortisol levels, whereas poor discrimination was associated with higher cortisol levels (Ray & Sapolsky, 1992). Furthermore, elevated hypothalamic–pituitary axis activity is believed to underlie baseline anticipatory arousal to novel situations (Rosen & Schulkin, 1998).

Impact of Temperament on Physiology

Of late, research efforts have been directed at the physiological response of startle and its relationship to risk factors for anxiety disorders. Two studies show an overall elevated baseline startle in at-risk children and adolescents of parents with anxiety disorders in comparison with offspring of other parents (Grillon, Dierker, & Merikangas, 1997; Grillon *et al.*, 1998), albeit limited to at-risk females in the second study. A psychiatric comparison group of offspring of parents with alcoholism did not posses overall elevation in startle magnitude, although they did show a reduced habituation to startle (Grillon *et al.*, 1997). Also, individual differences in familial risk or negative affect seem to summate with negatively valent stimuli in potentiating the startle response. Grillon *et al.* (1998) found that males at high risk for anxiety by virtue of parental anxiety showed greater startle potentiation during aversive emotional states than low-risk males. Similarly, Corr, Kumari, Wilson, Checkley, and Gray (1997) found that individuals scoring in the upper range on the Harm Avoidance Scale, a construct very similar to neuroticism, showed more potentiation of startle when viewing unpleasant scenes such as mutilated bodies, in comparison with low scorers. Even among infants of only 9 months of age, Schmidt and Fox (1998) reported greater modulation of startle, via the presence of a stranger, in those originally classified as behaviorally inhibited at the age of 4 months. Corr, Wilson, Kaviani, Thornton, Checkley, and Gray (1996) failed to find a relationship between Eysenck's personality factors and modulation of startle. However, in a reanalysis of these findings, Wilson, Kumari, Gray, and Corr (2000) noted that the results had been confounded by slides of disgusting versus fearful scenes. In other words, low-neuroticism participants showed inhibited startle to fearful film clips relative to disgusting images, whereas those with high neuroticism did not differentiate between the two, indicating a heightened sensitivity across the board. These findings have been replicated in individuals who are at risk by virtue of high trait anxiousness or fearfulness, but who do not meet criteria for anxiety disorders. That is, Cook, Hawk, Davis, and Stevenson (1991) found significant startle potentiation during aversive imagery compared with pleasant imagery in high-fear subjects, and replicated the same basic effect using aversive and neutral pictures (Cook, Davis, Hawk, Spence, & Gautier, 1992). Thus, the evidence for negative affectivity to increase startle reactivity is steadily accruing.

   In addition to startle, evidence exists for particular physiological characteristics in individuals with an anxious-prone temperament as well as offspring of anxious parents. As already mentioned in Chapter 3, a behaviorally inhibited temperament is associated with various features of sympathetic, parasympathetic, and hypothalamic–pituitary axis activation. For example, the earliest manifestation of inhibited behavior, according to Kagan (1997), is high reactivity as seen in frequent vigorous motor activity (i.e., arousal) combined with distress cries (i.e., negative valence) to visual, auditory, and olfactory stimuli. In response to moving mobiles, smells of alcohol, and tape-recorded voices, these children (Kagan, Snidman, & Arcus, 1992, p. 172):

> extend their arms and legs in momentary spasticity, display bursts of vigorous limb activity, and on occasion arch their backs to the presentation of the stimulus events. Further, during some of the periods of vigorous motor activity, these infants fret or cry, suggesting that the distress is a consequence of becoming highly aroused.

More high-reactive than low-reactive infants have fetal heart rates over 140 beats per minute in the few weeks *before* birth. Also, high-reactive infants had higher sleeping heart rates at 2 weeks of age while being held erect (Snidman, Kagan, Riordan, & Shannon, 1995), although baseline heart rate and blood pressure did not discriminate between the groups after 4 months of age (Kagan, Reznick, & Snidman, 1988). In addition to their characteristic profile of high and stable heart rates (Turner *et al.*, 1996), behaviorally inhibited children also show greater magnitudes of heart rate acceleration and pupillary dilation to cognitive stress and larger postural increases in diastolic blood pressure than the uninhibited (Kagan *et al.*, 1988). Similarly, inhibited three-year-olds from the island of Mauritius were differentiated from uninhibited children by a faster heart rate and higher skin conductance in response to a tone stimulus (Scarpa, Raine, Venables, & Mednick, 1997). In addition, Kagan *et al.* (1995) found that inhibited 21-month-olds and 4-year-olds had significantly greater asymmetry in skin temperature, with a cooler temperature on the right-hand ring finger than on the left side. This paralleled findings of a cooler right forehead in high-reactive infants when they reached the age of 21 months. Asymmetry in body temperature is the result of sympathetically mediated vasoconstriction of the arterioles mediated by α-adrenergic receptors. Given that the sympathetic nervous system is more reactive on the right than on the left side of the body, children who cool more on the right than on the left are presumed to possess a more reactive sympathetic system. In related work, McManis, Kagan, Snidman, and Woodward (2002) observed greater right frontal activation in 10–12-year-olds who were classified as high reactive at 4 months and as highly fearful at 14 and 21 months of age. Moreover, they also showed faster latency to wave V of the brain stem auditory evoked response (Woodward *et al.*, 2001). Finally, as with high-trait-anxious adults, behaviorally inhibited children show sustained cortisol responding to daily stressors in comparison with normal habituation patterns in controls (Flinn & England, 1995; Gunnar, 2001). Further evidence for the role of the hypothalamic–pituitary axis is that high-reactive infants aged 4 months had narrower faces at 14 and 21 months of age compared with low-reactive infants, controlling for other aspects of stature; narrow face width has been connected with high levels of circulating glucocorticoids (Arcus & Kagan, 1995). Thus, sympathetic, parasympathetic, and hypothalamic–pituitary axis functioning may all be involved in proneness to anxiety.

Studies of offspring of anxious parents similarly show signs of elevated sympathetic tone, such as greater skin conductance response at the baseline and under threat, in comparison with offspring of non-anxious parents (Merikangas *et al.*, 1999). In addition, their higher resting homeostatic regulation of central and peripheral vascular systems and lower sensitivity to orthostatic challenge (i.e., lower changes in pulse and blood pressure) were viewed as increased autonomic tone, representing hypervigilance of the autonomic nervous system to environmental stimuli. These patterns were not evident in offspring of parents who abused substances. Moreover, offspring of anxious parents who also met the criteria for anxiety disorders exhibited greater differences on all of these measures than offspring of parents without anxiety disorders (Merikangas *et al.*, 1999). These findings could suggest that the manifestation of anxiety itself enhances the processes of anxiousness, in this case a physiologically prepared set. Alternatively, those who develop anxiety disorders may possess stronger vulnerabilities and stronger autonomic tone even before the onset of anxiety disorders.

Impact of Physiology on Anxiety

Either way, elevated startle and sympathetic and parasympathetic autonomic functioning in those at risk for anxiety disorders is likely to contribute to the development of anxiety in a number of ways. Most of the evidence pertains to sympathetic functioning. For example, high arousability enhances the impact of aversive stimuli, which in turn enhances conditionability (Hugdahl, Fredrikson, & Öhman, 1977). That is, stronger physiological responses to aversive stimuli generally elicit stronger conditioning (e.g., Hugdahl *et al.*, 1977; Öhman & Bohlin, 1973). In fact, intensity of bodily response to aversive stimuli is found to mediate conditioning in humans (Forsyth & Eifert, 1998). In a similar fashion, experimental studies with non-primates and monkeys indicate that high levels of prior stress (i.e., stress sensitization) and the associated state of physiological arousal enhance the acquisition, strength and generalizability of conditioned responding (e.g., Rosen & Schulkin, 1998; Sullivan *et al.*, 1999). These effects have been similarly observed in traumatized adults with posttraumatic stress disorder (Grillon & Morgan, 1999; Orr *et al.*, 2000), and are described in more detail in Chapter 6. Conversely, impaired conditioning of warning signals and impaired avoidance learning of painful stimuli in individuals with antisocial personality disorder has been attributed in part to deficits in autonomic or cardiac reactivity to aversive stimuli (e.g., Lykken, 1975; Raine, Venables, & Williams, 1995). Also, the level of arousal mediates differences in the avoidance behavior of different strains of rats (Satinder, 1977).

In addition, high levels of arousal are likely to elevate the salience of aversive stimuli and thereby slow the rate of habituation (Groves & Thompson, 1970). Indirect support includes the enhancing effects of injections of epinephrine enhance physiological as well as emotional responding to film clips known to induce fear (Mezzacappa, Katkin, & Palmer, 1999). Although there is no direct evidence that elevated autonomic state increases reactivity to future stressors, there is evidence for heart rate activity within a few hours of a physical trauma to predict the later onset of posttraumatic stress disorder (Bryant, Harvey, Guthrie, & Molds, 2000). Also, as already mentioned, elevated or sustained hypothalamic–pituitary axis activation in response to stressors is likely to contribute to the generalizability of anxious responding to contexts associated with threat.

Finally, as reviewed in Chapter 4, low tonic levels of cardiac vagal tone due to elevated parasympathetic functioning correlate with poor emotion regulation, poor orienting to, and discrimination among, external stimuli, and later emotional distress. That is, individuals who have difficulty discriminating among which external stimuli are associated with threat and which are not are more likely to respond indiscriminantly with generalized anxious responding to broad contextual cues than individuals who are able to more clearly discriminate and attribute their negative affect to circumscribed objects or situations. The effects cited in support of this model include the dampening effect of low cardiac vagal tone upon the orienting response and the loss of differential conditioning by virtue of diminished orienting (see Chapter 4). The effects may be mediated by unpredictability, given that both poor orienting and limited contingency awareness yield similar effects (Grillon, 2002a). To summarize, elevated sympathetic responding to non-specific stressors, low cardiac vagal tone, and sustained hypothalamic–pituitary axis activation may contribute to the development of excessive and pervasive anxiety. Once manifest, the anxiety disorders are characterized by a state of general physiological hypervigilance rather than particularly intense physiological responding to acute stressors.

Avoidance of Threat

The third anxious process of avoidance, like attentional and judgmental biases and supportive physiology, is presumed to contribute to anxiousness in a self-perpetuating cycle. Such avoidance includes behavioral retreat from potential threat, extra cautiousness and preparation, reliance on safety signals, superstitious forms of self-protection, reassurance seeking, and "trying not to think about" fear-related cues. In addition, lowered vagal tone in association with limited orienting to discrete external cues has been conceptualized as another type of avoidance of negative affect (Friedman & Thayer, 1998b). Avoidance clearly serves the protective function of terminating, undoing, or preventing exposure to threat, but of course by so doing, avoidance also blocks corrective experience that could lessen the threat value of avoided stimuli.

Impact of Temperament on Avoidance

Avoidance is evident early on in the retreat to familiarity in behaviorally inhibited children, as well as in highly excitable or reactive strains of non-primates and rhesus monkeys, reviewed in Chapter 3. Although a step removed from temperament, trait anxiety also correlates with avoidance behavior. Chorpita *et al.* (1996) found that trait anxiety positively associated with avoidant coping responses in children. Similarly, Bell-Dolan (1995) found that high-trait-anxious children were more likely to propose maladaptive coping strategies for threatening circumstances conveyed by vignette (such as appeal to authority versus approach-based solutions). Moreover, Vasey, Daleiden, and Williams (1992) found that clinically anxious 9–14-year-olds selected more distraction and avoidance responses than controls, even though the groups had equivalent amounts of knowledge of possible alternative coping responses. The fact that anxious and control children were equally likely to choose avoidant solutions once they made threatening interpretations of situations (Barrett *et al.*, 1996) illustrates the link between avoidant solutions and danger-laden expectations. Indeed, in his model of response expectancy, Kirsch (1985) emphasized the role of not only expected likelihood of fear but also the expected aversiveness of the fear response and the expected harm or danger from the stimuli (which he called the primary reinforcement value) as the major determinants of avoidant behavior. That is, the more likely fear is expected to occur, and the more harmful the fear response and the stimulus are expected to be, the stronger the probability of avoidance. Fear expectancy may be closely linked to negative affectivity, and "reinforcement value" may be closely linked to a threat-based style of emotion regulation. As described in Chapter 4, parenting factors are likely to be particularly influential upon "reinforcement value", partly through encouragement of threat expectations and partly through direct encouragement of avoidant responding, especially in anxious-prone children. Thus, high negative affectivity and/or a threat-based style of emotion regulation seem to contribute to avoidant solutions to potential stressors. Of course, avoidance also can be trained independently of predisposing anxious prone temperaments, as shown in experimental studies of avoidance learning.

Impact of Avoidance on Anxiety

The self-perpetuating nature of avoidant reactions has been alluded to throughout. Very telling in this regard is that phobic avoidance behavior is more stable than other symptoms of anxiety in both adults (Tyrer *et al.*, 1987) and youths (Last *et al.*, 1996), even though circumscribed phobias load less heavily on broad vulnerabilities toward anxiousness (Mineka *et al.*, 1998). From the standpoint of conditioning theory, fear persists because avoidance of the conditioned stimulus prevents the extinction that normally occurs through repeated non-reinforced exposures. For example, phobic individuals typically overestimate fear or the likelihood of panicking in specific situations (e.g., Rachman & Lopatka, 1986; Taylor & Rachman, 1994a), although some exceptions are noted (e.g., Arntz, van den Hout, Lousberg, & Schouten, 1990; Telch, Valentiner, & Bolte, 1994). These estimates predict more avoidance behavior, which in turn reduces disconfirmatory opportunities, so that expectations remain high (Rachman, 1994). Moreover, avoidance is presumed to maintain itself over time. For example, fear reduction experienced as a result of avoidance or escape behavior is likely to instrumentally reinforce future avoidant responding, although rather than accounting for all avoidance, as initially hypothesized by Mowrer (1939), instrumental conditioning via fear reduction is assumed to operate as an avoidance motivator only for some of the time (Reiss, 1980). More recently, emphasis has been given to the role of safety signals in maintaining avoidance. That is, behavior is motivated not only by escape from fear but also by approach to safety (Rachman, 1984). Stimuli that are present when escaping or avoiding feared stimuli serve as safety signals because they provide information that safety has been achieved (McAllister, McAllister, Scoles, & Hampton, 1986). According to this perspective, avoidant behavior at any given time is jointly determined by perceived danger and availability of safety; avoidance increases when safety signals are not present. In fact, a sense of diminished safety may explain why unexpected or unpredictable events generate more fear and avoidance than expected events because without predictability, periods of safety are not clearly demarcated (Seligman, 1968)). Unpredictable events include the experience of fear itself, and thus Rachman and Levitt (1985) proposed that the degree of *mismatch* between predicted fear and actual fear contributes to phobic avoidance by diminishing safety. In support, underprediction of fear (i.e., unexpectedly high levels of fear) increases subsequent fear predictions, anticipatory anxiety, and avoidance (e.g., Arntz, Hildebrand, & van den Hout, 1994; Arntz, van Eck, & Heijmans, 1990; Rachman, Levitt, & Lopatka, 1988; Rachman & Lopatka, 1986; Schmidt, Jacquin, & Telch, 1994; Telch, Ilai, Valentiner, & Craske, 1994; van Hout & Emmelkamp, 1994). These effects go beyond random distribution or regression to the mean (e.g., Arntz *et al.*, 1990a, 1994). In other words, overpredictions of fear maintain avoidant behavior, and underpredictions of fear are particularly potent reinforcers of avoidance as well as future overpredictions of fear.

From a perspective broader than avoidance of circumscribed phobic stimuli, Hayes, Strosahl, and Wilson (1999) view avoidance as an attempt to control aversive internal experiences of fear and anxiety. In turn, these attempts are a primary source of the psychological dysfunction that propels one in the direction of a clinically severe disorder, in much the same way as is proposed to result from attempts to suppress unwanted thoughts (Wegner & Smart, 1997). Corroborating evidence exists in the domains of panic disorder and obsessive–compulsive disorder. In both cases, the shift from a non-clinical state of occasional episodes of distress (i.e., infrequent panic attacks or occasional intrusive thoughts) to a "disordered" state appears to be influenced by reactions to such episodes of acute distress, and in particular reactions designed to avert or control their occurrence. In relation to intrusive thoughts, which occur very commonly in the population (see Chapter 1), a variety of reactions have been found in unselected samples, including doing nothing, self-reassurance, analyzing the thought, seeking reassurances, replacement with another thought or action, and thought stopping (Ladouceur *et al.*, 2000). Thoughts appraised as more eogdystonic were associated with greater use of escape or avoidance strategies (Langlois, Freeston, & Ladouceur, 2000), and attempts to deal with intrusive thoughts by escaping or avoiding them were associated with more distress overall and more difficulty in removing the intrusions than "non-effortful" or minimal reactions to intrusive thoughts (Freeston, Ladouceur, Thibodeau, & Gagnon, 1991). Similarly, reactions designed to "neutralize" or undo intrusive thoughts are associated with more distress and more urges to neutralize upon re-exposure to those thoughts than is doing nothing (Salkovskis, Westbrook, Davis, Jeavons, & Gledhill, 1997).

These data are consistent with the extensive body of experimental work on thought suppression. Specifically, suppression-related thoughts are enhanced when suppression is voluntarily relinquished or disabled by cognitive demands (Wenzlaff & Wegner, 2000). Thought suppression is speculated to involve both an intentional operating process that seeks thoughts to promote the preferred state (i.e., not the unwanted thoughts), and an ironic monitoring process that remains in the background of consciousness and searches for mental contents that signal the failure to achieve the desired state (i.e., the unwanted thoughts). It is ironic because it opposes the overall goal of suppression by remaining vigilant for the unwanted item, but is necessary because it alerts the operating process of the need to renew distraction when the unwanted thought is detected. Hence, through ironic monitoring, attempts at thought suppression result in what Wegner and Smart (1997) refer to as "deep cognitive activation" — the notion that a thought is accessible or primed (as measured by its influence on other thoughts) and yet is not reportably conscious. Full activation, in this model, refers to thoughts that are both accessible and consciously present. Surface activation refers to conscious thinking but limited accessibility, as might occur when attempting to concentrate on something that is not very interesting or on a distractor in order to avoid thinking about something else that is more accessible. Intentional activation of thoughts — such as attempts at thought suppression or concentration — increases the accessibility of thoughts that are least desired in consciousness (e.g., trying not to think of "house" decreases the speed with which the color of the printed word is named during a Stroop interference task). The ironic process is especially strong under a mental load, such as during parallel tasks or when under stress, that interferes with strategic mental control activities so that the more automatic ironic monitoring process predominates. According to this model, the use of distraction or any other suppression attempt to erase an unwanted thought results in surface level activation of the distraction but deep activation of the unwanted thought that primes its resurgence. In addition, suppression induces autonomic reactivity. For example, Gross and Levenson (1993) found that participants instructed to suppress their emotions while watching a distressing film showed greater blood vessel constriction and skin conductance reactivity than those not instructed to suppress. Also, individuals who chronically suppressed their thoughts tend to respond with heightened skin conductance to reminders of unwanted thoughts (Wegner & Zanakos, 1994).

Mirroring the detrimental impact of attempts to suppress obsessive-type intrusive thoughts, attempts to suppress thoughts about traumas appear to be more pronounced in those who develop distress after trauma. For example, more attempts at thought suppression were reported by individuals who developed acute stress disorder versus those did not after a motor vehicle accident (Harvey & Bryant, 1998), and in those who developed posttraumatic stress disorder following rape versus those who did not (Shipherd & Beck, 1999). In addition, Ehlers, Mayou, and Bryant (1998) found that the tendency to suppress accident-related thoughts at 3 months was a predictor of posttraumatic stress disorder symptoms 1 year later. There is also good evidence that avoidance of trauma reminders in general (versus trauma-related thoughts specifically) contribute to posttraumatic stress disorder. In a well-conducted longitudinal study, Gilboa-Schechtman and Foa (2001) found that women who were traumatized and showed a delayed peak reaction (indicative of avoidance) to the trauma had elevated trauma pathology in the long term. Others report that avoidant reactions to trauma are one of the strongest predictors of the development of posttraumatic stress disorder (e.g., Bryant & Harvey, 1995; Joseph, Williams, & Yule, 1995). Finally, the use of worry as a verbal strategy for suppressing and avoiding unpleasant fear-based autonomic arousal is hypothesized to contribute to the cycle of chronic worry and generalized anxiety disorder (e.g., Borkovec & Roemer, 1995; Freeston, Rheaume, Letarte, Dugas,

& Ladouceur, 1994), as described in detail in Chapter 7. Thus, not only avoidance of phobic stimuli but also avoidance of negative symptoms in general appear to contribute to the cycle of ongoing distress.

Stressor Exacerbation

Two types of data suggest that processes of anxiety are exacerbated by ongoing stressors. First, variations in symptom levels over time are influenced by environmental factors (Eaves & Eysenck, 1976). Mackinnon *et al.* (1990) studied 254 twin pairs on five separate occasions. The variability in symptoms of anxiety and depression over time did not have a significant genetic basis but rather appeared to be under environmental influence. Second, life stressors over periods of months and years predict later anxious and depressive symptoms (Cohen, McGowan, Fooskas, & Rose, 1984) in adult samples, although the same may not be true of adolescents (Cohen, Burt, & Bjork, 1987; Rueter *et al.*, 1999). There is also evidence for heightened stressors in the months preceding the onset of anxiety disorders, although the research falls short of the stress-related research in other areas of psychopathology. For example, panic disorder patients report significantly more life events than controls in the months preceding onset of panic symptoms (Faravelli, 1985; Faravelli & Pallanti, 1989; Pollard *et al.*, 1989; Roy-Byrne *et al.*, 1986), although the findings are not always replicated (e.g., Rapee *et al.*, 1990) and the effects are often small in magnitude. One study found that men reporting four or more life events in the prior year were 8.5 times more likely to meet criteria for generalized anxiety disorder than men who reported three or fewer life events, although the same was not the case for women (Blazer, Hughes, & George, 1987), and diagnostic status was not measured at the baseline.

Summary

Hypervigilance to threat, a prepared physiological state, danger-laden judgments, and avoidance behavior are viewed as manifestations of anxiety, which contribute to further anxiousness. Hypervigilance is well documented in the form of preferential allocation of attentional resources to threat-relevant information, most consistently seen when inhibitory regulation is prevented by conditions of restricted awareness. There is some evidence for highly anxious individuals to exhibit slowed disengagement from threat, at least when faced with the demand of ongoing cognitive tasks, plus eventual avoidance of threat with sufficiently long periods of time, presumably to avoid negative affect. Consistent with theories of emotion regulation, a higher-level executive system of attention processing influences involuntary preattentive mechanisms of engagement and disengagement. Attentional selectivity appears to be driven by an executive system that determines the threat value of stimuli, and highly trait-anxious individuals assign higher threat values to stimuli in studies of judgment of risk, judgment of association, and judgment of meaning. In addition, certain stimuli (such as angry and fearful faces) may innately possess elevated threat value due to their biological significance. Among youths, the evidence suggests that attentional bias only becomes a discriminating feature in older children, as if to imply that all children preferentially attend to threat, but, with development, non-anxious youths inhibit such attentional biases whereas anxious-prone youths do not. However, the data remain inconsistent. Among adults, evidence for magnification of attentional biases in individuals with high negative affectivity is limited. Nonetheless, attentional biases are trainable, and acquisition of a negative attentional bias predicts distress to later stressors. Similarly, judgmental biases are more apparent in those with high trait anxiety, and they too are trainable and influence levels of state anxiety. These findings reflect the contributory role of attentional and judgmental biases toward anxiousness, although their significance for the development of anxiety disorders is not known. The demonstrations of "trainable" attentional and judgment biases also imply that high negative affectivity is not a necessary precursor to threat-biased information-processing styles, thus rendering the parental influences and emotion regulation factors described in Chapter 4 all the more important.

Physiological arousal, in its varied forms, is seen as supporting a state of hypervigilance. Individuals with anxiety disorders generally do not exhibit elevated acute stress responding (with the exception of specific phobias) but instead exhibit elevated sympathetic and hypothalamic–pituitary axis activation in anticipation of stress, possibly combined with tonic levels of low cardiac vagal tone. Although the effects of such a state upon attentional and interpretive biases have not been fully studied, there is evidence that heightened autonomic arousal enhances conditioning to aversive stimuli and good reason to believe that it slows habituation. Elevated hypothalamic–pituitary axis activation may contribute to generalized anticipation of stressors, and tonically low cardiac vagal tone may contribute to overgeneralized anxious responding to a broad array of reminders of threat. Moreover, there is evidence that such features are enhanced by negative affectivity, or behavioral inhibition, and youths at risk for anxiety are characterized by elevated sympathetic and cortisol reactivity to non-specific stressors as well as lowered vagal tone. These early aspects of psychophysiological functioning may contribute to a state of overall physiological preparedness for threat.

Avoidant coping is the third anxious process that is motivated not only by the expectancy for fear but also the threat value of fear and associated stimuli. Again, the vulnerability factors of negative affectivity and a threat-based style of emotion regulation are presumed to heighten avoidant responding, as seen in retreat from unfamiliarity or novelty in anxious-prone primates and non-primates. addition, avoidant coping is trainable, according to the extensive literature on avoidance learning, and the role of parental influences may be paramount in the development of an avoidant style of responding. Moreover, avoidance contributes to ongoing distress in the form of fearful expectations and further avoidance of phobic stimuli, and in the form of overall anxiousness. For example, several investigations link avoidant responding to occasional symptoms as critical to the transition to further and more pervasive distress, and the extensive experimental research on thought suppression demonstrates the negative impact, physiologically and emotionally, of such attempts.

In summary, the anxious processes are fueled by broad vulnerability factors, such that greater vulnerability is expected to elicit more pervasive hypervigilance, physiological preparation for stressors, threat-based judgments, and avoidant behaviors. Ongoing stressors appear to exacerbate anxious processes as well. At the same time, anxious processes contribute to ongoing anxiety, and thus are likely to explain the chronicity of anxiety disorders throughout adulthood.

Chapter 6

Specificity in Salience and Threat Value

Factors that are common to the manifestation of anxiety disorders have been addressed up until this point, these being vulnerability factors of negative affectivity and a threat-based style of regulating negative affect, and the resultant anxious processes of hypervigilance or preferential attentional allocation to potential threat, a physiological state of preparedness in anticipation of stressors, and avoidant responding to potential threats. The issue addressed in this chapter is how these anxious processes become tied to specific classes of stimuli; or the individual learning histories through which particular sets of stimuli acquire or retain their threat value. Both associative and non-associative pathways are considered. The magnifying impact of broader vulnerabilities upon these pathways is described as well.

Associative Learning

Traumatic Conditioning

Early learning theorizing relied heavily on contiguous classical conditioning models to explain the development of fears and phobias. In this view, a neutral stimulus develops fear-provoking properties by virtue of close temporal pairing with an aversive stimulus. These early theories were criticized (e.g., Rachman, 1978). The two-factor theory (Mowrer, 1939), in which subsequent to initial classical conditioning of fears avoidance was reinforced by its fear-reducing properties, was similarly discredited because a series of studies have shown that avoidance behavior continues after extended trials despite diminution of conditioned fear (Siddle & Bond, 1988). Recent revisions to conditioning theorizing of fear and anxiety seem to correct the earlier pitfalls. Rachman (1991a), Davey (1992), and Mineka and Zinbarg (1995) provide excellent reviews of the newer conditioning models and their application to human fear and anxiety. Within these newer "dynamic" models, traumatic conditioning remains a prominent explanation for phobic responding given the evidence for traumatic causation of anxiety. Examples of such causation include classical conditioning of anxiety in humans using electric shocks as the unconditioned stimulus (e.g., Öhman, Fredrikson, & Hugdahl, 1978). More dramatic results are obtained with more intense stimuli, of which naturalistic examples include the development of anticipatory nausea and vomiting due to chemotherapy, fears of drugs due to negative or allergic reactions during drug ingestion (Siddle & Bond, 1988), or posttraumatic stress disorder from life-threatening traumas.

Recollections of traumatic experiences as the initiator of phobic responding is often cited as evidence for traumatic conditioning, with estimates as follows: animal fears, 26.7–67 percent (Fredrikson, Fischer, & Wik, 1997; King, Clowes-Hollins, & Ollendick, 1997; Merckelbach, Arntz, Arrindell, & de Jong, 1992; Merckelbach, Arntz, & de Jong, 1991; Öst & Hugdahl, 1981); claustrophobia, 69 percent (Öst & Hugdahl, 1981); dental and blood, and injury and injection, phobias, 49–100 percent (de Jongh, Muris, Ter Hurst, & Duyx, 1995; Kleinknecht, 1994; Lautch, 1971; Moore, Brodsgaard, & Birn, 1991; Öst, 1991; Öst & Hugdahl, 1985); social phobia, 58 percent (Öst & Hugdahl, 1981); driving phobia, 70 percent (Munjack, 1984); agoraphobia, 88 percent (Öst & Hugdahl, 1981, 1983). Unfortunately, this type of recollection is fraught with imprecision, and confounding factors include the influence of the current mood state on memory, the assumption of conscious awareness of factors that may have not been consciously appraised at the time, and unreliability in general. For example, Taylor, Deane, and Podd (1999) found considerable variation in retrospective accounts of fear onset, with only 54 percent of etiological attributions (i.e., traumatic versus vicarious etc) remaining stable over a 1 year period and with most change occurring in the "cannot remember" group. In a similar vein, the correlation between retrospective reports at 18 years of age and the actual number of major childhood injuries reported at 9, 11, 13, and 15 years of age was only 0.42 (Henry, Moffitt, Caspi, Langely, & Silva, 1994).

Moreover, the results from retrospective reports are affected by the particular instrument and the way questions are posed. Hence, Kirkby, Menzies, Daniels, and Smith (1995) obtained substantially different rates of traumatic onsets from different instruments. Instruments that include unexpected panic as a type of direct traumatic conditioning yield more support for traumatic onset (e.g., Öst & Hugdahl, 1981, 1983) than instruments that exclude unexpected panics (e.g., Menzies & Clarke, 1993, 1995c). Much less contaminated than recollection of course is prospective longitudinal research, but such studies are almost non-existent. In the Dunedin Multidisciplinary data set, Poulton, Waldie, Thomson, and Locker (2001) found that late-onset dental fear was related to earlier aversive conditioning experiences in the form of decays and tooth loss. Although supportive of traumatic conditioning, this report remains one of a kind. Much more telling is the body of experimental evidence for traumatic conditioning that is reviewed below.

Vicarious Acquisition and Informational Transmission

Obviously, some fears develop in the absence of direct personal traumatic experience. Over 20 years ago, Rachman (1978) proposed that fears can be acquired through at least three pathways: traumatic conditioning, informational transmission (more recently labeled transmission of verbal information), and vicarious observation. Examples of vicarious and information transmission were provided in the discussion of parent influences upon the transmission of fear in Chapter 4. Informational transmission refers to conveyance of threatening information about specific objects, as occurs with parental warnings or media reports about dangers inherent in specific situations. Retrospective estimates for informational transmission as the source of phobic responding are as follows: animal fears, 6.7–15 percent (Fredrikson *et al.*, 1997; King, Clowes-Hollins, & Ollendick, 1997; Merckelbach *et al.*, 1991, 1992; Öst & Hugdahl, 1981); claustrophobia, 11 percent (Öst & Hugdahl, 1981); dental and blood, and injury and injection, phobias, 6 percent (de Jongh *et al.*, 1995; Kleinknecht, 1994; Lautch, 1971; Moore, Brodsgaard, & Birn, 1991; Öst, 1991; Öst & Hugdahl, 1985). Although the notion of informational transmission is face valid and consistent with the role of parental expectations in generating offspring anxiety, these estimates of onset again remain subject to severe biases of retrospection.

Vicarious observation refers to observing a model respond fearfully or be traumatized in the presence of a specific stimulus. Retrospective estimates for the vicarious acquisition of phobias are as follows: animal fears, 28–71 percent (Fredrikson *et al.*, 1997; King, Clowes-Hollins, & Ollendick, 1997; Merckelbach *et al.*, 1991, 1992; Öst & Hugdahl, 1981); claustrophobia, 9 percent (Öst & Hugdahl, 1981); dental and blood, and injury and injection, phobias, 12 percent (de Jongh *et al.*, 1995; Kleinknecht, 1994; Lautch, 1971; Moore, Brodsgaard, & Birn, 1991; Öst, 1991; Öst & Hugdahl, 1985). The same criticism of retrospective data collection applies. Less biased is the evidence described in Chapter 4 for childrens' fears to vary as a function of the extent to which mothers express their fears in the presence of their children (Muris *et al.*, 1996b), and for toddlers to express more negative affect and avoidance of a toy toward which the mother expressed a negative versus a positive reaction (e.g., Gerull & Rapee, 2002).

As mentioned in Chapter 4 also, Mineka and colleagues provide the strongest experimental evidence to date for vicarious fear acquisition in their sample of rhesus monkeys (e.g., Cook & Mineka, 1987, 1989, 1990; Mineka & Cook, 1993; Mineka *et al.*, 1984). Laboratory-reared young adult monkeys, not previously exposed to snakes, observed unrelated, wild-reared monkeys react fearfully in the presence of live and toy snakes and non-fearfully in the presence of neutral objects. The majority showed rapid acquisition of an intense fear of snakes, nearly as strong as the fear usually observed in wild monkeys, and the fear persisted for at least 3 months. Mineka and Cook (1993) argued that processes involved in vicarious acquisition are very similar to those involved in direct traumatic conditioning: the observer monkey's response (unconditioned response) directly parallels the model monkey's display of fear (unconditioned stimulus) in the presence of the snake (conditioned stimulus). Earlier, Siddle and Bond (1988) similarly proposed that vicarious fear acquisition is a type of conditioning, given that electrodermal responses can become conditioned through observation of facial expressions of emotion. They also consider informational transmission to be a type of conditioning, given that certain responses can be conditioned through instruction alone. An alternative but overlapping conceptualization of the effect of observing another person exhibiting fears is social referencing, whereby one's perception of another's interpretation of a stimulus is used to form one's own appraisal of that stimulus. Either way, facial expressions provide a major source of information that effects the modeling and vicarious acquisition of fear and anxiety and the communication of a sense of present threat.

Stress in a Dynamic Context

Simple, or one-trial traumatic experiences, informational transmission, and vicarious acquisition are rarely sufficient to account for the development of significant fears and phobias. For example, albeit again based on retrospective recall of past experiences, non-phobic individuals report as many aversive experiences with a stimulus as individuals who become phobic of the same stimulus. DiNardo, Guzy, and Bak (1988) found that dog-phobic individuals did not differ from those without phobia with respect to their number of aversive encounters with dogs (approximately two-thirds in each case). Merckelbach *et al.* (1992) found that relatively equal proportions of spider-phobic and non-spider-phobic individuals reported conditioning-type events with spiders (60–66 percent). Also, Ehlers, Hofmann, Herda, and Roth (1994) found that a sample of 56 individuals with driving phobias had no more accidents than a control sample. Nor did the former group report more models who were anxious, nor report witnessing, hearing or reading about accidents or driving dangers more than control participants. Finally, Menzies and Clarke (1995b) found that an acrophobic sample did not differ from controls in terms of prevalence of direct conditioning experiences, vicarious learning, or negative information from fearful friends, and in fact controls had a stronger history of trauma events. Although these retrospective data are susceptible to error, they raise the possibility that the trauma experience is indeed relatively consistent between phobic and non-phobic individuals, then it is clear that the same traumatic event is experienced differently by different people, and probably differently by the same person at different times. To account for this variation, Mineka and Zinbarg (1995) proposed a "stress-in-dynamic-context anxiety model" in which psychological and historical contextual influences upon conditioning are emphasized. Specifically, they emphasize: constitutional factors such as temperament, past history of exposure to uncontrollable life events and prior traumatic conditioning events; current contextual factors at the time of the stressor; and future modification of the impact of the stressor through processes such as forgetting or other memory changes and other experiences. Each area is summarized briefly, and although the discussion refers mostly to direct exposure to aversive stimuli (i.e., direct traumatic conditioning), the concepts may be equally applicable to vicarious acquisition and informational transmission versions of conditioning processes.

Constitutional Factors

The learning that takes place as a result of negative events has long been considered in part determined by pre-existing variables of a constitutional nature as well as learning history (Eysenck, 1967; Gray, 1970; Mineka & Zinbarg, 1995). That is, certain constitutional or historic variables moderate the influence of traumas and the development of conditioned anxiety. One such constitutional factor is neuroticism. Eysenck (1967) originally proposed that "neurotic introverts" are at risk for acquiring conditioned anxiety responses because of central and peripheral hyperarousal. Introverts were hypothesized to possess heightened cortical arousal, leading to greater cortical excitation, which facilitates acquisition and depresses extinction of aversive learning. Nonetheless, neuroticism also was judged to contribute to conditioning due to stronger and longer-lasting sympathetic nervous system reactions to stressful stimuli, thereby energizing cortical mechanisms, leading to increased conditionability and resistance to extinction (Eysenck, 1967).

Some indirect support comes from the evidence already mentioned in Chapter 5 for enhanced threat learning with heightened arousal, although heightened arousal *per se* is not a direct index of neuroticism. Öhman and Bohlin (1973) showed that more aroused individuals, as defined by the number of spontaneous fluctuations in skin conductance, showed better aversive conditioning. Hugdahl *et al.* (1977) found that similarly defined highly aroused subjects showed a diffuse responding style during acquisition trials of pairing a neutral stimulus with an unconditioned stimulus — not differentiating between reinforced and non-reinforced cues — and in addition showed the most resistance to extinction over a subsequent series of 20 trials. In a more direct test of Eysenck's theory, Fredrikson and Georgiades (1992) found that introverts conditioned accelerative heart rate (i.e., defensive) responses to a stimulus paired with electric shock whereas extraverts conditioned decelerative heart rate (i.e., orienting) responses. They did not find differences in terms of electrodermal activity, leading them to conclude that the increased heart rate reactivity and conditionability among introverts was due to reduced vagal tone rather than increased sympathetic activation. However, neuroticism did not relate to conditioning in their study. Avila, Parcet, Ortet, and Ibanez-Ribes (1999) examined whether high sensitivity to punishment, as defined by Gray's model of the behavioral inhibition system, led to impairment in learning to associate a future reward with an aversive event. In their study, punishment (loss of points in a game task) was followed by a larger reward than conditions without punishment. As hypothesized, low scorers on the sensitivity to punishment scale more quickly learned how to gain more rewards.

Several studies report greater conditionability in high-trait-anxious individuals, which is relevant because trait anxiety is viewed as a lower-order component of negative affectivity (Zinbarg, 1998). Some time ago, Spence and Spence (1966) noted that high trait anxiety was typically associated with superior eyelid conditioning performance to a puff of air paired with a tone. Zinbarg and Mohlman (1998) also found that highly trait-anxious participants formed aversive expectations to avoidance cues more quickly than low-trait-anxious individuals. Furthermore, college students who scored high on a measure of obsessive–compulsive behavior (that presumably correlates with trait anxiety) acquired a conditioned eye blink response faster than low scorers (Tracy, Ghose, Stecher, McFall, & Steinmetz, 1999). Notably, however, not all results indicate elevated conditionability among highly trait-anxious samples (e.g., Davidson, Payne, & Sloane, 1964; Guimaraes, Hellewell, Hensman, Wang, & Deakin, 1991).

Stronger effects have been obtained in more severely distressed samples, and especially those with posttraumatic stress disorder, although the results cannot be attributed completely to vulnerability factors in these kinds of studies. For example, clinically anxious individuals show slower extinction of skin conductance responses conditioned to angry facial expressions in comparison with non-anxious individuals

(Pittman & Orr, 1986). Also, Grillon and Morgan (1999) found that veterans with posttraumatic stress disorder exhibited greater conditioning to shock compared with healthy controls. Interestingly, this was only true in a second assessment session. Initially, the posttraumatic stress disorder group showed heightened reactivity overall as seen by non-differential responding between conditioned and neutral stimuli, thus replicating the findings of Hugdahl *et al.* (1977) with highly aroused subjects. We are reminded of the data presented in previous chapters for more indiscriminant responding in relation to chronically low levels of vagal tone (e.g., Friedman & Thayer, 1998a), poor contingency awareness, and unpredictability (Grillon, 2002a). In addition to initial non-differential responding were signs of increased anticipation of shock over trials, and elevated baseline responding from the first to the second assessment session. Together, these represent a state of generalized anxious responding that resembles the experimental evidence for greater generalization and less cue specificity of fear learning in non-primates under conditions of high stress (Rosen & Schulkin, 1998) and startle potentiation during anticipation of stressors due to enhanced contextual conditioning (see Chapters 4 and 5; Grillon, 2002a).

Orr *et al.* (2000) also studied conditioning in traumatized individuals, some of whom met the criteria for posttraumatic stress disorder. The latter group showed stronger differential conditioning immediately, even after correcting for baseline elevations in heart rate and skin conductance responding. The use of autonomic indices may account for the discrepant findings relevant to the earlier study by Grillon and Morgan (1999), who used startle instead. The posttraumatic stress disorder group in the study by Orr *et al.* (2000) exhibited stronger heart rate reactivity to the unconditioned stimulus (although equivalent skin conductance reactivity), suggesting that they experienced the aversive stimulus more intensely than the non-posttraumatic stress disorder group. This is relevant because, as already mentioned in Chapter 5, the salience of aversive stimuli increases the intensity of conditioned fear reactions (Mackintosh, 1974), and may be a critical pathway through which negative affectivity potentiates aversive learning. In other words, the stronger the emotional response to stimuli, the greater the learning that takes place (Forsyth & Eifert, 1996), and the intensity of the body's response to an aversive stimulus was even found to mediate conditioning in another study (Forsyth & Eifert, 1998). Combine stronger emotional responding with a basic drive to understand lawful relationships and to explain emotional reactions ("it was *that* that made me anxious"), then heightened conditioning seems even more probable. Again, however, it is very likely that superior conditionability in clinically anxious groups derives from the stress of anxiousness (i.e., of posttraumatic stress disorder), and the role of negative affectivity *per se*, while likely, is not delineated by these types of study.

Constitutional variables also may influence the evaluation of conditioning experiences as more or less favorable, resulting in more or less conditioned fear expression (Davey, 1992). "In particular, individuals may adopt generalized coping strategies that allow them to cognitively neutralize or devalue threats, with the implication that such individuals will be less likely to acquire durable anxiety-based disorders" (Davey, Burgess, & Rashes, 1995, p. 424). Threat devaluation refers to demotion of a stressor through cognitive reappraisal of its significance, and is thus an exemplar of emotion regulation, which, like high negative affectivity, is likely to contribute to the impact of aversive events. Some support was found in that participants with more phobic fear reported using threat devaluation significantly less often than those with less phobic fear, as did clinical groups of individuals with specific phobias and panic disorder patients in comparison with normal controls (Davey *et al.*, 1995). Obviously, these types of between-group comparisons cannot signify a *contributory* role for threat appraisal. The more telling evidence is that cognitive appraisals of the meaning of traumatic events, at least within 4 months of the event, predict the severity of posttraumatic stress disorder symptoms at a later point in time (Dunmore, Clark, & Ehlers, 2001), consistent with the cognitive model of Ehlers and Clark (2000). These and related findings are presented in more detail in Chapter 7. The most telling evidence of all — appraisal systems at the time of the aversive event — is yet to be reported.

Less broad constitutional factors include a history of experience with the to-be-conditioned stimulus. For example, the concept of "latent inhibition" alluded to when describing the detrimental effects of overrestrictive parenting refers to prior exposure to a conditioned stimulus (before it is ever paired with an unconditioned stimulus), reducing the amount of subsequent conditioning. Latent inhibition is attributed to loss of conditioned stimulus salience or associability because it initially predicts nothing of importance (Mackintosh, 1983). Latent inhibition can occur vicariously as well as through direct experience. For example, Mineka and Cook (1986) examined the degree to which prior vicarious exposure to a monkey behaving non-fearfully prevented or immunized the development of fear when monkeys subsequently observed a fearful monkey in the presence of a snake. Indeed, prior experience fully prevented the acquisition of fear in six out of eight monkeys. Prior non-fearful exposure, either directly or vicariously, offers one explanation for why fears do not *always* develop after traumatic experiences. For example, Davey (1989) reported that individuals with a history of painful dental treatments who did not develop dental anxiety had a number of relatively painless treatments prior to the painful experiences. De Jongh *et al.* (1995) found that those who had always been fearful of dentists had relatively short durations between their first dental treatment and their first painful treatment, suggesting they lacked positive experiences to buffer the development of long-lasting fear when a painful treatment occurred. Again, however, these data are based on verbal retrospection. As Mineka and Zinbarg (1995) note, latent inhibition may also explain why familial concordance rates are not higher; observation of one family member behaving fearfully is probably buffered by other family members responding non-fearfully to the same stimulus.

Current Contextual Factors and Preparedness

Whereas constitutional factors relate to individual differences that influence rates of responding to a given experience, current contextual factors refer to factors that influence rates of responding across types of experience for everyone. These include controllability and escapability of the aversive event. Not only are uncontrollable aversive events more distressing, as illustrated by the effects of perceived control or lack thereof over carbon dioxide inhalations for non-clinical participants with elevated anxiety sensitivity (a facet of trait anxiety) (Zvolensky, Eifert, Lejuez, & McNeil, 1999) and panic disorder patients (Sanderson, Rapee, & Barlow, 1989), but conditioned responding is generally stronger as a result of uncontrollable versus controllable shock in non-primate and primate samples (e.g., Mineka, Cook, & Miller, 1984). Uncontrollable shocks, for example, lead to increased cortisol levels and gastric ulceration (Weiss, 1971a, 1971b, 1971c), and heightened anxiety in novel situations (Peterson, Maier, & Seligman, 1993) in non-primates. The conclusions made in 1976 (Maier & Seligman, 1976) that uncontrollable events produce motivational, cognitive, and emotional disturbances have withstood the test of time. Thus, rape and other forms of sexual molestation during which the victim has very little control may be particularly likely to generate subsequent fear, in contrast to other forms of abuse, all other factors being equal. Another current contextual factor is the intensity of the aversive experience, with more intense aversive experiences resulting in more conditioning, as illustrated by the higher rates of posttraumatic stress disorder with more direct combat exposure (e.g., Litz, King, King, Orsillo, & Friedman, 1997). It is easy to see where individual differences in negative affectivity may interact with the intensity factor because negative affectivity heightens the intensity of aversive experiences. Furthermore, the degree of conditioning is influenced by how much reliable and non-redundant information is provided about the unconditioned stimulus (e.g., Mackintosh, 1983; Rescorla, 1988b). For example, if an aversive event occurs only sometimes in relation to a neutral stimulus, and sometimes occurs in the absence of the neutral stimulus, then the latter is not a reliable predictor of the aversive event and is unlikely to become conditioned. For example, nursing assistants who are only occasionally present during chemotherapy procedures are less likely to become feared than nursing assistants who are reliably present.

Also influential upon conditioning are principles of belongingness and preparedness. The preparedness hypothesis developed originally from findings regarding conditioned taste aversion, illustrating that certain conditioned–unconditioned stimulus combinations are more easily learned than others. For example, Garcia and Koelling (1966) demonstrated that organisms more easily associate taste with illness than with electric shock. Also, pain is more readily associated with auditory and visual stimuli than with gustatory stimuli, and gastric distress is more easily associated with taste than with vision (Rachman, 1991a). This effect is referred to as belongingness. Hamm, Vaitl, and Lang (1989) found that belongingness, objectified as ratings of the relative closeness or similarity in meaning of two concepts, affected conditioning. High belongingness pairs (e.g., an angry face and a loud scream) showed superior acquisition and resistance to extinction relative to low belongingness pairs (e.g., a landscape and a loud scream). Thus, traumatic experiences are more likely to lead to conditioned fear if the traumatic event "belongs" with the stimulus with which it is associated; yet another explanation for variability in the extent to which conditioning occurs.

The study of preparedness has shed much light on the nature of fear. Originally, Seligman (1970) argued that we possess a biologically based preparedness to rapidly associate certain objects, such as snakes, spiders, enclosed places, and angry faces —

those which may have been dangerous or posed a threat to our early ancestors — with aversive events, and that a similar disposition has not yet developed for more modern dangers. The category of preparedness includes reptiles, given that the predatory defense system is assumed to have its evolutionary origin in a prototypical fear of reptiles in early mammals. Social fears are viewed as a second evolved behavioral system related to conspecific attack and self-defense, which serves to control the interaction between individuals in a group by defining a hierarchy of submission and dominance. That is, repeated social defeat leads to increased submissiveness and lowering of position in the dominance hierarchy. Mineka and Zinbarg (1995) emphasize the power of social defeat as an uncontrollable stressor because repeated social defeat produces many of the effects seen with inescapable (uncontrollable) shock, including escape deficits in the face of aversive stimuli and potentiated conditioned fear responses. It is for these reasons that a facial expression of threat is a particularly potent fear stimulus, as indicated by the evidence reviewed earlier for rapid detection of facial stimuli and selective attention to angry faces (see Chapter 5). As a third category, Seligman (1970) proposed that rituals of washing and checking once promoted survival and reproduction, and subsequently became genetically coded in the form of prepared learning mechanisms that can be easily triggered. Thus, humans may be biologically prepared to obsess or ruminate about certain stimuli that posed a threat to our early ancestors, and to perform certain kinds of responses to reduce such distress (Mineka & Zinbarg, 1995). In agreement, de Silva, Rachman, and Seligman (1977) noted that obsessive–compulsive content and behaviors fall predominantly in the range of prepared stimuli. Finally, Rachman (1991a) hypothesized that unusual, unexpected, or novel bodily sensations also represent prepared stimuli. Thus, almost all objects feared in the context of anxiety disorders represent evolutionarily prepared stimuli, which may explain the non-random nature of phobic stimuli (de Silva, Rachman, & Seligman, 1977). (Note that the terms "prepared", "evolutionarily primed" or "evolutionarily significant", and "fear relevant" are used interchangeably throughout the following discussion.)

"Prepared" conditioning was posited to involve rapid, one-trial acquisition, slow extinction, and to be non-cognitive (Seligman & Hager, 1972). Although extant data with humans do not always show a reliable difference in the rate of acquisition between prepared and unprepared stimuli paired with electric shock (Öhman, Fredrikson, Hugdahl, & Rimmo, 1976), they mostly show greater resistance to extinction for prepared (animal and social) stimuli (e.g., Dimberg, 1986a; Hugdahl & Öhman, 1977; Mazurski, Bond, Siddle, & Lovibond, 1996; Öhman, 1986; Schell, Dawson, & Marinkovic, 1991). Some contradictory data exist (e.g., Merckelbach, van den Hout, & van der Molen, 1987), but Öhman and Mineka (2001) question the methodology involved in those studies. Good evidence exists for superior conditioning to angry faces compared with happy or neutral faces paired with electric shocks (Öhman & Dimberg, 1978), at least with respect to skin conductance measures, and when the angry faces are angled toward participants (Dimberg & Öhman, 1983). There is even evidence for stronger conditioning of stimuli with evolutionary preparedness versus stimuli with cultural, ontogenetic mediated fear relevance (i.e., reptiles versus guns or electric outlets) (e.g., Cook, Hodes, & Lang, 1986; Hugdahl & Kaerker, 1981). In addition, extinction is more resistant for angry faces than for happy faces (e.g., Esteves, Dimberg, & Öhman, 1994). A particularly interesting finding is that conditioned *responses* to fear-relevant stimuli differ from those to fear-irrelevant stimuli — conditioned heart rate is typically acceleratory in the former case and deceleratory in the second, potentially representing true conditioned defensive responding versus conditioned orienting responding.

As already mentioned, Cook and Mineka (1989, 1991) and Mineka and Cook (1993) examined the degree to which laboratory-reared monkeys developed fear from observing other monkeys show fear. They compared prepared (e.g., snakes) versus unprepared (e.g., flowers) stimuli, via ingenious use of videotapes and splicing. The concept of preparedness was supported: monkeys became fearful of snakes but not of flowers, despite observing equally fearful performances with respect to each stimulus. They noted that this result was particularly important because previous studies of preparedness effects were limited to measures of autonomic functioning, and relatively short-lived responding. In addition, because these monkeys had no prior exposure to the elements used in the conditioning trials, the results could not be attributed to ontogenetic/experiential factors over and above phylogenetic selection. Furthermore, these results pertained to fear acquisition rather than fear extinction. The strength of their results in comparison with the human studies reported above may lie in the fact that for monkeys to observe other monkeys behaving fearfully is a more naturalistic and intense aversive experience than for humans to receive electric shocks. This suggests that the investigation of true fear in humans is greatly limited by ethics and laboratory settings: weaker results in human laboratory studies should not be judged as evidence against traumatic conditioning to prepared stimuli.

Evidence for the *automaticity* or non-cognitive nature of prepared learning comes from several reports of superior conditionability to masked or non-reportable fear-relevant (i.e., prepared) stimuli compared with fear-irrelevant stimuli (e.g., Esteves, Dimberg, & Öhman, 1994; Katkin, Wiens, & Öhman, 2001; Öhman & Soares, 1993, 1998; Parra, Esteves, Flykt, & Öhman, 1997; Wong, Shevrin, & Williams, 1994). Similarly, extinction is more resistant for facial expressions than for non-prepared stimuli, even when stimuli are backward masked (e.g., Esteves, Dimberg, & Öhman, 1994). The automaticity notion was also supported by studies of faster detection of fear-relevant stimuli within an array of stimuli, although the true automaticity of such biases is debated (see Chapter 5).

Accompanying the pre-conscious if not automatic attentional biases for fear-relevant stimuli is explicit judgment bias. Tomarken *et al*. (1989) examined covariation biases, or distortions in the perceived relation between two events, to demonstrate that preparedness is related to elevated risk estimates for negative outcomes. Using an illusory correlation paradigm, high- and low-fear participants were exposed to slides of snakes, spiders, mushrooms, or flowers, which were followed by shock, tone, or nothing. Although the shock delivery was random, participants overestimated the relationship between the fear slides (i.e., snakes and spiders), and shock and were generally accurate with regards to non-fear slides. These findings have since been replicated and extended to other fear stimuli (de Jong & Merckelbach, 1991; Pury & Mineka, 1997; Tomarken, Sutton, & Mineka, 1995). Several experiments also demonstrate stronger covariation bias with phylogenetic than with ontogenetic fear-relevant stimuli (e.g., Tomarken *et al.*, 1995). Expectancies for shock sometimes are elevated initially for both types of stimuli, but the covariation bias remains over trials for phylogenetic fear-relevant stimuli whereas it reduces for ontogenetic stimuli (Amin & Lovibond, 1997; de Jong, Merkelbach, & Arntz, 1995; Kennedy, Rapee, & Mazurski, 1997;). Overall, covariation biases of this sort are viewed as a type of adaptive conservatism because "the long-run cost to an organism that would be incurred by mistakenly treating a threatening stimulus or situation as nonthreatening is greater than the cost that would be incurred by mistakenly treating a safe stimulus or situation as threatening" (Tomarken *et al.*, 1989, p. 391).

The notion of evolutionary driven response selection has been questioned by Davey (1995), who argues that covariation biases may arise from pre-existing beliefs about certain relationships, including culturally generated beliefs. In support, expectancies for delivery of shock are stronger for prepared than unprepared stimuli even *prior* to exposure to shock–stimulus pairings (e.g., Davey & Craigie, 1997; Kennedy, Rapee, & Mazurski, 1997; McNally & Heatherton, 1993). In addition, Davey (1995) posited that "preparedness" results can be most parsimoniously understood as non-associative, namely selective sensitization rather than selective associative learning. In their comprehensive review of the literature, Öhman and Mineka (2001) recognize the potential for sensitization as an account, especially given evidence for elevated physiological responding to prepared stimuli even before pairing with aversive stimuli. However, they maintain that associative learning is the more primary means of preparedness responding, and non-associative effects cannot account for the longevity of prepared fear responding. They also discount the possibility that preparedness is the result of latent inhibition which has been put forth because many of the stimuli used to represent preparedness are rare whereas unprepared stimuli are more familiar and therefore histories of trauma-free experiences with the latter type of stimuli would limit their conditionability (Bond & Siddle, 1996). The work of Mineka and Cook (1993) and Cook and Mineka (1989) with vicarious learning in monkeys implies otherwise, as these monkeys had had no prior experience with any of the experimental stimuli and yet superior conditioning occurred to the prepared stimuli.

To distinguish between preparedness and other types of fear and anxiety, Öhman and Mineka (2001) propose two levels of learning. On one level, prepared stimuli are processed via a fear module characterized much as Seligman originally proposed by selectivity (i.e., sensitized to respond to evolutionarily primed stimuli), automaticity (i.e., because of the origin of this type of learning and responding in primitive brains, the behaviors are not typically under voluntary control, and elicited whether or not the stimulus is represented in consciousness), encapsulation (i.e., once activated, the fear module runs its course, and is resistant to conscious cognitive influences), and a specific neural circuitry involving the amygdala. As an illustration of encapsulation, instructions that no more aversive stimuli would be presented immediately extinguished conditioned skin conductance responses to fear-irrelevant stimuli but not to prepared stimuli (Hugdahl & Öhman, 1977). This was replicated by Soares and Öhman (1993b) using masked presentations of the conditioned stimulus during extinction and instructions that no more aversive stimuli would be forthcoming.

Öhman and Mineka (2001) place cognitive learning on a second level of learning, similar to Razran (1961), who argued that higher levels of learning (e.g., cognitive contingency learning) emerged later in ontogeny and phylogeny relative to lower levels of learning (e.g., habituation, sensitization, and basic classical conditioning). Conditioning with non-prepared stimuli, arbitrary pairings between neutral and aversive stimuli, or less aversive stimuli are posited to engage only the cognitive level of learning and not the emotional level of learning. Notably, most of the anxiety disorders are judged to involve prepared stimuli and thus emotional learning. However, the surrounding contexts and stimuli with which prepared stimuli become associated probably represent cognitive learning, which Öhman and Mineka (2001) attribute to circuits centered around the hippocampus. Thus, their association of the amygdala with fear-relevant, emotional learning, and the hippocampus with fear-irrelevant, cognitive learning, overlaps with other models reviewed in Chapters 2 and 4 for the amygdala to be central to cue-explicit conditioning and the hippocampus to be more involved in contextual conditioning.

Post-conditioning Events

Following conditioning, a variety of processes may influence the persistence of fear. These too appear to interact with constitutional factors. One post-conditioning factor is expectancies for aversive outcomes. For example, as described in Chapter 5, phobic individuals typically overestimate fear or the likelihood of panicking in specific situations (e.g., Rachman & Lopatka, 1986b; Taylor & Rachman, 1994) that motivate avoidance behavior that in turn prevents disconfirmatory opportunities and maintains the threat value of outcomes. Ironically, one source for overestimation of fear are instances of unexpectedly high fear (see Chapter 5). Conceivably, the vulnerability to unexpectedly high fear in the first place is tied to negative affectivity.

Another possible post-conditioning factor is termed "inflation", whereby mild fear conditioned to a mildly aversive stimulus can be greatly strengthened by subsequent independent exposure to a strong aversive stimulus. For example, fear responding to a conditioned stimulus is potentiated by administration of corticosteroids as well as non-contingent unconditioned stressors (Izquierdo, Barros, Medina, & Izquierdo, 2002; Rescorla, 1974; Sullivan *et al.*, 1999). In a series of clinical case studies, Davey, de Jong, and Tallis (1993) noted instances of a mild fear later growing in magnitude due to non-contingent exposure to a powerful unconditioned stressor not paired with the conditioned stimulus. Similarly, Bouton, Mineka, and Barlow (2001) give the example of the excitatory strength of interoceptive cues associated with several mild panic attacks being escalated by later major stressors in the form of intense panic attacks unconnected to the earlier interoceptive cues. Interestingly, inflation is more likely to happen with lengthier intervals between original conditioning and higher-intensity events (Hendersen, 1985). Inflation provides one mechanism through which stressful events enhance pre-existing fears, such as might occur when a mild fear of heights is intensified following major surgery. Thus, inflation may contribute to the insidious development of some phobias. Given that stressors are more frequent and more impactful in individuals with high negative affectivity, constitutional variables may interact with post-conditioning reinstatement effects as well. Inflation effects have been attributed to stress sensitization, but Davey (1992) posits a cognitive representational model of incubation effects that emphasizes the ability to disengage from and/or to devalue threat. He proposes that inflations of fear sometimes occur with rehearsal or mental reflection about aversive events, in the absence of direct or vicarious experience with aversive stimuli. To illustrate this, Jones and Davey (1990) established a conditioned fear to a triangle (by pairings with a 115 dB tone), and then asked participants to think about the loud tone and their reactions to it, think about a neutral object, or think about another unrelated aversive event (someone trying to stick a pin in your eye). Rehearsals occurred over six occasions, each lasting only 6 seconds. Responses to the triangle versus another unpaired neutral stimulus were then tested. Differential fear conditioning was only apparent for the group that rehearsed the loud tone. Albeit limited in scope, these data suggest that rehearsal of the aversive stimulus strengthened retention of conditioned fear. Generalization to prepared stimuli remains to be evaluated. Field and Davey (2001) suggest that inflation effects may be modulated by individual differences in rumination about or distraction from aversive events. They hypothesized that ruminators are more likely to inflate the severity of aversive events, resulting in more phobic responding than distractors. Davey and Matchett (1994) employed the same cued–unconditioned stimulus rehearsal procedure with high- and low-trait-anxious groups; the high-trait-anxious group exhibited significantly greater conditioned responses following rehearsal than the low-trait-anxious group. Thus, a threat-based style of emotion regulation and/or negative affectivity may enhance the detrimental effect of rehearsal, possibly by enhancing the threat value of the aversive event.

Inflation via stress sensitization or rehearsal may explain some of the findings regarding return of fear after treatment. That is, after an initial decline, fear and anxiety are susceptible to at least partial recovery even in the absence of relearning. Return of fear has been observed following treatment of specific phobias (e.g., Connolly, 1979; Grey, Rachman & Sartory, 1979; Grey, Sartory, & Rachman, 1981; Philips, 1985; Rachman, 1966; Rachman & Levitt, 1988; Rachman & Lopatka, 1988; Rachman, Robinson, & Lopatka, 1987; Rachman & Whittal, 1989a, 1989b; Salkovskis & Mills, 1994; Sartory, Rachman, & Grey, 1982; Shafran, Booth, & Rachman, 1993), obsessive–compulsive disorder (Foa, 1979; Likierman & Rachman, 1980), agoraphobia (Craske, Sanderson, & Barlow, 1987), and performance anxieties (Craske & Rachman, 1987). Return of fear as a concept is relevant to the current discussion to the degree that it represents waxing of fears after having waned even in the absence of treatment. Rachman (1989) posited that alongside treatment and post-treatment variables (the latter including inflation effects), individual difference variables may predispose certain individuals to return of fear. The most studied such variable is an elevated heart rate, which associated positively with return of fear in several studies (Craske *et al.*, 1987; Grey *et al.*, 1981; Sartory *et al.*, 1982). The only study to specifically test *a priori* the effects of initial heart rate compared anxious musical performers with a relatively low versus a relatively high heart rate at the baseline (Craske & Rachman, 1987). Performers with relatively high anticipatory heart rates showed the most return of fear 3 months after treatment ended. However, the findings are not fully consistent as at least two other studies failed to find a relationship between heart rate and return of fear (e.g., Grey *et al.*, 1979; Shafran *et al.*, 1993). Still, the potential for the magnification of return of fear by an elevated anticipatory heart rate complements the evidence for stronger and more generalized aversive conditioning with a higher heart rate (see Chapter 5).

We suggested that the occasions when the heart rate did predict return of fear were attributable to certain styles of thinking (Craske & Rachman, 1987). Individuals with elevated anticipatory heart rates may be more vulnerable to remembering exposures to feared stimuli more negatively, and this memory inflation generates more fear upon re-testing. The overlap with Davey's notion of rehearsal is obvious. In support, high-heart-rate participants tended to overestimate their previous level of fear whereas low-heart-rate participants did the opposite (Craske & Rachman, 1987). Bower (1981) proposed that intense emotional experiences are likely to be cognitively rehearsed between exposures more often than less intense experiences. Therefore, performers who experienced more intense arousal may have rehearsed their performance experiences more often than performers who were less aroused. Again, distortions may occur during these cognitive rehearsals, inflating the negativity of prior experiences. In support, high-heart-rate participants thought mostly about "uncomfortable moments" of their previous performance in the anticipation phase of their next performance, whereas low-heart-rate participants thought more about comfortable moments or did not think about their level of discomfort at all, despite comparable self-reported discomfort throughout performances (Craske & Rachman, 1987). The role of negatively inflated representations about feared stimuli is further supported by the finding that claustrophobic participants whose beliefs in their fearful cognitions increased just prior to re-assessment showed more return of fear (Booth & Rachman, 1992). This was replicated by Shafran *et al.* (1993). Thus, reinstatement of the threat value of aversive experiences may contribute to return of fear. Although the research to date pertains to treatment effects, these notions seem applicable to the "spontaneous" return of fear after its "spontaneous" decline, as appears to occur with the waxing and waning of fears over time.

Summary of Associative Factors

In summary, three associative pathways have been proposed to explain how certain stimuli (objects, people, places or internal events) become more threatening than other stimuli. These include direct traumatic association, vicariously observing others be traumatized or model distress, and informational transmission. With the exception of extreme traumas, phobic fears are rarely acquired by one-trial conditioning. The impact of traumatic events, of observing trauma, or frightening pieces of information is influenced by individual difference variables such as negative affectivity and threat-based styles of emotion regulation as well as a history of experience with the stimulus with which negative events take place. Thus, two different individuals may react very differently to the same trauma or piece of information given their own temperament and learning history. Higher negative affectivity, stress reactivity, anxiousness, and, perhaps, lower vagal tone are associated with stronger conditioning that is also more generalized, such that distressed individuals show more indiscriminant responding in contexts of potential threat. As outlined in Chapter 5, the effects of low cardiac vagal tone and poor discrimination among discrete stimuli mimic the effects of unpredictability, and may indeed be mediated by unpredictability. Moreover, individual difference variables in the form of expectancies and inflations of the negativity of aversive experiences (directly, vicariously, or via information) may influence the durability of a conditioned response and the waxing of responding following a waning in intensity. Similarly, stressors may influence the durability and strength of conditioned responding over time, and as outlined previously, the impact of stressors is in turn influenced by individual differences in negative affectivity. Conditionability is also influenced by contextual variables at the time of the aversive experience, including controllability, intensity, informational value, and evolutionary significance. Contextual variables are relevant for everyone, but these too interact with individual difference variables such as when anxious-prone vulnerabilities contribute to the intensity or perceived uncontrollability of an aversive event. In addition to the complex myriad of contextual and individual difference variables that impact a given aversive experience, each learning event influences the state of vulnerability to future learning in a type of complication model, thus shifting the threat value of stimuli over time and explaining the insidious onset of most phobias and anxiety disorders. For example, a history of warnings about the dangers of unexpected physical sensations, combined with the vicarious traumatization of seeing one's parent die of a heart attack, may shift an individual closer to becoming fully conditioned to fear changes in his/her heart rate with the occurrence of an unexpected panic attack.

Non-associative Factors

Menzies and Clarke (1993) proposed a model of fears and phobias that is not at all dependent on conditioning. Justification for their model draws heavily from the fact that many phobic individuals (0–77 percent, 25.3 percent on average) report being unable to recall events related to the onset of their fears (Kleinknecht, 1994). In addition, they criticize studies that purport to assess conditioning onset for failing to establish the essential elements of conditioning of pairing of a previously neutral stimulus with an independent unconditioned stimulus (Kirkby *et al.*, 1995). By so doing, any traumatic experience is classified as direct conditioning, leading to an overestimation of conditioned cases. Using their own scale, Menzies and Clarke (1993) found that the majority of 50 parents believed that their children's water phobias developed without direct experience or information, and had been present from the very first time their children had contact with water. Only 2 percent directly attributed their child's phobia to classical conditioning episodes of being distressed by something while in or near water. With this same scale, Menzies and Clarke (1995b) found that the majority (56 percent) of 148 individuals seeking treatment for acrophobia claimed that they had always been fearful of heights, and only 11 percent reported direct conditioning experiences. Kirkby *et al.* (1995) directly compared the initial fear origins scale developed by Öst and Hugdahl (1981) with their new scale with respect to the etiology of spider phobia. The corresponding rates for direct conditioning, vicarious acquisition, and informational transmission using the two forms were as follows: 51.5 versus 6.1 percent, 54.5 versus 6.1 percent, and 48.5 versus 3 percent, respectively. The corresponding figures for a group of individuals with mixed phobias seeking treatment were: 48.8 versus 9.7 percent, 43.9 versus 7.3 percent, and 43.9 versus 4.9 percent, respectively (Menzies, 1996). More recently, Menzies and Parker (2001) asked height-fearful and non-fearful participants to recollect their history of experiences using the revised scale. Height-fearful individuals claimed more often they had always been afraid or that their fear had arisen in a non-associative traumatic event rather than associative events.

Menzies and colleagues conclude that while lack of recall may be due to memory failure, the more likely possibility is that fears have non-associative, Darwinian origins, or evolutionary pressures that have endowed certain stimulus configurations with fear-evoking qualities innately. These include fear of conspecific threat in primates (i.e., social anxiety), separation anxiety, and fear of heights, odors, and novelty. As with preparedness notions, these stimuli are considered prepotent, meaning that they once posed a challenge to our survival, and fear of them increased our fitness. In contrast to preparedness notions, however, the expression of fear in relation to those stimuli is *not* dependent on aversive learning or information. Moreover, Menzies and Clarke (1993) propose that individual differences in fearfulness lie not in the acquisition of fear but in the readiness to fear and the elimination of fear. Specifically (Menzies & Clarke, 1993, p. 500):

> given maturational processes and normal background experiences, most members of the species will show fear to a set of evolutionary-relevant stimuli on their first encounter .... [T]his initial fearful response will typically diminish across time due to repeated, non-traumatic exposure to the feared object or situation (i.e., habituation). However ... poor habituators and those who do not get the opportunity for safe exposure will remain fearful of such stimuli from their first encounter often appearing for treatment at a later age.

In other words, the non-associative model proposes that phobias develop out of innate fears shared by all humans, with adult phobias attributable to enhanced genetic readiness in some individuals to fear particular situations or deficits in mechanisms to eliminate fear responses.

As noted, the evidence for a non-associative account rests largely on the inability of phobic individuals to recall specific conditioning onsets. However, retrospective recall of etiological factors is very suspect. We found some support for a non-associative model using a prospective longitudinal study (Poulton *et al.*, 2001a). Specifically, we found no relationship between putative aversive conditioning experiences during the first 3 years of life (e.g., overnight hospitalizations or separation from parents) and level of separation anxiety at the age of 3 years. Similarly, parental death and separations from parents did not predict separation anxiety at 11 or 18 years of age. These results could indicate that separation anxiety is not dependent on conditioning experiences. However, we did not measure other conceivable forms of associative learning that may have influenced separation anxiety such as parental modeling or transmission of information. Overall, evidence for the non-associative account remains very sparse, and data from the revised Origins of Phobias Scale remain highly questionable, no matter how the questions are asked, due to the reliance on retrospective report. It is this which makes the experimental evidence in support of conditioning paradigms so convincing.

Moreover, there are several reasons to refute the notion of non-associative fears. For example, just because conditioning factors cannot be recalled does not mean they did not exist. Mineka and Öhman (2002) describe the ways in which traumatic conditioning events may occur without being consciously recalled. For example, phobic responses may be connected with implicit (i.e., without conscious awareness) rather than explicit memories centered on the amygdala rather than via cognitive and conscious pathways centered on the hippocampus (Öhman & Mineka, 2001). In addition, a contiguous but delayed relationship might be obscured through processes of sensory preconditioning, or "behaviorally silent learning". In this set of circumstances, pairings of two neutral stimuli are followed by pairings of one of the neutral stimuli with an aversive unconditioned stimulus. Subsequent presentation of the unpaired neutral stimulus alone elicits a conditioned response appropriate to the unconditioned stimulus, even though the second neutral stimulus was never directly paired with the unconditioned stimulus. Thus, anxiety may emerge in response to a particular stimulus not because of a direct traumatic association but because that stimulus was previously associated with another stimulus with which there were traumatic associations. Sensory preconditioning thus offers one avenue for fears that emerge for no apparent reason. Also, as already mentioned, associations may develop insidiously.

Forsyth and Eifert (1996) and Forsyth and Chorpita (1997) criticize the non-associative model from the standpoint of relying on an unsubstantiated view of traumatic conditioning; that Menzies and colleagues fail to realize that conditioning is dependent on the unconditioned response to the unconditioned stimulus versus the unconditioned stimulus itself. In the absence of a response, the identification of a clear external unconditioned stimulus only is of limited value for explaining human phobias. "From the subject's or client's perspective, however, it is the response that is experienced as traumatic and not the environmental UCS capable of evoking it" (Forsyth & Eifert, 1996, p. 457). In support, as already mentioned, intensity of bodily responses to aversive stimuli (carbon dioxide inhalations) mediated conditioning (Forsyth & Eifert, 1998). Thus, identification of an episode of intense fear is more important in evaluating conditioning history than is identification of the aversive stimulus. It is for this reason that Barlow (1988) argued that fear itself may be an unconditioned stimulus, especially if it is unexpected. Menzies and colleagues define conditioning events solely based on respondent conditioning, and define descriptions of being terrified in the absence of a clear external unconditioned stimulus as examples of "non-trauma" conditioning. This category of "terror in the absence of a clear external unconditioned stimulus" constituted a relatively large subset of their samples (27 and 30 percent; Kirkby *et al.*, 1995; Menzies, 1996). Finally, Mineka and Öhman (2002) criticized the assumption of a genetic readiness for phobias by referring to the evidence to date for only a moderate heritability of specific phobias, with a large portion of the variance explained by unique, non-shared environmental factors (plus error).

That being said, certain childhood fears — such as of heights, strangers, and separation, and, perhaps, loud noises, darkness, and animals — are so common at particular stages of development (see Chapter 1) that they may well indeed represent innately prepotent fears. Hypothetically, failure to eliminate such developmental fears may represent high loading on the vulnerability factors of negative affectivity and a threat-based style of emotion regulation; a possibility which resonates with the earlier description of attentional biases toward spider and snake stimuli among youths that fade with age and remain only in those prone to more anxiety (e.g., Kindt *et al.*, 2000). Indeed, Lonigan and Phillips (2001) specifically hypothesized that children high in negative affect are less likely to habituate to normal fears and/or to dishabituate fears. Furthermore, a style of responding to negative affect that encourages threat evaluation and avoidance may serve to retain such developmentally appropriate fears over time.

Non-associative fears of this type constitute only a minority of persistent fears and phobias, and thus cannot account for the majority of anxiety disorders, although they may directly facilitate the associative onset of other types of fear due to stress sensitization effects. That is, stress reactivity to developmentally prepotent stimuli may increase the impact of traumatic, vicarious or informational transmission experiences that generate excessive fears of other stimuli. Thus, non-associative retention of fears may simply represent the *vulnerability* to associative acquisition of fears of specific stimuli, and even contribute to such associative fear acquisition due to stress sensitization.

Summary

According to associative principles of fear acquisition, stimuli gain elevated threat value due to traumatic conditioning, vicarious acquisition, and/or informational transmission of threat. The strongest evidence for these pathways to fear acquisition comes from experimental studies, given the fallibility of retrospective accounts of fear origins. However, the potency of each aversive experience is embedded within a broad context of constitutional variables, contextual variables, and post-conditioning variables. Negative affectivity and a threat-based style of emotion regulation present as strong candidates for constitutional variables that also influence post-conditioning and contextual variables. For example, negative affectivity enhances conditionability, perhaps because of stronger fear responding to unconditioned stimuli, and expectancies of fear and evaluations of threat seem to influence longevity of conditioned responding. With more distress comes more generalized responding and less clear discrimination among which cues possess threat value and which do not — instead, the entire context in which aversive events have or could occur becomes more threatening. Thus, both anticipatory and contextual conditioning is enhanced at the cost of cue-specific differentiation among conditioned and non-conditioned stimuli. Poor contingency awareness and impaired orientation to and discrimination among external stimuli, indicative of lowered cardiac vagal tone and inflexible responding, may contribute to the generalizability of anxious responding, and may do so by enhancing unpredictability. Also, a history of experience with a wide array of situations may buffer against aversive conditioning and yet may be limited in anxiety-prone individuals. In terms of contextual variables, lack of control increases the likelihood of aversive conditioning, and belonginginess and preparedness factors explain the non-randomness of phobias and the greater vulnerability for all of us to learn to fear those stimuli associated with biological survival, be it predators, social alienation, contamination, or novel bodily sensations. Reflecting the ever-present role of vulnerability factors, it is conceivable that evolutionarily prepared learning is more likely in those with higher negative affectivity. In terms of post-conditioning variables, expectancies and tendencies to ruminate and inflate the meaning of negative experiences and stressors may contribute to the retention of learned fear responding. Again, these factors are potentially magnified in vulnerable individuals. In other words, vulnerabilities that inflate the salience/intensity of negative affect (negative affectivity) and its threat value as well as that of associated stimuli (threat-based style of emotion regulation) seem to magnify associatively acquired fears of specific stimuli. However, this is not to suggest that phobic responding is dependent on vulnerabilities toward anxiousness. Certain very circumscribed phobias may indeed arise in the absence of generalized vulnerability, and hence are more likely to exhibit cue-specific conditioned responding rather than reactivity to contexts associated with threat cues, whereas more pervasive anxiety disorders are presumed to possess greater generalized vulnerability. Importantly, conditioning and associative models emphasize a dynamic unfolding of the threat value of certain classes of stimuli over time, with each new experiencing molding the reactivity to subsequent experiences. In this way, the mostly insidious build up of phobic and anxious responding over time is explained.

The non-associative model refutes the role of learning in phobic responding, and instead posits that phobias are innate and that their failure to diminish over time is representative of the vulnerability to anxiety. Unfortunately, support for this argument is limited to retrospective recall, which is unreliable and assumes full conscious awareness of precipitating factors that in fact may not be obvious to the individual even at the time of their occurrence. In contrast, the associative model is supported by experimental demonstrations of the impact of direct traumatization, and of vicarious observation of others being distressed or traumatized. Also, the non-associative model emphasizes respondent conditioning, which has been criticized. Nonetheless, certain developmental fears, such as fears of strangers and separation, animals, and heights, may have non-associative origins, consistent with the normalcy of these fears during certain stages of development, and with the evidence, albeit still preliminary, that all children exhibit attentional bias toward snakes and spiders initially, and that these biases subside with age except in those prone to anxiety. Indeed, non-associative fears may represent the persistence of developmentally appropriate fears due to elevated negative affectivity and/or a threat-based style of emotion regulation. Moreover, by virtue of the stress sensitization generated by their own manifestation, such non-associative fears may amplify the acquisition of learned anxiety responding to specific classes of stimuli via traumatic, vicarious, or informational pathways. Whereas

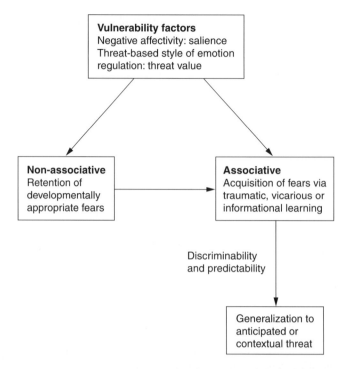

Figure 6.1: Associative and non-associative pathways and vulnerabilities.

associatively acquired anxious and phobic responding may be acquired in the absence of generalized vulnerabilities toward anxiousness, the retention of developmentally appropriate non-associative fears may be much more closely dependent on generalized vulnerabilities. Hence, we are brought back to the argument posed in Chapter 1 that the childhood expression of fear *per se* is of little relevance for future anxiety, whereas excessive fearfulness in childhood represents a broader vulnerability factor toward anxiety disorders. A summary of the associative and non-associative pathways is provided in Figure 6.1.

The associative and non-associative pathways explain responding to specific classes of stimuli, and it is at the level of these classes of stimuli, along with differential loading on the vulnerability factors, that much of the differentiation among the anxiety disorders is assumed to occur. Thus, social stimuli possess elevated threat value for the socially anxious individual whereas bodily sensations possess elevated threat value for the panic disorder individual (see Chapter 7). Anxious responding to more than one class of stimuli, as measured by the co-occurrence of anxiety disorders, is presumably enhanced by higher loadings on negative affectivity and a threat-based style of emotion regulation that result in a greater array of stimuli becoming salient and inbued with threat value.

Chapter 7

Anxiety Disorders

Overview

In the last chapter the means by which specific classes of stimuli retained and/or acquired a threat value were considered. The anxiety disorders are presumed to differ primarily in the particular class of stimuli that possesses elevated threat value, whether it be social, physical, or mental. Also, loading on generalized vulnerability factors is likely to differentiate among the anxiety disorders. In this chapter, each anxiety disorder is described, with specific reference to the learning experiences and biological propensities that contribute to the elevated threat value of the class of stimuli unique to that disorder.

As outlined in the previous chapter, the salience and threat value of stimuli is likely to be affected by the broad-based vulnerabilities of negative affectivity and a threat-based style of emotion regulation, as well as history of experience with related stimuli and ongoing contextual variables. Salience and threat value of stimuli is likely to be additionally affected by developmental stages. For example, social stimuli become more prominent upon first entering school (around 5–6 years of age) and upon first entering romantic relationships (during teenage years) for everyone. Similarly, mental processes (thoughts, images, and impulses) may be more salient at times of development that coincide with greater responsibility for one's thoughts and actions, such as upon leaving home or having a family. In fact, such developmental shifts may help explain the modal ages of onset for each anxiety disorder.

Stimuli judged to be threatening will naturally become the target of vigilance, danger-laden beliefs, and avoidance behavior (i.e., anxious processes). These processes in turn maintain the threat value of the relevant set of stimuli, creating a self-perpetuating cycle of distress and avoidance (i.e., anxiety disorders), as well as magnifying the vulnerability toward continuing anxiety. The maintaining influences for each disorder are described in this chapter.

Panic Disorder

Salience and Threat Value of Bodily Sensations

Central to current theorizing about panic disorder is the notion of anxiety sensitivity (Reiss, 1980), or the belief that anxiety and its associated symptoms may cause deleterious physical, social, and psychological consequences that extend beyond any immediate physical discomfort during an episode of anxiety or panic. Despite disagreement from others (e.g., Lilienfield, Jacob, & Turner, 1989), anxiety sensitivity is posited to differ from trait anxiety (Reiss, 1991), with which it correlates only moderately (0–36 percent variance overlap). For example, anxiety sensitivity accounts for unique variance in fear after controlling for the effects of trait anxiety (e.g., Reiss, Peterson, Gursky, & McNally, 1986). Hence, Zinbarg and Barlow (1996), later elaborated by Zinbarg, Mohlman, and Hong (1999), view anxiety sensitivity as a lower-order vulnerability in their hierarchical model. Specifically, negative affectivity is conceptualized as a higher fourth-order trait that is related to the general tendency to react with negative affect to stressful stimuli. Trait anxiety is a third-order facet of negative affectivty related to the slightly less general tendency to react anxiously to potentially threatening stimuli. Anxiety sensitivity is a second-order facet of trait anxiety related to the more specific tendency to react anxiously to one's own anxiety and anxiety-related sensations. Finally, anxiety sensitivity is divisible into three still lower-order facets relating to concerns about different domains: physical concerns, mental incapacitation concerns, and social concerns.

Anxiety sensitivity is elevated across most anxiety disorders, but it is particularly elevated in panic disorder (e.g., Taylor, Koch, & McNally, 1992; Zinbarg & Barlow, 1996), especially the physical concerns subscale (Zinbarg & Barlow, 1996; Zinbarg, Barlow, & Brown, 1997). Therefore, beliefs that physical symptoms of anxiety are harmful seem to be particularly relevant to panic disorder. Theoretically, anxiety sensitivity may contribute to the onset of panic disorder because it primes reactivity to bodily sensations. In support, several longitudinal studies indicate that high scores on the Anxiety Sensitivity Index predict the onset of panic attacks over 1–4 year intervals in adolescents (Hayward *et al.*, 2000), college students (Maller & Reiss, 1992), and community samples with specific phobias or no anxiety disorders (Ehlers, 1995). The predictive relationship remains after controlling for prior depression (Hayward *et al.*, 2000). In addition, Anxiety Sensitivity Index scores predicted spontaneous panic attacks, and worry about panic (and anxiety more generally), during an acute military stressor (i.e., 5 weeks of basic training), even after controlling for a history of panic attacks and trait anxiety (Schmidt, Lerew, & Jackson, 1997, 1999). However, it is important to note that anxiety sensitivity accounted for only a relatively small portion of the variance and neuroticism was a better predictor of panic attacks. Equally if not more compelling is the evidence that anxiety sensitivity predicts subjective distress and reported symptomatology in response to procedures that induce strong physical sensations such as carbon dioxide inhalation (Forsyth, Kollins, Palav, Duff, & Maher, 1999), balloon inflation (Messenger & Shean, 1998), and hyperventilation (Sturges, Goetsch, Ridley, & Whittal, 1998), in non-clinical samples, even after controlling for the effects of trait anxiety (Rapee & Medoro, 1994).

What are the origins of anxiety sensitivity, and particularly the physical concerns element of anxiety sensitivity that is most relevant to panic disorder? Consistent with the notions presented in Chapter 6, we (Craske & Rowe, 1997) posited that anxiety sensitivity is acquired insidiously from a lifetime of direct aversive experiences (such as personal history of significant illness or injury), vicarious observations (such as exposure to significant illnesses or death among family members, or family members who display fear of body sensations through hypochondriasis), and/or informational transmissions (such as parental warnings or overprotectiveness regarding physical well-being). This hypothesis was based indirectly on earlier research by Ehlers (1993), who found that infrequent panickers and panic disorder patients reported that their parents were more likely to suffer from chronic illnesses that required treatment and physical symptoms typical of anxiety, in comparison with parents of patients with other anxiety disorders and controls. In addition, patients with panic disorder observed sick-role behavior related to panic symptoms in their parents more often than control participants. This was not true for sicknesses such as the common cold, suggesting specificity to anxiety-related symptoms. Although the role of anxiety sensitivity (physical concerns) was not directly evaluated, it is reasonable to assume that childhood experiences such as these would elevate the salience and threat value of bodily sensations associated with anxiety. In support, Watt, Stewart, and Cox (1998) reported that levels of anxiety sensitivity in young adulthood were positively correlated with retrospectively reported learning experiences related to anxiety symptoms in the form of parental reinforcement (instrumental) and parental modeling (classical). However, in contrast to the findings of Ehlers (1993), Watt *et al.* (1998) also reported more learning experiences related to cold symptoms. Similarly, Watt and Stewart (2000) found that elevated anxiety sensitivity related to retrospectively reported parental responses to somatic symptoms in general and not specifically to anxiety-related symptoms. Unfortunately, data from all of these studies are retrospective and thus vulnerable to errors.

Other studies highlight the role of medical illnesses in predicting later panic disorder, again suggesting that the history of events influences the salience and threat value of bodily cues, which in turn primes panic disorder. For example, using the Dunedin Multidisciplinary Study database, we found that experience with personal respiratory disturbance and parental ill-health as a youth predicted panic disorder at the ages of 18 or 21 years (Craske *et al.*, 2001). In addition, more respiratory disturbance is reported in the history of panic disorder patients compared with other anxiety-disordered groups (Verburg, Griez, Meijer, & Pols, 1995). As reviewed in Chapter 3, medical adversity as a child has been related to increased risk for later anxiety disorders, and there may be a particular affinity with panic disorder. Finally, panic attacks themselves elevate anxiety sensitivity over a 5 week period in adults (Schmidt *et al.*, 2000), and over a 1 year period in adolescents, albeit to a lesser extent (Weems, Hayward, Killen, & Taylor, 2002).

Two other factors may also contribute to the salience and threat value of bodily sensations — those being interoceptive awareness and lability in autonomic responding. Panic disorder patients as well as non-clinical panickers appear to have heightened awareness of, or ability to detect, bodily sensations of arousal (e.g., Ehlers & Breuer, 1992, 1996; Ehlers, Breuer, Dohn, & Feigenbaum, 1995; Zoellner & Craske, 1999). Discrepant findings (e.g., Antony, Meadows, Brown, & Barlow, 1994; Rapee, 1994a) exist, but have been attributed to methodological artifact (Ehlers & Breuer, 1996). Ability to perceive heart beat, in particular, appears to be a relatively stable individual difference variable, given that it does not differ between untreated and treated panic disorder patients (Ehlers & Breuer, 1992), or from before to after successful treatment (Antony, Meadows, Brown, & Barlow, 1994; Ehlers *et al.*, 1995). Thus, interoceptive accuracy may be a predisposing trait for panic disorder. Ehlers and Breuer (1996, p. 174) conclude that "although good interoception is considered neither a necessary or a sufficient condition for panic disorder, it may enhance the probability of panic by increasing the probability of perceiving sensations that may trigger an attack if perceived as dangerous".

Separate from interoception is the issue of physiological propensity to acute and intense autonomic activation. As noted in Chapter 3, some evidence points to a unique genetic influence upon the reported experience of breathlessness, heart pounding, and a sense of terror (Kendler *et al.*, 1987). Perhaps cardiovascular reactivity presents a unique physiological predisposition for panic disorder. Consistent with this notion is the evidence that panic disorder patients report having experienced panic-like and cardiac sensations, although less intense and frightening, prior to their first panic attack (Craske, Miller, Rotunda, & Barlow, 1990; Keyl & Eaton, 1990). Conceivably, such prior experiences reflect a state of autonomic reactivity that develops into full-blown panic when instances of autonomic arousal occur in threatening contexts or stressful conditions (i.e., when the sensations are more likely to be perceived as threatening). In fact, the large majority of initial panic attacks are recalled as occurring outside of the home, while driving, walking, at work, or at school (Craske, *et al.*, 1990), in public in general (Lelliott, Marks, McNamee, & Tobena, 1989), and on a bus, plane, subway, or in social evaluative situations (Shulman *et al.*, 1994). Thus, situations that set the scene for initial panic attacks may be ones in which bodily sensations are perceived as particularly threatening due to impairment of functioning (e.g., driving), entrapment (e.g., air travel, elevators), negative social evaluation (e.g., job, formal social events), or distance from safety (e.g., unfamiliar locales). Entrapment concerns may be particularly salient for subsequent development of agoraphobia (Faravelli, Pallanti, Biondi, Paterniti, & Scarpato, 1992). Consistent with the principles reviewed in Chapter 6, the *impact* of episodes of autonomic cardiac reactivity may even intensify over time, with the potentiating influences of additional stressors or ruminative rehearsals that inflate their threat value. Unfortunately, all of the data about autonomic reactivity derive from report of symptoms, which is not a good index of actual autonomic state (Pennebaker, 1992) and may instead reflect interoception. Another physiological factor that may increase the salience of bodily symptoms of arousal pertains to vestibular dysfunction. That is, space and motion discomfort and impaired sensory integration of spatial information are found to be more characteristic of patients with panic disorder/agoraphobia than other anxiety or depressive disorders (Jacob, Furman, Durrant, & Turner, 1996, 1997). Furthermore, vestibular dysfunction is believed to contribute to autonomic dysfunction (Furman, Jacob, & Redfern, 1998), and thereby contribute to panic attacks. Although these findings are derived from objective recordings, there are no extant data for a contributory role of vestibular dysfunction in the generation of panic attacks, panic disorder, or agoraphobia.

In summary, learning experiences about bodily sensations, heightened interoceptive awareness, and, perhaps, a physiological propensity to experience intense and acute autonomic activation are hypothesized to increase the salience and threat value of bodily cues of arousal (represented by the physical concerns subscale of the Anxiety Sensitivity Index). The reason why hazard rate curves for panic disorder prevalence show a clear point of inflection between 15 and 19 years of age (Burke, Burke, Regier, & Rae, 1990) may be explained by the added salience of bodily cues at that point due to sexual development and hormonal changes (Buchanan, Eccles, & Becker, 1992).

Maintaining Influences

Acute "fear of fear" that develops after initial panic attacks in *vulnerable individuals* refers to fear of certain bodily sensations associated with panic attacks (e.g., racing heart, dizziness, paresthesias) (Barlow, 1988; Goldstein & Chambless, 1978). Conceptually, individuals primed by their life experiences and biological propensities to view bodily sensations associated with anxiety in general as threatening are more likely to panic and more likely to develop excessive anxiety over the particular sensations involved in panic attacks. Acute fear of panic-related bodily sensations is attributed to two factors. The first is interoceptive conditioning, or conditioned fear of internal cues, such as elevated heart rate, because of their association with intense fear, pain, or distress (Razran, 1961). Specifically, interoceptive conditioning refers to low-level somatic sensations of arousal or anxiety becoming conditioned stimuli so that early somatic components of the anxiety response come to elicit significant bursts of anxiety or panic (Bouton *et al.*, 2001). In the original work by Razran (1961), dogs were administered aversive stimulation at the same time as bowel movements occurred. Consequently, the dogs learned to fear visceral sensations. An extensive body of experimental literature attests to the robustness of interceptive conditioning (e.g., Dworkin & Dworkin, 1999), particularly with regard to early interoceptive drug onset cues becoming conditioned stimuli for larger drug effects (e.g., Sokolowska, Siegel, & Kim, 2002). In addition, like the conditioned responses to prepared stimuli (see Chapter 6), interoceptive conditioned responses are not dependent on conscious awareness of triggering cues (Razran, 1961). In support, conditioned responses to interoceptive stimuli have been observed under anesthesia in animals (e.g., Lennartz & Weinberger, 1992; Shibuki, Hamamura, & Yagi, 1984; Uno, 1970) and humans (e.g., Block, Ghoneim, Fowles, & Kumar, 1987), although the acquisition of interoceptive conditioned responding may require conscious awareness initially (Irie, Maeda, & Nagata, 2001; Lovibond & Shanks, 2002). Within this model, then, slight changes in relevant bodily functions that are not consciously recognized may elicit conditioned fear and panic due to previous pairings with the terror of panic (Barlow, 1988; Bouton *et al.*, 2001). Our own work on nocturnal panic attacks provides indirect evidence for the role of learned anxiety and reactivity to bodily sensations in the absence of conscious appraisals of such sensations at the time of their occurrence (Craske & Freed, 1995; Craske *et al.*, 2002a). Specifically, we measured reactivity to signals of arousal during sleep. Before sleep, biofeedback signals were ostensibly calibrated to reflect each individual's level of physiological arousal. During stages 2 and 3 of sleep, an ascending decibel series (35–80 dB, 2 second duration, 3 minute inter-trial intervals) of signals was experimentally induced (Craske *et al.*, 2002a). Panic disorder patients with recurrent nocturnal panic attacks and panic disorder who, before sleep, were led to believe that changes in their physiology would be indicative of "abnormality" failed to achieve as deep a sleep (Figure 7.1), woke with more distress and endorsed more panic attacks (Figure 7.2) than participants who were led to believe that such changes were "normal" or participants who were presented with a distinctly different signal unrelated to their physiological arousal. Again, this is only indirect evidence for "unconscious" interoceptive reactivity because we did not experimentally induce physiological arousal during sleep; only signals of arousal.

The second factor offered by D. M. Clark (1986) to explain acute fear of panic-related body sensations is catastrophic misappraisals of bodily sensations (i.e., misinterpretation of sensations as signs of imminent death, loss of control, and so on). As with interoceptive conditioning, this cognitive appraisal factor can be viewed as a sensitization of pre-existing tendencies to view anxiety as being harmful. Also as with interoceptive conditioning, misappraisals are believed to operate at both conscious and subconscious levels of awareness, such that individuals may judge bodily sensations in a catastrophic manner without being aware of so doing, and thus experience "out of the blue" panic attacks.

Debate continues as to the significance of catastrophic misappraisals of bodily sensations versus conditioned (emotional, non-cognitively mediated) fear responding.

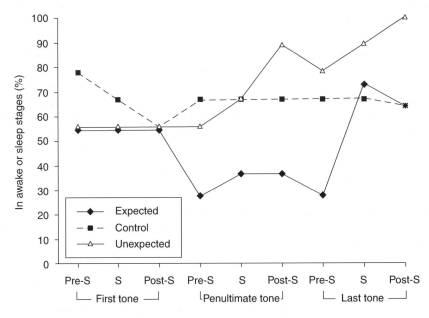

Figure 7.1: Percentages per group in the awake state or in sleep stage 1 or 2 across pre-stimulus (Pre-S), stimulus (S), and post-stimulus (Post-S) phases for first tone, penultimate tone, and last tone. (Redrawn by permission of the American Psychological Association from Craske *et al.* (2002a).)

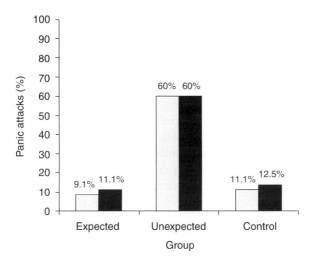

Figure 7.2: Percentages per group who met the criteria for panic attacks. (Redrawn by permission of the American Psychological Association from Craske *et al.* (2002a).)

Bouton *et al.* (2001) take argument with the purely cognitive model of panic disorder by stating that it cannot account for panic attacks that are devoid of conscious cognitive appraisal without turning to constructs such as "automatic appraisals" that prove to be untestable. In addition, Bouton *et al.* (2001) defend criticisms of conditioning models by clarifying the relations among conditioned and unconditioned stimuli and responding. By so doing, they emphasize the differences between anxiety and fear/panic, much as was outlined in Chapter 2. In brief, Bouton *et al.* (2001) state that the similarity between conditioned and unconditioned stimuli, as occurs in interoceptive conditioning and when the early symptomatic signs of panic (conditioned stimulus) signal the rest of the panic attack (unconditioned stimulus), creates very robust, easily conditioned responding, which potentially overshadows other exteroceptive predictors of the unconditioned stimulus. Also, since the early onset of panic symptoms as a conditioned stimulus is in close proximity to the unconditioned stimulus, the conditioned response is likely to be very similar to the unconditioned response. This contrasts to other forms of conditioning, where the conditioned response is quite distinct from the unconditioned response because it is in response to a reminder of the unconditioned stimulus and not to the unconditioned stimulus itself. Consequently, conditioned responses typically become more preparatory rather than active defense behaviors. Moreover, as noted in previous chapters, conditioned stimuli that represent evolutionary significance (prepared) tend to elicit conditioned responses that are closer to the unconditioned response (i.e., are more defensive) than non-prepared stimuli. For example, prepared stimuli tend to elicit conditioned heart rate acceleration in contrast to heart rate deceleration for non-prepared stimuli (Cook *et al.*, 1986; Dimberg, 1987). Since bodily sensations are believed to represent prepared stimuli, it is not surprising that Forsyth and Eifert (1998) found conditioned heart rate accelerations to a video clip of a heart beating arrythmically. For both of these reasons (proximity and preparedness), panic attacks themselves are believed to develop properties of conditioned fear responding.

Conditioned *anxiety* develops to other less proximal cues for panic attacks, such as contexts and places. Whereas conditioned anxiety motivates instrumental acts that have been learned through negative reinforcement to protect the organism, such as avoidance and reliance on safety signals, conditioned panic motivates behavior of escape or fight. At the same time, conditioned anxiety enhances conditioned and unconditioned responding to other stimuli, thus augmenting minor panic reactions to other stimuli. Hence, in their view, conditioned anxiety may lower the threshold for subsequent panic reactions. Bouton *et al.* (2001) offer explanations for why conditioned fear is not always produced by interoceptive cues, including the presence of safety signals, context effects (so that performance in one context does not necessarily generalize to performance in other contexts), and occasion setters (discrete stimuli that can turn off or on, responding to conditioned stimuli).

In summary, Bouton *et al.* (2001) emphasize differences between the states of panic and anxiety and elaborate upon conditioning theory that has been represented far too simplistically to date in applied models for panic and other anxiety disorders. The experience of panic attacks, in their model, leads to conditioning of anxiety to cues associated with panic so that in their presence conditioned anxiety occurs. Moreover, panic itself may become conditioned to a set of specific bodily cues in close proximity to panic, and this conditioning may occur in parallel with conditioning of anxiety to other cues.

While accepting that conditioning clearly involves cognition in the form of attention, expectancy, short-term memory and rehearsal, as is certainly demonstrated in studies of attentional bias to masked stimuli (see Chapter 5), Bouton *et al.* (2001) argue against the notion that conditioning inevitably involves propositional, declarative knowledge, as is implied by the cognitive theory of panic. As described in Chapter 6, Öhman and Mineka (2001), along with others such as LeDoux (1996), have argued persuasively that aversive emotional learning can occur without conscious representation of learning, and that implicit emotional memories can activate fear systems without individuals being aware of the reasons. In fact, there is abundant evidence for conditioned fear responding to masked presentations of previously conditioned stimuli that are prepared, or evolutionarily significant (e.g., Esteves *et al.*, 1994; Katkin, Wiens, & Öhman, 2001; Öhman & Soares, 1993, 1998; Parra *et al.*, 1997; Wong, Shevrin, & Williams, 1994), and as noted earlier, unusual or novel bodily sensations are presumed to represent an evolutionarily prepared stimulus (Rachman, 1991a). Thus, the role of catastrophic cognitions is questioned, and at the very least is not considered necessary for a learned emotional response.

Bouton *et al.* (2001) propose that catastrophic misappraisals may accompany panic attacks because they are a natural part of the constellation of responses that go with panic or because they have been encouraged and reinforced much like sick-role behaviors during childhood. In addition, such thoughts may become conditioned stimuli that trigger anxiety and panic, as demonstrated via panic induction through presentation of pairs of words involving sensations and catastrophic outcomes (Clark, Salkovskis, & Anastasiades, 1990) may simply represent words becoming conditioned stimuli for panic attacks. In this case, catastrophic cognitions may well be sufficient to elicit conditioned panic attacks but not necessary.

Whether cognitively or non-cognitively based, an excessive anxiety over panic-related bodily sensations in panic disorder is well supported. Individuals with panic disorder have strong beliefs and fears of physical or mental harm arising from bodily sensations that are associated with panic attacks (e.g., Chambless, Caputo, Bright, & Gallagher, 1984; McNally & Lorenz, 1987). They are more likely to interpret bodily sensations in a catastrophic fashion (Clark *et al.*, 1988), and to allocate more attentional resources to words that represent physical threat, such as "disease" and "fatality" (e.g., Ehlers, Margraf, Davies, & Roth, 1988; Hope, Rapee, Heimberg, & Dombeck, 1990), and catastrophe words, such as "death" and "insane" (e.g., Maidenberg, Chen, Craske, Bohn, & Bystritsky, 1996; McNally *et al.*, 1992). Also, they are more likely to fear procedures that elicit bodily sensations similar to the ones experienced during panic attacks, including benign cardiovascular, respiratory, and audiovestibular exercises (Jacob, Furman, Clark, & Durrant, 1992; Zarate, Rapee, Craske, & Barlow, 1988), as well as more invasive procedures such as carbon dioxide inhalations, compared with patients with other anxiety disorders (e.g., Perna, Bertani, Arancio, Ronchi, & Bellodi, 1995; Rapee, 1986; Rapee, Brown, Anthony, & Barlow, 1992) or healthy controls (e.g., Gorman *et al.*, 1994). The findings are not fully consistent, however, as they did not differ from patients with social phobia in response to an epinephrine challenge (Veltman, van Zijderveld, Tilders, & Dyck, 1996). Nonetheless, patients with panic disorder also fear signals that ostensibly reflect heightened arousal and false physiological feedback (Craske & Freed, 1995; Craske *et al.*, 2002a; Ehlers, Margraf, Roth, Taylor, & Birnbaumer, 1988). On the other hand, direct manipulation of declarative cognition can also impact the level of distress over physical symptoms. For example, individuals with panic disorder and non-clinical panickers report significantly less fear and panic during laboratory-based panic provocation procedures, such as hyperventilation and carbon dioxide inhalation, when they perceive that the procedure is safe and/or controllable (e.g., Rapee, Mattick, & Murrell, 1986; Sanderson *et al.*, 1989), when accompanied by a safe person (Carter, Hollon, Carson, & Shelton, 1995), or after cognitive-behavioral treatment that reduces fears of bodily sensations (Craske *et al.*, 2003, in press; Schmidt, Trakowski, & Staab, 1997). In contrast, contextual variables of perceived safety and controllability were not significant in the study of epinephrine challenges (Veltman, van Zijderveld, van Dyck, & Bakker, 1998).

An acute fear of bodily sensations is likely to generate ongoing distress for a number of reasons. First, in the immediate sense, autonomic arousal generated by fear in turn intensifies the sensations that are feared, thus creating a reciprocating cycle of fear and sensations that sustains until autonomic arousal exhausts or safety is perceived. In contrast, fear of external stimuli generally does not intensify the object of fear. Second, because bodily sensations that trigger panic attacks are not always immediately obvious, they may generate the perception of unexpected or "out of the blue" panic attacks (Barlow, 1988). Furthermore, even when interoceptive cues are identifiable, they tend to be less predictable than external stimuli. For example, an accelerated heart rate may be produced by excitement, anger, fear, sexual arousal, stimulants, stress, inefficient breathing, or natural variations in heart rate, to name a few, and may shift rapidly and independently of veridical contextual variables, thus creating unpredictability. As reviewed in Chapter 4 when discussing predictability in relation to emotion regulation, a body of experimental evidence illustrates heightened distress with unpredictable aversive events (Mineka & Kilhlstrom, 1978; Mineka *et al.*, 1984a). Consistent with this literature, we found that general worry about recurrent panic attacks and daily anxiety were higher the day after unpredicted attacks and lower the day after predicted panic attacks in a sample with panic disorder (Craske, Glover, & DeCola, 1995). Interestingly, this effect was only observed in patients who experienced both types of attacks, and was not observed when comparing subgroups of patients who experienced only predicted versus only unpredicted attacks. Perhaps the impact of unpredictability is stronger when within the context of prediction; as suggested by the experimental evidence showing that unpredictable events generate more emotional disturbance when preceded by predictable events (Mineka & Kihlstrom, 1978). The overall benefits of prediction have been attributed to several factors, including conditioned inhibition, counter conditioning, and safety signals (Rosellini, DeCola, & Warren, 1986). The safety signal hypothesis (Seligman, 1968; Seligman & Binik, 1977) is particularly appealing, and posits that when a stimulus reliably predicts danger, its absence predicts safety, allowing relaxation to occur during times when the stimulus is absent. The inherent erosion of perceived safety that comes from unpredictable fear has already been mentioned (see Chapter 5).

Not only are bodily sensations less predictable, but like other internally generated stimuli such as threat-related images, they are also less controllable than clearly discernible external stimuli. That is, the ability to terminate a bodily sensation is likely to be substantially weaker than the ability to terminate a clearly defined external situation, if by only physically escaping the situation. As reviewed earlier, uncontrollability of aversive stimuli also elevates distress (e.g., Maier, Laudenslager, & Ryan, 1985; Mineka *et al.*, 1984a). Unpredictability and uncontrollability, then, are seen as enhancing general levels of anxiety about "when is it going to happen again" and "what do I do when it happens". Furthermore, like imagery, bodily sensations are more likely to represent unexpected close proximity to threat (e.g., sensations of suffocation, flashbacks to near death experiences) than external stimuli (e.g., a height, a dog), thus constituting repeated re-exposures to unconditioned aversive experiences that reinstate and strengthen conditioned anxiety and occasions of abrupt fear. For all these reasons — unpredictability, uncontrollability, and imminence of threat — fears of bodily sensations are likely to generate more pervasive distress than fears of external cues, thereby contributing to high levels of chronic anxious apprehension (Barlow, 1988). In turn, as already mentioned, anxious apprehension increases the likelihood of panic, by directly increasing the availability of sensations that have become conditioned cues for panic and/or by increasing attentional vigilance for these bodily cues. Thus, a maintaining cycle of panic and anxious apprehension develops. Also, subtle avoidance behaviors are believed to maintain negative beliefs about feared bodily sensations (Clark & Ehlers, 1993). Examples include holding onto objects or people for fear of fainting, sitting and remaining still for fear of heart attack, and moving slowly or searching for an escape for fear of acting foolish (Salkovskis, Clark, & Gelder, 1996). Finally, anxiety may develop over specific contexts in which the occurrence of panic would be particularly troubling (i.e., situations associated with impairment, entrapment, negative social evaluation, and distance from safety). These anxieties could contribute to agoraphobia, which in turn maintains distress by preventing disconfirmation of catastrophic misappraisals and extinction of conditioned responding.

Not all individuals who panic develop agoraphobia, and the extent of agoraphobia that emerges is highly variable (Craske & Barlow, 1988). Various factors have been investigated as potential predictors of agoraphobia. Although agoraphobia tends to increase as history of panic lengthens, a significant proportion of individuals panic for many years without developing agoraphobic limitations. Nor is agoraphobia related to age of onset or frequency of panic (Cox, Endler, & Swinson, 1995; Craske & Barlow, 1988; Rapee & Murrell, 1988). Some studies report more intense physical symptoms during panic attacks when there is more agoraphobia (e.g., de Jong & Bouman, 1995; Goisman *et al.*, 1994; Noyes, Clancy, Garvey, & Anderson, 1987; Telch, Brouilard, Telch, Agras, & Taylor, 1989). Others fail to find such differences (e.g., Cox *et al.*, 1995; Craske *et al.*, 1990). Nor do fears of dying, going crazy, or losing control relate to the level of agoraphobia (Cox *et al.*, 1995; Craske, Rapee, & Barlow, 1988). On the other hand, concerns about social consequences of panicking may be stronger when there is more agoraphobia (Amering *et al.*, 1997; de Jong & Bouman, 1995; Rapee & Murrell, 1988; Telch *et al.*, 1989). Consistent with expectancy theories (see Chapter 5), the degree of anticipation of panic in specific situations predicts the degree of avoidance of those situations as well (Cox *et al.*, 1995; Craske *et al.*, 1990). However, whether the social evaluation concerns and anticipation of panic attacks are precursors or are secondary to agoraphobia remains to be determined.

Occupational status also predicts agoraphobia, accounting for 18 percent of the variance in one study (de Jong & Bouman, 1995). Perhaps the strongest predictor of agoraphobia is sex. As described in Chapter 1, the ratio of males to females shifts dramatically in the direction of female predominance as the level of agoraphobia worsens (e.g., Thyer *et al.*, 1985). Possible reasons for this sex difference are addressed in the next chapter.

Summary

The primary focus of threat in panic disorder is bodily sensations associated with fearful arousal. Such threat is believed to arise following from an initial unexpected panic attack, and is more likely in individuals with vulnerabilities of negative affectivity and a threat-based style of emotion regulation in general, and more specifically in individuals whose learning history and biological propensity have raised the salience and threat value of bodily sensations. Anxiety over panic-related bodily sensations and repeated panic attacks are likely to be maintained by conditioned anxiety to contextual reminders, and conditioned fear responding to somatic signals and associated vigilance for them, misappraisals of the threat value of bodily sensations, which may in and of themselves induce panic but are not a necessary precondition for panic attacks, and avoidant behavior. In other words, the anxious processes of vigilance, threat-laden beliefs, and avoidant reactions perpetuate the disorder.

Social Anxiety Disorder

Salience and Threat Value of Social Stimuli

Heightened salience and threat value of social cues, beyond that which is universally influenced by biological preparedness, may prime individuals toward social anxiety disorder. Social sensitivity is not exclusive to social anxiety disorder, however, and may be highly relevant to the progression of agoraphobia and generalized anxiety disorder as well as other disorders. As already described, persistent fears of strangers at an early age (i.e., behavioral inhibition) predict the onset of anxiety disorders. Conceivably such consistent fear responding to strangers is indicative of non-associative retention of developmentally appropriate fears due to high loadings on the vulnerability toward anxiousness (see Chapter 6).

Another contributory factor has been proposed by Wells and Clark (1997) as specific beliefs and assumptions that inflate the threat value of social stimuli. The first are rigid rules for governing social behavior (e.g., "I must always sound fluent and intelligent"). Second are conditional assumptions about the consequences of one's social behavior (e.g., "If people see me shake they will think I am stupid"), and third are core beliefs concerning self as a social object, such as "I am boring". Presumably, as with anxiety sensitivity regarding physical concerns, these beliefs derive from a lifetime history of traumatic (such as being ridiculed for choice of attire), vicarious (such as parental modeling of overconcern with other's opinions), or informational (such as parental warnings regarding the dangers of social disapproval) experiences. Direct experiences with being ridiculed or rejected may be a particularly potent pathway for elevation of threat value in social situations because social defeat is assumed to represent a very powerful unconditioned stimulus akin to uncontrollable stressors (Mineka & Zinbarg, 1995). The role of informational transmission and vicarious acquisition for elevated threat value of social cues is supported by the finding that parents of offspring with social phobia are more likely to score high on social concerns (Bruch, Heimberg, Berger, & Collins, 1989). Also, retrospective studies show that adults with social phobia are more likely to report that their parents placed greater emphasis on the opinion of others than do adults with agoraphobia or controls (Bruch & Heimberg, 1994; Bruch et al., 1989). In general, however, the evidence for longitudinal predictors of social phobia is meager. The one exception is behavioral inhibition, which increases the risk for social evaluative disorders but is not unique to the onset of social phobia.

Social sensitivity is very much tied to the concept of dominance and submission hierarchies. Öhman (1986) views social fears as originating in concerns over dominance and submission in groups, and in that regard different from other predatory fears (e.g., specific phobias). Competitive encounters that generate dominance hierarchies often involve ritualized displays of threat from the dominant animal, and fear and submissiveness on the part of the defeated animal. The expression of fear in social situations therefore both represents the emotion as well as communicates defeat. Given the communication functions of fear in social situations, the physiological propensity to exhibit visible signs of autonomic arousal, such as the propensity to blush or sweat, may independently contribute to the salience or threat value of social situations. However, there is no direct supportive evidence for this proposal. That is, generalized social anxiety does not reliably involve more autonomic arousal than is observed in healthy controls in social settings. For example, Puigcerver, Martinez-Selva, Garcia-Sanchez, and Gomez-Amor (1989) failed to find differences between individuals with social phobia and controls in terms of skin conductance in social situations, and concluded that the main group difference lies in the internal evaluation of psychophysiological responses. In fact, one potential maintaining influence for social phobia is catastrophic misinterpretation of "usual" physical sensations in social and performance situations. Moreover, Gerlach, Wilhelm, Gruber, and Roth (2001) found that social-phobic individuals with primary complaints of blushing did not physiologically blush more than social-phobic individuals without such a complaint, under conditions of equivalent amounts of embarrassment and anxiety in three experimentally contrived situations (watching an embarrassing video, giving a talk, and holding a conversation). Again, differences in the perception of physiological reactions seemed more important than the reactions themselves. On the other hand, those who were most concerned with blushing did have higher heart rates during the three social tasks compared with the social-phobic individuals who were not concerned about blushing. Perhaps the intensity of their heart rate reactivity led them to become more concerned about visible signs of distress, the blushing, even though they were not more physiologically prone to blush.

Interestingly, specific social phobia (i.e., social anxiety in one or two circumscribed social situations, most often of a performance nature) is characterized by more autonomic arousal and plasma catecholamines during public speaking and interaction tests relative to controls and to generalized social phobia (Heimberg, Hope, Dodge, & Becker, 1990; Hofmann *et al.*, 1995; Levin *et al.*, 1993). Hofmann *et al.* (1995) offered several mechanisms for why patients with generalized social phobia show less arousal in performance situations than do those with specific social phobia. First, generalized social fears may result in less "coherent" fear structures, which according to the research of Lang and colleagues would mean less intense autonomic reactivity. Second, pervasive worry may inhibit processing of phobic material, as outlined in Chapter 2, and dampen the generalized group's responses to acute challenges. Third, Hofmann *et al.* (1995) cite McNeil, Vrana, Melamed, Cuthbert, and Lang (1993), who showed that associated emotions of shame and embarrassment result in cardiac decreases. McNeil *et al.* (1993) proposed that a competing parasympathetic shame response may summate with fearful sympathetic activation to attenuate heart rate increase in generalized social phobia. In a related vein, Öhman (1986) earlier suggested that shame and "losing face" inherent to social defeat mitigate escape behavior and acute arousal, compared with predatory fears. If so, this difference between social and predatory fear systems exemplifies variations in response profiles for different types of threat stimuli, as suggested in Chapter 2. Another possibility for explaining the difference between generalized and specific forms of social phobia is that the latter, like other forms of specific phobias, is generally associated with a lower loading on broader vulnerabilities toward anxiousness. Consequently, specific threat–cue conditioning is likely to be stronger, whereas a more generalized conditioned reactivity to a broader array of contextual cues is likely to characterize the more generalized social phobic.

The elevated salience and threat value of social cues may also derive from deficits in social skills (e.g., Trower, Yardley, Bryant, & Shaw, 1978), given that inappropriate responses to social situations increase the likelihood of undesired outcomes and distress. However, this may apply to only a subset with social anxiety disorder as skill deficits are not present in the majority with social phobia (e.g., Emmelkamp, Mersch, Vissia, & van der Helm, 1985). In summary, generalized social phobia may be related to a behaviorally inhibited temperament and social sensitivity combined with dysfunctional beliefs about social behavior that in turn derive from a learning history that validates the threat value of social situations. There is little evidence for a specific biological propensity toward social phobia. As with other threat stimuli, a dynamic relationship probably exists between predisposing traits of social sensitivity and beliefs about negative evaluation, on the one hand, and ongoing aversive social events on the other hand. In other words, stronger social sensitivities and beliefs about negative evaluation (that derive from histories of direct, vicarious and informational experiences and non-associative failure to habituate) will increase the chances of intense and prolonged distress from a given aversive social experience, whether it is direct, vicarious, or informational. In addition, social sensitivities may contribute to the impact of other aversive events, such as an unexpected panic attack in a crowded or otherwise public situation. Not only might this experience be sufficiently aversive to enhance the development of other types of anxiety such as panic disorder and agoraphobia, but unexpected panic attacks may become critical to the onset of fully fledged social phobia, especially in someone already primed by experience to judge social situations as more threatening. As already noted, social situations appear to vary in salience based on psychosocial development. Thus, entering school at around the age of 5 years may be a prime time for social situations to become more salient. The same may be true of puberty and adolescence, when peer relations and romantic relations gain prominence. In accord, the modal age of onset for adult social phobia tends to be during late adolescence (see Chapter 1).

Maintaining Influences

Because the object that is being evaluated in social situations is the self, social anxiety is likely to enhance self-focus of attention in social contexts, and such self-directed attention is likely to contribute to ongoing anxiousness (Ingram, 1990b; Wood, Saltzberg, & Goldsamt, 1990). As outlined by Woody (1996), self-focus produces internal attributions for failure because the self and self-flaws become the most salient source for attributions. Also, self-focus may impede performance. That is, preoccupation with negative evaluation may lead to skill deficit by detracting attention from and thus interfering with prosocial behaviors such as listening, generating comments, or attending to meta-communications such as voice tone. Self-focus of attention is characteristic of all anxiety disorders (Woodruff-Borden, Brothers, & Lister, 2001), but a particular type of self-focus is believed to characterize social anxiety. Similar to the concept of public self-consciousness presented by Buss and Scheier (1976), Wells and Clark (1997) emphasize dysfunctional awareness of how one appears to others. That is, individuals with social phobia attend to self-generated images of themselves, and their behavior in social situations, as if they were viewing themselves from an external point of view. In fact, Wells and Clark (1997) propose that it is this awareness of how one appears to others that causes a shift of attention to the self, and generates fears of "not only other people's reactions to the self, but also potential failure to meet personal goals for publicly acceptable performance. Failure to meet these goals, which could lead to disapproval from others, is profoundly threatening because it undermines one's positive sense of self" (Wells & Clark, 1997, p. 16–17). In accord, when asked to form an image of a social situation in which they felt anxious, social-phobic individuals were more likely than controls to rate the image as if from an observer's perspective, although they did not show this bias with respect to anxious non-social situations (Wells, Clark, & Ahmad, 1998). In another study, patients with social phobia were more likely to report spontaneously occurring and negative images dominated by an observer perspective in social situations, compared with controls (Hackman, Surawy, & Clark, 1998). Similarly, Wells and Papageorgiou (1999) found that only patients with social evaluative concerns reported observer perspectives for recalled images of socially anxious situations, whereas individuals with blood/injury/injection phobias and normal controls did not. This is especially important given evidence that field of perspective relates to causal attributions for an event — actors tend to make situational attributions for their own behavior whereas observers tend to make more dispositional attributions for the same actor's behaviors. In addition, like Clark and Wells (1995), Coles, Turk, Heimberg, and Fresco (2001) suggest that such an observer perspective, which they again recorded from socially phobic individuals, may interfere with the processing of external information that is contrary to one's negative beliefs. That is, any type of internal dialogue, whether defined by the self as a social object or not, is likely to divert attention away from external cues about performance. This in turn is likely to lead to a self-evaluation of social performance that is largely dependent on preconceived notions of inadequacy rather than actual behavior (Dodge, Hope, Heimberg, & Becker, 1988). In support of this notion, several studies indicate that socially anxious individuals rely on global self-appraisals versus specific information in social contexts (Rapee & Lim, 1992). For example, they judge their own social performance more negatively than do controls (Alden & Wallace, 1995; Rapee & Lim, 1992; Stopa & Clark, 1993; Tran & Chambless, 1995). In particular, Alden and Wallace (1995) found that socially phobic individuals appraised specific aspects of their own non-verbal behavior (i.e., visibility of anxiety, warmth, and interest) negatively regardless of whether their interactions were successful or not. With a self-directed attention focus, recall for aspects of a social situation should be impaired, and indeed Hope, Heimberg, and Klein (1990) found that socially anxious undergraduates recalled less partner information and made more recall errors than non-anxious peers. Similar findings were reported by Daly, Vangelisti, and Lawrence (1989), although others failed to find such differences (Stopa & Clark, 1993). Finally, Papageorgiou and Wells (2002) found that feedback about heart rate rising prior to a conversational task elicited greater anxiety, more observer perspective imagery, and more negative evaluations of their own performance in individuals with high fears of negative evaluation compared with those with low fears and those who did not receive such feedback about their heart rate. These data were consistent with the notion that socially anxious individuals assume that "the way they feel in feared situations must reflect the way they are perceived" (Papageorgiou & Wells, 2002, p. 182).

Alongside evidence related to self-focus of attention, there is abundant evidence for overly negative judgments and attentional biases toward socially relevant threat in social phobia, and, as noted in Chapter 5, these processes are assumed to contribute to ongoing anxiety in social situations. That is, socially anxious groups show longer response times for social evaluative words in modified Stroop tasks. This bias is specific, being stronger for social evaluative words than physically threatening words (Hope et al., 1990b; Lundh & Öst, 1996; Maidenberg et al., 1996; Mattia et al., 1993). Also, in dot probe detection tasks, socially anxious individuals show a bias toward social threat words relative to neutral or physical threat words (Asmundson & Stein, 1994). More recent studies indicate an attentional bias toward angry faces among high trait socially anxious individuals (Mogg & Bradley, 2002) perhaps followed by an avoidant diversion of attention away from such stimuli (Chen, Ehlers, Clark, & Mansell, 2002), consistent with the vigilance avoidance hypothesis described in Chapter 5. Also, high trait socially anxious individuals were superior to low trait socially anxious individuals in classifying emotional expressions of "morphed" facial images when the images included fear (Richards et al., 2002). Other studies indicate biased interpretations of the meaning of social situations. That is, socially anxious individuals are clearly fearful of being judged negatively by others, and perceive themselves very negatively. For example, they are more likely to remember negative interpersonal interactions (O'Banion & Arkowitz, 1977), tend to evaluate their social behavior negatively and to make internal attributions for social failure (e.g., Girodo, Dotzenroth, & Stein, 1981), and perceive themselves as unable to deal with embarrassing situations. Also, socially anxious patients judge negative social events to be more likely, and positive social events to be less likely, than normal controls (Foa et al., 1996; Lucock & Salkovskis, 1988), report more negative self-evaluative thoughts throughout a conversation than other anxious patients or healthy controls (Stopa & Clark, 1993), and interpret ambiguous social events as more negative, and mildly negative social events as more catastrophic, than other anxious patients or controls (Wells & Clark, 1997). Moreover, there is now evidence for a ruminative process that maintains negative judgments of social performance over time in individuals with social phobia compared with controls whose initial negative appraisals tend to subside over time (Abbott & Rapee, 2003 in press). Evaluations of social situations may be particularly resistant to modification because, in contrast to other fears and phobias, social cognitions are "largely inaccessible to disconfirmation" (Foa *et al.*, 1996, p. 438). In other words, socially anxious individuals are reliant on *estimates* of what they believe others think of their behavior.

In addition to inflated risk and valence of negative social events, Cloitre, Heimberg, Liebowitz, and Gitow (1992) found that socially phobic individuals were more likely to attribute control to "powerful others". Brown, Heimberg, and Juster (1995) and Leung and Heimberg (1996) obtained similar results. In other words, socially phobic individuals perceive events as unpredictable and uncontrollable, but not random. Instead, events are determined by powerful others in social situations. This is consistent with the emphasis placed by Öhman (1986) on dominance submission hierarchies and the potency of social defeat as a stressor (Mineka & Zinbarg, 1995). Thus, social defeat generates effects similar to uncontrollable aversive encounters, and the latter generate social defeatist behaviors — to be socially defeated may represent uncontrollability, and hence attribution of control to dominant or powerful others.

Safety and avoidant behaviors are also likely to maintain social anxiety because even though they are intended to reduce the risk of social failure and humiliation, they serve to maintain erroneous beliefs. For example, light-colored clothes might be worn to avoid the visible signs of sweating, and statements may be thoroughly rehearsed before being stated to avoid mispronunciations. These behaviors exacerbate symptoms of anxiety, prevent disconfirmation of negative beliefs, maintain self-perception as a social object, and sometimes impact negatively on the social encounter.

Summary

The elevated salience and threat value of social cues may arise from varied traumatic, vicarious, or informational transmission experiences that accumulate over time. They may be enhanced or complemented by a vulnerability to anxiousness in the form of failure to habituate the developmentally appropriate "stranger fear" response. The role of a specific biological propensity to react more strongly to social situations has not been supported. Social anxiety is maintained by the anxious processes of vigilance toward threat of social situations, and of oneself in social situations, threat-laden beliefs about social situations and of oneself in social situations, and avoidant behavior. An over-awareness of how one appears to others may be critical to the maintenance of social anxiety.

Posttraumatic Stress Disorder

Symptoms of fear and avoidance, re-experiencing the trauma and anxious arousal are almost normative immediate responses to an assault. Thus, most victims show signs of posttraumatic stress immediately after traumatic events, often meeting criteria for acute stress disorder (i.e., dissociative symptoms, persistent re-experiencing, marked avoidance of reminders, anxiety, and increased arousal for a minimum of 2 days and a maximum of 4 weeks within at least 4 weeks of a traumatic event). However, these symptoms subside for most within a few months. For example, rates for posttraumatic stress symptoms are 70–94 percent immediately after non-sexual assault and rape, and decrease to 48–64 percent 1 month later, and 22–47 percent 3 months later (e.g., Riggs, Rothbaum, & Foa, 1995; Rothbaum, Foa, Riggs, Murdock, & Walsh, 1992; Valentiner, Foa, Riggs, & Gershuny, 1996). The same occurs for victims of motor vehicle accidents (e.g., Blanchard *et al.*, 1995; Brom, Kleber & Hofman, 1993; Mayou, Bryant, & Duthie, 1993). Thus, only a proportion of traumatized individuals develop posttraumatic stress disorder. Lifetime prevalence of posttraumatic stress disorder in women is 35 percent after rape and 39 percent after aggravated assault (Kilpatrick & Resnick, 1993). Also, only 8–41 percent of victims of motor vehicle accidents meet the criteria for posttraumatic stress disorder (Blanchard *et al.*, 1995; Mayou *et al.*, 1993), as do 31 percent of Vietnam male veterans at some time in their lives (Jordan *et al.*, 1991), and 24 percent of younger adults exposed to various traumas (Breslau *et al.*, 1991). Various factors moderate the influence of trauma, and many of these were discussed in general as moderators of aversive conditioning in the previous chapter.

Trauma Intensity

One of the predictors of the development of posttraumatic stress disorder is the intensity of the stressor. For example, the level of exposure to war zones predicts posttraumatic stress disorder among Vietnam veterans (e.g., Jordan *et al.*, 1991) and peace-keeping missions (Litz *et al.*, 1997). Similarly, injury or wounding, and perception of trauma severity, is predictive of posttraumatic stress disorder among combat veterans (e.g., Helzer *et al.*, 1987), female crime victims (e.g., Bownes, O'Gorman, & Sayers, 1991; Kilpatrick *et al.*, 1989), and motor vehicle accident victims (Blanchard *et al.*, 1995). Prevalence of posttraumatic stress disorder is 3.4 percent in Vietnam veterans who were not wounded versus about 20 percent in those who were wounded (Helzer *et al.*, 1987). Furthermore, the general aversiveness of the environment in which trauma occurs is also predictive of posttraumatic stress disorder, at least with respect to war trauma (Litz *et al.*, 1997). Not to be forgotten is the role of negative affectivity in magnifying trauma intensity.

In addition, the degree to which traumas are perceived as uncontrollable and unpredictable is believed to predict posttraumatic stress disorder (Foa, Zinbarg, & Rothbaum, 1992; Mineka & Zinbarg, 1995). However, the evidence is drawn mainly from experimental investigations of uncontrollable stressors — very few studies exist of humans in naturalistic settings. In one study, motor vehicle accident victims who were viewed by themselves and others as "responsible" for the accident (a proxy for predictability or controllability) showed less distress and marginally less incidence of posttraumatic stress disorder 12 months later than those who were not personally responsible for the accident (Delahanty *et al.*, 1997). Unfortunately, a more direct test of the controllability hypothesis failed to find an association between perceptions of control during criminal assault and posttraumatic stress symptoms (Kushner, Riggs, Foa, & Miller, 1993).

Negative Affectivity

Aside from the severity of the trauma itself, the discriminating features of those who recover versus those who go on to develop posttraumatic stress disorder tend to fall into three main categories: negative affectivity, prior stress, and coping with the trauma. As reviewed in previous chapters, negative affectivity, along with a prior history of stress, predict not only the probability of encountering stressors but also reactivity to stressors, and thus it is not surprising that negative affectivity predicted posttraumatic stress disorder among a traumatized group of young adults (adjusted odds of 1.53), as did factors conceptually tied to neuroticism, such as pre-existing anxiety or depression (odds of 2.46), and a family history of anxiety (odds of 2.89). Other predictors were a family history of instability and deviance (i.e., antisocial behavior; odds of 2.05) and early separation from parents (odds of 3.49) (Breslau *et al.*, 1991). The cross-sectional nature of these data limits causal inferences, but there exists other evidence for a genetic contribution to posttraumatic stress disorder that is likely to reflect the role of negative affectivity. For example, among 4042 monozygotic and dizygotic twin pairs who were in military service during the Vietnam war era, genetic variance accounted for up to a third of symptom variance, even after controlling for concordance in the amount of combat exposure between twin pairs (True *et al.*, 1993).

Also as reviewed in earlier chapters, repeated stressors increase reactivity to future stressors, a phenomenon known as stress sensitization. This has been demonstrated physiologically in non-primates and in rhesus monkeys (see Rosen & Schulkin, 1998; Sullivan, Coplan, & Gorman, 1998) and in terms of increased rates of posttraumatic stress disorder with multiple traumas (e.g., Breslau *et al.*, 1999a). Prior experiences with uncontrollable stress in particular may sensitize organisms to deleterious effects of subsequent uncontrollable trauma (Drugan, Moye, & Maier, 1982). It is for this reason that Foa *et al.* (1992) predicted that repeated childhood abuse in particular may predispose survivors to develop posttraumatic stress disorder following later traumatization, although Breslau *et al.* (1999a) did not find a unique relationship between early sexual abuse and later reaction to trauma. Instead, violence in general, and particularly multiple incidents of violence, was an important predictor of later reactivity.

Emotion Regulation: Threat Valuation and Avoidant Coping

Emotion regulation may be a central mediator of the response to trauma. That is, intensity and uncontrollability of the stressor aside, the interpretation placed on the event (the meaning of the event) and the way in which it is managed (e.g., avoidance) seem to be critical elements, consistent with factors that contribute to the durability of conditioned responding reviewed in Chapter 6. Threat valuation of traumas has been studied from a number of perspectives. Some have studied "finding meaning" as a way of buffering symptom development following traumatization (Taylor, 1983). However, the concept "finding meaning" is vague. According to the premises of hopelessness theory (Abramson, Metalsky, & Alloy, 1988), the attribution of causes of negative events to internal, global, and stable factors correlates with posttraumatic stress symptoms. This is illustrated in scripts from survivors of naval disasters, where internal and controllable attributions were associated with subsequent posttraumatic distress (Joseph, Brewin, Yule, & Williams, 1991, 1993). Falsetti and Resick (1995) attempted to improve on previous research by examining causal attributions for hypothetical events as well as actual traumas in victims of crimes and non-victims. In their sample of female students, they did not find clear differences between their victims and non-victims in terms of attributions for hypothetical negative events, although internal, stable, and uncontrollable attributions for actual traumatic events correlated with symptomatology among victims. These findings raise the possibility that attributions are epiphenomal to the emotional reaction. On the other hand, the effects of attributional style have been detected longitudinally as well. Mikulincer and Solomon (1988) examined the influence of attributional style on the development of posttraumatic stress symptoms 2–3 years after Israeli combat veterans fought throughout the Lebanon war. Symptomatology related to prior attribution of positive events to more external and uncontrollable causes and attribution of negative events to more external, stable and uncontrollable causes. Although their method for rating attributional style is questioned by Joseph *et al*. (1995), other supportive findings exist as well. These include more symptomatology after traumas in individuals with prior external locus of control, at least when traumas are below a certain intensity threshold (Solomon, Mikulincer, & Benbenishty, 1989). Above that threshold the locus of control had little impact on post-trauma emotional reactions. Joseph *et al*. (1995b) conclude from their review that attributions about traumatic events may represent a complex interaction of the nature of the event and pre-existing individual differences in attributional style, with the latter not being necessary for posttraumatic stress disorder, but may "help shape the specific cognitions about the trauma, which in turn, determine the nature and intensity of emotional states, such as fear, rage, guilt or shame, which, in turn, influence the choice of coping and the level of crisis support received" (Joseph *et al*., 1995, p. 537).

Another approach emphasizes pre-existing beliefs. Extending from notions presented by Horowitz (1976, 1980), Janoff-Bulman (1985) hypothesized that global positive beliefs may predispose to greater symptomatology after traumatic events. Specifically, the more globally positive beliefs are, the more likely that they will be shattered by traumatic events, and the more likely will be the development of overly global negative beliefs and posttraumatic stress disorder. Somewhat related is the notion that prior experience with control can sometimes increase negative reactions to subsequent uncontrollable stress relative to no prior experience with control (Mineka & Zinbarg, 1995). Conceivably, control generates safety associations, which are violated by uncontrollable aversive experiences in much the same way that Janoff-Bulman (1985) speculated that prior positive beliefs render subsequent traumas more negatively impactful. On the other hand, prior control can also buffer against subsequent stressors. Mineka and Kelly (1989) integrated these findings by suggesting that prior control may sensitize organisms to subsequent aversive, uncontrollable events if experienced in the same context where control was previously learned, but immunize against such events if they occur in dissimilar contexts, because safety associations are more likely to be violated in the first than the second case. If so, then posttraumatic stress disorder would be most likely to develop if traumas occurred in previously safe or pleasant contexts, or in contexts associated with a sense of control. In accord, Foa *et al.* (1992) note that posttraumatic stress disorder is more likely to follow childhood sexual abuse from fathers than from strangers or older children (McLeer, Deblinger, Atkins, Foa, & Ralphe, 1988), presumably because abuse from fathers is representative of greater violation of expectations of safety. For the same reasons, Foa and Riggs (1994) propose that not only are women who view themselves as incompetent or unable to control the world at high risk for the development of posttraumatic stress disorder following a traumatic incident, but also women who believe they are competent and always in control, because the traumatic incident disconfirms these assumptions. Women not at high risk for posttraumatic stress disorder are hypothesized to hold neither extreme views of the world nor of themselves, but instead recognize that sometimes they cannot control aversive events.

More recently, Ehlers and Clark (2000) proposed a cognitive model of posttraumatic stress disorder in which persistent symptomatology is predicted by appraisals of "serious current threat", such as appraisals of reactions during the trauma (e.g., mental defeat, mental confusion) and appraisals of reactions after the trauma. The concept of mental defeat is particularly interesting, referring to a perceived loss of psychological autonomy and a sense of not being human any more, and has been associated with the severity of posttraumatic stress disorder (e.g., Ehlers, Maercker, & Boos, 2000). Dunmore, Clark, and Ehlers (1999) evaluated certain aspects of this model by asking victims to appraise various features of the trauma and their reaction to the trauma within 4 months of the event and 6 and 9 months later. Various cognitive factors predicted the severity of posttraumatic stress symptoms, and again 6 and 9 months later, including mental defeat, mental confusion, and detachment recalled as occurring during the trauma, as well as negative appraisals of initial symptoms and perceived permanent change as a result of the trauma. The degree to which these types of cognitive appraisals reflect broader predisposing factors of negative affectivity and/ or a threat-based style of emotion regulation was not tested but is clearly in need of investigation.

Presumably, the greater the threat that is judged, the greater the likelihood of avoidant coping (Joseph *et al.*, 1995). As reviewed in previous chapters, an avoidant reaction is presumed to contribute to the development of a disorder. In support, attempts at thought suppression have been found to predict posttraumatic stress disorder or to be characteristic of those who develop the disorder versus those who do not (e.g., Ehlers *et al.*, 1998; Harvey & Bryant, 1998; Shipherd & Beck, 1999). For example, Bryant and Harvey (1995) examined 56 hospitalized motor vehicle accident victims 12 months after the accident. Avoidant coping style (e.g., attempts to avoid thinking about the incident) as well as pending compensation were strong predictors (accounting jointly for 41 percent of the variance) of intrusive recollections of the accident (as measured by the intrusion subscale of the Impact of Events Scale; Horowitz, Wilner, & Alvarez, 1979). Valentiner *et al.* (1996) examined coping responses of 215 females who were sexually and non-sexually assaulted, 2 weeks to 3 months after being assaulted. Three coping factors were analyzed: mobilizing support, positive distancing, and wishful thinking. The major finding was a strong positive association between wishful thinking (e.g., self-blame and denial by fantasy) and the severity of posttraumatic symptoms. Foa and Riggs (1995) found that numbing, dissociation, and anger predicted the chronicity of posttraumatic stress symptoms, which they attributed to avoidance and failure to emotionally process events. Similarly, a meta-analysis of 68 studies found that peritraumatic dissociation yielded the largest effect size for predicting posttraumatic stress disorder (Ozer, Best, Lipsey, & Weiss, 2003). Most of the studies analyzed relied upon retrospective reporting of dissociative experiences, and Marshall and Schell (2002) make the argument that recall of dissociation rather than dissociation *per se* is representative of those suffering from posttraumatic stress because dissociation (derealization and depersonalization) within a few days of community violence trauma was not predictive of posttraumatic stress symptoms in their sample ($n = 250$) at either 3 months or 12 months after the trauma. On the other hand, in another prospective longitudinal evaluation, delayed reaction to trauma, indicative of numbing or avoidance, was predictive of elevated trauma pathology in the long term (Gilboa-Schechtman & Foa, 2001). Thus, the role of dissociation *per se* remains somewhat controversial, whereas avoidance is both conceptually and empirically more strongly linked with development of disorder.

Sensory and Verbal Processing

Basic behavioral conceptualizations of posttraumatic stress disorder emphasize traumatic conditioning from the initial trauma, causing conditioned emotional responding to reminders of the event, "vivid flashbulb memories", and avoidance behavior. More specifically, conditioned fear is elicited by memories or reminders of the unconditioned stimulus, or the trauma, in much the same way that conditioned fear is elicited by bodily sensations in close proximity to panic attacks: fear occurs as the trauma is reprocessed or re-experienced. Conditioned anxiety is elicited by more distal reminders and through processes of stimulus generalization. The intense distress results in learned avoidance behavior, which brings some immediate relief but, at the same time, reinforces fear and prevents habituation or correction of the threat value of intrusive recollections. Thus, through avoidance and maintenance of threat value, reappearance of traumatic memories after long intervals without recollection is likely to occur. In addition, contexts that were integrally linked with the original trauma (such as certain locations or mood states) may reinstate fear when they are re-encountered, even many years after the original trauma. Brewin (2001) extends upon this basic model in his dual-representation theory. In this theory, traumatic memories are divided into two types that are stored in different representational formats that in some ways overlap with the distinction drawn by Joseph *et al.* (1995) between event cognitions versus appraisals. In Brewin's more comprehensive and neurocognitively based model, verbally accessible memory is the memory system that supports ordinary autobiographical memories, that can be edited, and that interacts with other autobiographical memories, and receive sufficient conscious processing to be transferred to long-term memory stores that can be deliberately retrieved. Verbally accessible memory is connected with the hippocampus. In contrast, situationally accessible memories are those memories that support trauma-related dreams and flashbacks; they contain information about perceptual processing of the trauma scene and bodily response to the trauma. Situationally accessible memories are connected with the amygdala, and thereby Brewin's conceptualization fits with models of emotional learning proposed by LeDoux (1996) and Öhman and Mineka (2001).

In normal response to trauma, Brewin proposes that sufficiently detailed verbally accessible memories are fully integrated with pre-existing knowledge structures, by deliberate focusing on flashback content and repeated conscious processing of detailed information about the trauma. By so doing, the verbally accessible memory system eventually inhibits the situationally accessible memory system. These normal processes, however, can be impeded by high levels of stress, as would occur with very intense or prolonged traumas, and the associated secretion of glucocorticoids that impair declarative memory in the hippocampus, resulting in poor verbal integration of the trauma. In accord with this hypothesis, trauma memories in posttraumatic stress disorder are usually fragmented (Foa, Molnar, & Cashman, 1995). In an overlapping model, Joseph *et al.* (1995) suggested that traumatic events produce extreme emotional arousal that cannot be immediately processed, and instead are stored in immediate memory as pictorial or iconic representations. Krystal, Southwick, and Charney (1995) also proposed that the initial encoding of traumas involves less verbal and more emotional, pictorial, and sensory memory systems. Sensory and emotional memories are considered to be more involuntary and thus more likely to intrude into consciousness unwantedly (LeDoux, 1987). Thus, Joseph *et al.* (1995) posited that imagery based "event cognitions" and internal cues of emotional state linked with the initial trauma (as indicated by studies using yohimbine; Southwick *et al.*, 1993) form the basis for re-experiencing phenomena, such as intrusive thoughts and flashbacks.

To explain the development of long-lasting distress following trauma, Brewin (2001) proposes that verbally accessed memories remain impoverished when there is marked avoidance of trauma reminders and flashbacks. Under such impoverished conditions, there is a lack of inhibition over the amygdala and situationally accessible memories, and hence recurrent flashbacks, nightmares, and emotional responses to situational reminders continue to occur. Thus, Brewin's model takes into account the two factors believed to be central to the predisposition to negative reaction to trauma: high levels of stress, the accompaniment being high negative affectivity, and avoidant coping or a threat-based style of emotion regulation.

Maintaining Influences

In the case of posttraumatic stress disorder the factors described as central to the development of the disorder are also the factors responsible for its maintenance over time, those being avoidant coping and threat valuation. Threat valuation may extend beyond trauma-related stimuli to the world in general. For example, Foa *et al.* (1995)

propose that posttraumatic stress disorder involves perceptions of the world as dangerous, and self-perceptions of incompetence and helplessness. Obviously, such themes would generate ongoing anxiety and arousal. Similarly, Resick and Schnicke (1990) describe cognitive distortions that generate beliefs about the world as a dangerous place or of oneself as powerless.

There is evidence for elevated vigilance as measured psychophysiologically and attentionally in those who develop posttraumatic stress disorder. Such vigilance is likely to contribute to ongoing distress, avoidance, and threat appraisal. For example, Vietnam veterans with posttraumatic stress disorder are physiologically hyper-reactive to combat-related stimuli relative to veterans without posttraumatic stress disorder (e.g., Blanchard, Kolb, Pallmeyer, & Gerardi, 1982; Gerardi, Blanchard, & Kolb, 1989; Malloy, Fairbank, & Keane, 1983; Pitman, Orr, Forgue, de Jong, & Claiborn, 1987). Also, Bryant, Harvey, Gordon, and Barry (1995) found that motor vehicle accident victims with posttraumatic stress disorder ($n = 10$) showed more eye fixation on threat words (blood, ambulance, and death) than healthy controls, as if they were preferentially processing threat-related stimuli. However, for reasons that are not clear, not all posttraumatic victims show signs of hyperarousal to threat-related stimuli (Bryant *et al.*, 1995; Pitman *et al.*, 1990). Perhaps, affective shut-down through numbing is occasionally sustained throughout exposure to direct trauma reminders.

In addition, heightened physiological reactivity has been observed independently of trauma reminders. As mentioned in Chapters 5 and 6, the debate is whether such arousability reflects non-cue-dependent sensitization or high levels of contextual conditioning. For example, Bryant *et al.* (1995) found that their posttraumatic stress disorder group was more physiologically reactive to neutral stimuli as well as threat stimuli in a way that is consistent with other evidence for indiscriminant responding to threat with higher levels of distress. Also, yohimbine, which activates noradrenergic neurons, produced more panic attacks and larger elevations in plasma 3-methoxy-4-hydroxyphenylethyleneglycol (MHPG) and blood pressure in patients with posttraumatic stress disorder than controls (Southwick *et al.*, 1993). Southwick *et al.* (1993) suggest that the noradrenergic system is involved in behavioral sensitization, such that with repeated stressors, re-exposure to a lower-intensity stressor elicits a stronger norepinephrine release than expected. Thus, the exaggerated MHPG response to yohimbine may reflect a noradrenergic system that is sensitized due to severe stress. However, any reaction in the laboratory setting is just as easily attributed to contextual factors. For example, that combat veterans with posttraumatic stress disorder exhibited stronger startle at the baseline and larger potentiation of startle by yohimbine than healthy controls was attributed by Morgan *et al.* (1995) to posttraumatic patients being more reactive to the stress of a drug challenge. As reviewed previously, Grillon and Morgan (1999) reached similar conclusions from their observations of non-differential responding between conditioned and neutral stimuli, as measured by startle reactivity. The authors attributed this profile to a tendency to react with fear and anxiety to innocuous events presented in stressful contexts. Similar to the profile of increasing anticipation of shock reported by Orr *et al.* (2000), Grillon and Morgan (1999) found that baseline startle increased in posttraumatic stress disorder veterans from session 1 to session 2, which again was interpreted as enhanced contextual fear conditioning (to the place where they previously received an aversive stimulus) and enhanced generalization of fear learning. The fact that baseline responding normalized during the conditioning and post-conditioning phases of the second laboratory session was not consistent with overall sensitization.

Yehuda and colleagues propose chronic sensitization of the hypothalamic–pituitary axis, given their extensive body of research indicating lowered 24 hour urinary cortisol excretion (Kellner *et al.*, 2002; Yehuda *et al.*, 1995), a higher concentration of glucocorticoid receptors on circulating lymphyocytes, augmented cortisol suppression in dexamethasone suppression testing (Kellner *et al.*, 2002; Yehuda, Boisoneau, Lowy, & Giller, 1995), and higher excretions of dopamine, epinephrine, and norepinephrine (Geracioti, Baker, Ekhator *et al.*, 2001; Yehuda, Southwick, Giller, Ma, & Mason, 1992). They suggest a hyper-responsiveness of the hypothalamic–pituitary axis, which usually is accompanied by a down-regulation of the system, but in the case of posttraumatic stress disorder is accompanied by an up-regulation of glucocorticoid receptors, thus maintaining a state of hyperresponsivity to the environment (Yehuda, 1999). Nonetheless, these data too may reflect "frequent and prolonged emotional response to conditioned stimuli" (Davidson & Baum, 1986, p. 307). Even the evidence for greater sleep disturbance, with higher incidence of phasic increases of electro-myographic activity (i.e., periodic movements) during REM and non-REM sleep in posttraumatic stress disorder patients relative to controls (Ross *et al.*, 1990), and reduced sleep efficiency due to relatively frequent awakenings and movement time (e.g., Glaubman, Mikulincer, Porat, Wasserman, & Birger, 1990; Hefez, Metz, & Lavie, 1987; Lavie, Hefez, Halperin, & Enoch, 1979; Mellman, Kulick-Bell, Ashlock, & Nolan, 1995), can be viewed as contextual conditioning. That is, sleep can be a "dangerous context" due to the absence of the powers of vigilance needed for self-protection (Grillon, 2002a) or by virtue of association with trauma-related nightmares.

Sullivan *et al.* (1999) combine the notions of sensitization and contextual conditioning in a reciprocal model whereby stress enhances fear memories and conditioning by strengthening learned fear and generalization of new learning; in turn accumulating fear memories enhance stress sensitivity and sensitization. Clearly, such processes maintain ongoing distress and reactivity to even very degraded versions of the traumatic event, and encourage avoidance behavior.

Summary

Even though posttraumatic stress disorder is predicted by the intensity of traumas, individual differences play a significant role in modulating trauma reactivity. Factors found to predict the development of posttraumatic stress disorder include negative affectivity and a history of prior stress, consistent with a stress sensitization model. In addition, avoidant coping and threat appraisals (i.e., emotion regulation skills) appear to moderate the reaction to traumas. As with the other anxiety disorders, posttraumatic stress is maintained by elevated vigilance and associated physiology, threat-laden beliefs, and avoidant behavior, which generalize to contextual cues and could involve sensitization processes (seen in elevations in sympathetic and hypothalamic–pituitary axis activation across 24 hour recordings and non-differential responding in laboratory settings) more than for other anxiety disorders due to the severely high levels of distress.

Obsessive–compulsive Disorder

Salience and Threat Value of Unwanted Mental Processes

The occurrence of unwanted thoughts, images, or impulses *alone* does not seem to predict the onset of obsessive–compulsive disorder (see Chapter 1). That is, as much as 80–90 percent of community samples experience intrusive thoughts at some time (e.g., Salkovskis & Harrison, 1984), and yet the prevalence of obsessive–compulsive disorder remains in the realm of 1–2 percent. Clark and Purdon (1995, p. 967) comment:

> The sudden intrusion of unwanted or unwillful thoughts, images, or impulses is a frequent and natural occurrence within our stream of consciousness. In fact at times we seem almost helpless in our efforts to consciously control the content or direction of our thoughts … as evidenced by the unwanted intrusion of a variety of mental events from a mundane tune or rhyme to a negative, possibly even disgusting or abhorrent thought or image. This intrusive quality of cognition may be a particularly adaptive aspect of human nature when it involves the spontaneous occurrence of positive cognitions associated with creativity, inspiration, problem-solving, and relief from boredom leading to increased motivation for productive work and social interaction.

The commonality of intrusive thoughts extends to compulsive behaviors, given that 55 percent of the community exhibits some ritualistic behavior (Muris *et al.*, 1997a) and 10–27 percent exhibit significant compulsive behavior (e.g., Frost, Lahart, Dugas, & Sher, 1988).

Nor can the development of obsessive–compulsive disorder be attributed to more negative intrusive material than is experienced normally, because the content of obsessions does not differ between clinical and non-clinical samples. For example, mental health professionals were unable to distinguish "obsessions" transcribed from clinical versus non-clinical samples (Rachman & deSilva, 1978). A similar pattern occurs in the comparison between non-clinical and clinical compulsions, given that although obsessive–compulsive patients engage more frequently in washing, cleaning, and ordering whereas normal individuals engage in more magical, protective behaviors, overall a close correspondence was noted between the content of compulsions across the two groups (Muris *et al.*, 1997a).

Intrusive thoughts are more likely under conditions of stress, such as in mothers whose children are about to undergo surgery (Parkinson & Rachman, 1981b). The intrusions subside relatively quickly as stress dissipates (Parkinson & Rachman, 1981c). It is hypothesized that those whose intrusive thoughts do not dissipate, but instead become more frequent and distressing (i.e., develop into obsessive–compulsive disorder), *react* more negatively to their intrusions. Individuals with obsessive–compulsive disorder certainly find the intrusive mental processes more discomforting than do control groups (Parkinson & Rachman, 1981a). The range of reactions to intrusive thoughts was documented by Freeston *et al.* (1991), who found that the most common responses to intrusions among an unselected university student sample were "no effortful response" or self-reassurance (26 percent), attentively thinking about the thought or seeking reassurance from others (34 percent), and escape/avoidance (40 percent). The last of these strategies refers to attempts to replace the thought with another, to become distracted by other activities, or telling oneself to stop thinking. Overall, those who employed the last two strategies were more anxious and reported more difficulty removing the intrusions. Also, these two strategies were associated with more sadness, worry, guilt, and disapproval, in comparison with the "no effortful response" strategy. In a replication study, the strategies again ranged from doing nothing, to self-reassurance, analyzing the thought, seeking reassurances, replacement with another thought or action, and thought stopping (Ladouceur *et al.*, 2000). Thoughts appraised as more egodystonic (i.e., the content is experienced as inconsistent with the individual's belief system and thus perceived as irrational) were associated with greater use of escape or avoidance strategies (Langlois *et al.*, 2000), and attempts to deal with intrusive thoughts by escaping or avoiding them were associated with more distress overall and more difficulty removing the intrusions than "non-effortful" or minimal reactions to intrusive thoughts (Freeston *et al.*, 1991). These data suggest that distress about intrusive cognitions is tied in with attempts to remove them.

In comparison with controls, patients with obsessive–compulsive disorder are more likely to attempt to resist or remove their unwanted thoughts and images (Parkinson & Rachman, 1981a). Furthermore, patients with obsessive–compulsive disorder react to their intrusive thoughts with more punishment (e.g., "I get angry at myself for having the thought") and worry (e.g., "I dwell on other worries") than do controls (Amir, Cashman, & Foa, 1997). Thus, the progression from non-clinical to clinical states may be mediated by negative reactions to intrusive mental processes. The negative reactions may in turn be based on appraisals about mental processes, a concept first put forth by Rachman (1976) and elaborated by Salkovskis (1985, 1989). Salkovskis distinguished between intrusions and negative automatic thoughts (i.e., appraisals) about intrusions. The former are egodystonic, whereas the latter are relatively autonomous, idiosyncratic, and are experienced as reasonable and egosyntonic. Similarly, Wells and Morrison (1994) distinguish between obsessions and worries about obsessions. Worry is viewed as "a more strategically driven conceptual activity than obsessions" (Wells & Morrison, 1994, p. 860). More specifically, Salkovskis (1985, 1989) proposed that negative thoughts about intrusive thoughts, images, or impulses are characterized by an inflated sense of responsibility, which derives from basic assumptions about one's thoughts or images such as: having a thought about an action is equivalent to action (first proposed by Rachman (1976), who later termed it "thought–action" (Rachman, Thordarson, Shafran, & Woody, 1995)); failing to prevent or trying to prevent harm to oneself or others is the same as having caused harm in the first place; responsibility is not attenuated by other factors such as a low probability of occurrence; failing to neutralize an intrusion about harming others is similar to seeking or wanting to harm others; and one should and can exercise control over one's thoughts. Others (e.g., Rachman, 1997; Wells & Morrison, 1994) give less emphasis to an inflated sense of responsibility because the evidence regarding responsibility and obsessiveness is mixed (Freeston, Ladouceur, Gagnon, & Thibodeau, 1993; Rachman *et al.*, 1995; Rheaume, Freeston, Dugas, Letarte, & Ladouceur, 1995; Scarrabelotti, Duck, & Dickerson, 1995 versus Jones & Menzies, 1997). Nonetheless, responsibility remains a viable construct given that sense of responsibility predicted the level of distress over intrusive thoughts (Scarrabelotti *et al.*, 1995) and that diffusion of responsibility lessened distress and urges to ritualize after an intrusive thought or image (Ladouceur *et al.*, 1995; Lopatka & Rachman, 1995).

Most of the available research pertains to thought–action fusion, or the belief that thinking about an unacceptable event makes that event more probable, and the interpretation that obsessional thoughts and forbidden actions are morally equivalent: that thinking of causing harm to another increases the likelihood of causing harm to another, and thinking of causing harm to another generates the same moral responsibility as if harm had actually been caused to another. These types of thought–action fusions correlate moderately with obsessive–compulsive features (Rachman *et al.*, 1995). In addition, Rassin, Merckelbach, Muris, and Spaan (1999) found that thought–action fusion correlated with reactivity to an intrusive idea. That is, participants who were led to believe that thinking the word "apple" could result in administration of an electric shock to another person reported more intrusive thoughts about apples, discomfort, and resistance than those who did not expect an aversive outcome from thinking the word "apple". Importantly for the current discussion, the level of distress and report of intrusive thoughts in the first group correlated positively with the level of thought–action fusion. Other research has shown that whereas thought–action fusion correlates with various symptoms of anxiety in adolescents and with excessive worry and symptoms of generalized anxiety disorder (Hazlett-Stevens, Zucker, & Craske, 2002), the relationships are strongest with symptoms of obsessive–compulsive disorder (Muris *et al.*, 2001).

In summary, sensitivity to intrusive mental processes is believed to contribute to the transition from subclinical to clinical levels of obsessionality. Unfortunately, it is almost impossible to directly test the degree to which *initial* appraisals of intrusive thoughts or images predict later obsessive–compulsive disorder, but the evidence reviewed herein is strongly suggestive of the influence of the threat value of unwanted thoughts and images upon levels of distress. What might be the origins of the heightened threat value of intrusive mental processes? Shafran, Thordarson, and Rachman (1996) posited that thought–action fusion and other features that represent overvaluation of the importance of thoughts may arise from cultural factors such as religions that emphasize the sinfulness of having blasphemous, adulterous, or aggressive thoughts, or a chance pairing between a thought and a negative event, such as thoughts of wishing one's parent were dead followed shortly by the actual death of the parent. In accord with the first hypothesis, Sica, Novara, and Sanavio (2002) found that individuals with a high degree of religiosity reported more obsessionality, overimportance of thoughts, control of thoughts, perfectionism, and responsibility than those with low religiosity even after controlling for levels of anxiety and depression. Similarly, in a college student sample, we found a strong relationship between religiousity and thought–action fusion (Zucker, Craske, Barrios, & Holguin, 2002). Cultural factors are also apparent in the heightened prevalence of intrusive thoughts about contamination among groups where religious emphasis is placed upon purity and where many rituals and practices are used to avoid pollution and cleanse the self (Kirmayer, Young, & Hayton, 1995). Along the same lines, Rachman (1997) posited that obsessional content derives in large part from personal values. For example, intrusive thoughts of harming others are particularly distressing for people who value kindness toward others, and intrusive thoughts of sinful actions are particularly distressing for those with high religious standards, and hence these thoughts, possessing the highest threat value, would be most likely to enter the cycle of thought–action fusion, attempts to resist, and distress.

Salkovskis, Shafran, Rachman, and Freeston (1999) put forth other life experiences that may contribute to an inflated sense of responsibility, such as high levels of responsibility or being led to believe at a young age that one was responsible for negative consequences over which one had little control. Conversely, having no responsibility as a child due to overprotective parenting may similarly lead to an inflated sense of responsibility upon entering the world alone, and finding the responsibilities of independence very difficult. Finally, incidents in which one's actions or inactions contribute to a serious misfortune or even a near-critical incident where a catastrophe to which the person contributed was only averted by unlikely circumstances or good luck may be another source of an inflated sense of responsibility. As can be seen, the types of life experiences that increase the salience and threat value of intrusive thoughts or images remain very speculative, with the possible exception of religiousity.

The discussion so far has highlighted potential sources of elevated threat value for unwanted intrusive thoughts, images, or impulses. The salience of unwanted mental processes may be additionally influenced by a physiological propensity to repetition of cognitive material, in the same way that vulnerability to blood phobias may be influenced by a propensity to faint at the sight of blood, and vulnerability to panic disorder may be influenced by a propensity to experience acute and intense autonomic reactivity. This possibility relates to a large body of research on the neurobiology and neuropsychology of obsessive–compulsive disorder. Perhaps more than any other anxiety disorder, obsessive–compulsive disorder has been judged to involve specific neurological deficits. These have been studied from the perspective of brain structure and function, neuropsychological test performance, and even autonomic state, given that some have conjectured that non-specific autonomic overactivation contributes to the repetitiveness of intrusive mental processes. In support, autonomic activity is elevated when confronted with obsessive–compulsive stimuli such as contaminated objects (e.g., Boulougouris, Rabavilas, & Stefanis, 1977), but the most important question is whether a generalized state of hyperarousal inhibits the dismissal of intrusive thoughts. If so, as Hoehn-Saric *et al.* (1995) note, individuals with obsessive–compulsive disorder should be more "autonomically activated" in general and respond more strongly to non-specific stressors. However, despite earlier positive findings (e.g., Beech & Liddell, 1974; Boulougouris *et al.*, 1977), later studies have failed to find support for this contention. For example, Hollander *et al.* (1991) found no evidence for elevated noradrenergic functioning in general, and Chappell *et al.* (1996) failed to find differences in levels of corticotropin-releasing factor, taken from cerebrospinal fluid from lumbar punctures, between patients with obsessive–compulsive disorder and healthy controls. Similarly, Zahn, Leonard, Swedo, and Rapoport, (1996) found no heart rate or skin conductance differences under resting and non-specific stress conditions (innocuous tones and a reaction time task) in 55 youths with obsessive–compulsive disorder compared with 58 controls. Thus, as with most other anxiety disorders (except posttraumatic stress disorder), signs of autonomic activation in obsessive–compulsive disorder may be restricted to anticipation of or exposure to specific threat cues.

Others have evaluated basic deficits or dysregulations in cognitive processing, such as general memory deficits. For example, using scales modified from a standard intelligence battery, Savage *et al.* (1996) found evidence for impaired recall of non-verbal memory in obsessive–compulsive patients compared with 20 healthy controls, although this deficit was not apparent with verbal material nor with recognition memory. Importantly, these findings may be mediated by excessive self-doubt rather than basic deficits in memory functioning. For example, Clayton, Richards, and Edwards (1999) compared individuals with obsessive–compulsive disorder, individuals with panic disorder, and controls on a battery of psychometric tests of selective attention, to find poorer performance for obsessive–compulsive disorder patients. A very important caveat noted by the authors was that these deficits were found on timed tasks but not on untimed tasks, raising the distinct possibility that performance may have been hindered by excessive caution or slowness of responding. Furthermore, in direct contrast to the memory deficit model, Radomsky and Rachman (1999) found that patients with obsessive–compulsive disorder had superior memory for contaminated objects compared with clean ones, whereas anxious and non-anxious controls did not. Moreover, such patients exhibited a positive memory bias for a prior checking scenario, particularly when the checking was conducted under conditions of high responsibility (Radomsky, Rachman, & Hammond, 2001).

Another deficit model posits that individuals with obsessive–compulsive disorder discriminate poorly between memories for events and memories for images (Johnson, 1988). Although this notion fits with patient reports of inability to recall whether a behavior was actually performed or not, the evidence generally is very weak. For example, obsessive–compulsive patients were less confident than controls about their memories, although the two groups did not differ in terms of reality monitoring when evaluating actual versus imagined performance of tracing a line-drawn picture or word (McNally & Kohlbeck, 1993). Using a signal detection task, Brown, Kosslyn, Breiter, Baer, and Jenike (1994) asked 28 patients with obsessive–compulsive disorder and 18 controls to compare the heights of the first and last letters of words either written or imagined in lower case, and then later asked them to recall which words had been presented in writing. Similarly to McNally and Kohlbeck (1993), Brown *et al.* (1994) did not find support for an actual deficit in reality monitoring. In fact, the patient group tended to discriminate between real and imagined stimuli better than control participants. Also, Constans, Foa, Franklin, and Mathews (1995) compared 12 patients with checking compulsions and seven healthy controls in terms of a series of action sequences, half of which ended with instructions to perform an action and half with instructions to imagine performing an action. Some of the action sequences were relevant to obsessive–compulsive fears (e.g., lighting and blowing out a candle, sheathing and unsheathing a knife) whereas others were neutral (e.g., pushing out or pulling in a chair). Later, participants were asked to recall whether the last action for each task was real or imagined. As with previous studies, obsessive–compulsive patients were not deficient in reality monitoring with either fear-relevant or -neutral stimuli.

Some suggest that individuals with obsessive–compulsive disorder are impaired in their ability to dismiss or selectively attend to extraneous sensory stimuli, internally generated cognitive stimuli, or random thoughts. This hypothesis has been tested using negative priming, which involves naming of a target item that was previously presented as a distractor to be ignored; naming is usually slowed under these conditions due to the response cost of having to overcome the inhibition before further processing is possible. Studies generally demonstrate the absence of negative priming in obsessive–compulsive disorder even though it is evident in other anxiety disorders (Enright & Beech, 1990, 1993a, 1993b). For example, Enright, Beech, and Claridge (1995) compared 32 patients with obsessive–compulsive disorder to 32 patients with various other anxiety disorders using a Stroop task, in which color naming occurred under various conditions of prior distractors. Obsessive–compulsive patients showed less negative priming (i.e., less interference caused by distractors) than other anxiety patients, at least with presentations at speeds below conscious awareness. This was interpreted as a fundamental deficit in cognitive inhibition at a preattentive level. At slower speeds, the authors conclude that more attended strategies of cognitive processing may mask preattentive deficits in inhibition. Failed inhibition may also account for directed forgetting effects. The standard effect of instructions to forget is poorer recall of such words, and this effect was observed in patients with obsessive–compulsive disorder as well as healthy controls. However, in contrast to healthy controls, obsessive–compulsive patients also recalled more negative "forget words" compared with positive or neutral "forget words" (Wilhelm, McNally, Baer, & Florin 1996). Poor cognitive inhibition is hypothesized to cause a greater number of intrusions into consciousness, making deliberate attempts to suppress those intrusions more difficult. These findings are complemented by another study in which instructions to suppress a neutral thought of "white bears" resulted in faster lexical decision times for recognizing "bear" as a word in comparison with other words that had not been suppressed in patients with obsessive–compulsive disorder (Tolin, Abramowitz, Przeworski, & Foa, 2002). Socially anxious individuals and non-anxious controls did not show this bias. The authors concluded that obsessive–compulsive problems involve deficits in ability to suppress neutral thoughts due to inhibitory failures because attempts to suppress were associated with increased priming of the target thoughts.

In line with this conclusion are various results from investigations of neuroanatomy and brain functioning. A series of neuroimaging studies suggest that certain sections of the brain are implicated in obsessive–compulsive disorder (e.g., Baxter *et al.*, 1992; Insel, 1992; Rauch *et al.*, 1994; Swedo *et al*, 1992). The most consistent findings are increased glucose metabolism or other indices of activation in the orbitofrontal cortex and caudate nuclei, which are normalized with successful pharmacological or behavioral treatments (e.g., Schwartz, Stoessel, Baxter, Martin, & Phelps, 1996). The orbitofrontal cortex, cingulate cortex, and caudate nuclei are part of a circuit that may be involved in regulation of repetitive thoughts and behaviors, such as occurs with fixed-action patterns in response to key releasing stimuli (Rapoport, 1989). Baxter *et al.* (1992) suggested that the caudate nucleus is underactive in obsessive–compulsive disorder, so that thoughts, sensations, and actions generated by the orbital frontal cortex are not suppressed. A "pass through" of orbital cortical inputs to the globus pallidus and thalamus may then occur, and increased thalamic input to the orbital cortex results in an abnormal, self-reinforcing circuit. In support, Robinson *et al.* (1995) found evidence for smaller volumes of the caudate nucleus in 26 obsessive–compulsive patients compared with 26 healthy controls, although volume did not correlate with the duration or severity of obsessive–compulsive disorder.

Li *et al.* (2000) used a neuropsychological task — the "Schroder staircase" — to assess the degree to which disinhibitory processes in the corticostriatal circuitry would facilitate involuntary perceptual reversals (i.e., the staircase appears to flip upside down). During a 30 second interval, the average number of perceptual shifts was 9.3, 7.1, and 4.3 for obsessive–compulsive disorder, generalized anxiety disorder, and normal control groups, respectively. Also, the number of shifts correlated with anxiety and obsessiveness in the obsessive–compulsive disorder group only. This was interpreted as evidence for different neural mechanisms across disorders. Again, however, the number of shifts could as well be explained by self-doubt and indecisiveness on the part of obsessive–compulsive patients, who may simply possess more such self-doubt in relation to visual stimuli than do patients with generalized anxiety disorder, who still possess more self-doubt than controls.

Moreover, the findings from brain scanning studies remain far from conclusive. For example, the finding of smaller volumes of the caudate nucleus has not been replicated (Stein *et al.*, 1993). In addition, Cottraux *et al.* (1996) compared positron emission tomography (PET) scans of 10 obsessive–compulsive patients with predominant checking features while they were resting and obsessing (e.g., "you forget to turn off an electrical apparatus and while you are out your home is set on fire") to 10 normal subjects while they were resting and thinking about normal obsessions (e.g., "you are going out alone and inadvertently you may bully older people, children, or weaker people on the street or in the crowd"). Interestingly, both groups showed increased activity in orbitofrontal areas with obsessive stimulation, suggesting that the act of obsessing was responsible for changes in brain functioning. However, some other differences were noted: during rest, obsessive–compulsive patients had more activity in superior temporal regions, and during obsessing, and activity in the superior temporal region correlated with activity in the orbitofrontal region for obsessive–compulsive patients only. Obviously, further comparisons with other anxiety disorders and mood disorders, and well as studies of high-risk groups, are warranted before drawing strong conclusions about neurobiological pathways of obsessive–compulsive disorder.

In addition, purely biological models are unable to account for the restriction of obsessive–compulsive behaviors to specific classes of stimuli. As noted by Rachman (1997), obsessions of causing harm to others always target the helpless — the elderly, disabled, and young — whereas "there are no Arnold Schwartzenegger obsessions". The fact that there are many stimuli about which patients do *not* obsess suggests that deficits in cognitive processing, if they do exist, must interact with learning and psychological factors such as appraisals of mental content mentioned earlier. Nonetheless, the previously reviewed studies of negative priming and directed forgetting indicate a potential contributory role for difficulty filtering or inhibiting intrusive mental processes, although their role in the *onset* of obsessive–compulsive disorder is far from empirically validated.

The peak ages of onset for obsessive–compulsive disorder tend to be in childhood as well as in the early 20s (see Chapter 1). What are the developmental factors that may contribute to the salience and threat value of intrusive mental processes around those times? Perhaps the early 20s is the developmental phase associated with elevated responsibility for one's own thoughts and actions because it is the expected time for leaving home and having a family, at least in Western cultures. At those times, the salience and threat value of intrusive thoughts and images may become more prominent for everyone, and particularly for those with a history and/or physiological propensity to already possess an elevated salience and threat value. However, a developmental explanation for intrusive thoughts is less obvious in childhood, primarily because childhood obsessive–compulsive disorder typically involves much less obsessive rumination and much more compulsive rituals than is true of adults (e.g., Rapoport *et al.*, 1992). Indeed, others have argued that mental processes are less relevant to anxious pathology in early childhood due to cognitive capacities (Nelles & Barlow, 1988). Perhaps childhood onset of obsessive–compulsive disorder represents a failed attempt at emotion regulation of negative affect in general rather than an attempt to control unwanted mental processes *per se*. If so, childhood obsessive–compulsive disorder may parallel the compulsive ritualistic-like behavioral effects of repeated frustration seen in animals when exposed to insoluble discrimination problems or high stress (Mineka, Suomi, & Delizio, 1981). These are referred to as displacement behaviors in reaction to high arousal or conflict, and are hypothesized to give animals time to adjust and make decisions about whether to flee or fight (Stein, Shoulberg, Helton, & Hollander, 1992). Conceivably, then, childhood-onset obsessive–compulsive disorder may be less tied in with the threat value of unwanted mental processes and more tied in with elevated negative affectivity, with compulsive behaviors representing a maladaptive method of attempting to regulate high negative affect.

Maintaining Influences

Catastrophic appraisals of intrusive thoughts as exemplified in thought–action fusion are presumed to increase the repetitiveness of intrusions and associated distress for a number of reasons. For example, negative affect that results from such catastrophic appraisals may increase the "availability" of intrusive thoughts (e.g., Reynolds & Salkovskis, 1992). Also, negative appraisals may increase the number of retrieval cues for such intrusions in memory (Wells & Morrison, 1994), and both factors increase the frequency of intrusions. Also, Rachman (1998b) proposed that catastrophic interpretations of intrusive thoughts convert previously neutral stimuli into threatening stimuli. His example is very illustrative: when one misinterprets images of causing harm as evidence for being a dangerous individual, then sharp objects are converted into potential weapons. Anxiety reactions may be misinterpreted in the same way. For example (Rachman, 1998b, p. 386),

> if the person interprets the intrusive thoughts as signifying that he is dangerous and may lose control and harm a child, it follows that sensations of discomfort/anxiety (e.g., trembling, sweating) in the presence of children are interpreted as signs of serious loss of control.

The recurrence of an intrusive thought itself may be misinterpreted (e.g., "That this horrible thought continues to recur must mean that I really am a horrible person"). Thus, an increasing array of previously neutral external and internal stimuli become sources of potential threat that provoke continued obsessions.

In addition, catastrophic misappraisals of intrusive mental processes are likely to drive strong attempts to control the intrusive covert material, as has been observed in the link between thoughts appraised as egodystonic and avoidant/escape strategies in non-clinical samples (Langlois *et al.*, 2000). Attempts at avoidance may be especially likely if combined with other beliefs that thoughts should and could be controlled (Clark & Purdon, 1993). Wells (1997) argues that such a drive to control thoughts leads to a state of hypervigilance to thought cues and an inability to attend to information that disconfirms negative appraisals. In addition, such efforts at control are likely to increase the level of associated distress and possibly the frequency of intrusive thoughts. The body of research on thought suppression rebound (reviewed in Chapter 5) suggests a similar pathway through which attempts at control are counterproductive and may engender more of the very thing that is being suppressed. Specifically, thought suppression generates vigilance for unwanted material, and such vigilance contributes to resurgence of that material (Wenzlaff & Wegner, 2000). Salkovskis and Campbell (1994) assigned non-clinical participants who had recently experienced three or more distressing, intrusive thoughts to conditions of thought suppression, mention control, or three different types of distraction regarding a personal intrusive thought. In the thought suppression condition, participants were informed "it is very important that you try as hard as you can to suppress the thought 'X' ", although they were also to record the thought if it occurred. The mention control condition entailed recording only. After 5 minutes, each condition was followed by a period of "think anything". The suppression group experienced more intrusive thoughts during suppression and the subsequent interval of "think anything" in comparison with the mention control group. Distraction only reduced the frequency of intrusions when a specific distracting task was provided. Trinder and Salkovskis (1994) conducted a more naturalistic follow-up study. Students who had experienced negative intrusive thoughts in the past month were asked to either suppress, simply record, or concentrate upon idiosyncratic, personally relevant, negative intrusions over 4 days. The suppression group reported more intrusive thoughts and more distress over those thoughts during the 4 days. However, concentrating upon thoughts also produced more discomfort than recording only, leading the authors to conclude that neither suppression nor dwelling on unwanted thoughts is therapeutically beneficial.

Several studies have been unable to replicate immediate enhancement or rebound effects from thought suppression of obsessive material (Merckelbach, Muris, van den Hout, & de Jong, 1991; Muris, Merckelbach, & Horselenberg, 1996). For example, Smari, Birgisdottir, and Brynjolfsdottir (1995), Rutledge (1998), and McNally and Ricciardi (1996) failed to find robust evidence for thought suppression rebound, but as noted by Purdon and Clark (2001) the degree to which obsessional material was targeted fully in those studies is not clear. Using a clinical sample, Janeck and Calamari (1999) again failed to find evidence for thought suppression rebound of obsessional material. Purdon and Clark (2001) found evidence for more distress with suppressed thoughts but not more frequency of suppressed thoughts. Possibly none of these studies provided sufficient cognitive load to truly test for the ironic monitoring process presumed to lead to thought suppression rebound (Wenzlaff & Wegner, 2000), as described in Chapter 5. Alternatively, patient samples may not be able to comply with non-suppression instructions against which to compare the effects of suppression, as suggested by a study by Purdon (2001) in which normal subjects were asked to suppress and then not suppress their most distressing thoughts. Consistent with the data already reviewed regarding catastrophic misappraisals, the greater the concern that thought reoccurrences signified undesirable personal characteristics, poor mental functioning, and negative future events, the more negative the mood state. Importantly, despite instructions not to suppress, participants who appraised the thoughts negatively engaged in efforts to control their thoughts. Thus, it is conceivable that the effects of thought suppression have not been observed reliably in subclinical and clinical patients because the comparison "non-suppression" condition remains a "suppression" condition due to strong emotional–motivational influences.

Another type of avoidance is neutralization, or attempts to "put things right", or tactics for undoing or averting perceived catastrophes (Rachman, 1997), such as counter images, counting or praying sequences, ritualized internal dialogue, and reassurance seeking. For example, the person who misinterprets sexual images as evidence for immorality may neutralize via praying sequences, and the person who misinterprets violent imagery as evidence for dangerousness may neutralize via counter images of sainthood. Attempts to control intrusive thoughts by neutralizing are assumed to increase their salience and persistence because neutralizing is another form of suppression. Also, neutralizing is hypothesized to increase preoccupation with intrusions, prevent discovery that feared outcomes do not occur, temporarily alleviate negative affect and therefore become an instrumental reinforcer, and increase the salience of such intrusions and their priority for processing (Salkovskis, 1985). The temporary reduction in distress was demonstrated by Rachman, Shafran, Mitchell, Trant, and Teachman (1996) who asked healthy controls to think "I hope ____ is in a car accident" (inserting the name of a friend or relative). Then, participants either did whatever they wanted to neutralize or cancel the effects of the sentence, or were delayed from neutralization for 20 minutes by reading a magazine. Neutralization resulted in prompt anxiety reduction compared with delay, although anxiety eventually declined in the latter condition too. Also, Salkovskis *et al.* (1997) selected individuals who reported frequent intrusive thoughts and tendencies to neutralize. Then, while listening to audio-taped presentations of their intrusive thoughts, they either

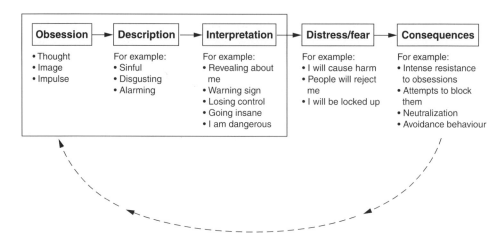

Figure 7.3: The postulated sequence of descriptions, interpretations, and actions. (Redrawn by permission of Elsevier from Rachman (1997).)

distracted (i.e., counted backward mentally) or neutralized every time they heard the thought. Subsequent responses to audio-taped presentations were evaluated. As predicted, the group that neutralized experienced more discomfort when re-exposed to the same thought, and stronger urges to neutralize and distract during re-exposure. These effects were recently replicated in a sample of patients with obsessive–compulsive disorder (Salkovskis, Thorpe, Wahl, Wroe, & Forrester, 2003 in press).

Finally, avoidance of stimuli associated with obsessional content (e.g., avoidance of sharp objects for the person who fears harming someone else), like neutralizing, contributes to the maintenance of obsessions by preventing discovery that feared outcomes do not occur. The self-perpetuating nature of attempts to control intrusive thoughts is depicted by Rachman (1997) (Figure 7.3).

Summary

The tendency to react negatively to intrusive thoughts or images may be critical to the transition from occasional intrusive thoughts to obsessive–compulsive problems, at least in adults. Negative reactions are characterized by attempts to control unwanted thoughts, images, or impulses, which in turn have been linked with appraisals of unwanted thoughts as being representative of something bad that has happened or could happen in the future. Hence, the threat value of unwanted mental processes is elevated. The types of life experiences and biological propensities that increase the salience and threat value of unwanted thoughts and images, which tend to occur commonly in the population at large, are largely untested. However, religiosity appears to relate to obsessiveness, and may exemplify learning histories that increase the threat value of negative thoughts and images. Similarly, early critical learning incidents in which catastrophes or near catastrophes were attributed to coincidental thinking are speculated to increase the threat value of such internal mental processes. Much research attention has been directed at possible biological markers of obsessive–compulsive disorder. Although studies of neuroanatomy are mixed, and studies of neuropsychological functioning are often confounded by the effects of excessive self-doubt, tasks of directed forgetting and negative priming point to a potential biological propensity to repetitive thought connected with difficulty inhibiting cognitive input. Such inhibition may contribute to the salience of intrusive material. However, the data are cross-sectional and do not indicate a contributory role. Moreover, such broad-based deficits in inhibition alone are insufficient explanations for obsessions given that they do not explain their selective nature — why some thoughts or images become repetitive and others do not.

Once anxiety is clearly associated with intrusive thoughts, images, or impulses, distress appears to be maintained by ongoing efforts to avoid the unwanted material, and continuing misappraisal of their meaning. Moreover, attempts at thought suppression, and presumably other forms of avoidance as well, are believed to enhance vigilance for unwanted mental processes. In general, this model is more applicable to adult-onset obsessive–compulsive disorder, where the role of intrusive mental processes is much more prominent than is true of childhood-onset obsessive–compulsive disorder. The latter is potentially more closely linked with negative affectivity and a maladaptive attempt to cope with high negative affect, although this possibility remains speculative and without empirical support.

Specific Phobias

Salience and Threat Value of Anxiety and Bodily Sensations

Specific phobias refer to fears and avoidance of circumscribed objects or situations. These stimuli tend to fall into clusters that vary in terms of age of onset (Curtis, Hill & Lewis, 1998; Öst, 1987), rates of co-occurrence with other disorders (Himle, McPhee, Cameron, & Curtis, 1989), pathways to fear acquisition (Himle, Crystal, Curtis, & Fluent, 1991), response profiles (Craske, Zarate, Burton, & Barlow, 1993), familial aggregation data (Himle *et al.*, 1989), and genetic variance data (Kendler *et al.*, 1993). Consequently, blood/injury/injection phobias, animal phobias, natural environment phobias (storms, water, heights), and situational phobias (closed-in places, tunnels, bridges, and public transportation) are now recognized as distinct types of specific phobias.

Situational phobias, particularly claustrophobia, overlap with panic disorder and agoraphobia (Craske *et al.*, 1993). That is, panic attacks are common in individuals with claustrophobia when they confront enclosed places (e.g., Rachman, Levitt, & Lopatka, 1988), as are fears of suffocation and entrapment (Rachman *et al.*, 1988; Rachman & Taylor, 1993), as well as fears of loss of control (Febbraro & Clum, 1995), both of which are common to panic disorder. In fact, entrapment, suffocation, and loss of control are considered to be core cognitions for claustrophobia because their modification accounts for significant fear reduction (Shafran *et al.*, 1993). In addition, individuals who fear enclosed places have higher anxiety sensitivity and stronger fears of bodily sensations, independent of the phobic context, than individuals who fear animals (Craske & Sipsas, 1992). Driving phobias, another type of situational specific phobia, are strongly connected to panic attacks as well. Ehlers *et al.* (1994) found that 81 percent of a group of 56 individuals with driving phobias had experienced panic attacks, and 65 percent ranked panic attacks as one of the three most important reasons for their driving fear. We also found that, like panic disorder and phobias of enclosed places, phobias of driving were characterized by strong "fear of fear" (Craske *et al.*, 1993). Fears of heights correlate with tendencies to misinterpret bodily sensations as dangerous also (Davey, Menzies, & Gallardo, 1997). Thus, experiences that render bodily sensations more salient and more threatening may contribute to situational phobias and some natural environment phobias (i.e., heights) as well. Unfortunately, all of the evidence to date is cross-sectional, and there is no longitudinal evidence to support the contributory role of the elevated threat value of bodily sensations to the development of situational phobias. Nor have there been studies of the *types* of life experiences and biological propensities that may influence the salience and threat value of bodily sensations as they pertain to the eventual development of situational phobias, although it is conceivable that some of the same factors that have been proposed for panic disorder may apply to situational phobias as well (e.g., illnesses). Of course, as reviewed in Chapter 6, it is also possible for specific phobias to emerge following an intense aversive experience, such as a panic attack or any other direct intense trauma (such as a car accident). Thus, a history of experiences that elevate the salience and threat value for bodily sensations may not be necessary for the onset of situational phobias.

Individuals who are phobic of animals show less "fear of fear" than individuals who are claustrophobic (Craske *et al.*, 1993). Verburg, Griez and Meijer (1994) compared individuals with animal phobias, situational or natural environment phobias, and non-anxious controls in response to carbon dioxide inhalations (seven breaths of 35 percent carbon dioxide). Animal-phobic individuals did not differ from non-anxious controls, whereas situational or natural-environment-phobic individuals showed greater increases in anxiety and a trend toward more panic symptoms than non-anxious controls. On the other hand, animal phobias are not completely devoid of anxiety expectancy or anxiety sensitivity. For example, severe animal-phobic individuals are concerned about panicking or losing control (McNally & Steketee, 1985). Furthermore, overestimation of the amount of fear to be experienced when faced with one's phobic stimulus is characteristic of animal-phobic individuals as well as claustrophobic individuals, and is believed to maintain phobic anxiety and avoidance (e.g., Rachman, 1994).

Salience and Threat Value of Disease

Certain animal phobias and phobias of blood, injury, and injection may be tied to disgust sensitivity or heightened rejection of potential contaminants (Davey, Forster,

& Mayhew, 1993). A series of studies provides some support for this hypothesis. For example, measures of disgust and contamination sensitivity correlate with fear of animals, and particularly animals that are fear-relevant but harmless (e.g., rats, spiders, cockroaches, maggots, and snakes) whereas animals that are considered predatory and likely to attack (e.g., shark, tiger, lion, bear) do not correlate with this dimension (Matchett & Davey, 1991). Video presentations that evoke emotions of disgust increase fear of the first type of animal while videos of violence increase fear of the second type of animal (Webb & Davey, 1992). Davey *et al.* (1993) proposed that the relationship between certain animals and disgust sensitivity represents a disease avoidance process that is evolutionarily tied to the prevention of transmission of disease. Furthermore, they suggested that some animals acquire their disgust-evoking status by directly spreading disease and therefore being a source of contamination (e.g., rats), by contingent association with contamination or dirt (e.g., cockroaches or spiders), and by possessing features which naturally elicit disgust such as those which resemble feces or mucus (slugs, or slimy-appearing snakes). In contrast to conditioning models that attribute phobic responding to aversive experiences with a *given* animal, disgust sensitivity implies that large classes of animals are feared, and that this is transmitted culturally rather than by direct aversive experience. Davey *et al.* (1993) refer to the work of Rozin and Fallon (1987) to outline the ways in which disgust is transmitted. Thus (Davey *et al.*, 1993, p. 48):

> At an early age, the transmission of disgust may be mediated by the facial or verbal expression of disgust in relation to a disgusting object. This may occur as a result of the disgust reaction in the parent eliciting a similar reaction in the offspring ... or merely by enabling the offspring to identify disgusting objects through social referencing .... Eventually, as the offspring learns to associate more and more specific objects with disgust, this enables them to develop a cognitive schema for disgust and contamination by establishing that disgust is related to certain general properties (e.g., mucosity, decayed material, etc.). Hence, levels of disgust and contamination sensitivity in the offspring will be determined by the range and nature of the objects to which the parents exhibit disgust reactions.

Davey *et al.* (1993) found the predicted relationship between parental disgust sensitivity and offspring fears of animals known to be associated with disgust, albeit in a small sample.

The notion of disgust sensitivity has been extended to blood, injury, and injection phobias. Rachman (1990) argued that blood-phobic individuals are more likely to experience disgust, nausea, or repulsion than fear. Disgust was certainly more present in the facial expressions of phobic individuals as they observed scenes of surgeries than for control subjects (Lumley & Melamed, 1992). Others have failed to replicate the significance of disgust in fear responding (Thorpe & Salkovskis, 1995), and suggest that disgust may have little relevance to phobias in general, and may become amplified only in relation to stimuli normally associated with disgust. For example, Thorpe and Salkovskis (1998) found that although animal-phobic individuals had disgust-related beliefs about their phobic objects, measures of global disgust sensitivity were not closely linked to the phobic response and did not influence attentional biases toward phobia-relevant stimuli. In another study of reactivity to pictures of surgical operations, spiders, other contaminants, and neutral stimuli, analog spider-phobic individuals rated spider stimuli as more fear- than disgust-provoking, whereas analog blood-, injury-, and injection-phobic individuals rated surgical operations as more disgust- than fear-provoking. Also, both groups rated other non-fear-related contaminants as more disgusting than did a non-phobic control group (Sawchuk, Lohr, Westendorf, Meunier, & Tolin, 2002). Thus, like Thorpe and Salkovskis (1995), Sawchuk *et al.* suggest that disgust sensitivity may be elevated in general by phobic states but is not primary in relation to spider phobias. On the other hand, disgust may play a more central role for blood, injury and injection phobias, given their earlier finding that blood-, injury-, and injection-phobic individuals scored higher on a scale of contamination fears than spider-phobic individuals, and contamination fear scores correlated with blood phobia measures but not with spider phobia measures (Sawchuk, Lohr, Tolin, Lee, & Kleinknecht, 2000).

Salience and Threat Value of Blood, Injury, and Injections

Most phobic individuals experience increased autonomic activation as they approach their phobic stimulus (although, in contrast to the more pervasive anxiety disorders, circumscribed phobias are less likely to exhibit elevated anticipatory responding to stressors in general). For example, relative to a laboratory resting heart rate, driving-phobic individuals had a significantly increased heart rate during a standardized drive in comparison with control participants (Sartory, Roth, & Kopell, 1992). Also, McNeil *et al.* (1993) found stronger heart rate and skin conductance responses to imagery of phobic scenarios among dental-phobic individuals in comparison with control participants. A unique physiological difference occurs with respect to blood, injury, and injection phobias that is characterized by a bi-phasic physiological response of sympathetic arousal followed quickly by parasympathetic hypotension and bradycardia that results in faintness and actual fainting (e.g., Öst, Sterner, & Lindahl, 1984). The vulnerability to fainting is attributed to more vagal control and less sympathetic modulation of cardiac response than occurs for other anxiety disorders, such as panic disorder (Friedman *et al.*, 1993). Interestingly, individuals who faint in response to blood, needles, or injury exhibit a normal psychophysiological response when exposed to other fear-inducing situations (Hoehn-Saric & McLeod, 1988). Hence, a stimulus specificity of the vagal response is apparent. Some discordance has been observed between reports of faintness and objective indices of blood pressure. Lumley and Melamed (1992), for example, found that many blood-phobic individuals reported increased faintness at the same time that their blood pressures elevated. Nevertheless, overall, fainting is much more common in blood, injury, and injection phobias than other phobias or anxiety disorders. A physiological propensity to fainting may increase the salience of blood, injury, and injection cues, and interact with disgust sensitivity or independently contribute to phobic responding. This is not to suggest, however, that proneness to fainting is a necessary precursor to blood, injury, and injection phobias. Panic attacks or severe pain during medical procedures, for example, may be sufficient to engender a phobic response independent of other vulnerabilities.

Salience and Threat Value for Other Phobic Stimuli

There is little reason to believe that the remaining circumscribed phobias, of predatory-type animals and natural environment stimuli, such as the dark, thunder, lightning, and water, are related to particular propensities that elevate the threat value of such stimuli. It is conceivable that some of these fears represent developmentally appropriate fears that have not habituated, in accord with non-associative principles, for reasons of being highly prone to anxiousness (see Chapter 6). The typical childhood onset of phobias of animals, storms, and water is consistent with a non-associative hypothesis, whereas situational phobias tend to develop throughout adolescence and early adulthood, and blood, injury, and injection phobias tend to emerge during later childhood and adolescence (Craske *et al.*, 1996). On the other hand, there is no evidence to date that specific phobias of the natural environment are associated with more pervasive anxiousness than other phobias, as would be expected if they were fueled by higher loadings on broad vulnerability factors. Moreover, the non-associative hypothesis does not negate the possibility of associative learning events (via direct conditioning, vicarious, or informational acquisition) for animal phobias and natural environment phobias.

Maintaining Influences

The maintenance of phobic anxiety appears to reside in vigilance and associated physiology, danger-laden beliefs, and avoidance behavior — or, as defined throughout, a threat-based style of emotion regulation. The role of avoidance behavior in maintaining phobic fear has been referenced already, and is generally presumed to minimize fear reduction processes that come about with sustained interaction with the object of fear, through habituation, extinction, or cognitive reprocessing (e.g., Foa & Kozak, 1986); in other words, avoidance is assumed to sustain the salience and threat value of whatever it is that is being avoided.

   The evidence for attentional vigilance and associative supportive physiology was reviewed in Chapter 5, and extends from modified Stroop and dot probe performance tasks of attention to measures of central nervous system reactivity to visual presentations of phobic stimuli. In contrast to some of the other anxiety disorders, these processes tend to be more circumscribed to presentations of phobic stimuli. Similarly, potentiation of startle is recorded in the presence of phobic stimuli but does not generalize to anticipatory or contextual cues as much as occurs for other anxiety disorders (Grillon, 2002a). These results are interpreted as evidence for less generalized anxiety in specific phobias compared with other anxiety disorders, perhaps due to a lower loading on broad vulnerability factors (Mineka *et al.*, 1998) as already mentioned. Moreover, by virtue of being circumscribed, specific phobic stimuli tend to be more predictable and controllable compared with other stimuli, such that the anxious process itself generates less distress than is usually the case (see the section on panic disorder above).

   As predicted originally by Beck, Emery, and Greenberg (1985), several studies illustrate a pivotal role for danger-laden appraisals in specific phobias. These appraisals can be categorized as perceived dangers of the stimulus and of one's own reaction to the stimulus (Craske *et al.*, 1993). Hence, acrophobic individuals overestimate the danger inherent in heights relative to controls (Menzies & Clarke, 1995a). Their estimates of danger increase more dramatically upon entering the phobic situation as well (Menzies & Clarke, 1995a), although other studies fail to demonstrate this proximity function (e.g., Andrews, Freed, & Teeson, 1994). In addition, individuals with specific phobias overestimate the likelihood of negative outcomes in relation to their feared stimuli in a series of studies of covariation bias described in an earlier chapter (e.g., Tomarken *et al.*, 1989). Moreover, the intensity of spider fear relates to the strength of conviction in beliefs to do with harm and coping (Thorpe & Salkovskis, 1995). DiNardo *et al.* (1988) found that expectation of harm was more important than aversive experience *per se* in the maintenance of fears of dogs. Furthermore, catastrophizing thoughts were the strongest predictor of avoidance behavior in a group of acrophobic individuals (Marshall, Bristol, & Barbaree, 1992).

The latter finding was in direct contrast to an earlier report by Williams and Watson (1985) that irrational thinking was a weak predictor of acrophobic avoidance behavior. Marshall *et al.* (1992) criticized their limited method for measuring cognitions, asking only about likelihood of falling instead of analyzing thought content in full. Nevertheless, other studies by Williams and colleagues in which cognitions are assessed more broadly similarly illustrate that cognitions of danger are weak predictors of avoidance behavior (e.g., Williams, Kinney, & Falbo, 1989; Williams, Turner, & Peer, 1985). Instead of danger appraisals, they have shown the importance of self-efficacy judgments. Self-efficacy refers to confidence in one's ability to accomplish a given task (Bandura, 1977). A large literature on self-efficacy and specific phobias, beginning with Bandura, Adams, and Beyers in 1977, consistently shows a strong correlation between self-efficacy and actual *phobic behavior* (e.g., Bandura & Adams, 1977; Bandura, Reese, & Adams, 1982; Emmelkamp & Felten, 1985). In fact, self-efficacy explains one-third to three-quarters of the variance in phobic behavior (Williams, 1992), and is a much stronger predictor of avoidance behavior than estimates of danger or of anxiety (e.g., Williams, Dooseman, & Kleifield, 1984; Williams *et al.*, 1989, 1985; Williams & Rappaport, 1983; Williams & Watson, 1985).

Clearly, then, there is an abundance of evidence for phobic fear and behavior to correlate with conscious appraisals of danger, expectations of fear, or lowered self-efficacy. How can these data be reconciled with notions of emotional learning that is outside the control of conscious intentions and evaluations (Öhman & Mineka, 2001; Soares & Öhman, 1993a)? Are such conscious appraisals secondary to phobic fear — merely *post hoc* tendencies to rationalize fear reactions? Very relevant to this issue is a carefully conducted study by Williams *et al.* (1997). Although their phobic sample was comprised of agoraphobic individuals, the findings may well generalize to other phobic responding. They found a general absence of danger appraisals or expectations of anxiety or panic as agoraphobic individuals confronted their most feared driving and claustrophobic situations, replicating previous findings with more limited methodologies (Kenardy, Oei, Weir, & Evans, 1993; Last, Barlow, & O'Brien, 1985). In other words, at the height of fear, conscious appraisals of danger were minimal. In contrast, data regarding danger appraisals typically are gathered from self-report scales in anticipation of a phobic stimulus, or during exposure to mildly intense phobic stimuli, or during post-exposure contemplation. In all cases, self-ratings are made under conditions of potential threat as opposed to very imminent threat. As outlined in Chapter 2, the state of potential threat and worry is likely to involve more complex cognitive processing than is the emotion of fear in response to imminent threat; a conclusion that is supported by the higher cortical versus lower brain stem pathways that have been connected with each state, respectively. Thus, patients in the study by Williams *et al.* (1997) rated high estimates of danger before and after their actual confrontation with "scary tasks", despite the absence of danger appraisals during the encounter. Such anticipatory cognitions certainly contribute to ongoing distress and decisions to avoid future encounters, and therefore contribute to the maintenance of phobias, although they may not be very influential in the midst of intense fear.

Summary

As reviewed in Chapter 6, fears of circumscribed objects or situations are explainable by a history of traumatic, vicarious, or informational experiences that have occurred in relation to that stimulus. Non-associative processes may contribute to the persistence of developmentally appropriate fears, but there is no empirical evidence. In general, broad vulnerability factors of negative affectivity and a threat-based style of emotion regulation may be less relevant to the onset of circumscribed phobias than to other anxiety disorders, but may still play a contributory role given the evidence reviewed in Chapter 6, for them to amplify the impact of traumatic, vicarious, and informational pathways to fear acquisition.

A history of experiences that elevate the salience and threat value of bodily sensations may contribute to the onset of situational phobias and possibly acrophobia, although the research remains cross-sectional, and there is no reason to assume that such historical features are a prerequisite. A traumatic car accident or fall may be sufficient to generate phobic responding independent of the threat value of bodily sensations. A connection possibly exists between sensitivity to disgust or contamination sensitivity and fears of blood, injury, and injection, although the data are preliminary, and, again, such sensitivities are not presumed necessary. Observing significant others display obvious distress around blood or slimy animals may be sufficient to generate phobic responding. Proneness to fainting appears to be specific to blood, injection, and injury phobias, and may indeed contribute to the salience of medical type stimuli. The remaining classes of phobias, animals and the natural environment, could conceivably fall into the category of non-associative fears that fail to habituate, especially given their early age of onset. However, traumatic, vicarious, or informational pathways may equally well explain their onset, and these pathways are more empirically supported.

Maintaining influences involve the primary elements of a threat-based style of emotion regulation — attentional vigilance and physiology (although possibly moderated by the relative predictability and controllability of circumscribed phobic stimuli), danger-laden beliefs (although most operative in anticipation of or in reflection about phobic stimuli rather than at the height of phobic fear), and avoidance behavior.

Generalized Anxiety Disorder

As described in previous chapters, generalized anxiety disorder is the disorder for which fear cues are the least circumscribed, or the most diffuse, and the disorder that loads most highly on neuroticism (Mineka *et al.*, 1998). High negative affectivity, especially when combined with a threat-based style of emotional regulation, generates a broad net of threat and pervasive anxious processes that lead to continuous detection and interpretation of potential threats. One consequence of such diffuse and apparently uncontrollable negative reactivity across a broad array of unpredictable situations may be self-representation as permanently anxious and "out of control" (Chorpita, 2001). In fact, the central domain of threat for generalized anxiety disorder may be negative affectivity itself and its meaning for sense of self. Specifically, excessive negative affectivity erodes perceived self-competency in managing life effectively. In a self-perpetuating cycle, excessive negative affectivity is viewed as evidence of personal ineffectiveness, which in turn generates more distress and negative affectivity. The threat to personal effectiveness potentially explains the overlap in symptom patterns for generalized anxiety disorder and major depression/dysthymia.

The Broad Net of Threat

The notion of a broad net of threat is substantiated by various theories and data sets. Borkovec (1994) attributes the origins of excessive worry to a tendency to misperceive future events as catastrophic and to misperceive future catastrophes with a high likelihood of occurrence. Similarly, Eysenck (1992) attributes dysfunctional worry, which he calls hypervigilance, to tendencies to overestimate probabilities of aversive events, their imminence, their aversiveness, and a perceived inability to control them. Notice that in both cases the reference is to aversive events in general rather than specific classes of aversive stimuli.

Extensive research, reviewed in Chapter 5, demonstrates that over-readiness to perceive threat is a core characteristic of general anxiety. For example, high-trait-anxious individuals as well as individuals diagnosed with generalized anxiety disorder show an attentional bias toward threatening information, as measured via a slowed response latency to color naming of threat words in modified Stroop paradigms (e.g., Mathews & MacLeod, 1985; Mathews, Mogg, Kentish, & Eysenck, 1995; Mogg *et al.*, 1989), faster reaction times to detect probes that follow threat words versus neutral words in visual probe detection tasks (e.g., MacLeod *et al.*, 1986), and impaired tracking of a neutral stimulus when threatening information is conveyed auditorally in dichotic listening tasks (e.g., Mathews & MacLeod, 1986). Thus, various cognitive tests suggest that anxiousness is associated with diversion of attention toward threatening material, even when the material is not consciously perceived (e.g., Mogg *et al*., 1993b). Also, as reviewed earlier, such diversion appears to be determined by the threat value of stimuli (Mogg *et al*., 2000b). Thus, individuals with generalized anxiety disorder appear to assign higher threat value to an array of stimuli in comparison with controls.

Consistent with this possibility is the evidence for a negative bias in judgments regarding the likelihood and meaning of negative events. That is, as reviewed in Chapter 5, individuals with high trait anxiety tend to inflate the risk of negative events, particularly under state-anxious conditions (Butler & Mathews, 1983), and overestimate the association between negative events and neutral stimuli (Chan & Lovibond, 1996; Lovibond & Chan, 1990). Individuals with high trait anxiety or generalized anxiety disorder also tend to interpret ambiguous events as threatening (Eysenck, MacLeod, & Mathews, 1987; Eysenck *et al*., 1991; Mathews *et al*., 1989b). More recently, we demonstrated such a bias in an analog generalized anxiety disorder group as they articulated their thoughts in an ongoing format to ambigious scenarios pertaining to social situations and academic performance (Sachs, Davison, & Craske, 2003 in press).

Worry about Worry

Recently, emphasis has been given to metacognitions about worry. Davey, Tallis, and Capuzzo (1996) isolated five factors for perceived consequences of worrying: three negative (worry disrupts effective performance, exaggerates the problem, and causes emotional distress) and two positive (worry motivates and helps analytical thinking). Interestingly, both negative and positive factors accounted for variance in measures of psychopathology. Hence, dysfunctional beliefs not only about the negative consequences but also about the positive consequences of worrying may contribute to excessiveness of worry. Positive consequences include superstitious beliefs ("worrying about an event makes it less likely that it will occur"), or beliefs that worry anticipates future events ("worrying makes me reflect on life by asking questions that I might not usually ask when happy"), which may encourage attribution of eventual non-occurrence of anticipated catastrophes to worry activity. Cartwright-Hatton and Wells (1997) developed a self-report scale of positive and negative consequences of worry. Although small samples of patients with generalized anxiety disorder were not distinguishable from patients with obsessive–compulsive disorder on either dimension (Cartwright-Hatton & Wells, 1997), individuals with generalized anxiety disorder held stronger negative beliefs but not stronger positive beliefs about worry in comparison with individuals with panic disorder, individuals with social phobia, and controls in a subsequent larger study (Wells & Carter, 2001). Hence, negative metacognitions about worry may be more unique to generalized anxiety disorder than are positive metacognitions.

Wells and Mathews (1994) proposed that negative metacognitions about worry, such as "worrying could make me go crazy" or "worrying is abnormal", give rise to worry about worry, which in turn leads to attempts to suppress worrying. Such attempts increase the salience of worry-related activity, and prevent disconfirmation of beliefs concerning the dangers of worrying, or maintain its threat value (Wells, 1995). In an elaboration of their model, Wells and Carter (2001) proposed that given positive metacognitive beliefs about worry, individuals with generalized anxiety disorder are presumed to use worry as a way of coping with their wide array of potential threat. This is referred to as type 1 worry, which again may not differentiate generalized anxiety disorder from other anxiety disorders. The worrying continues until it is displaced by goals that compete for attention or until it is safe to stop worrying — a felt sense or knowing that all possibilities have been contemplated. However, negative metacognitive beliefs, or negative appraisal of worry, become central to the excessiveness of worry in generalized anxiety disorder. The latter is referred to as type 2 worry, and involves worry about the uncontrollability and dangerousness of worry for physical and mental well-being. Consistent with the findings already reported, type 2 worry is a stronger predictor of pathological worry that is type 1 worry (Wells & Carter, 1999). Type 2 worry is hypothesized to elicit such intense anxiety that it is difficult to attain the internal state that signals that worry can cease — the felt sense of knowing. In addition, worry may interfere with effective problem-solving, and, by generating negative scenarios, trigger more worry. Worry may also lead to intrusive thoughts, which in turn are viewed as a sign of loss of control. One way of interrupting this cycle is to engage in behaviors intended to avert the need to worry, such as avoidance of news or reassurance seeking. However, as with all avoidant strategies, these behaviors can worsen the cycle. For example, reassurance seeking can lead to conflicting information and more uncertainty. Also, avoidance interferes with gathering disconfirming information or practice of non-worry-based coping. There may also be attempts to suppress or remove from consciousness thoughts that may trigger worry, but such suppression is rarely effective.

As already mentioned, type 2 negative metacognitions may be parsimoniously attributed to high levels of negative affectivity and a threat-based style of emotion regulation that results in the expression of unpredictable and uncontrollable negative affect across a broad array of situations. In earlier work, we established that typical worry episodes were rated by individuals with generalized anxiety disorder as more uncontrollable than by healthy controls (Craske, Rapee, Jackel, & Barlow, 1989). We recently replicated these findings in a comparison of individuals with generalized anxiety disorder to those with subclinical features of generalized anxiety disorder (Craske, 2002). In addition, a certain amount of worry is experienced as unpredictable or as occurring for no apparent reason. Unpredictability of worry is reported more often by patients with generalized anxiety disorder than healthy controls when they monitor their typical worries (Craske *et al.*, 1989): 36 percent of generalized anxiety disorder patients versus 11.8 percent of controls endorsed "unprecipitated" worries. Similarly, in our recent work, individuals with generalized anxiety disorder reported higher rates of unprecipitated worry than those with subclinical features of generalized anxiety disorder (Craske, 2002).

As noted in previous chapters, unpredictable and uncontrollable aversive events (of which negative affect itself is one example) are generally distressing, particularly when aversive events are awarded high threat value, as would be the case when anxiety and worry are viewed as evidence for personal ineffectiveness. The ever-widening set of threat cues and the unpredictability and uncontrollability of anxious responding that characterizes high levels of negative affectivity generates the inevitable perception of not being in control of one's own emotions. According to Chorpita's (2001) developmental model of overanxiousness in youths, this may lead to the attribution of anxious responding to an invariant aspect of oneself — "I am permanently anxious" or "I am incompetent" — which in turn contributes to anxious responding. Thus, children who view themselves as anxious, given their negative reactivity to a wide variety of potentially threatening cues and inability to cope, may view this trait as stable, and be more likely to perceive themselves as unable to control their own fearful reactions. The development of effective skills for managing negative affect, particularly as modeled or transmitted by parental figures, would presumably be essential to offset such a negative cycle. Lonigan and Phillips (2001) similarly emphasize that negative affectivity and a broad-based attention to threatening aspects of the world may lead to a self-representation of incompetence that contributes to more generalized and stable anxious responding. Trust in oneself to manage in the world, to make decisions, and to fulfill responsibilities effectively is severely threatened by extreme, unpredictable negative affect.

Personal Ineffectiveness

Various pieces of evidence point to an eroded sense of personal effectiveness in generalized anxiety disorder, including ratings of confidence, analysis of common themes in catastrophizing cycles, evidence requirements for decision-making, and sources of iteration in catastrophizing. Questionnaire studies show that the tendency to worry excessively is associated with lack of confidence in problem-solving and avoidance coping (Davey, 1993, 1994; Davey *et al.*, 1992; Dugas, Letarte, Rhéaume, Freeston, & Ladouceur, 1995; Ladouceur, Blais, Freeston, & Dugas, 1998). Importantly, Davey *et al.* (1992) attributes this effect to high trait anxiety rather than worry *per se*; once trait anxiety is statistically controlled, worry is associated with more constructive features such as problem-focused coping and information seeking. Thus, Davey *et al.* (1992) speculated that high trait anxiety prevents acceptance of solutions generated by the act of worrying, because high trait anxiety generates poor problem-solving confidence, perceived lack of control over problem-solving, and catastrophizing tendencies. In the model presented herein, high trait anxiety as a lower-order trait of negative affectivity generates unpredictable and uncontrollable anxiety, and it is that which threatens self-competency and lowers self-confidence.

Others have also posited that chronic worry reflects a sense of personal incompetence (Kendall & Ingram, 1987). In support, worriers often couch their worries in terms of personal ineptness (Davey & Levey, 1998). Vasey and Borkovec (1992) conducted content analyses on all steps from "catastrophizing" interviews in which participants were asked to state all the negative consequences of areas of worry (e.g., "If I received a negative evaluation at work, then ..."). Worriers generated proportionally more "failure/ineffectiveness" content than non-worriers. These results were consistent with a follow-up study by Davey and Levy (1998), in which trait worry scores correlated positively with both the number of catastrophizing steps generated and independent judges' ratings of the content as "feelings of personal inadequacy". We replicated this finding in our study of content of catastrophizing across six different domain areas of threat among controls and analog generalized anxiety disorder samples (Hazlett-Stevens & Craske, 2003 in press). Responses were coded by blind raters into content categories. Not only did the worriers generate more catastrophizing steps, but "negative emotion" and "personal failure" were the most frequently coded categories in each of the six domains for the analog-generalized anxiety disorder group. Moreover, the analog-generalized anxiety disorder group was independently rated as more often worrying about personal failure.

Thus, a sense of personal inadequacy may be integral to persistent catastrophizing. In an experimental manipulation, Davey, Jubb, and Cameron (1996) provided false feedback regarding proposed solutions to real-life problem scenarios. Those whose feedback suggested poor performance had increased anxiety and stronger tendencies to catastrophize a personal worry, generating more bad outcomes and defining a problem as progressively worsening, in comparison with those whose feedback bolstered confidence in problem-solving. The authors suggested that poor problem-solving confidence may facilitate catastrophizing by preventing effective closure of the catastrophizing process (Davey *et al.*, 1996a) whereas negative mood contributes to catastrophizing by facilitating access to mood-congruent information that is counterproductive to problem-solving (Vasey & Borkovec, 1992). In support, Johnston and Davey (1997) found that exposure to negative news reports increased negative mood and personal catastrophizing relative to neutral or positive news reports.

Perceived personal inadequacy may explain two other sets of findings, the first one being elevated evidence requirements. Tallis, Eysenck, and Mathews (1991) suggested that worriers experience delays in problem-solving decisions and thus perseverance of the worry state due to elevated evidence requirements for making decisions. The evidence to date rests on findings that induced worry slows response times to ambiguous concept categorization tasks and delays decision-making in stimulus categorization (Metzger, Miller, Cohen, Sofka, & Borkovec, 1990; Tallis *et al.*, 1991). Elevated evidence requirements may arise from lower perceived competency in decision-making.

Second, personal ineffectiveness may explain the iterative style in worrying. Johnston and Davey (1997) found that induced negative mood resulted in a tendency to persist in generating catastrophizing steps, as did experimentally reduced problem-solving confidence (Davey *et al.*, 1996a). In a series of six studies, Davey and Levy (1998) established that the persistent catastrophizing style transferred to hypothetical situations, and that the general iterative style was equally likely to persist in elucidating what was good as well as what was bad about a topic. Startup and Davey (2001) expanded on these findings to show that negative mood induction resulted in more iteration on a positive topic (i.e., "What is good about being the Statue of Liberty?") as would be expected according to a "mood as input" rule of functioning. That is (Startup & Davey, 2001, p. 87), negative mood will influence judgments about whether the individual believes he or she satisfactorily completed the task. Thus, negative mood induction provides the individual with information that the task may not yet be satisfactorily completed, which would result in perseveration regardless of the valence of the iterative task.

In the terms proposed by Wells and Carter, negative mood interferes with the felt sense of knowing, and therefore worrying continues. A related rule of generate "as many as you can" before stopping may be motivated by the notion that worrying is a necessary process for preventing negative events from happening. Thus, as Startup and Davey (2001, p. 93) state,

> because of their need to be reassured that all aspects of problems have been adequately addressed, worriers will tend to persist at the task until they feel they have adequately considered all of the possible outcomes of the "what if?" questions generated during the catastrophizing process.

It seems reasonable to speculate that a sense of personal inadequacy, which is generated from high levels of unpredictable and uncontrollable negative affect, will contribute to a rule of "as many as you can". By the same token, a limited flexibility in responding to environmental demands, which has been attributed by others to a limited awareness of ongoing environmental contingencies due to engagement in future-oriented worry, may in fact represent a preference for relying on rigid rules for governing behavior because of perceived incompetence and self-doubt in judgments of prevailing conditions (Craske & Hazlett-Stevens, 2002).

In summary, high negative affectivity and a threat-based style of emotion regulation are presumed to lead to a broad net of threat, and unpredictable and uncontrollable anxious responding across a wide array of situations that contributes to a sense of personal ineffectiveness. Such self-judgment is presumed to magnify worry about worry, or negative metacognitions about worry, which in turn may generate attempts to suppress worrying and various other behaviors that contribute to worry in the long term. In addition, alongside negative mood state, a sense of personal inadequacy may contribute to catastrophizing, elevate evidence requirements, and contribute to the iterative style of worrying by motivating the need to generate as many outcomes as possible, all leading to impaired problem-solving and further erosion of self-competency.

Maintaining Influences

The output of chronic worry maintains worry, particularly ongoing catastrophizing and avoidance. As already reviewed, chronic worriers perceive events as more catastrophic, and generate significantly more catastrophizing scenarios for potential problems, even hypothetical problems (such as being the Statue of Liberty) (Davey & Levey, 1998; Vasey & Borkovec, 1992), and more reasons for negative events (Macleod, Williams, & Bekerian, 1991). Vasey and Borkovec (1992) suggest that chronic worriers possess elaborated memory stores for answers to catastrophic questions, and being able to retrieve an answer to "what if..." questions serves to prolong the catastrophic worry sequence. Very telling is the experimental evidence reviewed in Chapter 5 for negative interpretive biases to elevate state anxiety (Mathews & Mackintosh, 2000), thus indicating their contributory role.

Avoidance, as usual, is likely to have a maintaining influence as well, and in addition to attempts to avoid worry or topics that may elicit worry (Wells & Carter, 2001), worry itself may become a form of avoidance. Specifically, worry is not only a way of avoiding unwanted future environmental threats (such as job loss and ill health); it becomes a way of avoiding immediate somatic responses to perceived threat (such as accelerated heart rate and sweating). The notion of avoidance of somatic responses is very much linked with worry being a largely verbal state. The abstract reasoning quality of worry, as reviewed in Chapter 2, is supported by evidence for worriers reporting proportionately less visual and more verbal cognitive processing than non-worriers under relaxing, baseline conditions (Borkovec & Inz, 1990; Meyer, Miller, Metzger, & Borkovec, 1990). Also, the act of worrying for unselected groups is associated with proportionate increases in the amount of verbalizing (e.g., Stober *et al.*, 2000; Wells & Morrison, 1994). Although there are limitations to this research, such as the problems associated with retrospective measurement of time spent worrying or imagining (Wells & Papageorgiou, 1995), the predominance of verbalizing is detected by more behavioral indices of cognitive activity as well (Rapee, 1993).

The possible competition between worry and conceptual reasoning on the one hand, and fear imagery and autonomic arousal on the other hand, was described in Chapter 2. In brief, this proposition stems in large part from experimental work by Lang and colleagues, in which imagery of fearful stimuli (especially imagery that incorporates aspects of the stimulus, response to the stimulus, and meaning of the stimulus) elevates autonomic responding, in comparison with a relative absence of autonomic responding to verbal descriptions of the same material (Lang, 1985; Vrana, Cuthbert, & Lang, 1986). Evidence exists to suggest that worry is in fact associated with suppression of autonomic reactivity (Thayer *et al.*, 2000) and that individuals with generalized anxiety disorder show restricted autonomic reactivity to non-specific stressors (Hoehn-Saric *et al.*, 1989). We extended this finding to suppressed immune response (number of natural killer cells in the blood) to a phobic stimulus in high worriers versus low worriers who were all fearful of spiders (Segerstrom *et al.*, 1999). Also, a preceding interval of worry appears to dampen subsequent physiological responding to imagined fearful stimuli relative to prior intervals of relaxation (Borkovec & Hu, 1990; Borkovec *et al.*, 1993; Peasley-Miklus & Vrana, 2000), and high scorers on a worry questionnaire exhibited less cardiac reactivity to personally fearful imagery than low scorers (Szollos *et al.*, 1990). However, the results are not always positive (e.g., Hazlett-Stevens & Borkovec, 2001).

Closer examination of the nature of autonomic dysregulation shows that worry in generalized anxiety disorder is associated with chronically lowered cardiac vagal tone that dampens autonomic responding. For example, Lyonfields *et al.* (1995) found that individuals with generalized anxiety had less variation in their heart rate (measured via mean successive differences of interbeat interval) than controls at rest. Also, the state of worry was associated with a greater decline in vagal tone than were aversive images, although these effects were mostly evident in non-anxious individuals because the generalized anxiety group tended to show lower levels of vagal tone at the baseline as well as during tasks. Thus, Lyonfields *et al*. (1995) suggest that generalized anxiety disorder individuals are chronically deficient in cardiac vagal tone, consistent with their relatively constant state of worrying. Similarly, Thayer *et al*. (1996) compared the vagal tone of the heart rate in 34 patients with generalized anxiety disorder (in the absence of panic disorder) and 32 non-anxious controls during resting baseline, relaxation, and worry conditions. Again, the generalized anxiety group showed lower cardiac vagal tone across all phases of the experiment, including the baseline, and the act of worrying reduced vagal tone (despite acceleration of respiration rate) in both groups relative to baseline or relaxation conditions. As already reviewed, these findings extend beyond generalized anxiety disorder to panic disorder (e.g., Hoehn-Saric *et al*., 1991; Yeragani *et al*., 1990) and obsessive–compulsive disorder (Hoehn-Saric *et al*., 1995). Moreover, heart rate variability is negatively associated with trait anxiety scores (Yeragani *et al*, 1998), and sometimes, although not always, with depression (e.g., Rechlin *et al*., 1995). Thus, lowered heart rate variability may be a gauge of general negative rumination and distress, perhaps particularly elevated in generalized anxiety disorder due to an overall elevated level of anxiousness. Friedman and Thayer (1998b) present a functional model that integrates systems theory with the principles of non-linear dynamics for explaining the relevance of restricted heart rate variability to the anxiety disorders. In short, the model associates reductions in heart rate variability with behavioral and affective restrictions via the principle of self-similarity; that restrictions occurring at the level of cardiovascular functioning parallel restrictions in affective experiences and behavior due to "symptom avoidance". Thus, again, heart rate variability may index attempts to avoid negative affect. Noteworthy is the link between lowered vagal tone and poor discriminability among external stimuli (see Chapter 4), which in turn is believed to contribute to the generalizability of anxious responding. As described already, Grillon (2002a) outlines the way in which poor contingency awareness in connection with poor orienting to and discrimination among external stimuli impedes differential conditioned responding to discrete threat stimuli and enhances generalized conditioned responding to contextual cues associated with threat. In addition, such effects mimic and are perhaps mediated by the lack of predictability. Under these conditions of limited discrimination and unpredictability of discrete threat cues, avoidance would be an even more likely outcome. As mentioned in Chapter 4, lowered vagal tone may derive from familial influences (such as early synchronicity with parental behaviors and the effects of such synchronicity upon attention) as well as biological propensities. Hence, the tendency to perceive many things as threatening may emerge as a combination of high levels of negative affectivity as well as impaired orienting and attention. Of course, these pathways are as yet to be empirically supported, but they are consistent with the growing body of literature pertaining to attachment styles and interpersonal dysregulation in generalized anxiety disorder (see Borkovec, Newman, Pincus, & Lytle, 2002).

Whatever the underlying contributors, the association between worry and restricted autonomic reactivity has led Borkovec and colleagues (Borkovec, Shadick, & Hopkins, 1991) to suggest that by suppressing imagery and associated autonomic activation, worry inhibits access to, and modification of, underlying fear. In other words, worry becomes a form of avoidance. Consequently, catastrophic images are presumed to continue to emerge periodically, in turn motivating continued cognitive avoidance in the form of worry. Hence, the successful reduction of fearful arousal by worrying negatively reinforces worry activity. As a result of this negative reinforcement cycle, pre-attentive biases toward threat and further catastrophic images, with the associated drive to shift to worry in order to avoid them, are reinforced.

Some limited support exists for this reinforcement cycle. For example, Butler, Wells, and Dewick (1995) showed participants distressing films. In comparison with instructions to form images or to "settle down", worrying about the film reduced anxiety immediately afterward, but increased intrusive images in the following 3 days. Also, Wells and Papageorgiou (1995) exposed students to a gruesome film of an accident, followed by one of five conditions: worry about the film and its implications in a verbal form; image the film and its implications; distraction; worry about usual topics of worry; and "settle down". The first condition resulted in the most intrusive images about the film over the next 3 days. The fact that imaging the film resulted in less subsequent intrusive images was interpreted as more successful emotional processing. However, instructions to imagine the film still yielded more subsequent intrusions than the control condition of "settling down", presumably because the former condition stimulated more tagging of threat-related material with other material in memory, which stimulated retrieval of threat-related material (Wells, 1994), albeit less than the verbal conceptual analysis induced by worrying verbally. However, the key premise of Borkovec's model is yet to be tested: does suppression of catastrophic imagery and associated autonomic arousal by the act of worrying generate further worry?

In addition to suppressing somatic arousal, worry may serve to avoid other more emotional issues (Freeston *et al.*, 1994). Borkovec and Roemer (1995) go so far as to suggest that perhaps worry avoids negative affect associated with memories of past aversive events, such as prior traumatic events or unhappy childhoods. On the other hand, they also recognize that individuals who tend to worry excessively may conclude that they are avoiding more distressing thoughts by worrying in order to make sense of the worry process that is uncontrollable. Furthermore, there is no direct evidence that worriers worry to avoid past traumas.

Summary

In summary, it is posited that high levels of negative affectivity and a threat-based style of emotion regulation creates pervasive, unpredictable, and uncontrollable negative affect, which in turn leads to a sense of lack of personal control over one's own emotions and an assumption of trait invariance of being permanently anxious or out of control. This leads to increasing negative reactivity and a spiraling cycle of pervasive anxiety. The end result is a sense of personal ineffectiveness, or a doubt about one's own competency and decision-making, of which one manifestation is worry about worry. The ongoing experience of worry, panic, and intrusive images repeatedly confirms the sense of personal incompetency, leading to poorer problem-solving and avoidance.

Ongoing perceptions of threat and impaired problem-solving is likely to contribute to excessive worry. Moreover, worry itself may become a form of avoidance, not only of future unwanted events but of intense somatic arousal generated by catastrophic fear imagery. By so doing, worry becomes reinforced, and at the same time prevents possible habituation or correction to fear imagery such that fearful imagery reappears and motivates further worry.

General Summary

Processes in common across the anxiety disorders include vigilance and supportive physiology, danger-laden beliefs, and avoidance behaviors. The anxiety disorders are differentiated primarily by the type of stimuli to which these anxious processes become attached, as well as the role of broad vulnerability factors. That is, there is reason to believe that higher loadings on negative affectivity and perhaps a more pervasive threat-based style of emotion regulation are more likely to manifest as generalized anxiety disorder than specific phobias. In the previous chapter, *ways* in which stimuli become threatening — via conditioning, vicarious acquisition, informational transmission, or lack of habituation to developmentally appropriate fears — were covered. In this chapter, the *content* of experiences that lead to one set of stimuli being awarded higher threat value over other stimuli have been reviewed in relation to each anxiety disorder. In addition, particular biological propensities that may contribute to the salience of classes of stimuli were considered. Notably, whereas negative affectivity raises salience, and a threat-based style of emotion regulation raises the threat value of negative affect and associated *stimuli in general*, certain biological propensities and learning histories raise the salience and threat value of *particular classes of stimuli*. The former are assumed to potentiate but not be necessary for the latter.

Once a particular set of stimuli is sufficiently threatening, their threat value is maintained by the anxious processes of ongoing vigilance and associated physiology, danger-laden beliefs, and avoidance behavior. These take slightly different forms, dependent on the nature of the threat stimulus. Thus, avoidance of negative affect associated with an intrusive thought may involve ritualizing and neutralizing, whereas avoidance of negative affect associated with a social situation may involve submissive behaviors, and avoidance of a circumscribed external stimulus may involve refusal to approach the stimulus. Also, internally generated threat stimuli (images, thoughts, sensations) are likely to elicit more anxious distress overall than externally generated stimuli, due to factors of unpredictability, uncontrollability, and proximity to threat. Moreover, in a reciprocal fashion, anxious processes strengthen higher-order vulnerabilities toward ongoing distress: the greater the vulnerability the more pervasive the anxiety, and the more pervasive the anxiety the greater the vulnerability.

Panic disorder is influenced by high negative affectivity combined with a high threat value assigned to bodily sensations. Anxiety sensitivity, particularly the physical concerns subscale, has been the most directly studied in this regard, and has been found to contribute to the prediction of panic attacks and panic-related worry. The award of high threat value to bodily sensations may derive from histories of medical distress, or parental overprotectiveness and modeling regarding health concerns. In addition, high levels of interoception and possibly individual differences in propensity to peaks of autonomic activation may contribute to the salience and threat value of bodily sensations. Once established as acutely fear-provoking, bodily sensations are likely to continue to elicit distress as a result of cognitive misappraisals of their harmfulness, attentional vigilance to them, and avoidance behaviors. In addition, by virtue of being internally generated, fears of bodily sensations elicit pervasive generalized distress, which in turn contributes to the cycle of panic and panic disorder. Whether panic attacks can be elicited without declarative knowledge of danger is a debated point, but there is considerable evidence for "unconscious" conditioned responding to bodily cues, as is evident with other evolutionarily prepared stimuli.

Histories of conditioning, vicarious acquisition, and informational transmission may contribute to the threat value of social stimuli, although this body of research is not as well developed as that of anxiety sensitivity and panic disorder. High negative affectivity and its manifestation in behavioral inhibition may also contribute to the salience of unfamiliar social stimuli. A physiological propensity to visibly express fear in social situations (e.g., blushing, sweating), which serves an important communication function of defeat, has not been well supported as a contributory factor. The finding that social anxiety disorder has modal ages of onset that coincide with important developmental stages in social development (5 years, upon entering school, and teenage years, upon entering independent peer and romantic relationships) attests to the universally elevated salience of social stimuli at critical times. For vulnerable individuals, these times become even more critical. Maintaining influences most studied in relation to social anxiety disorder include vigilance for the self and, in particular, the view of oneself as a social object, in addition to overly negative beliefs about failure to meet socially expected standards of performance. Presumably, avoidance plays an important role also.

Posttraumatic stress disorder is influenced mostly by the intensity of the trauma *per se* as well as predisposing elements of high negative affectivity, stress sensitization (which parallels the effects of negative affectivity) and avoidant responses to trauma, which appear to enhance the likelihood of subsequent emotional distress, as well as the threat valuation of the event and its meaning for safety in the future. Avoidance and high threat valuation, along with high stress reactivity, may coincide with a tendency for pictorial or sensory memory systems (i.e., flashbacks, nightmares) to dominate without modulation from verbally accessible memory systems. In addition, elevated conditionability to potential threat, even threat unrelated to the original trauma, and/ or elevated physiological sensitization, are likely to support continued distress in victims of trauma. The evidence points to a more "physiologically stressed" state than for other anxiety disorders.

Obsessive–compulsive disorder has been associated with high threat value being awarded to intrusive thoughts and images. Consistent with this position is the growing body of evidence that avoidant or otherwise distressed reactions to intrusive thoughts contribute to their recurrence and development into repetitive obsessions. Negative reactions to intrusive mental content may be associated with life experiences that raise their threat value such as highly religious backgrounds. Similarly, a variety of cultural factors may influence the "importance" of thoughts. Others have suggested that critical incidents of coincidence between intrusive thoughts and actual negative events may contribute to the threat value of intrusive material, although all but religiousity remain very speculative at this point. In addition, the salience of intrusive thoughts/ images may be enhanced by central attentional system failure to inhibit irrelevant information, as shown in cognitive tasks such as directed forgetting and negative priming. Much research on central nervous system function and structure in obsessive–compulsive disorder has been interpreted as evidence for dysregulation of a central inhibiting unit, the caudate nucleus. However, studies to date are fraught with methodological problems, and the results are not fully replicable, and even if such structural or functional dysregulation exists it does not explain the selectivity of obsessional material. It is also noteworthy that this model of sensitivity to intrusive thoughts and images seems less applicable to childhood onset of obsessive–compulsive disorder, which involves considerably less obsessive content than occurs for adults.

The subtypes of specific phobias are influenced by different factors. Situational phobias are connected with elevated threat value for bodily sensations, whereas this is much less the case for animal phobias. Blood, injury, and injection phobias may be primed by disgust sensitivity, although the evidence remains preliminary. On the other hand, a very specific physiological propensity to fainting appears to contribute to the salience and threat value of blood, injury, and injection cues. Other animal phobias and natural environment phobias are possibly tied with non-associative pathways in the form of failures of habituation, although there is no supporting evidence, and associative pathways remain viable. Specific phobias are associated with less distress overall than other anxiety disorders, possibly due to lower loading on broad vulnerability factors and the circumscribed nature of the fear stimuli.

Critical to generalized anxiety disorder is unpredictable and uncontrollable experiences of negative affect in a wide array of situations, generated by high loadings on negative affectivity. This experience may lead to perceptions of being permanently anxious, out of control, and, most importantly, incapable of managing oneself and one's life. The personal incompetency is reinforced by continuing cycles of uncontrollable and excessive worry. In addition, worry may become self-reinforced by its tendency to inhibit the experience of acute fear and associated autonomic arousal.

Chapter 8

Why More Women than Men?

To summarize the origins model thus far, the anxiety disorders are believed to share in common with depressive disorders and other forms of emotional distress a non-specific proneness to negative affectivity. Such negative affectivity is presumed to enhance the salience of fear and anxiety as well as other negative emotions. When combined with a style of responding to negative affect that is characterized by high threat value and avoidance, the proneness to anxiety in particular is enhanced. The higher the loading on negative affectivity and the more pervasive the threat-based style of responding, the greater the chances of becoming anxious over a broader array of stimuli.

Anxiousness is manifested as hypervigilance to sources of threat, a physiology that supports such vigilance, danger-laden judgments, and avoidant behaviors, all of which contribute to ongoing anxiety in a self-perpetuating manner. The classes of stimuli that become most anxiety-producing are selected by the history of traumatic, vicarious, and informational associative experiences that elevate the threat value of particular stimuli, and biological propensities that elevate their salience. Failure to habituate to developmentally appropriate fears may render additional stimuli anxiety-provoking. Associative and non-associative pathways are amplified by vulnerability factors, and the manifestation of anxiety itself may amplify the vulnerability to further distress, especially when it is experienced in an unpredictable or uncontrollable fashion.

As reviewed in Chapter 1, females are at greater risk than males for anxiety disorders as well as depression. The divergence between males and females increases post-puberty, when female propensity intensifies whereas male risk for anxiety as well as depression remains relatively unchanged. Results from longitudinal analyses confirm the hazard rate curves, in that childhood anxiety predicts adolescent anxiety in girls only, and that anxiety is more stable in females than males throughout adolescence and early adulthood. The divergence may progressively widen through later middle-age as well. Closer examination suggests that most sex differentiation occurs not in the propensity to fear *per se* but in the level of anxious and avoidant responding. In this chapter, the parts of the origins model at which greater risk is conferred upon females than males and the social and evolutionary underpinnings of such risk are considered.

Negative Affectivity

Presuming that at least some of the risk for anxiety disorders derives from negative affectivity, one might hypothesize differences between males and females in this regard and that such differences would be apparent from a very young age. Therefore, it is surprising that males exhibit more emotional reactivity than females in the very first few months of life. For example, female newborns, 40–75 hours old, showed signs of less emotional distress in their superior orienting responses and conditioned heart rate decelerations to a 70 dB sine wave (conditioned stimulus) paired with blinking lights (Stamps & Porges, 1975). In an assessment that involves separation from primary caregivers, the Neonatal Behavior Assessment Scale, Davis and Emory (1995) found that infant girls had no change in cortisol levels following the procedures, whereas boys had significant changes from the baseline and higher cortisol levels than girls during and following the procedures. The results are not always consistent, as Gunnar *et al.* (1992) found no sex differences in cortisol levels when 38 infants (8–10 months old) were separated from a caregiver. Nonetheless, Weinberg, Tronick, Cohn, and Olson (1999, p. 175) concluded that *most*

> Studies using the Neonatal Behavioral Assessment Scale or naturalistic observations have shown that male infants smile less than female infants and display more irritability, crying, facial grimacing, and lability of emotional states …. Male neonates also show a more rapid buildup of arousal and a quicker peak of excitement.

In their own investigation of negative affect in 6-month-olds during the "still face" paradigm (i.e., 2 minute interval in which the mother looks at the infant with a still face and does not smile, talk, or touch interspersed between two other 2 minute intervals of face-to-face play interaction between mother and child), Weinberg *et al.* (1999) again found that male infants responded with more negative affect than female infants. In general, male infants are rated as showing greater irritability and more intense expressions of happiness, anger, sadness, and fear even when raters are blind as to the sex of the infants (Eisenberg, Martin, & Fabes, 1996). Beyond the first few months, temperament seems to equalize between the sexes. For example, in the large Australian Temperament Project (longitudinal study of 2443 infants) very few sex differences were noted in the first few years of life in terms of temperament, activity level, or non-compliance (Prior, Smart, Sanson, & Oberklaid, 1993). Similarly, mothers' ratings of their 21-month-old children indicated no sex differences in rates of inhibition or withdrawal from novelty (Garcia-Coll, Kagan, & Resnick, 1984), which, as reviewed in Chapter 3, are behaviors that are closely linked to neuroticism and negative affectivity. Also, no sex differences were found in parent ratings of toddler's behavior when norming the Child Behavior Checklist (Achenbach, & Edelbrock, 1984).

The stronger female propensity to negative affectivity begins to appear around 2 years of age. That is when "low-reactive" girls begin to appear more inhibited than boys (Arcus & Kagan, 1995). Boys are generally rated as more angry whereas girls are rated as more fearful throughout toddler and preschool years (Eisenberg *et al.*, 1996b). Signs of elevated anxiousness and inhibition in females increase throughout childhood, and hence whereas parents did not rate their toddlers differently, they did rate their 4–5-year-old boys and girls differently, so much so that sex-specific scales and norms were developed for the Child Behavior Checklist (Achenbach & Edelbrock, 1984). During late elementary and high school, girls report more surprise, sadness, shame, shyness, and guilt, whereas boys report more contempt and are more likely to deny the other emotions endorsed more frequently by girls (Eisenberg *et al.*, 1996b). Moreover, girls become progressively more prone to negative affectivity with age. For example, Eysenck and Eysenck (1976) found that whereas boys showed no change, girls showed a distinct upward slope in their neuroticism scores from 7 through 15 years of age. This profile was replicated in a recent combined longitudinal and cross-sectional study of changes over a 4 year period between the ages of 12 and 18 years (McCrae *et al.*, 2002). Hence, adolescent girls report higher levels of emotional intensity (Eisenberg *et al.*, 1996b) and of neuroticism than adolescent boys (e.g., del Barrio, Moreno-Rosset, Lopez-Martinez, & Olmedo, 1997; Goodyear, Ashby, Altham, Vize, & Cooper, 1993). Similarly, in our own study of over 800 high school juniors, females scored higher on the neuroticism scale of the Costa-McCrae questionnaire (R. E. Zinbarg, S. Mineka, & M. G. Craske, unpublished findings). Sex differences are very stable by adulthood. For example, women obtained higher mean scores on neuroticism than did men in all of 37 countries (Lynn, R. & Martin, 1997). From another analysis of 26 different cultures ($n = 23\,031$), women reported themselves to be higher on neuroticism, agreeableness, warmth, and openness to feelings, whereas men rated themselves as higher on assertiveness and openness to ideas (Costa, Terracciano, & McCrae, 2001).

As alluded to in Chapter 3, biological factors appear to be most influential at a very young age, but with development, temperament is increasingly influenced by experience and context (Lonigan & Phillips, 2001). Thus, social influences may well contribute to the development of heightened negative affectivity in females. Consistent with the age at which the first signs of increased negative affectivity in females occur, the developmental literature indicates that the effects of socialization upon gender role behaviors become *evident* at around the age of 2 years and increase thereafter at a faster rate in girls than boys (Martin, Ruble, & Szkrybalo, 2002). It may be for this reason that concordance for behavioral inhibition among same-sex monozygotic twin pairs was similar between girls and boys at 14 months of age, whereas by 20 months of age the concordance rates were almost twice as high for boys than girls (Robinson *et al.*, 1992). That is, environmental influences upon behavioral inhibition were stronger for girls than boys at the later age. The nature of such social influences is described in detail in a later section of this chapter.

Interestingly, the developmental shift in temperament is paralleled by shifts in reactivity to facial expressions. Specifically, males appear to be more attuned than females to parental (maternal) facial expressions during infancy (e.g., Weinberg *et al.*, 1999) whereas females become more attuned to facial expressions at a later developmental stage. For example, by the age of 11 years, boys exhibit less reactivity to faces than girls, as measured by rates of decline in amygdala activation over repeated exposures to fearful faces (Thomas *et al.*, 2001). Similarly, adult females show more activation of the limbic system than males during exposure to facial stimuli, as measured by electrophysiology (Orozco & Ehlers, 1998). Some studies even find that females are more accurate at classifying facial expressions (Thayer & Johnsen, 2000). Meta-analyses indicate that whereas there may be no differences in emotion recognition (Elfenbein & Ambady, 2002), females show superior *processing* of facial expressions (McClure, 2000). These findings relate to other evidence for females being more facially expressive than males in emotionally provoking situations. For example, in their evaluation of facial muscle activity among males and females exposed to happy and angry faces, Dimberg and Lundquist (1990) found that females responded with more distinct facial muscle responses to happy faces, although other research has shown that sex differences of this type interact with ethnicity (Vrana & Rollock, 2002).

As described in Chapters 5 and 6, facial expressions are prepotent stimuli for the communication of present danger and acquisition of anxiety and fear. Hence, by virtue of sensitivity to facial expressions, females may be more likely to acquire anxiety of specific stimuli by observing others express fear or anger, and may be more attuned to surrounding dangers in general. One might also surmise that sensitivity to facial expressions places females at particularly greater risk for social phobia, but in fact that is the anxiety disorder where least sex differences are observed. Paradoxically, the "down-regulation" of female anxiousness in social situations may be a consequence of the same factors that explain their heightened sensitivity to facial expressions; a point returned to below.

In summary, although females score higher than males on measures of negative affectivity, and progressively more so over childhood and adolescence, temperament during the first year to year and a half seems indistinguishable between the sexes. If anything, male newborns show signs of stronger emotional reactivity than females. The shift to female predominance seems to occur around 2 years of age, coinciding with the developmental phase at which gender role behaviors first begin to be observed. One particularly interesting aspect of this developmental progression is a heightened sensitivity to facial expressions in females. The female propensity to negative affect is likely to contribute to their risk for anxiety disorders as well as depression.

Genetic Influences

As reviewed in Chapter 3, the proneness to negative affectivity appears to be influenced by heritability as well as life traumas. The heritability is shared with the heritability for symptoms of anxiety and depression, and is described as being largely non-specific in its effects upon the development of anxiety disorders. Hence, it is conceivable that genetic factors may be relevant to different risks for anxiety disorders between the sexes. One model of genetic factors attributes heightened risk for anxiety among females to a lower threshold and greater liability for anxiety disorders. Within this framework, a male proband would be more deviant in his liability than a female proband, as males in general would have a higher threshold for the disorder. If so, the distribution of liability would be more deviant for the relatives of male probands than for relatives of female probands: the former group would be more likely to have anxiety disorders than the latter group (Rhee, Waldman, Hay, & Levy, 1999). Hence, fathers with anxiety disorders would be more likely to transmit risk to their offspring than would mothers. However, in contrast to this model, the risk for anxiety disorders in offspring is equal whether the mother or father has an anxiety disorder, according to recent studies as well as meta-analyses (Connell & Goodman, 2002; Dierker *et al.*, 1999).

In another model, the slower rate of psychosocial and physical development in boys is emphasized as leading to a different genetic influence because "interactions with the environment during their relative immaturity may lead to more information being derived from the genome" (Rhee *et al.*, 1999, p. 26–27). By implication, heritability may account for more of the variance in male than female anxiety. However, in their study of genetic influences upon neuroticism, Lake *et al.* (2000) found that the overall contribution of genetic factors to individual differences was greater for females (broad heritability 41 percent) than males (broad heritability 35 percent), consistent with previous large twin and family studies (e.g., Finkel & McGue, 1997). Similarly, research with child and adolescent samples reliably indicates higher heritability estimates for fears and phobias for girls than for boys (Eley, 2001). (Studies of symptom ratings and diagnostic groups in adult samples show no differences in the genetic and environmental variance patterns for men versus women (Hettema, Prescott, & Kendler, 2001; Kendler *et al.*, 1987; Roy *et al.*, 1995), but heritability estimates are more meaningful for traits and temperament than for disorders.) That heritable factors account for less of the variance in boys' negative affectivity might reflect strong counteractive environmental influences; conversely, environmental influences may support heritable tendencies toward negative affectivity, more so for girls than boys. In other words, by being encouraged to be active, independent, and to repeatedly face anxiety-provoking situations, boys are exposed to experiences that, in a complication-type model, weaken a genetically influenced vulnerability toward negative affect. However, if this were the case, the gap between female and male negative affectivity should progressively widen across generations, and to date there is no evidence to support this proposition. Thus, the significance of sex by genetic interactions for explaining negative affectivity remains unclear.

Life Stressors

As reviewed in Chapter 3, major adversities contribute to reactivity to future stressors (i.e., stress sensitization) and thereby enhance negative affectivity. Some have argued that sex differences in anxiety arise from a higher incidence of acute and/or chronic traumas or stressors in women as a result of their lower status politically, economically, and socially in most cultures. The results regarding life stressors are contradictory: some studies show that women report more stressful life events (e.g., Bebbington, Tennant, & Hurry, 1991; Bebbington *et al.*, 1993); others using different methodologies do not find such differences (Uhlenhuth & Paykel, 1973). More importantly for the stress sensitization hypothesis, males are exposed to a *greater* number of major adversities or traumas than females (Breslau *et al.*, 1991).

One exception is that sexual abuse is a greater threat for females. For example, female youths and adolescents born in Christchurch, New Zealand (*n* = 1265) were exposed to higher rates of sexual violence than males (Fergusson, Swain-Campbell, & Horwood, 2002). Similarly, female youths were more often subjected to sexual abuse, but not physical abuse, than males in a large survey across 19 states in the United States (Cappelleri, Eckenrode, & Powers, 1993). Even when not the victim of rape or assault, the potential risk for such events may influence womens' perceptions of threat. Koss and Mukai (1993) reviewed evidence showing that fear of rape is highly prevalent among women, and it is a fear not shared by men. Sexual assault is a particularly potent trauma due to its high degree of uncontrollability, and therefore may be especially significant to female anxiety proneness. In support, statistical removal of the variance attributable to sexual abuse in the Christchurch study significantly lessened the female-to-male discrepancy for later anxiety disorders (Fergusson *et al.*, 2002). Nonetheless, the fact that a sex discrepancy still remained suggests that sexual abuse is not the full explanation.

Even though women are subjected to fewer traumas overall in comparison with men, they appear to be more impacted by them in terms of internalizing symptoms. This is especially true for "social network crises", such as the death of a loved one or a close relative, which elicits considerably more distress in females than males (Kessler & McLeod, 1984). But differences in reactivity extend to other traumas as well. For example, more women (27 percent) than men (13 percent) in the "high exposure" category developed major depression, generalized anxiety, or posttraumatic stress disorder following the Mount Saint Helen's volcano eruption (Shore, Tatum, & Vollmer, 1986). In a naturalistic study of the incidence of new psychiatric diagnoses within 7–9 months for victims of two traumatic events in Belgium (a major hotel fire, and a major car accident involving 150 cars), sex was a predictor of any type of disorder (anxiety disorders, depression, or substance abuse), as was loss of control, type of trauma, and seeing a close friend or relative being injured (Maes, Mylle, Delmeire, & Altamura, 2000). Unfortunately, the onset of "disorder" in that study was determined retrospectively. Breslau and colleagues have conducted a number of investigations of trauma. From a sample of 21–30-year-olds (*n* > 1000), males were 1.46 times more likely to encounter traumatic events, but among those exposed to traumatic events, women were 1.77 times more likely than men to develop posttraumatic stress disorder (Breslau *et al.*, 1991). In another study they conducted a random sampling of index life events from participants in the Detroit Area Survey of Trauma (Breslau, Chilcoat, Kessler, Peterson, & Lucia, 1999). The conditional risk for posttraumatic stress disorder associated with any trauma was 13 percent in females and 6.2 percent in males. Thus, the conditional risk for posttraumatic stress disorder was approximately two times higher in females, and this ratio remained even when sex difference in type of trauma was controlled. Others have shown similar findings when the "type" of trauma event is controlled (Breslau, Andreski, Davis, Peterson, & Schultz, 1997; Kessler *et al.*, 1995), again highlighting the fact that differential rates of sexual abuse do not account for all of the sex differences in anxiety proneness. Moreover, Breslau *et al.* (1997) found that pre-existing anxiety disorders or depression played only a small part in the observed sex difference in posttraumatic stress disorder after exposure to trauma. Nor were women more likely to report multiple events or more likely to be affected by cumulative effects of multiple events than males. Instead, reaction to the given trauma seemed to be most important differentiating factor. In some ways, this is consistent with another set of findings showing that predictors of posttraumatic stress disorder derive mostly from war zone stressors for male Vietnam war veterans in contrast to post-war resiliency factors for female Vietnam war veterans (King, King, Foy, Keane, & Fairbank, 1999).

In summary, females are no more vulnerable than males to the occurrence of major life traumas, with the exception of sexual assault. In fact, males are exposed to more traumas than females — a fact which may be explained by the various evolutionary and social pressures for males to face threats, as described below. However, females are at greater risk for developing posttraumatic stress disorder and other internalizing symptoms following traumatic events. Evidence presented in earlier chapters would suggest that heightened negative affectivity and style of responding to traumas are crucial to these sex differences. Along these lines, it is also conceivable that the impact of trauma is just as strong for males but that the manifestation of such an impact is more likely to be in the arena of externalizing problems due to different ways of coping with negative affect. The greater distress generated by social network crises for females may be indicative of their prosocial gender role described below. Finally, the greater anxiogenic impact of traumas upon females is consistent with their profile of progressive elevation in negative affectivity over time, but is unlikely to explain their proneness to a more anxious and inhibited temperament as early as 2 years old. Social influences are likely to be very critical at early ages, and it is such influences to which attention is now turned.

Threat-based Style of Emotion Regulation

The expression of negative affect is moderated by one's reaction to it. As reviewed in Chapter 4, the regulation of emotion is initially biologically driven but soon comes under the influence of environmental factors, including parent–child interactions. An intrusive or negative parenting style seems likely to contribute to offspring distress overall, but the added features of parenting that reinforce avoidant behavior and threat-based expectations may have a more unique role in the development of pathological anxiety. It is here that much of the separation between female and male risk for anxiety disorders may occur. Differences in the parenting of male versus female offspring can be viewed from both evolutionary and social constructivist models. As summarized by Wood and Eagly (2002), the evolutionary model links sex differences in behavior to reproductive pressures. That is, men are more aggressive than women due to the reproductive advantage of being stronger and bigger; women are intrinsically oriented to seek mates with the resources that can support them and their offspring; and males are oriented to compete with other males in dominance contests. From the social constructivist point of view, gender is a product of societal role assignments and self-selection into social roles rather than of biological differences between the sexes. Whether evolutionarily or socially driven, parents reinforce their children's behavior in gender-biased ways.

Synchronicity During Infancy

As proposed in Chapter 4, synchronicity between parent and infant may be critical to infant distress, the initial establishment of a sense of prediction and control, including instrumental control over others' behaviors as well as one's own emotional state. These are the very processes that are critical to the moderation of negative affect. Moreover, the effect of synchronicity upon orienting and sustained attention overlaps with other evidence for low vagal tone and poor responsivity or inflexibility in response to environmental demands. Limited flexibility and attentional discrimination are hypothesized to contribute to overgeneralized anxious responding.

Even though the research connecting parent–infant synchronicity to later anxiety disorders is yet to be conducted, it is worthwhile addressing whether sex differences exist in parent–infant synchronicity in a way that could contribute to female risk for anxiety. Several studies indicate that mother–son dyads are more often in coordination than mother–daughter dyads, whether defined by matching facial expressions (Malatesta & Haviland, 1982), matching direction of attention at each other or at objects (Tronick & Cohn, 1989), or consistency in moving affectively over time (Tronick & Cohn, 1989). As described previously, Weinberg *et al.* (1999) examined 81 6-month-old infants using the "still face" paradigm. Although mothers did not use more frequent or different strategies to regulate emotional states in boys versus girls, there was greater coordination in mother–son than in mother–daughter dyads in the 2 minutes preceding the still face paradigm. According to Weinberg *et al.* (1999, p. 185):

> This finding suggests that mothers and sons more carefully tracked each other's behavior and facial expressions than mothers and daughters. This greater coordination, which takes place at a subtle microtemporal level, may function to help boys maintain self regulation.

In another study, maternal positivity in the interval preceding the still face paradigm correlated with a greater range of affective "bids" in male infants but not in female infants (Mayes & Carter, 1990), again suggestive of more involvement with the parent in male compared with female infants.

Sex differences in parent–infant synchronicity may relate to infant temperament. As reviewed already, there is some evidence that male newborns are more irritable than female newborns. Assuming that their elevated irritability is not in relation to mothers' attempts to console (Lowinger, 1999; see Chapter 4), and instead is more general, as it indeed seems to be, then the male newborns' temperament may in part account for the greater coordination in mother–son dyads compared with mother–daughter dyads. If these findings prove to be robust, the heightened vulnerability to anxiety disorders and other emotional disorders in females may arise *partly* from lower synchronicity between mother and daughter, and the resultant weakened base of predictability and controllability, despite beginning their lives with less emotional reactivity than males. However, it is unlikely to account for all of female propensity to anxiety, especially as the level of desynchrony may have to be quite extreme for its impact to be detrimental. Furthermore, the effects of excessive desynchrony are likely to be non-specific to all forms of emotional distress and not unique to the development of anxiousness. In addition, the specific pathways of confluence among parent–infant synchronicity, predictability, and controllability, and eventual generalizability of anxious responding, have yet to be comprehensively investigated. As described in Chapter 4, parent–infant synchronicity is presumed to influence attentional processes, of which orienting responses and discrimination among discrete cues are considered central to anxiousness. One index of attentional processing is cardiac vagal tone, but even here the evaluation of sex differences is very limited. One study found that depressed females had higher heart rate variability than non-depressed females, whereas the reverse pattern occurred for depressed males (Thayer, Smith, Rossy, Sollers, & Friedman, 1998), but another study showed no sex differences in heart rate variability at rest but greater reductions heart rate variability in response to stressors in females (Hughes & Stoney, 2000). Interestingly, Eisenberg and colleagues found that vagal tone correlated negatively with social functioning and positively with emotionality in kindergarten to second-grade girls (Eisenberg *et al.*, 1995), and again negatively with peer nominations of prosocial behavior in 8–13-year-old girls (Eisenberg *et al.*, 1996a), whereas the expected positive correlations with sociability and negative correlations with emotionality were found in boys. In these studies, ratings of sociability and emotionality were made by friends, teachers, or parents; they were not independent observations by blind raters. Thus, the authors attribute the interaction effects to gender stereotypes, in that boys' uninhibited, assertive behavior is viewed more positively than is girls', such that assertive girls are judged to be less socially appropriate and higher on emotionality. In support, they cite a study by Buck (1975), in which girls who exhibited spontaneous emotional reactions were judged by teachers as impulsive, domineering, and difficult to get along with whereas this was not true for boys. This brings us to the role of gender role socialization.

Gender Socialization and Parenting Expectations and Behaviors

Gender role traits are associated with anxiety, and in fact several studies show that it is low masculinity rather than high femininity that correlates with anxiousness and with mental health in general. For example, Chambless and Mason (1986) found that low masculinity (e.g., lack of assertiveness and activity) was associated with anxiety and avoidance whereas high femininity (e.g., kindness and nurturing) was not in their sample of patients with agoraphobia. Also, the number of fears endorsed on fear inventories in adult samples correlates negatively with more masculine role identities (Carey, Dusek, & Spector, 1988; Tucker & Bond, 1997). Even in children (aged 6–11 years) attending treatment, a negative relationship exists between masculinity and the number of fears (Ginsburg & Silverman, 2000). These data suggest that features of independence, activity, assertiveness, and other traits consistent with a masculine profile buffer against fear and anxiety. In addition to biological influences, such behavioral traits are greatly influenced by socialization, and, as mentioned earlier, gender-differentiated behavior generally begins to be exhibited around 2 years of age and to strengthen thereafter (Martin *et al.*, 2002).

Examples of differential reinforcement of behaviors in boys versus girls abound in the literature. For example, in an observational study of 3½-year-olds (*n* = 38), girls were more often ignored when they attempted to direct the interaction or make declarations and received positive attention more often when they were compliant, whereas boy's directive attempts received positive attention (Kerig, Cowan, & Cowan, 1993). Similarly, as noted above in the study by Buck (1975), teachers respond differentially to the same behavior patterns from girls versus boys, such as more negative responses for high activity levels in girls compared with boys (for a review see Keenan and Shaw, 1997). Expectations differ as well, in that mothers expect their boys to perform better than their girls. In a study of 11-month-olds, mothers were asked to estimate their child's crawling ability in a novel task of crawling down steep and shallow slopes (Mondschein, Adolph, & Tamis-LeMonda, 2000). There were no sex differences in actual performance, but mothers of boys expected their infants to be more successful than mothers of girls, and to attempt steeper and riskier slopes than girls. Parental expectations of their child's abilities are particularly important as they have a greater impact on children's achievement attitudes and academic performance than does the child's previous performance (Eisenberg *et al.*, 1996b).

Not only do parents socialize gender-conforming behaviors in their children, but several studies indicate that parents are more controlling of their female compared with their male offspring. For example, mothers rated themselves on daily checklists as being more likely to employ control without autonomy granting with their daughters (6–11 years old) and more likely to employ control with autonomy granting with their sons (Pomerantz & Ruble, 1998). As noted in Chapter 4, controlling and intrusive parenting styles are associated with offspring anxiety as well as conduct disorders. Unfortunately, the veracity of self-ratings of parenting style in the study by Pomerants and Ruble is questionable. More telling is evidence from Krohne and Hock (1991), who observed mothers of children aged 10–13 years to be more controlling if their girls had high versus low levels of anxiety, whereas mothers' behavior did not change relative to the level of anxiety in boys. In addition, because expression of anxiety is more consistent with the female gender role, such emotion and related behavior is tolerated, accepted, or encouraged in girls, whereas boys are expected to display instrumental traits of self-confidence and learn ways to reduce their fears (Bem, 1981; Golombok & Fivush, 1994). For example, in another observational study of 47 children aged 3½–4 years, shy behavior in girls was associated with positive parenting behavior such as acceptance and enjoyment of the child (Simpson & Stevenson-Hinde, 1985). In contrast, shyness was negatively associated with these types of parental behaviors for boys. Moreover, shyness in boys becomes less acceptable to parents as boys get older whereas the same is not true for girls (Stevenson-Hinde & Shouldice, 1993). Parents report greater acceptance of boys' anger (Eisenberg *et al.*, 1996b). As noted in Chapter 1, the differential acceptance of shyness and anxiousness in boys versus girls may explain why as many anxious boys as girls are brought to treatment by their caretakers when epidemiological studies indicate that girls suffer from more fear and anxiety than boys. Parents may be more likely to encourage anxious boys to overcome their anxiety and to receive professional help whereas anxious girls are more likely to be accepted as such.

By being encouraged to be more active and independent, boys are likely to build competency and self-efficacy in a wider array of domains than are girls. Also, they are more likely to encounter challenges that require persistence and problem-solving, thus contributing to an active coping style of managing negative affect. In addition, repeated exposures to a broad array of activities is likely to facilitate habituation to aversive stimuli, especially developmentally appropriate stimuli such as certain animals, the dark, or other aspects of the natural environment. Conversely, females may be at heightened risk for persistent fearfulness of such developmentally appropriate stimuli not only as a result of higher negative affectivity but also by being less strongly encouraged to face fear-provoking situations. Finally, breadth of experience generates a larger behavioral repertoire for buffering the later effects of aversive experiences, according to the principles of latent inhibition described in Chapter 6. For example, adolescent boys may be less prone to acquiring fears of bodily sensations (as in panic disorder) due to their involvement in sports and athleticism. Obviously, overly controlling parenting, lack of reinforcement of activity and assertiveness, and reinforcement of shy and anxious behaviors in girls severely limits these benefits.

For all these reasons, it is not surprising that even though boys typically score lower on scales of behavior regulation (i.e., impulsivity and delay of gratification; Eisenberg *et al.*, 1996b), they also typically perceive themselves as being stronger, more powerful, and more dominant than girls (Maccoby & Jacklin, 1974) and to have greater feelings of control (Dweck, 1990). Ohannessian, Lerner, Lerner, and Eye (1999) evaluated self-competence in the worth, appearance, social, academic, and athletic domains for 75 sixth-grade students across two assessments separated by 1 year. Overall, girls had lower self-competence than boys, and competency related negatively to depression and anxiety symptoms. Also, girls generally have lower expectancies for success, lower aspirations, greater anxiety about failure, and greater tendencies to attribute their failures to lack of ability and their successes to unstable factors (Eisenberg *et al.*, 1996b). These sex differences continue through adolescence (Allgood-Merten, Lewinsohn, & Hops, 1990) and adulthood. For example, Furst, Tenenbaum, and Weingarten (1985) found that women tended to underestimate their performance in tests whereas men overestimated their performance. Also, women report more fatalism and less sense of personal control over their lives than men (Thoits, 1987). Such lack of control and their submissive role in the submission dominance hierarchy of our species is likely to enhance females' perceived uncontrollability over stressors in general.

As reviewed previously, control is directly relevant to anxiety; early control appears to offset the later expression of fear and anxiety, and lack of control, real or not, enhances the impact of stressors (see Chapters 4 and 6). Thus, a lower sense of control in females may contribute to their heightened risk for anxiety disorders. In fact, perceived control seems to be central to various parenting differences between boys and girls: lower parental/child synchronicity in females relative to males in the first few months of life, more controlling parenting of girls than boys, and the expectations for less competency along with the reinforcement of anxiousness over the course of development for females may detract from a sense of personal control. Thus, as proposed by Chorpita and Barlow (1998), perceived control may be a mediator of parental influences and a subsequent moderator of anxiousness, and females experience and project less control than males.

In addition to being less positively reinforced for independence, assertiveness, and activity, girls are more strongly encouraged to be empathic and prosocial than are boys, who are more strongly encouraged to be autonomous (Eisenberg *et al.*, 1996b). Keenan and Shaw (1997) note that by 2 years of age, parents encourage daughters more than sons to relinquish toys to peers, take another's perspective, and behave prosocially. Zahn-Waxler, Robinson, and Emde (1992) observed the reactions of 200 pairs of monozygotic and dizygotic twin pairs to simulated distress by the mother and examiner. In contrast to the evidence presented earlier for girls to be less socially oriented toward their mothers than boys at 6 months of age (Weinberg *et al.*, 1999), 14–20-month-old girls engaged in significantly more enquiry and showed more empathic concern, prosocial behavior, and self-distress than boys. Although this may be attributable to developmental maturity, with females showing an advantage even at the toddler age in terms of language abilities, Keenan and Shaw (1997, p. 109) suggest that "Throughout girls' development, individual achievement has not been tied to their self concept. Instead, they have been socialized to guide themselves by understanding how their behavior affects others". They hypothesize that one of the reasons why girls experience an increase in internalizing disorders during adolescence is because their interpersonal orientation places them at a disadvantage to meet the challenges of adolescence when the primary tasks are individuation, independence from the family and achievement. Similarly, women and persons high in femininity show more empathic concern for others than males (Skoe, Cumberland, Eisenberg, Hansen, & Perry, 2002). As Almeida & Kessler (1998, p. 671) state:

> Women are in social roles that require them to provide more support to others, to be more empathetic, and to extend their concern to a wider range of people in ways that increase stressors, which ultimately lead to distress.

Thus, in daily diary studies, females endorse more distress due to interpersonal tensions and giving support to others whereas males are more distressed by work and financial problems (e.g., Almeida & Kessler, 1998).

Notably, boys and girls do not differ in their *ability* to understand another person's perspective, or to infer what others are thinking or feeling, but rather they differ in their *use* of "other" perspective: girls are more likely to put themselves in the "shoes of others" (Eisenberg *et al.*, 1996b). Hence, girls generally report more distress and exhibit more facial reactions to empathy-inducing stimuli (Eisenberg *et al.*, 1996b). These prosocial influences and effects are very consistent with other evidence for parents to talk more about emotions with their daughters, particularly positive emotions, which Eisenberg *et al.* (1996b) hypothesize might lead girls to attend to and express their emotions more. In contrast, boys are encouraged to minimize emotional expression (Quas *et al.*, 2000).

Even though self-reported nurturance does not correlate with trait anxiety (Chambless & Mason, 1986), prosocial and empathic socialization may be as important as the lack of independent assertiveness and the reinforcement of anxious, avoidant behaviors for risk for anxiety. For example, the prosocial and empathic emphasis goes hand in hand with females' heightened sensitivity to facial expressions, described earlier, which in turn enhances the vicarious acquisition of fear and anxiety and the general sense of threat in the environment. Thus, girls would be expected to be more influenced by parental modeling of fear and anxiety than are boys. Support for this hypothesis comes from the study by Gerull and Rapee (2002) (see Chapter 4), who coded the response of 15–20-month-old toddlers (*n* = 30, equal numbers of females and males) to their mothers' positive versus negative facial expressions toward a rubber snake/spider. Males and females did not differ on positive trials, but females were more fearful and avoidant following negative trials, suggesting that females indeed were more affected by observing their mothers showing fear and/or disgust reactions. More research is needed, especially given the potency of vicarious methods of fear acquisition and its explanatory significance for stronger familial aggregation for anxiety disorders for female compared with male offspring (see Chapter 4).

In summary, sex differences have been observed in terms of lower rates of coordination between mother and infant daughter interactions, possibly related to lower levels of emotional reactivity as newborns compared with males. In addition, higher degrees of parental control are exerted over girls than boys, particularly for anxious girls, although replication is sorely needed. Socialization patterns reinforce activity and independence, more so in boys than girls. Because shyness and anxiety are less accepted in boys than girls, anxious boys may be encouraged to be independent or to overcome their anxiety whereas anxious girls are positively reinforced for their anxiety. In addition, parents hold more negative expectations for their female than for their male offspring. Each of these factors may detract from a sense of competency and control for females, as is evident across a wide array of domains throughout adolescence, and that contributes directly to elevated anxiousness. Moreover, these reinforcement patterns may negate the development of effective strategies for managing negative affect, those being reappraisal, approach, and problem-solving behaviors. Social stereotyping may additionally limit the breadth of activities for females that would otherwise buffer against the impact of aversive experiences. Finally, alongside being reinforced for more prosocial and empathic skills, females are more responsive than males to parental facial expressions of fear and anxiety, and thus more vulnerable to vicarious fear acquisition in relation to specific stimuli and being alerted to a sense of present threat in general. More research on this potentially very important sex difference is needed. Socialization of the male and female gender roles appears to contribute to a threat-attendant and -avoidant style in females compared with an active and independent style in males; thus, gender role socialization (which is supported by physiological differences between the sexes described later) contributes specifically to proneness to anxiety in females whereas broader factors of elevated negative affectivity and emotional reactivity to major life adversities contribute to females' greater risk for emotional distress in general. Sex differences in the manifestation of anxious processes are examined next.

Anxious Processes

Anxious behaviors are certainly consistent with the female gender role of caregiver. That is, attending to potential threat, interpreting circumstances as threatening, and avoiding encounters with threat maintain the safety of the offspring: by not paying attention to potential threat, true threats may approach unnoticed, and thereby risk for offspring is increased; by actively confronting instead of avoiding potential threat, offspring are left unattended, and potentially permanently abandoned. Hence, we would expect females to exhibit more attentional biases toward threat, heightened judgments of threat, and avoidant responding in anticipation of threat.

Attention and Judgment Biases

Very little research has directly examined sex differences with respect to attentional and judgment processes using the paradigms described in Chapter 5, such as the dot probe task, the modified Stroop task, stimulus arrays, dichotic listening, or estimates of covariation, meaning, or probability. In one study, high- and low-test-anxious girls were faster attending to probes that followed threat versus neutral words in a dot probe task, at least in the lower probe location, whereas boys were slower following threat words (Vasey *et al.*, 1996). Among the low-anxious group in particular, girls were equally attentive to neutral and threat words whereas boys showed a bias away from threat words, suggestive of greater inhibitory control. Notably, this pattern is consistent with the evidence presented in Chapter 5 for inhibitory control being instituted at an earlier age in non-anxious compared with anxious youths. Perhaps boys inhibit or disengage from threat sooner than girls. Another study of fifth and sixth graders ($n = 277$), however, failed to find sex differences in proneness to interpret ambiguous or threatening situations as threatening or likely to occur to them (Suarez & Bell-Dolan, 2001). Obviously, it is difficult to draw conclusions on so little data.

On the other hand, chronic worry is associated with threat biases of attention and overestimations of threat. For example, worriers perceive events as more catastrophic and generate more catastrophizing scenarios for potential problems (see Chapter 7). Females score significantly higher on worry scales than men (Borkovec, Wilkinson, Folensbee, & Lerman, 1983), and females are more likely to develop generalized anxiety disorder. Sex differences in youths are not as robust as in adults; some find that girls endorse more worry than boys (Campbell & Rapee, 1994; Compas, Orosan, & Grant, 1993), whereas others find no sex differences in self-reported worry on the Penn State Worry Questionnaire (Suarez & Bell-Dolan, 2001). Again, the progressive increment in anxiety for females over the course of adolescence and later in adulthood probably accounts for less reliable differences among youth samples. As noted previously, worry is a state that is elicited by uncertainty about future threat, and excessive worry is linked with impaired confidence in problem-solving and elevated evidence requirements, as well as an iterative style of generating as many negative outcomes as possible before deciding an action. On both counts, worry is consistent with socialization of female behavior in the direction of wariness over potential threat, and avoidance rather than active problem-solving.

Worry shares features in common with "rumination", or behaviors and thoughts that focus attention on dysphoric symptoms or their consequences, in contrast to diversion of attention onto pleasant or neutral topics (e.g., Nolen-Hoeksema, 1991). Rumination exacerbates and prolongs dysphoric mood whereas active distraction alleviates it (Nolen-Hoeksema, Morrow, & Fredrickson, 1993). Morrow and Nolen-Hoeksema (1990) attributed the negative effects of rumination to its tendency to generate more negative interpretations and outcome expectancies and/or interfere with effective problem-solving and decision-making in a way that is very similar to the effects of excessive worry. As with depressed mood, we found that rumination prolonged anxious mood relative to distracting conditions (Blagden & Craske, 1996). In addition, we found that worry was the equivalent to "depressive rumination" (Segerstrom *et al.*,

2000), both being forms of repetitive ruminative thought that contribute to negative affect.

Just as females are more likely than males to worry, females are more likely than males to ruminate in response to dysphoric mood (Nolen-Hoeksema, 1991). Although sex differences have not been specifically measured with respect to rumination over anxious mood, rumination correlates with negative affectivity (Watson & Clark, 1984), which in turn is elevated in females. Thus, the tendency to ruminate or worry may predispose women to more depression and anxiety by generating more negative possibilities about which to worry, by interfering with problem-solving, and by activating other modes of negative thinking. Moreover, evidence reviewed in Chapter 5 indicates that the tendency to be distressed by symptoms of anxiety (i.e., intrusive thoughts, panic attacks) predicts their persistence over time and progression to a fully fledged disorder. Distress over symptoms probably is closely linked with states of rumination and worry. Conceivably, then, tendencies to worry and ruminate may render females more likely than males to transition from occasional symptoms to anxiety disorders. Unfortunately, there are no published data on sex as a moderator of response to occasional symptoms of panic and anxiety. In our own study of unselected college students, females reported more distress over intrusive thoughts than males (B. G. Zucker & M. G. Craske, unpublished findings), but clearly more research on this important topic is warranted.

Self-focus of attention — "an awareness of self-referent, internally generated information that stands in contrast to an awareness of externally generated information derived through sensory receptors" (Ingram, 1990b, p. 156) — also is intricately tied with worry and rumination. For example, rumination is theorized to include an analytical, evaluative cognitive style (i.e., worry) as well as a focus on symptoms and other aspects of the self-experience (i.e., self-focus) (Roberts, Gilboa, & Gotlib, 1998). Ingram (1990) proposed that excessive or overly rigid self-focus is characteristic of all emotional disorders, and in support correlational analyses indicate that it is positively associated with general psychopathology, and is negatively related to problem-solving (Woodruff-Borden *et al.*, 2001). A recent meta-analysis confirmed a moderate relation between self-focus and negative affect of various types (Mor & Winquist, 2002). In addition, Mor and Winquist established that depression was most strongly linked with private self-focus (evaluation of self unrelated to others' impressions) whereas social anxiety was most strongly linked with public self-focus (evaluation of self related to others' impressions of oneself), and generalized anxiety disorder was associated with both. As an aside, the effect sizes associated with generalized anxiety disorder were higher than those associated with depression or other types of anxiety. Such a result is predicted from the model of generalized anxiety disorder presented in Chapter 7 wherein a pervasive sense of personal ineffectiveness would generate ongoing self-evaluation across all domains, public and private. Most importantly for the current discussion, the relationship between negative affectivity and self-focus was elevated in samples that contained more females, suggesting that "when women engage in self focus, they do so in a more maladaptive manner than when men engage in self focus" (Mor & Winquist, 2002, p. 654).

Anxiety and other negative moods generate self-focused attention (Ingram, 1990; Wegner & Guiliano, 1980; Wood *et al.*, 1990), perhaps because they indicate that something could be wrong and focus is directed inwardly to identify and address the problem (Morris, 1999). In addition, self-focus induces negative affect. Several pathways have been proposed for this effect, such as by enhancing awareness of oneself falling short of personal standards (Duval & Wickland, 1972), especially if such standards are judged to be unattainable or a long way off (Carver & Scheier, 1998). Presumably, self-directed focus of attention also negatively impacts effective management of ongoing tasks that require attentional focus, such that, as with rumination and worry, problem-solving is impaired and subjective distress is maintained. Additionally one might hypothesize that overly self-focused attention impedes outward attention and discrimination among external cues, especially if internal and external cues compete for attention in the way proposed by Pennebaker (1982) such that those who are focused on internal cues perceive fewer external cues, and vice versa. As already mentioned in Chapter 4, discriminability among external cues facilitates flexibility in responding to environmental demands, and is considered to be an essential component of effective emotion regulation. Other research implies a connection between attention to external cues, levels of unpredictability, and overgeneralizability of anxious responding (see Chapter 4). Conceivably, self-focused attention not only elevates negative mood but also generalizes anxious responding by limiting predictable discrimination among discrete external threat cues. In this way, excessive self-focus of attention may also mimic the effects of excessive desynchronicity between infant and parent. However, direct investigations of these relationships are lacking.

One particular feature of self-focus of attention that differs between the sexes is the awareness of internal state. Females are more attentive to internal cues than males (Pennebaker, 1982, 2000). For example, females report more symptoms of physiological reactivity and greater interoceptive awareness than males (Pennebaker, 2000), even in adolescence (Eiser, Havermans, & Eiser, 1995; Kroenke & Spitzer, 1998). In a study of autonomic perception, males and females ($n = 417$) did not differ in the overall number of symptoms, but females reported more differential symptomatology across different emotional states (Shields, 1984). Relevant to the earlier discussion of greater sensitivity to facial expressions among females, those who report perceiving their own heart beats are also more facially expressive (Ferguson & Katkin, 1996). Both the James's (1890) and the Schachter-Singer (1962) theories imply that *autonomic perception* of this sort correlates with *emotion perception*. According to the James's perspective, emotions are perceived when specific physiological changes that are unique to each emotion are detected, and according to the Schachter–Singer perspective, a vague generalized arousal state precedes a search for emotion-relevant situational cues to determine the appropriate emotional response. In each case, awareness of one's internal state is likely to facilitate emotion perception. Moreover, emotion perception correlates with state and trait anxiety (Montgomery & Jones, 1984; Schandry, 1981), and intensity of physical responsiveness, whether perceived or real, contributes to conditioned anxiety responding (see Chapter 6). For example, when participants are led to believe they are emitting a stronger conditioned response than is the case, a larger conditioned response is emitted, and there is more resistance to

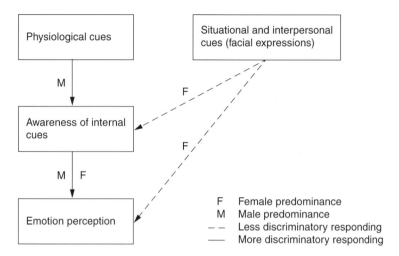

Figure 8.1: Female and male differences in emotion perception.

extinction compared with individuals with poor conditioned response discrimination (Davey, 1987). Hence, self-focused attention may enhance general negative affect as well as the acquisition and strength of conditioned anxiety and fear. By being more internally attuned, females may be more liable to all of these negative effects.

Notably, awareness of internal state is different from *interoceptive accuracy*, and in the latter case, males are clearly superior to females, as exemplified in their ability to detect heart beat (Harver, Katkin, & Bloch, 1993) and learning to detect heart beat (Katkin, 1985; Katkin, Blascovich, &, Goldband, 1981). Pennebaker and Roberts (1992) reviewed seven studies to find that the mean correlation between perceived and actual physiological levels for males was 0.29, but only 0.13 for females. Interestingly, Pennebaker and Roberts (1992) suggest that men and women use different sources of information for judging their physiological functioning, with men being more influenced by actual internal cues and therefore conforming to James' theory, whereas women are more influenced by situational cues and therefore conform more to the Schachter–Singer theory. This conclusion is reached after realizing that male superiority in physiological detection is limited to laboratory settings: sex differences are less apparent in naturalistic settings, where situational factors are more prominent. Clearly, direct empirical investigation of the salience of internal versus external cues in males' and females' emotion perception is warranted. If the proposed female–male difference withstands direct experimental investigation, it would imply that while females report being more aware than males of their physiological state, they rely more on external cues for judging their physiological responding and emotional state. If so, it would nicely complement the evidence for females being more empathic, and more attuned and sensitive to the facial expression of others, such that females may be more inclined to judge impending threat/safety on the basis of others' emotions whereas males may be more likely to use their own internal cues. These factors are depicted in Figure 8.1. Related to this is the evidence for girls to be more likely to attribute emotional reactions to interpersonal causes and for pre-school-aged boys to be more likely to attribute other's emotions to internal causes such as feeling sick (Eisenberg *et al.*, 1996b). Sensitivity to surrounding situational and interpersonal signals of threat for judging internal state is also consistent with females possessing lower self-efficacy and control: individuals who possess lower degrees of social power are more attentive to and skilled at understanding social–emotional cues in their environment than individuals higher in social status (Pennebaker & Roberts, 1992; Snodgrass, 1985).

At the same time, females may remain less discriminatory and more generalized in their judgment of what is threatening versus what is not in their surroundings. In contrast, males' stronger reliance on internal cues may result in better discrimination between what is threatening and what is not. In support, good heart beat discriminators were better able to differentiate masked reinforced versus unreinforced conditioned stimuli in terms of expectancy ratings (Katkin *et al.*, 2001), as if feedback from conditioned autonomic responses provided information about the emotional response that was used to guide verbal ratings. Hence, by being less reliant upon and less accurate in their detection of physiological cues and instead more reliant on situational cues in a poorly discriminated manner, females may be prone to judging themselves as anxious more of the time, especially given their socialization toward emotion expression in general.

Not to be forgotten, however, is that males generally experience stronger surges in autonomic arousal than females, and thus have more distinct physiological cues from which to derive emotion perception. As Pennebaker and Roberts (1992, p. 209) state:

> That is, at least in the case of stress-related emotions such as anger and anxiety, men may rely more than women on the relevant surges in heart rate or blood pressure to identify such emotional states because, on average, they experience these surges more forcefully.

Physiology

There has been considerable progress in research regarding sex dimorphism in brain structure and functioning in general, although its relationship to fear and anxiety and other emotions is only just beginning to be understtod. In their comprehensive review, De Vries and Boyle (1998) propose that sex differences in the brain cause sex differences in behavior and at the same time account for males and females displaying similar behaviors despite major differences in their physiological and hormonal conditions. Evidence to date indicates that male and female brains differ in terms of the corpus callosum, anterior commissure, size and shape of the left planum temporale, and in several clusters of neurons in the hypothalamus (De Vries & Boyle, 1998). Also, fundamental differences exist in the organization of cortical functions, as evident during language tasks in functional magnetic resonance imaging scans where activated left inferior frontal lobes in males compare to more diffuse and bilateral patterns of activation in the same frontal area in females, despite very few differences in male versus female abilities to execute the task (Shaywitz *et al.*, 1995). The obvious question is whether such differences relate to the vulnerability to anxiety. Unfortunately, research to date targets hormonal and physiological differences across the sexes with very little integration with brain structure and functioning.

From their comprehensive review of hormonal and physiological data, Taylor, Klein, Lewis, Gruenewald, Gurung, and Updegraff (2000) conclude that the female acute stress response is geared toward social affiliation and nurturing ("tend and befriend"), whereas the male acute stress response is geared toward attack and protect. They convincingly argue that the female stress response has selectively evolved to maximize survival of the self and offspring. Thus, females are seen as responding to acute stress by nurturing offspring in ways that protect them from harm, and reduce neuroendocrine responses that may compromise offspring health, and by befriending or affiliating with social groups to reduce risk. Tending refers to quieting and caring for offspring and blending into the environment. This pattern of behavior, that down-regulates sympathetic as well as hypothalamic pituitary adrenocortical responding to acute stress, is preferred to fight responses, which may place females themselves and their offspring at risk, and to flight behavior, which may be compromised by pregnancy and the need to care for offspring. Selectively affiliating during stress — befriending — maximizes the likelihood of multiple group members, which provides more eyes for detection of threat and deters predators. Group affiliation may be particularly strong for females because they have to defend against threats from males of their own species as well as external predators, as indicated by their higher rates of sexual abuse (see Chapter 7). Taylor *et al.* (2000) cite multiple studies to support the value of the group for females, including evidence that crowding stresses male rodents but calms female rodents; that women are more likely to cope with stress by seeking and using social support than are men; and that women prefer to affiliate with other women. As already mentioned, women also are more engaged in their social networks than are men, and are better at reporting network events such as major illnesses in children (Wethington, McLeod, & Kessler, 1987). In addition, theories exist for basic sex differences in orientation toward others, with women maintaining a collectivist orientation or connectedness and males remaining more individualistic (Cross & Madson, 1997; Niedenthal & Beike, 1997). Geary and Flinn (2002) attribute female group affiliation to philopatry (the tendency for members of one sex to stay in the birth group and members of the other sex to migrate to another group) that is male dominated, such that women migrate to their male partner's group. "In this circumstance, selection will favor women who have the social competencies needed to develop relationships with unrelated women and through this maintain a supportive social network" (Geary & Flinn, 2002, p. 748). As a result, females have more investment in relationships and are more disturbed when such relationships are in conflict, and are at greater risk for abuse when alliance with other women is not successful.

These data and theories are highly consistent with the evidence thus far for females to be socialized from a young age to be more social, express more empathy and take the perspective of others, to acquire superior sensitivity to facial expressions, to be more responsive to social networks and their needs and crises, and to rely more on surrounding situational and interpersonal cues for determing emotional state, all of which may reflect the greater protective value of the group for women than for men. Interestingly, these factors may explain in large part why males are almost as anxious as females in social situations, as measured by self-report and diagnostic status. That is, due to biological, environmental, and evolutionary driven systems, the threat value of social situations appears to be buffered for females, rendering them on a more equal par with males for the development of social anxiety disorder.

Taylor *et al.* (2000) relate the neuroendocrine system that underlies "tend and befriend" responding to the attachment/caregiving system, a stress-related system based on oxytocin and endogenous opioids. Presumably, the "tend and befriend" pattern is mediated by oxytocin and moderated by sex hormones and endogenous opioid peptide mechanisms. They propose that the basic neuroendocrine core of acute stress responding does not differ substantially between males and females — in both, stress triggers sympathetic adrenal medullary and hypothalamic pituitary adrenal activation — but the effects of these activations are different, with females having more oxytocin released, which enables more caregiving rather than fighting and fleeing. In support, females have a greater release of oxytocin and prolactin in response to an anxiogenic, serotonin agonist (meta-chlorophenylpiperazine (Arato & Bagdy, 1998). Oxytocin is a posterior pituitary hormone that is released to a broad array of stressors, is associated with parasympathetic functioning, enhances sedation and relaxation, reduces fearfulness, and decreases sympathetic activity. Oxytocin is enhanced by estrogen, whereas androgens inhibit oxytocin release under stress. Thereby, oxytocin calms the female who is physiologically aroused, and promotes affiliative behaviors, including maternal behavior. In support, Taylor *et al.* (2000) note that women who are lactating — when oxytocin levels are high — have lower levels of sympathetic arousal, more social behavior, and suppressed hypothalamic–pituitary axis response to stress. In addition, they cite research with non-primates where exogenous administration of oxytocin causes more social contact and grooming among rats. Interestingly, animals prefer to spend time with other animals in whose presence they have experienced high brain oxytocin levels in the past (Panksepp, 1998). Endogenous opioids released during stress appear to stimulate social interaction as well (Jalowiec, Calcagnetti, & Fanselow, 1989), and such opioids have different effects on the social behaviors of men and women, according to Taylor and colleagues (2000).

Oxytocin mediation may explain the relatively robust finding of weaker autonomic and endocrine reactivity to *acute* stressors in female versus male primates and non-primates. For example, female rats show fewer behavioral indications of fear, slower withdrawal latencies to heat and mechanical stimuli, higher ambulation in open-field tests, faster emergence from familiar into novel territory, and more exploration of novel territory (Gray, 1987). Even though the data are less consistent in humans (Gray & Lalljee, 1974), acute stress reactivity is stronger in males than females more often than not. In their study of human babies exposed to mild stress 20–58 hours after birth, Davis and Emory (1995) found greater heart rate increase and cortisol responses in males than females. These findings mirror the evidence presented in Chapter 3 for male newborns to have stronger peaks of physiological arousal in response to stressors than females newborns (Weinberg *et al.*, 1999). In a large anthropological study of 316 individuals aged 2 months to 58 years residing in a rural village in the West Indies, who were monitored over an 8 year period, Flinn, Quinlan, Decker, Turner, and England

(1996) found that male offspring were more at risk for unusual cortisol profiles than were female offspring in relation to unstable caretaking, especially during periods of father absence. Also, boys have heightened blood pressure reactivity (Tsao, Glover, Bursch, Ifekwanigwe, & Zeltzer, 2002) to acute laboratory stressors, including vicarious threat of observing others receive shock (Craig & Lowery, 1969).

Catecholamine studies yield similar findings. Early on, Frankenhaeuser (1975) concluded than when stressed (e.g., taking a test under a time pressure or performing an attention-demanding task), both adult men and boys increased their output of epinephrine, whereas epinephrine levels for women and girls remained relatively stable. Subsequent findings generally support this conclusion. Higher epinephrine and norepinephrine levels were observed in 18-year-old males undergoing a 6 hour exam (Rauste-von Wright, von-Wright, & Frankenhauser, 1981) and in 10–12-year-old boys before a classroom presentation (Elwood, Ferguson, & Thakar, 1986) compared with their female counterparts. Also, both males and females secrete more epinephrine during marital conflict, but the females' level of epinephrine returns to the baseline much faster than in males (Gottman, 1994; Gottman & Levenson, 1992).

Studies of skin conductance are less consistent. Several report stronger skin conductance reactivity in males, as measured via rates of habituation (Maltzman, Gould, Barnett, Raskin, & Wolff, 1979), responding during classical conditioning (Graham, Cohen, & Shmavonian, 1966), and during vicarious threat of observing others receive shock (Craig & Lowery, 1969). On the other hand, Katkin and Hoffman (1976) found no differences in skin conductance between equally fearful males and females when exposed to their feared object (spiders), and Haskins (1982) reported that female college students exhibited greater electrodermal activity than their male counterparts when presented with stressors of arithmetic problems and blood drawing from the antecubital vein.

Nonetheless, Taylor *et al.* (2000 pp. 421–422) conclude that

> women's responses to stress are characterized by patterns that involve caring for offspring under stressful circumstances, joining social groups to reduce vulnerability, and contributing to the development of social groupings, especially those involving female networks, for the exchange of resources and responsibilities. We maintain that aspects of these responses, both maternal and affiliative, may have built on the biobehavioral attachment/caregiving system that depends, in part, on oxytocin, estrogen, and endogenous opioid mechanisms, among other neuroendocrine underpinnings ... the fight-or-flight response [in males] may be heavily tied to androgenic prenatal or post-natal organization of an aggressive response to threat that is activated in part, by testosterone. A substantial neuroendocrine literature from animal studies with females suggests, in contrast, that sympathetic and HPA responses may be downregulated by oxytocin under stressful conditions, and that oxytocin, coupled with endogenous opioid mechanisms and other sex-linked hormones, may foster maternal and affiliative behavior in response to stress.

Of course, the female stress response may be moderated additionally by the nature of the stressor, and by critical reproductive related events in a woman's life, including the onset of puberty, pregnancy, lactation, and the menopause.

Very apparent from this discussion is the concordance between gender socialization influences and physiological reactions to acute stress. The reinforcement of assertive independence in males is well supported by their unmodulated "fight–flight" response. The reinforcement of anxious behaviors and prosocial orientation in females is well supported by their modulated "fight–flight" response to acute stress. Furthermore, the higher rate of conduct, oppositional, and antisocial personality disorders is partly explainable by the testosterone-mediated aggressive response of males to threat. As indicated in earlier chapters, boys and men are more vulnerable to these types of disorders, and the study by Barrett *et al.* (1996) highlighted the role of perceived threat as an instigator of aggressive responding. That is, oppositional children elected more threatening interpretations of ambiguous scenarios than did controls, and even more than did children with anxiety problems. However, their choice of coping was typically more aggressive than avoidant. Another important aspect to that study was the role of parental reinforcement, which serves to remind us that boys' tendencies toward aggression is fueled not only by testosterone activation when under threat but also by socialization of aggressive behaviors.

What is it about the "tend and befriend" response to stress that would contribute to more anxiety in females than males? Perhaps the befriending style generates more worrying about sources of threat in an avoidant and non-problem-solving style of group affiliation and congregation. Perhaps the seeking of support decreases self-efficacy and lessens the chances of active coping with perceived threats. By avoiding threats, the chances for corrective learning and habituation (see Chapter 5) are clearly diminished whereas encouragement to actively face perceived threats renders males not only more likely to be traumatized but also more likely to learn mastery and correct overappraisals of threat. In other words, the neurobiology of the female acute stress response, driven by evolutionary motivations for the protection of offspring and survival of the species and reinforced through socialization, supports worry and avoidance behavior. The higher levels of worry in females and the anxiogenic effects of such worry were described earlier in this chapter. The stronger pattern of avoidance behavior and the anxiogenic effects of such avoidance are described next.

Avoidance

As reviewed in Chapter 1, one of the most pronounced differences between males and females is avoidance behavior, a coping strategy that is reinforced culturally and, as just reviewed, is perhaps driven by evolutionarily based motivational systems that encourage a "tend and befriend" rather than a "fight or flight" response to acute stress. Thus, given the same level of fear of a circumscribed object, females are more prone to avoid than males. The contributory role of avoidance behavior is best evaluated by studying sex differences in reaction to initial experiences of distress. Unfortunately, there are almost no published data on this topic. As mentioned in Chapter 1, one relevant *post hoc* finding is that females endorse more control strategies than males in response to intrusive thoughts, as well as more difficulty eliminating the thoughts (Freeston *et al.*, 1991) but whether this results in females being more vulnerable to obsessive–compulsive disorder is yet to be directly evaluated. Indirect support derives from studies of self-reported coping with stressors in non-clinical samples. For example, Ptacek, Smith, and Zanas (1992) asked 186 college students to monitor over 21 consecutive days their most stressful event of the day, how the event was appraised, the coping methods they employed, and their perceived effectiveness. They found more problem-focused coping in males ($n = 42$) and more support-seeking and emotion-focused coping in females ($n = 110$). Problem-focused coping refers to cognitive and behavioral attempts to alter the stressful situation, and emotion-focused coping refers to more attempts to regulate emotional responses elicited by the stressor. Unfortunately, having participants themselves rate the nature of their coping response, whether it was problem focused or emotion focused or seeking support, renders the results vulnerable to artifactual bias (see Feingold, 1994).

The most direct evidence comes from studies of conditioning. That is, in contrast to responding to acute stress, there is reason to believe that females show elevated reactivity to contextual cues and reminders of stressors. Blanchard, Shepherd, de Padua Carobrez, and Blanchard (1991) studied natural defensive patterns in rats exposed to a cat (a natural predator of rats). Defensive patterns were assessed under two conditions: during the predator's presence ("actual threat") and following predator removal ("potential threat"). The potential threat condition involved exposure to cat odors, and other after effects of the cat's presence. When the cat was present, male and female rats behaved similarly, engaging in almost no movement or observable behavior, indicating high fear. However, under "potential threat" conditions, females behaved more defensively than males, suggesting greater female reactivity to risk of threat. This type of elevated anticipatory responding has been observed in girls and women as well. Spence and Spence (1966) noted that adult females had superior eyelid conditioning performance to a puff of air paired with a tone. Interestingly, however, when conditioning trials were masked as a probability-learning task (in which the experiment was described as a test of irrelevant distracting stimuli on the capacity to learn a problem task), sex was not important to conditionability. That is, females acquired conditioning responses to a greater degree than males, but this effect disappeared under masked conditions. The effects were attributed to differential levels of reactivity to the experimental setting. In the masked case, the *setting* was presented as less threatening, and therefore individual differences in response to threat were minimized. In youths at risk for anxiety by virtue of parental anxiety, Grillon *et al.* (1997, 1998a) found elevated baseline startle in females but not in males, despite equivalent degrees of fear potentiated startle in response to an explicit threat cue (Figure 8.2). An elevated baseline was interpreted as a state of anticipatory anxiety in relation to upcoming experimental procedures (see Chapter 5). In another study, high-risk female offspring again showed enhanced baseline startle, whereas high-risk male offspring displayed elevated potentiated startle to an explicit threat stimulus (a blast of air administered at the throat) (Merikangas *et al.*, 1999). Potentiation of startle was also tested using darkness, and even though darkness was presumed to represent potentiation via contextual stimuli as opposed to fear potentiation using the air blast, they found no sex differences in this case. More evaluation of sex differences in contextual reactivity is warranted, but the elevated baseline startle in high-risk female offspring remains a strong indicator of elevated

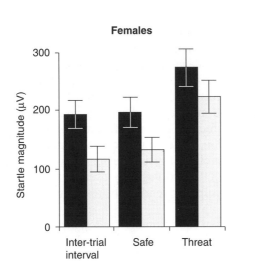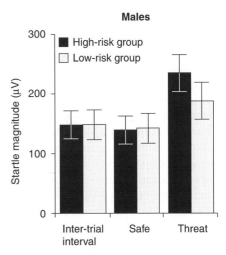

Figure 8.2: Magnitude of the startle reflex during the fear-potentiated startle procedure. (Redrawn by permission of Elsevier from Grillon *et al.* (1998a).)

reactivity to threatening aversive contexts (i.e., the experimental setting). In a related vein, unselected females, aged 7–23 years, showed greater startle potentiation to negative pictures than did males of the same ages (McManis, Bradley, Berg, Cuthbert, & Lang, 2001).

These findings resonate with the evidence cited earlier for stress reactivity and negative affectivity, again elevated in females compared with males, leading to more generalized conditioned anxiety responding. Broad anxiousness is connected with unpredictability and poor discrimination among external cues, and these features may be more characteristic of females due to poorer instrumental learning of attentional control during infancy, stronger encouragement for avoidant responding and ruminative self-focus of attention, and less accurate use of internal cues for judging emotional state and instead greater reliance upon external cues for such judgments. For any or all of these reasons, females are more prone to more generalized, anticipatory, and contextual anxiety responding. In turn, expectations of distress motivate avoidance behavior (see Chapter 5). Together, these data raise the distinct possibility that females are more prone to anxiety disorders because of elevated worry, anticipatory anxiety, and avoidant coping, but not because of elevated fear. Indeed, we are reminded here of the fact that males and females seem to be equally prone to true fear responding in the form of panic attacks, and it is only in the sequelae — the avoidance or distress — that sex differences occur (see Chapter 1).

One might speculate that females are more conditionable to explicit threat cues as well as contextual cues, given their elevated negative affectivity, higher assignment of threat value, and perceived intensity of physiological responding, all of which have been shown to amplify conditionabilty (see Chapter 6). However, the results are generally mixed. Higher rates of conditioning have been found for females in several adult samples (e.g., Guimares *et al.*, 1991), regardless of the potential confounding factor of menstrual phase (Hedlund & Chambless, 1990). Others report faster and/or stronger conditioning in males (Clark & Albino, 1975; Graham *et al.*, 1966), including non-primate studies (Maren, DeOca, & Fanselow, 1994), and other studies show no sex differences (Elder, Gamble, McAfee, & Van Veen, 1979; Fredrikson, Hugdahl, & Öhman, 1976). Perhaps males' stronger physiological response to acute stressors in the laboratory setting overrides female vulnerabilities to conditionability. Moreover, female conditionability, especially as it applies to the acquisition of long-lasting phobias and anxiety disorders, may be better indexed by rates of extinction or spontaneous recovery. Indeed, two studies indicate slower extinction among females than males (Guimaraes *et al.*, 1991; Johansen, 1993). A failure to replicate by Fredrikson *et al.* (1976) was attributed by Hedlund and Chambless (1990) to the use of variable levels of aversive stimuli, where one is less likely to see sex differences in conditioning perhaps because females choose a weaker unconditioned stimulus. In contrast, Guimaraes *et al.* (1991) used standardized 100 dB white noise for all participants. Unfortunately, there has been no systematic evaluation of sex differences in conditioned responding after an intervening period of time (e.g., spontaneous recovery). As described in Chapter 6, much of return of fear can be attributed to regained threat value of stimuli, whether via heightened arousal or anxious rehearsals about previously feared stimuli or lack of repeated exposure to previously feared stimuli. Since females tend to award higher threat value and have less opportunity or encouragement for repeated exposure to previously threatening stimuli, they may be more vulnerable to spontaneous recovery of fears and anxiety; a pattern that would fit with the longer durability of certain anxiety disorders for females (see Chapter 1).

Critical Developmental Phases

We are left with the question of why adolescence is a critical window in which the female propensity for anxiety increases so dramatically. Perhaps the combination of more negative life events occurring during adolescence in comparison with earlier ages (Hankin & Abramson, 2001), stronger gender role socialization pressures during adolescence compared with earlier ages (Keenan & Shaw, 1997), and greater evolutionary pressure toward procreation post-puberty for females than for men render adolescence the time at which all of the vulnerability factors described throughout become more prominent for females. Thus, the reinforcement of anxious behaviors versus assertive independence is stronger, the role of the social group for protection becomes greater, and the physiologically driven avoidant response to acute stressors (oxytocin mediated) is enhanced. The possibility of further risk for female anxiety during late middle age is not as clearly explained, although it does correlate with the time at which all offspring typically have left home. One might speculate that such a departure enhances perceived uncontrollability, which in turn increases current and future distress.

Summary

Greater risk for anxiety exists for females, especially in the transition from childhood to early adulthood, and perhaps again during later middle age. Consistent with the emphasis upon broad vulnerability factors that contribute to anxiousness, females tend to score higher than males on scales of neuroticism. However, the profile is one of few if any temperament differences in the very young, and even heightened emotional reactivity initially in males, with the female propensity to greater inhibition and negative affectivity emerging around 2 years of age, the time at which socialization of gender behaviors tends to be first observed. The sex differences in negative affectivity magnify from childhood through adolescence, in parallel with the higher rates of anxiety and depressive disorders in females over the course of adolescence. In tandem with the developmental shift in negative affectivity is a male-to-female cross-over in reactivity to facial expressions, such that girls and adult females are more reactive to facial expressions. Sensitivity to facial expressions is especially important because of its role in the vicarious acquisition of fear and anxiety as well as the communication of threat. In general, by virtue of elevated negative affectivity, females are at greater risk for detecting threat, learning threat associations, and retaining high levels of reactivity to aversive events.

The factors that contribute to negative affectivity were reviewed in Chapter 3 as genetic influences and major life adversities. Data regarding genetic factors in the transmission of negative affectivity for females suggests a greater genetic contribution for females than for males, but the meaning of this difference remains unclear at this point in time. In terms of major traumas, the results indicate that aside from sexual assault, females are no more prone to traumatic events than males, and in fact are exposed to fewer traumas overall. Thus, the number of major adversities does not appear to account for the elevated rate of negative affectivity in females. However, females are more prone to emotional distress following major traumas and network crises. Although such reactivity is likely to contribute to an ongoing cycle of negative affectivity and reactivity to future stressors, it seems unlikely to fully explain the female propensity to negative affectivity as early as 2 years of age.

Social patterns of reinforcement clearly differ for boys and girls. Differences in parenting are evident in the very first few months of life, where mothers show more synchronicity with their sons than their daughters, perhaps because of the greater emotional needs of their sons. Whatever the reason, synchronicity is potentially very important, as it establishes the base for predictability and controllability over the world and over one's own emotional responding as well as attentional control, which in turn are critical to levels of ongoing distress and ability to regulate emotional arousal. This base may be weaker in females than males. However, the relationship between synchronicity during infancy and proneness to anxiety disorders has not been directly studied, and furthermore may not be detectable given that relatively extreme levels of desynchronous parenting may be necessary before effects become observable in the child.

Gender behaviors are directly reinforced throughout childhood, as parents and others encourage boys to be more assertive, active, and independent than girls, whose behavior is more controlled and whose anxious behaviors are reinforced. Reinforcement patterns are accompanied by differential expectations of boys being more capable than girls. Consequently, boys are encouraged to face challenges in a wider variety of situations and thereby develop more mastery of skills of coping and persistence. In addition, breadth of experience of this kind is likely to facilitate habituation to naturally aversive stimuli and to build a repertoire of positive experiences that buffer later negative experiences. In addition, boys perceive themselves to be stronger, more dominant, and more in control than girls; a difference that extends throughout adolescence and adulthood. In light of the body of research on the effects of controllability, boys are thus presumed to be buffered from current distress and reactivity to future stressors.

Alongside low masculinity, girls are encouraged to be more prosocial and empathic than boys. Such prosocial training fits with their greater sensitivity to facial expressions, and while lowering their risk for social phobia, at the same time enhances females' vulnerability to modeling and vicarious acquisition of fears in relation to specific objects or stimuli, and to the detection of threat in general as communicated by others' facial expressions. Moreover, the negative reinforcement of assertiveness and independence combined with positive reinforcement for prosocial behaviors is likely to contribute to avoidance and retreat to social support as a way of coping with perceived threats.

For all these reasons, it is not surprising that girls exhibit more pervasive anxiousness than boys. Although there is a scarcity of research on attentional biases in females compared with males, women do worry and ruminate more than men, both of which interfere with active problem-solving and contribute to ongoing distressed mood in a self-perpetuating manner. Worry appears to be elicited by uncertainty about potential threat, and thereby excessive worry represents a wide net of potential threat. Also, women are more likely to engage in negative self-focus, which in turn generates more negative mood. Moreover, excessive self-focus may contribute to overgeneralizability of anxious responding by limiting discriminability among external cues, although this remains an untested hypothesis. In addition, under the umbrella of self-focus of attention, women report being more aware of their internal state than are men and such awareness correlates with emotion perception. The perceived intensity of internal responding also predicts the level of conditioned responding, such that internal awareness may generate more conditioned fear and anxiety in women. In combination with a greater awareness of internal cues are less accuracy in judging internal state and greater reliance upon situational cues for judging emotional state. This, in turn, is consistent with females' greater sensitivity to facial expressions, because facial expressions are an information source for judging surrounding danger and emotional state. Greater reliance on situational cues at the cost of accurate detection of internal cues, and especially if the reliance on situational cues is impeded by poorer discrimination among them so that the distinction of what is threatening and what is not becomes blurred (a hypothesis that remains to be directly tested), contributes to overgeneralizability of anxious responding. Added to this is the overestimation of threat that comes with the state of worry. Instead, by relying on internal cues more accurately to judge emotional state, males may be more able to discriminate between what is dangerous and what is not in the environment. In summary, the confluence of worry, self-focus, awareness of internal state but more reliance on situational cues to judge internal state may result in less discriminating and more overgeneralized anxious responding in females.

The study of physiology and behavior yields data very consistent with a profile of more generalized anxious responding in females, and also provides an evolutionarily based motivational analysis for such responding. That is, important differences appear to exist in the male and female response to acute stress. Whereas the sympathetic adrenal medullary and the hypothalamic–pituitary axis are activated in both sexes, the effects of such activation appear to be moderated in females by oxytocin and other endogenous opioids, the result of which is a down-regulation of the "fight–flight" system. Taylor and colleagues (2000) propose that such modulation of the "fight–flight" response is of evolutionary significance because it serves to protect the offspring. Instead of fighting or fleeing, the drive for females is to tend to offspring and befriend others as a way of achieving group protection. The evidence for prosocial training and the importance of the social network for females is consistent with this model, as is the relatively robust evidence for females to show a blunted physiological response to acute stressors in comparison with males. Importantly, the "tend and befriend" style may reinforce a worrisome and avoidant style of coping with perceived threat that contributes to proneness to anxiety disorders. In contrast, whereas the "fight–flight" response exposes males to more threats — hence their elevated rate of trauma exposure — it also provides the opportunity for mastery and threat value reappraisal in the same ways that derive from differential reinforcement of activity, independence, and assertiveness.

Consistent with the reasoning for more overgeneralized anxious responding in females, the evidence suggests that females are more reactive to reminders of threat or contextual threat cues than are males. Perhaps due to their stronger physiological reactivity and greater reliance on internal cues for judging internal state, males sometimes exhibit stronger conditioned responding to explicit threat cues in laboratory settings, although there is some evidence for a greater resistance to extinction in females, and a theoretical reason to suppose more spontaneous recovery of conditioned responses in females. Naturally, broader expectancies of threat motivate more pervasive avoidance behavior.

Overgeneralizability of anxious responding thus appears to be a key feature that separates female and male responding to threat. This difference is supported by a number of factors, including higher negative affectivity and a greater tendency to worry about potential threats, potentially lower synchronicity with parents during infancy leading to poorer attentional discrimination and more unpredictability or, by the same token, overly self-focus attention that detracts from discrimination among external cues, or indiscriminant reliance on external cues for judging threat.

As described in Chapter 5, an avoidant and worrisome style is presumed to maintain the *threat value* of negative affect and surrounding stimuli. At the same time, the *salience* of negative affect may be sustained in females by self-focus of attention and an elevated awareness of their internal state, plus their more pervasive anxious response to a wider array of stimuli that comes with negative affectivity. In contrast, despite the salience of their acute stress response and their greater exposure to trauma, the threat value of surrounding stimuli is lessened by males' more active, problem-solving, and non-avoidant coping that is supported by an unmodulated "fight–flight" reaction to threat and socialization of the male gender.

Chapter 9

Conclusion

The model proposed throughout offers an explanation for the various features of fear and anxiety presented in Chapter 1: for the modal ages of onset at which the different anxiety disorders are first noticed, for the typically insidious manner in which anxiety disorders emerge and for their enduring despite fluctuating symptom severities over time, for the durability of anxiety increasing with age or longevity, for the initial expression of anxiety to increase the risk for other forms of anxiety as well as depressed mood, and for females to be more prone to anxiety disorders than males. An underlying premise of the origins model is that fear and anxiety are functionally separable states characterized by different response profiles that are most adaptive for different stages of threat imminence. Fear is elicited once threat is certain or detected, with certainty ranging from contextual cues in close proximity to threat cues, to explicit threat cues associated with aversive events, to the aversive events themselves. Anxious worry, on the other hand, is elicited by undetected or uncertain threat, as would occur in response to contextual cues more distally associated with threat or even in the absence of any specific cues. To facilitate immediate action needed for self-preservation, fear is characterized by progressively increasing sympathetic autonomic nervous system activation and cortical or cognitive inhibition. In contrast, anxious worry involves suppression of autonomic reactivity and higher levels of verbal processing needed for preparatory strategizing to keep threat at bay. Anxious worry is thus connected with vigilance for threat and avoidant responding. Although fear is expressed within the context of anxiety disorders, the expression of fear itself is not a risk factor for anxiety disorders. Also, female and male differences occur less in the realm of fear *per se* than in the realm of anxiety and avoidance.

A temperament characterized by proneness to experience negative affect, referred to as neuroticism or negative affectivity, and overlapping with constructs of defensive motivational systems and behavioral inhibition, is a common link among the anxiety disorders and depressed mood. Indeed, this common temperament may account in large part for the high rates of co-occurrence among the anxiety disorders and depression. High negative affectivity is determined partly by genetic factors, although exactly what is genetically transmitted is not yet known, and partly by environmental influences. The genetic contribution is non-specific and in common with the vulnerability to anxiety and depression. An additional genetic influence is possibly exerted upon the vulnerability to fear and panic. Environmental influences include major adversities and traumas that enhance stress reactivity, a component of negative affectivity. In turn, high negative affectivity magnifies the negative impact of life traumas and even their likelihood of occurrence. Thus, the combination of negative affectivity and major adversity is presumed to generate a progressively worsening cycle of stress sensitization. The types of major adversities most relevant to anxiety may differ from those most relevant to depression. However, of even greater importance to the discrimination between anxiety and depression is the entirety of learning experiences that mold fearful and anxious ways of responding.

Overall, proneness to frequent and intense negative affect renders such negative affect highly *salient* or a prominent aspect of life functioning. Under such conditions, fear and anxiety will be stronger and more likely in all contexts that naturally prime such states, be it aversive stimuli, novel stimuli, evolutionarily prepared stimuli, developmentally appropriate fear stimuli, or reminders of any of them. Equally important for the anxiety disorders is what is "done" with fearful and anxious states. This is where the concept of emotion regulation, or the way in which arousal and distress are modulated, becomes relevant. Avoidance and danger-laden expectations represent a threat-based style of emotion regulation — or a style of responding that raises the *threat value* of negative affect and associated stimuli. The amount of anxiety that is manifested is influenced by both negative affectivity and a threat-based style of emotion regulation: neither vulnerability factor is necessary but both are contributory toward anxiety disorders.

Emotion regulation is partly biologically determined, especially by the maturing parasympathetic nervous system in the early stages of life, but environmental influences quickly become paramount. Parenting, in particular, impacts the child's skills at self-soothing and emotion regulation, although parenting styles and their impact upon offspring are very much determined by the temperament of the offspring as well. Synchronicity or coordination with the infant's signals, even in the first few months of life, seems critical to establishing a base of predictability and controllability. Very limited synchronicity, for example, may detrimentally impact the learning of contingencies between one's own behavior and outcomes that are external to oneself (e.g., parental responses) as well as internal to oneself (i.e., emotional state). The resultant unpredictability is directly intertwined with attentional processes, such as poor orienting to expected stimuli, and thereby mimics the effects of low cardiac vagal tone. In fact, parenting may directly contribute to chronically low cardiac vagal tone, and together they contribute to poor responsivity or inflexibility of responding to environmental stimuli. In contrast, high vagal tone and effective emotion regulation are seen as flexible and adaptive responding to environmental demands. Poor orienting and limited discrimination among discrete external cues in turn are connected with overgeneralizability of anxious responding to contextual cues; that is, the discrimination between what is threatening and what is not becomes blurred. Instead, the net of threat widens to more and more stimuli associated with negative experiences. Thus, predictability acquired through interactions with significant others in the beginnings of life may play a major role in the subsequent risk for anxiety disorders. However, these relationships remain without direct empirical support. Controllability in terms of personal exertion of contingencies — whereby infant's signals *influence* the parent's response — is also critical to instrumental learning of emotion regulation. Most importantly, early experiences with control buffer the effects of subsequent stressors.

In later childhood, parenting that is intrusive and high on criticism is characteristic of parents of anxious children, and to a certain degree of anxious parents, and may contribute to the child's progression toward anxiety. However, longitudinal evaluation remains to be done, and such parenting is not unique to anxiety but is characteristic of conduct disorders as well. Fearful and negative expectations from the parent as well as modeling of fearful behaviors may be more unique to offspring anxiety and thereby account for the specificity in familial transmission of anxiety disorders. Parenting influences of the latter kind may also contribute to environmental discrimination between anxiety and depression.

The stronger the vulnerabilities of negative affectivity and style of responding to negative affect that raises its threat value, the more pervasive is anxiety. Moreover, in a self-perpetuating cycle, anxious processes in and of themselves contribute to the underlying vulnerability to distress. The anxious processes are in common across the anxiety disorders, and include hypervigilance to threat, a physiology supportive of such vigilance, judgments that award high threat value, and avoidance behavior. Hypervigilance incorporates preferential allocation of attentional resources to threat material or slowed disengagement from threat under conditions of competing attentional demands, even without conscious awareness of what is being attended to. This includes attentiveness to angry or fearful facial expressions, which is an important target because such expressiveness communicates that danger may be looming and also contributes to vicarious acquisition of conditioned fear and anxiety. With sufficient lengths of time, anxious individuals exhibit an avoidance or diversion of attention away from threat material, presumably because of the distress provoked. The combination of initial attentional engagement followed by diversion is termed "vigilance avoidance". Attentional selectivity is driven by the threat value of a stimulus, something that is individually determined, although prepared stimuli of evolutionary significance (including angry and fearful faces) are more "attention" grabbing universally. Consequently, in tandem with attentional selectivity is the assignment of higher threat values by anxious prone individuals as seen in their judgments of risk for negative events, association of aversive stimuli with neutral stimuli, and judgment of meaning of ambiguous situations. Importantly, biases in attention toward and judgment of threat are "trainable", and thus possible to acquire even in the absence of high negative affectivity. This points to the importance of life experience factors that generate a threat-based way of responding. Moreover, "trained" biases of this sort elicit state anxiety or distress in response to stressors, indicating their exacerbating effect on levels of anxiousness.

With regard to physiology, the most robust finding in anxious populations is elevated baseline arousal measured through sympathetic adrenal medullary as well as hypothalamic–pituitary axis activation in anticipation of an upcoming stressor. Relative to non-anxious controls, anxious individuals do not show reliably heightened physiological reactivity to acute stressors. One exception is specific phobias, when the level of general anxiousness is lower compared with other anxiety disorders, and the reactivity to phobic stimuli is distinctively elevated. Otherwise, elevated baseline responding is consistent with a physiology that is supportive of hypervigilance to threat, and is also consistent with the notion that the anxiety disorders are defined mostly by elevated anxiety and worry rather than more intense fear responses *per se*. Individuals at risk for anxiety exhibit elevated sympathetic activation, chronically low cardiac vagal tone, and sustained or overactive hypothalamic–pituitary axis responding to stressors that eventually contributes to their state of vigilance and anticipatory arousal. The third anxious process is avoidance, motivated by the expectation of fear and its threat value. Avoidance plays a major role in the maintenance of anxiousness and may also explain much of the transition from subclinical symptoms to fully fledged anxiety disorders.

The broad vulnerability factors enhance the salience and threat value of stimuli associated with negative affect in general. In addition, particular stimuli acquire more salience and threat value as a result of life experiences and specific biological propensities. That is, stimuli gather threat value by virtue of direct traumatic events, by vicarious acquisition and by informational transmission, and gather additional salience in some cases as a result of biological propensities to react more strongly (as might occur in the case of fainting in response to blood, injury, or injections). The effect of such learning experiences is highly dependent on the entirety of learning in general and prior history with the particular stimulus, as well as the context in which learning occurs, such as the intensity of the aversive experience, its controllability, and the universal threat value (i.e., preparedness) of the stimulus. Moreover, the associative pathways to acquiring conditioned fear and anxiety over specific stimuli are typically enhanced by the broader vulnerabilities of negative affectivity and a threat-based style of emotion regulation. For example, negative affectivity enhances conditionability, and expectancies of fear and evaluations of threat contribute to persistence of conditioned responding. However, this is not to say that vulnerabilities to anxiety are necessary for phobic responding. With more distress comes more generalized responding and less clear discrimination among cues that are directly associated with threat versus surrounding contexts, thus mirroring the effects regarding unpredictability, poor orienting to and discrimination among external stimuli and chronically low cardiac vagal tone. Certain developmentally appropriate fears, such as fears of strangers, animals, and the natural environment, may have non-associative origins, meaning that they are innately experienced in the absence of aversive pairings. Anxious-prone individuals are theorized to fail to habituate to such fears. However, such fears do not account for the majority of adult phobias and anxiety, and the notion of non-associative fears remains without strong empirical support. On the other hand, there is reason to believe that the salience or threat value of certain stimuli are universally inflated at particular maturational points, and may thus explain why fears of social situations exacerbate during adolescence whereas situational fears of driving or flying, for example, increase during early adulthood.

The anxiety disorders are differentiated by the specific classes of stimuli that have acquired salience and high threat value and by their loading on the broader vulnerability factors. Generalized anxiety disorder loads more strongly on these factors than do specific phobias. Moreover, loading on the broader vulnerability factors is presumed to contribute to co-occurring anxiety disorders. That is, those possessing stronger negative affectivity will assign threat to a wider set of stimuli. In accord, neuroticism predicts multiple emotional disorders (Kreuger *et al.*, 1996). By the same token, pervasive anxiety across an array of situations is likely to contribute to the vulnerability to fearfulness and anxiety in other situations. Thus, whereas generalized anxiety disorder yields the highest rates of co-occurring anxiety disorders, specific phobia yields the least (Brown & Barlow, 1992). The ever-widening set of threat cues and the unpredictability and uncontrollability of anxious responding is posited to lead to negative self-judgments about the ability to control one's own emotions, leading to attribution of anxious responding to an invariant aspect of oneself (Chorpita, 2001), which in turn contributes to anxious responding. Co-occurring depressed mood may similarly be explained by the shared vulnerability of negative affectivity (see Chapter 3). The earlier manifestation of anxiety may even potentiate other manifestations of the same vulnerability.

Differences between males and females are apparent in the broad vulnerabilities of negative affectivity and style of responding to negative affect. That is, females possess elevated negative affectivity and a more avoidant and worrisome style of responding to negative affect. Given that parent–infant synchronicity is generally higher for mother–son than mother–daughter dyads, the early base of predictability controllability may be weakened for girls, although direct investigation of these possibilities is needed. Also, socialization influences throughout childhood and adolescence discourage female assertiveness, independence, and activity compared with males, and encourage prosocial, empathic behaviors that parallel females' stronger processing of facial expressions. Moreover, anxiety is more accepted and reinforced in girls than boys; instead, boys are more encouraged to overcome anxiety and are even more likely to be taken for professional treatment for anxiety. Thus, whereas girls may begin life as less emotionally reactive than male newborns, they become more inhibited in their behaviors by around the age of 2 years. Added to the reinforcement patterns are lower expectancies for competency in girls than boys across a wide array of domains that contributes to their lowered sense of control and heightened impact of negative life stressors.

The socialization influences map very closely onto evolutionary models in which offspring are better cared for by a system of avoidance and group affiliation than by "fight and flight". Thus, females show a modulated physiological response to acute stress and a behavioral retreat to the group, in comparison with the unmodulated "fight–flight" response of males. Retreat and avoidance contributes directly to female anxiety whereas, by directly facing perceived threats, males are not only exposed to more traumas but also given more opportunities for mastery and adaptive reappraisal of misjudged threat. Corollaries of retreat and affiliation are elevated sensitivity to facial expressions, which in turn contribute to vicarious acquisition of fear and a sense of environmental danger, and a lowered sense of control, which increases the impact of stressors. Other corollaries include greater worry, and rumination that contributes to the threat value of aversive stimuli, and heightened self-focus of attention and awareness of internal state that contributes to emotion perception, and when combined with greater reliance on situational–interpersonal cues for judgment of autonomic state results in overjudgment of anxiety and threat. Many of these corollaries yield effects similar to the effects of unpredictable aversive stimuli and chronically low cardiac vagal tone; that is, poor discrimination between what is threatening and what is not, or overgeneralizability of responding to contextual cues. Thus, females show elevated reactivity to contextual cues or reminders of threat in comparison with males' stronger response to acute stressors. The reasons why adolescence is the period of greatest divergence between female and male risk for anxiety are not fully clear but may be linked to enhanced socialization pressures and pressures for procreation at that time.

References

Abbott, B. B., Schoen, L. S., & Badia, P. (1984). Predictable and unpredictable shock: behavioral measures of aversion and physiological measures of stress. *Psychological Bulletin*, *96*, 45–71.

Abbott, M. J., & Rapee, R. M. (2003 in press). Post-event rumination and negative self-appraisal in social phobia before and after treatment. *Journal of Abnormal Psychology*.

Abe, K., & Masui, T. (1981). Age–sex trends of phobic and anxiety symptoms in adolescents. *British Journal of Psychiatry*, *138*, 297–302.

Abramson, L. Y., Metalsky, G. I., & Alloy, L. B. (1988). The hopelessness theory of depression: does the research test the theory? In L. Y. Abramson (ed.), *Social cognition and clinical psychology: a synthesis* (pp. 33–65). New York, NY: Guilford Press.

Achenbach, T. M., & Edelbrock, C. S. (1984). Psychopathology of childhood. *Annual Review of Psychology*, *35*, 227–256.

Agras, S. (1965). An investigation of decrements of anxiety responses during systematic desensitization treatment. *Behaviour Research and Therapy*, *2*, 267–270.

Agras, S. W., & Jacob, R. (1981). Phobia: nature and measurements. In M. Mavissakalian & D. H. Barlow (eds), *Phobia: psychological and pharmacological treatment* (pp. 35–62). New York, NY: Guilford.

Agras, S. W., Chapin, H. N., & Oliveau, D. C. (1972). The natural history of phobia: course and prognosis. *Archives of General Psychiatry*, *26*, 315–317.

Aikins, D., & Craske, M. G. (2003 in press). Ambulatory monitoring of sleep physiology in panic disorder with and without nocturnal panic attacks.

Akiskal, H. S. (1983). Dysthymic disorder: psychopathology of proposed chronic depressive subtypes. *American Journal of Psychiatry*, *140*, 11–20.

Albano, A. M., Chorpita, B. F., & Barlow, D. H. (1996). Childhood anxiety disorders. In E. J. Mash & R. A. Barkley (eds), *Child psychopathology* (pp. 196–241). New York, NY: Guilford Press.

Albus, M., Braune, S., Hoehn, T., & Scheibe, G. (1988). Do anxiety patients with or without frequent panic attacks differ in their response to stress? *Stress Medicine*, *4*, 189–194.

Alden, L. E., & Wallace, S. T. (1995). Social phobia and social appraisal in successful and unsuccessful social interactions. *Behaviour Research and Therapy*, *33*, 497–505.

Allen, A. J., Leonard, H., & Swedo, S. E. (1995). Current knowledge of medications for the treatment of childhood anxiety disorders. *Journal of the American Academy of Child and Adolescent Psychiatry*, *34*, 976–986.

Allen, N. B., Lewinsohn, P. M., & Seeley, J. R. (1998). Prenatal and perinatal influences on risk for psychopathology in childhood and adolescence. *Development and Psychopathology*, *10*, 513–529.

Allgood-Merten, B., Lewinsohn, P. M., & Hops, H. (1990). Sex differences and adolescent depression. *Journal of Abnormal Psychology*, *99*, 55–63.

Almeida, D. M., & Kessler, R. C. (1998). Everyday stressors and gender differences in daily distress. *Journal of Personality and Social Psychology, 75*, 670–680.

American Psychiatric Association. (1987). *Diagnostic and statistical manual of mental disorders* (3rd ed.) Washington, DC: American Psychiatric Press.

American Psychiatric Association. (1994). *Diagnostic and statistical manual of mental disorders* (4th ed.). Washington, DC: American Psychiatric Press.

Amering, M., Katschnig, H., Berger, P., Windhaber, J., Baischer, W., & Dantendorfer, K. (1997). Embarrassment about the first panic attack predicts agoraphobia in disorder patients. *Behaviour Research and Therapy, 35*, 517–521.

Amin, J. M., & Lovibond, P. F. (1997). Dissociations between covariation bias and expectancy bias for fear-relevant stimuli. *Cognition and Emotion, 11*, 273–289.

Amir, N., Cashman, L., & Foa, E. B. (1997). Strategies of thought control in obsessive–compulsive disorder. *Behaviour Research and Therapy, 35*, 775–777.

Amir, N., Foa, E. B., & Coles, M. E. (1998). Automatic activation and strategic avoidance of threat-relevant information in social phobia. *Journal of Abnormal Psychology, 107*, 285–290.

Anastasiades, P., Clark, D. M., Salkovskis, P. M., Middleton, H., Hackman, A., Gelder, M. G., & Johnston, D. W. (1990). Psychophysiological responses in panic and stress. *Journal of Psychophysiology, 4,* 331–338.

Anderson, J. C., Williams, S. M., McGee, R., & Silva, P. A. (1987). DSM-III disorders in preadolescent children: prevalence in a large sample from the general population. *Archives of General Psychiatry, 44*, 69–76.

Andrews, G., Freed, S., & Teeson, M. (1994). Proximity and anticipation of a negative outcome in phobias. *Behaviour Research and Therapy, 32*, 643–645.

Angst, J., & Dobler-Mikola, A. (1985). The Zurich Study: anxiety and phobia in young adults. *European Archives of Psychiatry and Neurological Sciences, 235*, 171–178.

Angst, J., & Vollrath, M. (1991). The natural history of anxiety disorders. *Acta Psychiatrica Scandinavica. Munksgaard Scientific Journal, 84*, 446–452.

Antony, M. M., Meadows, E. A., Brown, T. A., & Barlow, D. H. (1994). Cardiac awareness before and after cognitive–behavioral treatment for panic disorder. *Journal of Anxiety Disorders, 8*, 341–350.

Antony, M. M., Craske, M. G., & Barlow, D. H. (eds) (1995). *Mastery of your specific phobias.* San Antonio, TX: Harcourt Brace.

Arato, M., & Bagdy, G. (1998). Gender difference in m-CPP challenge test in healthy volunteers. *International Journal of Neuropsychopharmacology, 1,* 121–124.

Arcus, D., & Kagan, J. (1995). Temperament and craniofacial variation in the first two years. *Child Development, 66*, 529–1540.

Arnsten, A. F. T., & Goldman-Rakic, P. S. (1998). Noise stress impairs prefrontal cortical cognitive function in monkeys: evidence for a hyperdopaminergic mechanism. *Archives of General Psychiatry, 55*, 362–368.

Arntz, A., van den Hout, M. A., Lousberg, R. & Schouten, E. (1990a). Is the match/mismatch model based on a statistical artefact? *Behaviour Research and Therapy, 28,* 249–253.

Arntz, A., van Eck, M., & Heijmans, M. (1990b). Predictions of dental pain: the fear of any expected evil is worse than the evil itself. *Behaviour Research and Therapy, 28*, 29–41.

Arntz, A., Hildebrand, M., & van den Hout, M. (1994). Overprediction of anxiety, and disconfirmatory processes, in anxiety disorders. *Behaviour Research and Therapy, 32*, 709–722.

Asmundson, G. J. G., & Stein, M. B. (1994). Vagal attenuation in panic disorder: an assessment of parasympathetic nervous system function and subjective reactivity to respiratory manipulations. *Psychosomatic Medicine, 56*, 187–193.

Averill, J. R. (1973). Personal control over aversive stimuli and its relationship to stress. *Psychological Bulletin*, *80*, 286–303.

Avilla, C., Parcet, M. A., Ortet, G., & Ibanez-Ribes, M. I. (1999). Anxiety and counter-conditioning: the role of behavioral inhibition system in the ability to associate aversive stimuli with future rewards. *Personality and Individual Differences*, *27*, 1167–1179.

Baddeley, A. D. (1990). *Human memory: theory and practice.* Needham Heights, MA: Allyn & Bacon.

Balaban, M. T. (1995). Affective influences on startle in five-month-old infants: reactions to facial expressions of emotion. *Child Development*, *66*, 28–36.

Bandura, A. (1977). Self efficacy: toward a unifying theory of behavioural change. *Psychological Review*, *84*, 191–215.

Bandura, A., & Adams, N. E. (1977). Analysis of self-efficacy theory of behavioral change. *Cognitive Therapy and Research*, *1*, 287–308.

Bandura, A., Reese, L., & Adams, N. E. (1982). Microanalysis of action and fear arousal as function of differential levels of perceived self-efficacy. *Journal of Personality and Social Psychology*, *43*, 5–21.

Barlow, D. H. (1988). *Anxiety and its disorders: the nature and treatment of anxiety and panic.* New York, NY: Guilford Press.

Barrett, P. M., Rapee, R. M., Dadds, M. M., & Ryan, S. M. (1996). Family enhancement of cognitive style in anxious and aggressive children. *Journal of Abnormal Child Psychology*, *24*, 187–203.

Baxter, L. R., Schwartz, J. M., Bergman, K. S., Szuba, M. P., Guze, B. H., Mazziotta, J. C., Alazraki, A., Selin, C. E., Ferng, H. K., Munford, P., & Phelps, M. E. (1992). Caudate glucose metabolic rate changes with both drug and behavior therapy for obsessive–compulsive disorder. *Archives of General Psychiatry*, *49*, 681–689.

Bebbington, P. E., Tennant, C., & Hurry, J. (1991). Adversity in groups with an increased risk of minor affective disorder. *British Journal of Psychiatry*, *158*, 33–40.

Bebbington, P., Wilkins, S., Jones, P., Foerster, A., Murray, R., Toone, B., & Lewis, S. (1993). Life events and psychosis: initial results from the Camberwell Collaborative Psychosis Study. *British Journal of Psychiatry*, *162*, 72–79.

Beck, A. T., Emery, G., & Greenberg, R. L. (eds) (1985). *Anxiety disorders and phobias: a cognitive perspective*. New York, NY: Basic Books.

Becker, E. S., Roth, W. T., Andrich, M. & Margraf, J. (1999). Explicit memory in anxiety disorders. *Journal of Abnormal Psychology*, *108*, 153–163.

Beech, H. R. & Liddel, A. (1974). Decision-making, mood states and ritualistic behaviour among obsessional patients. In H. R. Beech (ed.), *Obsessional states* (pp. 143–160). London: Methuen.

Beidel, D. C., Fink, C. M., & Turner, S. M. (1996). Stability of anxious symptomatology in children. *Journal of Abnormal Child Psychology*, *24*, 257–269.

Bell-Dolan, D. J. (1995). Social cue interpretation of anxious children. *Journal of Clinical Child Psychology*, *24*, 2–10.

Bem, S. L. (1981). Gender schema theory: a cognitive account of sex typing. *Psychological Review*, *88*, 354–364.

Bennet, A., & Stirling, J. (1998). Vulnerability factors in the anxiety disorders. *British Journal of Medical Psychology*, *71*, 311–321.

Berg, C. Z., Rapoport, J. L., Whitaker, A., Davis, M., Leonard, H., Swedo, S. E., Braiman, S., & Lenane, M. (1989). Childhood obsessive–compulsive disorder: a two-year prospective follow-up of a community sample. *Journal of the American Academy of Child and Adolescent Psychiatry*, *28*, 528–533.

Bergman, R. L., & Craske, M. G. (2000). Verbalization and imagery during worry activity. *Depression and Anxiety, 11,* 169–174.

Bernstein, G. A., & Borchardt, C. M. (1991). Anxiety disorders of childhood and adolescence: a critical review. *Journal of the American Academy of Child and Adolescent Psychiatry, 30,* 519–532.

Biederman, J., Rosenbaum, J. F., Hirshfeld, D. R., Faraone, S. V., Bolduc, E. A., Gersten, M., Meminger, S. R., Kagan, F., Sidman, N., & Reznick, S. (1990). Psychiatric correlates of behavioral inhibition in young children of parents with and without psychiatric disorders. *Archives of General Psychiatry, 47,* 21–26.

Biederman, J., Rosenbaum, J. F., Bolduc-Murphy, E. A., Faraone, S. V., Chaloff, J., Hirshfeld, D. R., & Kagan, F. (1993). A three year follow-up of children with and without behavioral inhibition. *Journal of the American Academy of Child and Adolescent Psychiatry, 32,* 814–821.

Biederman, J., Faraone, S. V., Hirshfeld-Becker, D. R., Friedman, D., Robin, J. A., & Rosenbaum, J. F. (2001). Patterns of psychopathology and dysfunction in high-risk children of parents with panic disorder and major depression. *American Journal of Psychiatry, 158,* 49–57.

Birbaumer, N., Grodd, W., Diedrich, O., Klose, U., Erb, M., Lotze, M., Schneider, F., Weiss, U., & Flor, H. (1998). fMRI reveals amygdale activation to human faces in social phobics. *International Journal for the Rapid Communication of Research in Neuroscience, 9,* 1123–1226.

Blagden, J. C., & Craske, M. G. (1996). Effects of active and passive rumination and distraction: a pilot replication with anxious mood. *Journal of Anxiety Disorders, 10,* 243–252.

Blanchard, D. C., Shepherd, J. K., de Padua Carobrez, A., & Blanchard, R. J. (1991). Sex effects in defensive behavior: baseline differences and drug interactions. *Neuroscience and Biobehavioral Reviews, 15,* 461–468.

Blanchard, E. B., Kolb, L. C., Pallmeyer, T. P., & Gerardi, R. J. (1982). The development of a psychophysiological assessment procedure for post-traumatic stress disorder in Vietnam veterans. *Psychiatric Quarterly, 4,* 220–229.

Blanchard, E. B., Hickling, E. J., Vollmer, A. J., Loos, W. R., Buckley, T. C., & Jaccard, J. (1995). Short-term follow-up of post-traumatic stress symptoms in motor vehicle accident victims. *Behaviour Research and Therapy, 33,* 369–377.

Blazer, D., Hughes, D., & George, L. K. (1987). Stressful life events and the onset of a generalized anxiety syndrome. *American Journal of Psychiatry, 144,* 1178–1183.

Block, R. I., Ghoneim, M. M., Fowles, D. C., Kumar, V. (1987). Effects of a subanesthetic concentration of nitrous oxide on establishment, elicitation, and semantic and phonemic generalization of classically conditioned skin conductance responses. *Pharmacology, Biochemistry, and Behavior, 28,* 7–14.

Bolle, R. C. (1970). Species-specific defensive reactions and avoidance learning. *Psychological Review, 71,* 32–48.

Bond, N. W., & Siddle, D. A. T. (1996). The preparedness account of social phobia: some data and alternative explanations. In R. M. Rapee (ed.), *Current controversies in the anxiety disorders* (pp. 291–316). New York, NY: Guilford Press.

Booth, R., & Rachman, S. (1992). The reduction of claustrophobia: I. *Behaviour Research and Therapy, 30,* 207–221.

Borkovec, T. D. (1994). The nature, functions, and origins of worry. In G. C. L. Davey & F. Tallis (eds), *Worrying: perspectives on theory, assessment and treatment* (pp. 5–33). Chichester: Wiley.

Borkovec, T. D., & Sides, J. (1979). The contribution of relaxation and expectance to fear reduction via graded imaginal exposure to feared stimuli. *Behaviour Research and Therapy, 17,* 529–540.

Borkovec, T. D., & Hu, S. (1990). The effect of worry on cardiovascular response to phobic imagery. *Behaviour Research and Therapy, 28,* 67–73.

Borkovec, T. D., & Inz, J. (1990). The nature of worry in generalized anxiety disorder: a predominance of thought activity. *Behaviour Research and Therapy, 28*, 153–158.

Borkovec, T. D., & Lyonfields, J. D. (1993). Worry: thought suppression of emotional processing. In H. W. Krohne (ed.), *Attention and avoidance: strategies in coping with aversiveness* (pp. 101–118). Kirkland, WA: Hogrefe & Huber.

Borkovec, T. D. & Roemer, L. (1995). Perceived functions of worry among generalized anxiety disorder subjects: distraction from more emotionally distressing topics? *Journal of Behavior Therapy and Experimental Psychiatry, 26,* 25–30.

Borkovec, T. D., Wilkinson, L., Folensbee, R., & Lerman, C. (1983). Stimulus control applications to the treatment of worry. *Behaviour Research and Therapy, 21*, 247–251.

Borkovec, T. D., Shadick, R. N., & Hopkins, M. (1991). The nature of normal and pathological worry. In R. M. Rapee & D. H. Barlow (eds), *Chronic anxiety: generalized anxiety disorder and mixed anxiety-depression* (pp. 29–51). New York, NY: Guilford Press.

Borkovec, T. D., Lyonfields, J. D., Wiser, S. L., & Diehl, L. (1993). The role of worrisome thinking in the suppression of cardiovascular response to phobic imagery. *Behaviour Research and Therapy, 31*, 321–324.

Borkovec, T. D., Newman, M. G., Pincus, A. L., & Lytle, R. (2002). A component analysis of cognitive–behavioral therapy for generalized anxiety disorder and the role of interpersonal problems. *Journal of Consulting and Clinical Psychology, 70*, 288–298.

Boulougouris, J. C., Rabavilas, A. D., & Stefanis, C. (1977). Psychophysiological responses in obsessive–compulsive patients. *Behaviour Research and therapy, 15*, 221–230.

Bourdon, K. H., Boyd, J. H., Rae, D. S., Burns, B. J., Thompson, J. W., & Locke, B. Z. (1988). Gender differences in phobias: results of the ECA Community Survey. *Journal of Anxiety Disorders, 2*, 227–241.

Bouton, M. E., Mineka, S., & Barlow, D. H. (2001). A modern learning theory perspective on the etiology of panic disorder. *Psychological Review, 108*, 4–32.

Bowen, R. C., Offord, D. R., & Boyle, M. H. (1990). The prevalence of overanxious disorder and separation anxiety disorder: results from the Ontario Child Health Study. *Journal of the American Academy of Child and Adolescent Psychiatry, 29*, 753–758.

Bower, G. H. (1981). Mood and memory. *American Psychologist, 36*, 129–148.

Bowlby, J. (1969). Disruption of affectional bonds and its effects on behavior. *Canada's Mental Health Supplement, 59*, 12.

Bowlby, J. (1973). *Attachment and loss* (vol. 2). *Separation: anxiety and anger*. New York, NY: Basic Books.

Bowlby, J. (1980). By ethology out of psycho-analysis: an experiment in interbreeding. *Animal Behaviour, 28*, 649–656.

Bownes, I. T., O'Gorman, E. C., & Sayers, A. (1991). Assault characteristics and posttraumatic stress disorder in rape victims. *Acta Psychiatrica Scandinavica, 83*, 27–30.

Boyle, M. H., & Offord, D. R. (1991). Psychiatric disorder and substance use in adolescence. *Canadian Journal of Psychiatry, 36*, 699–705.

Bradley, B. P., Mogg, K., & Williams, R. (1994). Implicit and explicit memory for emotional information in non-clinical subjects. *Behaviour Research and Therapy, 32*, 65–78.

Bradley, B. P., Mogg, K., Millar, N. & White, J. (1995). Selective processing of negative information: effects of clinical anxiety, concurrent depression, and awareness. *Journal of Abnormal Psychology, 104*, 532–536.

Bradley, B. P., Mogg, K., Millar, N., Boham-Carter, C., Fergusson, E., Jenkins, J., & Parr, M. (1997). Attentional biases for emotional faces. *Cognition and Emotion, 11*, 25–42.

Bradley, B. P., Mogg, K., White, J., Groom, C., & de Bono, J. (1999). Attentional bias for emotional faces in generalized anxiety disorder. *British Journal of Clinical Psychology, 3*, 267–278.

Bradley, B. P., Mogg, K., & Millar, N. (2000). Covert and overt orienting of attention to emotional faces in anxiety. *Cognition and Emotion, 14,* 789–808.

Breiter, H. C., Rauch, S. L., Kwong, K. K., Baker, J. R., Weisskoff, R. M., Kennedy, D. N., Kendrick, A. D., Davis, T. L., Jiang, A., Cohen, M. S., Stern, C. E., Belliveau, J. W., Baer, L., O'Sullivan, R. M., Savage, C. R., Jenike, M. A., & Rosen, B. R. (1996). Functional magnetic resonance imaging of symptom provocation in obsessive–compulsive disorder. *Archives of General Psychiatry, 53,* 595–606.

Bremner, J. D., Southwick, S. M., Johnson, D. R., Yehuda, R., & Charney, D. S. (1993). Childhood physical abuse and combat-related posttraumatic stress disorder in Vietnam veterans. *American Journal of Psychiatry, 150,* 235–239.

Breslau, N., & Davis, G. C. (1992). Posttraumatic stress disorder in an urban population of young adults: risk factors for chronicity. *American Journal of Psychiatry, 149,* 671–675.

Breslau, N., Davis, G. C., Andreski, P., & Peterson, E. (1991). Traumatic events and posttraumatic stress disorder in an urban population of young adults. *Archives of General Psychiatry, 48,* 216–222.

Breslau, N., Davis, G. C., Andreski, P., Peterson, E. L., & Schultz, L. R. (1997). Sex differences in posttraumatic stress disorder. *Archives of General Psychiatry, 54,* 1044–1048.

Breslau, N., Chilcoat, H. D., Kessler, R. C., & Davis, G. C. (1999a). Previous exposure to trauma and PTSD effects of subsequent trauma: results from the Detroit Area Survey of Trauma. *American Journal of Psychiatry, 156,* 902–907.

Breslau, N., Chilcoat, H. D., Kessler, R. C., Peterson, E. L., & Lucia, V. C. (1999b). Vulnerability to assaultive violence: further speculation of the sex difference in post-traumatic stress disorder. *Psychological Medicine, 29,* 813–821.

Breslau, N., Chilcoat, H. D., Peterson, E. L., & Schultz, L. R. (2000). Gender differences in major depression: the role of anxiety. In E. Frank (ed.), *Gender and its effects on psychopathology* (pp. 131–150). Washington, DC: American Psychiatric Publishing.

Brewin, C. R. (2001). A cognitive neuroscience account of posttraumatic stress disorder and its treatment. *Behaviour Research and Therapy, 39,* 373–393.

Broadbent, D., & Broadbent, M. (1988). Anxiety and attentional bias: state and trait. *Cognition and Emotion, 2,* 165–183.

Broadhurst, P. L. (1975). The Maudsley reactive and nonreactive strains of rats: a survey. *Behavior Genetics, 5,* 299–319.

Brom, D., Kleber, R. J., & Hofman, M. C. (1993). Victims of traffic accidents: incidence and prevention of post-traumatic stress disorder. *Journal of Clinical Psychology, 49,* 131–140.

Brown, E. J., Heimberg, R. G., & Juster, H. R. (1995). Social phobia subtype and avoidant personality disorder: effect on severity of social phobia, impairment, and outcome of cognitive behavioral treatment. *Behavior Therapy, 26,* 467–486.

Brown, G. W., Harris, T. O., & Eales, M. J. (1993). Aetiology of anxiety and depressive disorders in an inner-city population: II. Comorbidity and adversity. *Psychological Medicine, 23,* 155–165.

Brown, H. D., Kosslyn, S. M., Breiter, H. C., Baer, L., & Jenike, M. A. (1994). Can patients with obsessive–compulsive disorder discriminate between percepts and mental images? A signal detection analysis. *Journal of Abnormal Psychology, 103,* 445–454.

Brown, T. A., & Barlow, D. H. (1992). Comorbidity among anxiety disorders: implications for treatment and DSM-IV. *Journal of Consulting and Clinical Psychology, 60,* 835–844.

Brown, T. A., Chorpita, B. F., & Barlow, D. H. (1998). Structural relationships among dimensions of the DSM-IV anxiety and mood disorders and dimensions of negative affect, positive affect, and autonomic arousal. *Journal of Abnormal Psychology, 107,* 179–192.

Brown, T. A., Campbell, L. A., Lehman, C. L., Grisham, J. R., & Mancill, R. B. (2001). Current and lifetime comorbidity of the DSM-IV anxiety and mood disorders in a large clinical sample. *Journal of Abnormal Psychology, 110,* 585–599.

Bruce, M., & Lader, M. (1991). DSM-III-R state anxiety symptoms in anxiety disorder patients. *Biological Psychiatry, 30,* 519–522.

Bruch, M. A., & Heimberg, R. G. (1994). Differences in perceptions of parental and personal characteristics between generalized and nongeneralized social phobics. *Journal of Anxiety Disorders, 8,* 155–168.

Bruch, M. A., Heimberg, R. G., Berger, P., & Collins, T. M. (1989). Social phobia and perceptions of early parental and personal characteristics. *Anxiety Research, 2,* 57–65.

Bryant, R. A., & Harvey, A. G. (1995). Avoidant coping style and post-traumatic stress following motor vehicle accidents. *Behaviour Research and Therapy, 33,* 631–635.

Bryant, R. A., Harvey, A. G., Gordon, E., & Barry, R. J. (1995). Eye movement and electrodermal responses to threat stimuli in post-traumatic stress disorder. *International Journal of Psychophysiology, 20,* 209–213.

Bryant, R. A., Harvey, A. G., Guthrie, R. M., & Moulds, M. L. (2000). A prospective study of psychophysiological arousal, acute stress disorder, and posttraumatic stress disorder. *Journal of Abnormal Psychology, 109,* 341–344.

Buchanan, C. M., Eccles, J. S., & Becker, J. B. (1992). Are adolescents the victims of raging hormones? Evidence for activational effects of hormones on moods and behavior at adolescence. *Psychological Bulletin, 111,* 62–107.

Buchel, C., Morris, J., Dolan, R. J., & Friston, K. J. (1998). Brain systems mediating aversive conditioning: an event-related fMRI study. *Neuron, 20,* 947–957.

Buck, R. (1975). Nonverbal communication of affect in children. *Journal of Personality and Social Psychology, 31,* 644–653.

Burke, J. D., Burke, K. C., & Rae, D. S. (1994). Increased rates of drug abuse and dependence after onset of mood or anxiety disorders in adolescence. *Hospital and Community Psychiatry, 45,* 451–455.

Burke, K. C., Burke, J. D., Regier, D. A., & Rae, D. S. (1990). Age at onset of selected mental disorders in five community populations. *Archives of General Psychiatry, 47,* 511–518.

Buss, A. M., & Plomin, R. (1984). *Temperament: early developing personality traits.* Hillsdale, NJ: Lawrence Erlbaum.

Buss, D. M., & Scheier, M. F. (1976). Self-consciousness, self-awareness, and self-attribution. *Journal of Research in Personality, 4,* 463–468

Butler, G., & Mathews, A. (1983). Cognitive processes in anxiety. *Advances in Behaviour Research and Therapy, 5,* 51–62.

Butler, G., & Mathews, A. (1987). Anticipatory anxiety and risk perception. *Cognitive Therapy and Research Special Issue: Anxiety: Cognitive Factors and the Anxiety Disorders, 11,* 551–565.

Butler, G., Wells, A., & Dewick, H. (1995). Differential effects of worry and imagery after exposure to a stressful stimulus: a pilot study. *Behavioural and Cognitive Psychotherapy, 23,* 45–56.

Bystritsky, A., Craske, M., Maidenberg, E., Vapnik, T., & Shapiro, D. (1995). Ambulatory monitoring of panic patients during regular activity: a preliminary report. *Biological Psychiatry, 38,* 684–689.

Bystritsky, A., Pontillo, D., Powers, M., Sabb, F. W., Craske, M. G., & Bookheimer, S. Y. (2001). Functional MRI changes during panic anticipation and imagery exposure. *Neuroreport: for Rapid Communication of Neuroscience Research, 12,* 3953–3957.

Calvo, M., & Castillo, M. D. (1997). Mood-congruent bias in interpretation of ambiguity: strategic processes and temporary activation. *Quarterly Journal of Experimental Psychology: Human Experimental Psychology, 50A,* 163–182.

Cameron, O. G., & Nesse, R. M. (1988). Systemic hormonal and physiological abnormalities in anxiety disorders. *Psychoneuroendocrinology, 13,* 287–307.

Cameron, O. G., & Hill, E. M. (1989). Women and anxiety. *Psychiatric Clinics of North America*, *12*, 175–186.

Campbell, M. A., & Rapee, R. M. (1994). The nature of feared outcome representations in children. *Journal of Abnormal Child Psychology*, *22*, 99–111.

Cantwell, D. P., & Baker, L. (1989). Stability and natural history of DSM-III childhood diagnoses. *Journal of the American Academy of Child and Adolescent Psychiatry*, *28*, 691–700.

Cappelleri, J. C., Eckenrode, J., & Powers, J. L. (1993). The epidemiology of child abuse: findings from the second national incidence and prevalence study of child abuse and neglect. *American Journal of Public Health, 83,* 1622–1624.

Carey, M. P., Dusek, J. B., & Spector, I. P. (1988). Sex roles, gender, and fears: a brief report. *Phobia Practice and Research Journal*, *1*, 114–120.

Carter, M. M., Hollon, S. D., Carson, R., & Shelton, R. C. (1995). Effects of a safe person on induced distress following a biological challenge in panic disorder with agoraphobia. *Journal of Abnormal Psychology*, *104*, 156–163.

Carter, W. R., Johnson, M. C., & Borkovec, T. D. (1986). Worry: an electrocortical analysis. *Advances in Behaviour Research and Therapy*, *8*, 193–204.

Cartwright-Hatton, S., & Wells, A. (1997). Beliefs about worry and intrusions: the meta-cognitions questionnaire and its correlates. *Journal of Anxiety Disorders*, *11*, 279–296.

Carver, C. S., & Scheier, M. F. (eds) (1998). *On the self-regulation of behavior.* New York, NY: Cambridge University Press.

Caspi, A., Elder Jr, G. H., & Bem, D. J. (1988). Moving away from the world: life course patterns of shy children. *Developmental Psychology*, *24*, 824–831.

Caspi, A., Henry, B., McGee, R. O., Moffitt, T. E., & Silva, P. A. (1995). Temperamental origins of child and adolescent behavior problems: from age three to age fifteen. *Child Development*, *66*, 55–68.

Caspi, A., Moffitt, T. E., Newman, D. L., & Silva, P. A. (1997). Behavioral observations at age 3 years predict adult psychiatric disorders: longitudinal evidence from a birth cohort. In M. E. Hertzig, & E. A. Farber (eds), *Annual progress in child psychiatry and child development* (pp. 319–331). Philadelphia, PA: Brunner/Mazel.

Cavanagh, K., & Davey, G. C. L. (2000a). UCS expectancy biases in spider phobics: underestimation of aversive consequences following fear irrelevant stimuli. *Behaviour Research and Therapy*, *38*, 641–651.

Cavanagh, K., & Davey, G. C. L. (2000b). The use of stimulus dimensions in judgement making in spider fearful and nonfearful individuals. *Behaviour Research and Therapy*, *39*, 1199–1211.

Chambless, D. L., & Mason, J. (1986). Sex, sex-role stereotyping and agoraphobia. *Behaviour Research and Therapy*, *24*, 231–235.

Chambless, D. L., Caputo, G., Bright, P., & Gallagher, R. (1984). Assessment of fear in agoraphobics: the Body Sensations Questionnaire and the Agoraphobia Cognitions Questionnaire. *Journal of Consulting and Clinical Psychology*, *52*, 1090–1097.

Chan, C. K. Y., & Lovibond, P. F. (1996). Expectancy bias in trait anxiety. *Journal of Abnormal Psychology*, *105*, 637–647.

Chappell, P., Leckman, J., Goodman, W., Bissette, G., Pauls, D., Anderson, G., Riddle, M., Scahill, L., McDougle, C., & Cohen, D. (1996). Elevated cerebrospinal fluid corticotropin-releasing factor in Tourette's syndrome: comparison to obsessive compulsive disorder and normal controls. *Society of Biological Psychiatry*, *39*, 776–783.

Chassin, L., Pitts, S. C., DeLucia, C., & Todd, M. (1999). A longitudinal study of children of alcoholics: predicting young adult substance use disorders, anxiety, and depression. *Journal of Abnormal Psychology*, *108*, 106–119.

Chen, E., & Craske, M. G. (1998). Risk perceptions and interpretations of ambiguity related to anxiety during a stressful event. *Cognitive Therapy and Research*, *22*, 137–148.

Chen, E., Lewin, M. R., & Craske, M. G. (1996). Effects of state anxiety on selective processing of threatening information. *Cognition and Emotion*, *10*, 225–240.

Chen, Y. P., Ehlers, A., Clark, D. M., & Mansell, W. (2002). Patients with generalized social phobia direct their attention away from faces. *Behaviour Research and Therapy*, *40*, 677–687.

Chorpita, B. F. (2001). Control and the development of negative emotion. In M. W. Vasey & M. R. Dadds (eds), *The developmental psychopathology of anxiety* (pp. 112–142). London: Oxford University Press.

Chorpita, B. F., & Barlow, D. H. (1998). The development of anxiety: the role of control in the early environment. *Psychological Bulletin*, *124*, 3–21.

Chorpita, B. F., Albano, A. M., & Barlow, D. H. (1996a). Child Anxiety Sensitivity Index: considerations for children with anxiety disorders. *Journal of Clinical Child Psychology*, *25*, 77–82.

Chorpita, B. F., Albano, A. M., & Barlow, D. H. (1996b). Cognitive processing in children: relation to anxiety and family influences. *Journal of Clinical Child Psychology*, *25*, 170–176.

Chorpita, B. F., Brown, T. A., & Barlow, D. H. (1998). Perceived control as a mediator of family environment in etiological models of childhood anxiety. *Behavior Therapy*, *29*, 457–476.

Clark, D. A. (1986a). Cognitive–affective interaction: a test of the "specificity" and "generality" hypotheses. *Cognitive Therapy and Research*, *10*, 607–623.

Clark, D. A. (1986b). Factors influencing the retrieval and control of negative cognitions. *Behaviour Research and Therapy*, *24*, 151–159.

Clark, D. A., & Purdon, C. (1993). New perspectives for a cognitive theory of obsessions. *Australian Psychologist*, *28*, 161–167.

Clark. D. A., & Purdon, C. L. (1995). The assessment of unwanted intrusive thoughts: a review and critique of the literature. *Behaviour Research and Therapy*, *33*, 93–102.

Clark, D. M. (1986). A cognitive approach to panic. *Behaviour Research and Therapy, 24*, 461–470.

Clark, D. M., & Ehlers, A. (1993). An overview of the cognitive theory and treatment of panic disorder. *Applied and Preventive Psychology*, *2*, 131–139.

Clark, D. M., & Wells, A. (1995). A cognitive model of social phobia. In R. G. Heimberg, M. R. Liebowitz, & F. R. Schreier (eds), *Social phobia: diagnosis, assessment, and treatment* (pp. 69–93). New York, NY: Guilford Press.

Clark, D. M., Salkovskis, P. M., Gelder, M., Koehler, C., Martin, M., Anastasiades, P., Hackmann, A., Middleton, H., & Jeavons, A. (1988). Tests of a cognitive theory of panic. In I. Hand & H.-U. Wittchen (eds), *Panic and phobias II: treatments and variables affecting course and outcome* (pp. 71–90). Berlin: Springer-Verlag.

Clark, D. M., Salkovskis, P. M., & Anastasiades, P. (1990). Cognitive mediation of lactate induced panic. In R. Rapee (Chair), *Experimental investigations of panic disorder.* Symposium conducted at the Association for Advancement of Behavior Therapy, San Francisco, CA.

Clark, D. M., Salkovskis, P. M., Öst, L. G., Breitholtz, E., Koehler, K. A., Westling, B. E., Jeavons, A., & Gelder, M. (1997). Misinterpretation of body sensations in panic disorder. *Journal of Consulting Clinical Psychology*, *65*, 203–213.

Clark, L. A., & Watson, D. (1991). Tripartite model of anxiety and depression: psychometric evidence and taxonomic implications. *Journal of Abnormal Psychology*, *100*, 316–336.

Clark, L. A., Watson, D. W., & Mineka, S. (1994). Temperament, personality, and the mood and anxiety disorders. *Journal of Abnormal Psychology*, *103*, 103–116.

Clarke, P. M., & Albino, R. C. (1975). Extraversion, attention and eyeblink conditioning. *Journal of Behavioural Sciences*, *2*, 183–191.

Clayton, I. C., Richards, J. C., & Edwards, C. J. (1999). Selective attention in obsessive–compulsive disorder. *Journal of Abnormal Psychology*, *108*, 171–175.

Cloitre, M., Heimberg, R. G., Liebowitz, M. R., & Gitow, A. (1992). Perceptions of control in panic disorder and social phobia. *Cognitive Therapy and Research*, *16*, 569–577.

Cloninger, C. R. (1986). A unified biosocial theory of personality and its role in the development of anxiety states. *Psychiatric Development*, *3*, 167–226.

Cloninger, C. R. (1987). A systematic method for clinical description and classification of personality variants: a proposal. *Archives of General Psychiatry*, *44*, 573–588.

Coan, J. A., Allen, J. J. B., & Harmon-Jones, E. (2001). Voluntary facial expression and hemispheric asymmetry over the frontal cortex. *Psychophysiology*, *38*, 912–925.

Cohen, L., McGowan, J., Fooskas, S., & Rose, S. (1984). Positive life events and social support and the relationship between life stress and psychological disorder. *American Journal of Community Psychology*, *12*, 567–587.

Cohen, L. H., Burt, C. E., & Bjorck, J. P. (1987). Life stress and adjustment: effects of life events experienced by young adolescents and their parents. *Developmental Psychology*, *23*, 583–592.

Cohen, P., Velez, C. N., Brook, J., & Smith, J. (1989). Mechanism of the relation between perinatal problems, early childhood illness, and psychopathology in late childhood and adolescence. *Child Development*, *60*, 701–709.

Cole, D. A., Peeke, L. G., Martin, J. M., Trugilo, R., & Seroczynski, A. D. (1998). A longitudinal look at the relation between depression and anxiety in children and adolescents. *Journal of Consulting and Clinical Psychology*, *66*, 451–460.

Cole, D. A., Peeke, L., Dolezal, S., Murray, N., & Canzoniero, A. (1999). A longitudinal study of negative affect and self-perceived competence in young adolescents. *Journal of Personality and Social Psychology*, *77*, 851–862.

Cole, D. A., Jacquez, F. M., & Maschman, T. L. (2001). Social origins of depressive cognitions: a longitudinal study of self-perceived competence in children. *Cognitive Therapy and Research*, *25*, 377–395.

Cole, F. C. (1991). The influence of role-taking on the convergent validity of the Family Adaptability and Cohesion Evaluation Scales III and the Parent Attitude Measure. *Dissertation Abstracts International*, *52*(2-B), 1053–1054.

Cole, P. M., Zahn-Waxler, C., Fox, N. A., Usher, B. A., & Welsh, J. D. (1996). Individual differences in emotion regulation and behavior problems in preschool children. *Journal of Abnormal Psychology*, *105*, 518–529.

Coles, M. E., Turk, C. L., Heimberg, R. G., & Fresco, D. M. (2001). Effects of varying levels of anxiety within social situations: relationship to memory perspective and attributions in social phobia. *Behaviour Research and Therapy*, *39*, 651–665.

Compas, B. E., Orosan, P. G., & Grant, K. E. (1993). Adolescent stress and coping: implications for psychopathology during adolescence. *Journal of Adolescence*, *16*, 331–349.

Connell, A. M., & Goodman, S. H. (2002). The association between psychopathology in fathers versus mothers and children's internalizing and externalizing behavior problems: a meta-analysis. *Psychological Bulletin*, *128*, 746–773.

Connolly, J. F. (1979). Tonic physiological responses to repeated presentations of phobic stimuli. *Behaviour Research and Therapy*, *17*, 189–196.

Constans, J. I. (2001). Worry propensity and the perception of risk. *Behaviour Research and Therapy*, *39*, 721–729.

Constans, J. I., Foa, E. B., Franklin, M. E., & Mathews, A. (1995). Memory for actual and imagined events in OC checkers. *Behaviour Research and Therapy*, *33*, 665–671.

Cook, E. W., Hodes, R. L., & Lang, P. J. (1986). Preparedness and phobia: effects of stimulus content on human visceral conditioning. *Journal of Abnormal Psychology*, *95*, 195–207.

Cook, E. W., Hawk, L. W., Davis, T. L., & Stevenson, V. E. (1991). Affective individual differences and startle reflex modulation. *Journal of American Psychology*, *100*, 5–13.

Cook, E. W., Davis, T. L., Hawk, L. W., Spence, E. L., & Gautier, G. H. (1992). Fearfulness and startle potentiation during aversive visual stimuli. *Psychophysiology, 29*, 633–645.

Cook, M., & Mineka, S. (1987). Second-order conditioning and overshadowing in the observational conditioning of fear in monkeys. *Behaviour Research and Therapy, 25,* 349–364.

Cook, M., & Mineka, S. (1989). Observational conditioning of fear to fear-relevant versus fear-irrelevant stimuli in rhesus monkeys. *Journal of Abnormal Psychology, 98*, 448–459.

Cook, M., & Mineka, S. (1990). Selective associations in the observational conditioning of fear in rhesus monkeys. *Journal of Experimental Psychology: Animal Behavior Processes, 16*, 372–389.

Coplan, J. D., Rosenblum, L. A., & Gorman, J. M. (1995). Primate models of anxiety: longitudinal perspectives. *Psychiatric Clinics of North America, 18*, 727–743.

Cook, M., & Mineka, S. (1991). Selective associations in the origins of phobic fears and their implications for behavior therapy. In P. R. Martin (ed.), *Handbook of behavior therapy and psychological science: an integrative approach* (vol. 164, pp. 413–434). Elmsford, NY: Pergamon Press.

Coplan, J. D., Trost, R. C., Owens, M. J., Cooper, T. B., Gorman, J. M., Nemeroff, C. B., & Rosenblum, L. A. (1998). Cerebrospinal fluid concentrations of somatostatin and biogenic amines in grown primates reared by mothers exposed to manipulated foraging conditions. *Archives of General Psychiatry, 55*, 473–477.

Corr, P. J., Kumari, V., Wilson, G. D., Checkley, S., & Gray, J. (1997). Harm avoidance and affective modulation of the startle reflex: a replication. *Personality and Individual Differences, 22*, 591–593.

Corr, P. J., Pickering, A. D., & Gray, J. A. (1997). Personality, punishment, and procedural learning: a test of J. A. Gray's anxiety theory. *Journal of Personality and Social Psychology, 73*, 337–344.

Costa, P. T., & McCrae, R. R. (1980). Influence of extraversion and neuroticism on subjective well-being: happy and unhappy people. *Journal of Personality and Social Psychology, 38*, 668–678.

Costa, P., Terracciano, A., & McCrae, R. R. (2001). Gender differences in personality traits across cultures: robust and surprising findings. *Journal of Personality and Social Psychology, 81*, 322–331.

Costello, E. J., & Angold, A. (1995). Epidemiology. In J. S. March (ed.), *Anxiety disorders in children and adolescents* (pp. 109–124). New York, NY: Guilford Press.

Cottraux, J., Gerard, D., Cinotti, L., Froment, J. C., Deiber, M. P., Le Bars, D., Galy, G., Millet, P., Labbe, C., Lavenne, F., Bouvard, M., & Mauguiere, F. (1996). A controlled positron emission tomography study of obsessive and neutral auditory stimulation in obsessive–compulsive disorder with checking rituals. *Psychiatry Research, 60*, 101–112.

Cox, B. J., Swinson, R. P., Shulman, I. D., Kuch, K., & Reichman, J. T. (1993). Gender effects and alcohol use in panic disorder with agoraphobia. *Behaviour Research and Therapy, 31*, 413–416.

Cox, B. J., Endler, N. S., & Swinson, R. P. (1995). An examination of levels of agoraphobic severity in panic disorder. *Behaviour Research and Therapy, 33*, 57–62.

Craig, K. D., & Lowery, H. J. (1969). Heart-rate components of conditioned vicarious autonomic responses. *Journal of Personality and Social Psychology, 11*, 381–387.

Craske, M. G. (1999). *Anxiety disorders: psychological approaches to theory and treatment.* Boulder, CO: Westview Press.

Craske, M. G. (2002). The role of spontaneity of panic in differentiating panic disorder and generalized anxiety disorder. *Anxiety Neuroses in the 21st Century.* Symposium conducted at the 9th International Current Issues and Controversies in Psychiatry, Barcelona, Spain.

Craske, M. G., & Craig, K. D. (1984). Musical performance anxiety: the three-systems model and self-efficacy theory. *Behaviour Research and Therapy, 22*, 267–280.

Craske, M. G., & Rachman, S. J. (1987). Return of fear: perceived skill and heart-rate responsivity. *British Journal of Clinical Psychology, 26,* 187–199.

Craske, M. G., & Barlow, D. H. (1988). A review of the relationship between panic and avoidance. *Clinical Psychology Review, 8,* 667–685.

Craske, M. G., & Sipsas, A. (1992). Animal phobias versus claustrophobias: exteroceptive versus interoceptive cues. *Behaviour Research and Therapy, 30,* 569–581.

Craske, M. G., & Freed, S. (1995). Expectations about arousal and nocturnal panic. *Journal of Abnormal Psychology, 104,* 567–575.

Craske, M. G., & Rowe, M. K. (1997). Nocturnal panic. *Clinical Psychology: Science and Practice, 4,* 153–174.

Craske, M. G., & Hazlett-Stevens, H. (2002). Facilitating symptom reduction and behavior change in GAD: the issue of control. *Clinical Psychology: Science and Practice, 9,* 69–75.

Craske, M. G., Sanderson, W. C., & Barlow, D. H. (1987). How do desynchronous response systems relate to the treatment of agoraphobia: a follow-up evaluation. *Behaviour Research and Therapy, 25,* 117–122.

Craske, M. G., Rapee, R. M., & Barlow, D. H. (1988). The significance of panic-expectancy for individual patterns of avoidance. *Behavior Therapy, 19,* 577–592.

Craske, M. G., Rapee, R. M., Jackel, L., & Barlow, D. H. (1989). Qualitative dimensions of worry in DSM-III-R generalized anxiety disorder subjects and nonanxious controls. *Behaviour Research and Therapy, 27,* 397–402.

Craske, M. G., Miller, P. P., Rotunda, R., & Barlow, D. H. (1990). A descriptive report of features of initial unexpected panic attacks in minimal and extensive avoiders. *Behaviour Research and Therapy, 28,* 395–400.

Craske, M. G., Zarate, R., Burton, T., & Barlow, D. H. (1993). Specific fears and panic attacks: a survey of clinical and nonclinical samples. *Journal of Anxiety Disorders, 7,* 1–19.

Craske, M. G., Glover, D., & DeCola, J. (1995). Predicted versus unpredicted panic attacks: acute versus general distress. *Journal of Abnormal Psychology, 104,* 214–223.

Craske, M. G., Barlow, D. H., Clark, D. M., Curtis, G. C., Hill, E. M., Himle, J. A., Lee, Y., Lewis, J. A., McNally, R. J., Öst, L., Salkovskis, P. M., & Warwick, H. C. (1996). Specific (simple) phobia. In T. A. Widiger, A. J. Frances, H. A. Pincus, R. Ross, M. B. First, & W. W. Davis (eds), *DSM-IV sourcebook* (pp. 473–506). Washington, DC: American Psychiatric Association.

Craske, M. G., Poulton, R., Tsao, J. C. I., & Plotkin, D. (2001). Paths to panic disorder/ agoraphobia: an exploratory analysis from age 3 to 21 in an unselected birth cohort. *Journal of the American Academy of Child and Adolescent Psychiatry, 40,* 556–563.

Craske, M. G., Lang, A. J., Rowe, M., DeCola, J. P., Simmons, J., Mann, C., Yan-Go, F., & Bystritsky, A. (2002a). Presleep attributions about arousal during sleep: nocturnal panic. *Journal of Abnormal Psychology, 111,* 53–62.

Craske, M. G., Lang, A. J., Tsao, J. C., Mystkowski, J., & Rowe, M. K. (2002b). Reactivity to interoceptive cues in nocturnal panic. *Journal of Behavior Therapy and Experimental Psychiatry, 32,* 173–190.

Craske, M. G., Lang, A. J., Aikins, D., & Mystkowski, J. (2003 in press). Cognitive behavioral therapy for nocturnal panic disorder.

Cross, S. E., & Madson, L. (1997). Models of the self: self-construals and gender. *Psychological Bulletin, 112,* 5–37.

Curle, C. E., & Williams, C. (1996). Post-traumatic stress reactions in children: gender differences in the incidence of trauma reactions at two years and examination of factors influencing adjustment. *British Journal of Clinical Psychology, 35,* 297–309.

Curtis, G. C., Hill, E. M., & Lewis, J. A. (1998). Heterogeneity of DSM-III-R simple phobia and the simple phobia/agoraphobia boundary: evidence from the ECA study. In T. A. Widiger,

A. J. Frances, H. A. Pincuss, R. Ross, M. B. First, W. Davis, & M. Kline (eds), *DSM-IV source book* (vol. 4, pp. 245–257). Washington, DC: American Psychiatric Association.

Dadds, M. R., Marrett, P. M., & Rapee, R. M. (1996). Family process and child anxiety and aggression: an observational analysis. *Journal of Abnormal Child Psychology, 24,* 715–734.

Daleiden, E. L. (1998). Childhood anxiety and memory functioning: a comparison of systemic and processing accounts. *Journal of Experimental Child Psychology, 68,* 216–235.

Dalgleish, T., Taghavi, R., Neshat-Doost, H., Moradi, A., Yule, W., & Canterbury, R. (1997). Information processing in clinically depressed and anxious children and adolescents. *Journal of Child Psychology and Psychiatry and Allied Disciplines, 38,* 535–541.

Dalgleish, T., Moradi, A., Taghavi, R., Neshat-Doost, H., Yule, W., & Canterbury, R. (2000). Judgements about emotional events in children and adolescents with post-traumatic stress disorder and controls. *Journal of Child Psychology and Psychiatry and Allied Disciplines, 41,* 981–988.

Dalgleish, T., Moradi, A. R., Taghavi, M. R., Neshat-Doost, H. T., & Yule, W. (2001). An experimental investigation of hypervigilance for threat in children and adolescents with post-traumatic stress disorder. *Psychological Medicine, 31,* 541–547.

Daly, J. A., Vangelisti, A. L., & Lawrence, S. G. (1989). Self-focused attention and public speaking anxiety. *Personality and Individual Differences, 10,* 903–913.

Davey, G. C. (1987). Integrating human and animal theories of conditioning. *Journal of Psychophysiology, 1,* 105–108.

Davey, G. C. (1989). UCS revaluation and conditioning models of acquired fears. *Behaviour Research and Therapy, 27,* 521–528.

Davey, G. C., & Matchett, G. (1994). Unconditioned stimulus rehearsal and the retention and enhancement of differential "fear" conditioning: effects of trait and state anxiety. *Journal of Abnormal Psychology, 103,* 708–718.

Davey, G. C., de Jong, P., & Tallis, F. (1993). UCS inflation in the etiology of anxiety disorders: some case histories. *Behaviour Research and Therapy, 31,* 495–498.

Davey, G. C. L. (1992). Classical conditioning and the acquisition of human fears and phobias: a review and synthesis of the literature. *Advances in Behaviour Research and Therapy, 14,* 29–66.

Davey, G. C. L. (1993). A comparison of three worry questionnaires. *Behaviour Research and Therapy, 31,* 51–56.

Davey, G. C. L. (1994). Worrying, social problem-solving abilities, and social problem-solving confidence. *Behaviour Research and Therapy, 32,* 327–330.

Davey, G. C. L. (1995). Preparedness and phobias: specific evolved associations or a generalized expectancy bias? *Behavioral and Brain Sciences, 18,* 289–325.

Davey, G. C. L. (1997). The merits of an experimentally testable model of phobias. *Behavioural and Brain Sciences, 20,* 363–364.

Davey, G. C. L., & Craigie, P. (1997). Manipulation of dangerousness judgements to fear-relevant stimuli: effects on *a priori* UCS expectancy and a posteriori covariation assessment. *Behaviour Research and Therapy, 35,* 607–617.

Davey, G. C. L., & Levy, S. (1998). Catastrophic worrying: personal inadequacy and a perspective iterative style as features of the catastrophizing process. *Journal of Abnormal Psychology, 107,* 576–586.

Davey, G. C. L., Hampton, J., Farrell, J., & Davidson, S. (1992). Some characteristics of worrying: evidence for worrying and anxiety as separate constructs. *Personality and Individual Differences, 13,* 133–147.

Davey, G. C. L., Forster, L., & Mayhew, G. (1993). Familial resemblances in disgust sensitivity and animal phobias. *Behavioural Research and Therapy, 31,* 41–50.

Davey, G. C. L., Burgess, I., & Rashes, R. (1995). Coping strategies and phobias: the relationship between fears, phobias and methods of coping with stressors. *British Journal of Clinical Psychology*, *34*, 423–434.

Davey, G. C. L., Jubb, M., & Cameron, C. (1996). Catastrophic worrying as a function of changes in problem-solving confidence. *Cognitive Therapy and Research*, *20*, 333–344.

Davey, G. C. L., Tallis, F., & Capuzzo, N. (1996). Beliefs about the consequences of worrying. *Cognitive Therapy and Research*, *20*, 499–520.

Davey, G. C. L., Menzies, R., & Gallardo, B. (1997). Height phobia and biases in the interpretation of bodily sensations: some links between acrophobia and agoraphobia. *Behaviour Research and Therapy*, *35*, 997–1001.

Davidson, J. R., Hughes, D., Blazer, D. G., & George, L. K. (1991). Post-traumatic stress disorder in the community: an epidemiological study. *Psychological Medicine*, *21*, 713–721.

Davidson, L. M., & Baum, A. (1986). Chronic stress and posttraumatic stress disorders. *Journal of Consulting and Clinical Psychology*, *54*, 303–308.

Davidson, P. O., Payne, R. W., & Sloane, R. B. (1964). Introversion, neuroticism, and conditioning. *Journal of Abnormal and Social Psychology*, *68*, 136–143.

Davidson, R. J. (1992). Prolegomenon to the structure of emotion: gleanings from neuropsychology. *Cognition and Emotion*, *6*, 245–268.

Davidson, R. J. (1998). Affective style and affective disorders: perspectives from affective neuroscience. *Cognition and Emotion*, *12*, 307–330.

Davis, M. (1998). Are different parts of the extended amygdala involved in fear versus anxiety? *Biological Psychiatry*, *44*, 1239–1247.

Davis, M., & Emory, E. (1995). Sex differences in neonatal stress and reactivity. *Child Development*, *66*, 14–27.

Deane, G. E. (1969). Cardiac activity during experimentally induced anxiety. *Psychophysiology*, *6*, 17–30.

DeCola, J. P., & Rosellini, R. A. (1990). Unpredictable/uncontrollable stress proactively interferes with appetitive Pavlovian conditioning. *Learning and Motivation*, *21*, 137–152.

DeCola, J. P., Rosellini, R. A., & Warren, D. A. (1988). A dissociation of the effects of control and prediction. *Learning and Motivation*, *19*, 269–282.

de Jong, G. M., & Bouman, T. K. (1995). Panic disorder: a baseline period. Predictability of agoraphobic avoidance behavior. *Journal of Anxiety Disorders*, *9*, 185–199.

de Jongh, A., Muris, P., ter Horst, G., & Duyx, M. P. M. A. (1995). Acquisition and maintenance of dental anxiety: the role of conditioning experiences and cognitive factors. *Behaviour Research and Therapy*, *33*, 205–210.

de Jong, P., & Merckelbach, H. (1991). Covariation bias and electrodermal responding in spider phobics before and after behavioral treatment. *Behaviour Research and Therapy*, *29*, 307–314.

de Jong, P., Merckelbach, H., & Arntz, A. (1995). Covariation bias in phobic women: the relationship between a priori expectancy, on-line expectancy, automatic responding, and *a posteriori* contingency judgment. *Journal of Abnormal Psychology*, *104*, 55–62.

del Barrio, V., Moreno-Rosset, C., Lopez, R. M., & Olmedo, M. (1997). Anxiety, depression and personality structure. *Personality and Individual Differences*, *23*, 327–335.

Delahanty, D. L., Herberman, H. B., Craig, K. J., Hayward, M. C., Fullerton, C. S., Ursano, R. J., & Baum, A. (1997). Acute and chronic distress and posttraumatic stress disorder as a function of responsibility for serious motor vehicle accidents. *Journal of Consulting and Clinical Psychology*, *65*, 560–567.

Derryberry, D., & Reed, M. A. (1994). Temperament and attention: orienting toward and away from positive and negative signals. *Journal of Personality and Social Psychology*, *66*, 1128–1139.

Derryberry, D., & Reed, M. A. (1996). Regulatory processes and the development of cognitive representations. *Development and Psychopathology, 8,* 215–234.

Derryberry, D., & Rothbart, M. K. (1997). Reactive and effortful processes in the organization of temperament. *Development of Psychopathology, 9,* 633–652.

Derryberry, D., & Reed, M. A. (2002). Anxiety-related attentional biases and their regulation by attentional control. *Journal of Abnormal Psychology, 111,* 225–236.

de Silva, P., Rachman, S., & Seligman, M. E. (1977). Prepared phobias and obsessions: therapeutic outcome. *Behaviour Research and Therapy, 15,* 65–77.

De Vries, G. J., & Boyle, P. A. (1998). Double duty for sex differences in the brain. *Behavioural Brain Research, 92,* 205–213.

Dienstbier, R. A. (1989). Arousal and physiological toughness: implications for mental and physical health. *Psychological Review, 96,* 84–100.

Dierker, L. C., Merikangas, K. R., & Szatmari, P. (1999). Influence of parental concordance for psychiatric disorders on psychopathology in offspring. *Journal of the American Academy of Child Adolescent Psychiatry, 38,* 280–288.

DiLalla, L. F., Kagan, J., & Reznick, J. S. (1994). Genetic etiology of behavioral inhibition among two-year-old children. *Infant Behavior and Development, 17,* 401–408.

Dimberg, U. (1986a). Facial expressions as excitatory and inhibitory stimuli for conditioned autonomic responses. *Biological Psychology, 22,* 37–57.

Dimberg, U. (1986b). Facial reactions to fear-irrelevant stimuli. *Biological Psychology, 23,* 153–161.

Dimberg, U. (1987). Facial reactions, autonomic activity and experienced emotion: a three component model of emotional conditioning. *Biological Psychology, 24,* 105–122.

Dimberg. U., & Öhman, A. (1983). The effects of directional facial cues on electrodermal conditioning to facial stimuli. *Psycholphysiology, 20,* 160–167.

Dimberg, U., & Lundquist, L. (1990). Gender differences in facial reactions to facial expressions. *Biological Psychology, 30,* 151–159.

di Nardo, P. A., Guzy, L. T., & Bak, R. M. (1988). Anxiety response patterns and etiological factors in dog-fearful and non-fearful subjects. *Behaviour Research and Therapy, 26,* 245–251.

di Nardo, P. A., Moras, K., Barlow, D. H., Rapee, R. M., & Brown, T. A. (1993). Reliability of DSM-III-R anxiety disorder categories: using Anxiety Disorders Interview Schedule Revised (ADIS-R). *Archives of General Psychiatry, 50,* 251–256.

Dodge, C. S., Hope, D. A., Heimberg, R. G., & Becker, R. E. (1998). Evaluation of the Social Interaction Self-Statement Test with a social phobic population. *Cognitive Therapy and Research, 12,* 211–222.

Drugan, R. C., Moye, T. B., & Maier, S. F. (1982). Opioid and nonopioid forms of stress-induced analgesia: some environmental determinants and characteristics. *Behavioral and Neural Biology, 35,* 251–264.

Dugas, M. J., Letarte, H., Rheaume, J., Freeston, M. H., & Ladouceur, R. (1995). Worry and problem solving: evidence of a specific relationship. *Cognitive Therapy and Research, 19,* 109–120.

Dumas, J. E., LaFreniere, P. J., & Serketich, W. J. (1995). "Balance of power": a transactional analysis of control in mother–child dyads involving socially competent, aggressive, and anxious children. *Journal of Abnormal Psychology, 104,* 104–113.

Dunham, P., & Dunham, F. (1990). Effects of mother–infant social interactions on infants' subsequent contingency task performance. *Child Development, 61,* 785–793.

Dunmore, E., Clark, D. M., & Ehlers, A. (1999). Cognitive factors involved in the onset and maintenance of posttraumatic stress disorder (PTSD) after physical or sexual assault. *Behaviour Research and Therapy, 37,* 809–829.

Dunmore, E., Clark, D. M., & Ehlers, A. (2001). A prospective investigation of the role of cognitive factors in persistent posttraumatic stress disorder after physical or sexual assault. *Behaviour Research and Therapy, 39*, 1063–1084.

Duval, S., & Wicklund, R. (1972). *A theory of objective self-awareness.* New York, NY: Academic Press.

Dworkin, B. R., & Dworkin, S. (1999). Heterotopic and homotopic classical conditioning of the boreflex. *Integrative Physiological and Behavioral Science, 34*, 158–176.

East, M. P., & Watts, F. N. (1994). Worry and the suppression of imagery. *Behaviour Research and Therapy, 32*, 851–855.

Eaton, W. W., Badawi, M., & Melton, B. (1995). Prodromes and precursors: epidemiologic data for primary prevention of disorders with slow onset. *American Journal of Psychiatry, 152*, 967–972.

Eaves, L., & Eysenck, H. (1976). Genetic and environmental components of inconsistency and unrepeatability in twins' responses to a neuroticism questionnaire. *Behavioral Genetics, 6*, 145–160.

Eaves, L. J., Silberg, J. L., Maes, H. H., Simonoff, E., Pickles, A., Rutter, M., Neale, M. C., Reynolds, C. A., Erikson, M. T., Heath, A. C., Loeber, R., Truett, K. R., & Hewitt, J. K. (1997). Genetics and developmental psychopathology: II. The main effects of genes and environment on behavioral problems in the Virginia Twin Study of Adolescent Behavioral Development. *Journal of Child Psychology and Psychiatry and Allied Disciplines, 38*, 965–980.

Echiverri, A., Shirinyan, D., Mystkowski, J., Hazlett-Stevens, H., & Craske, M. G. (2003 in press). A test of two approaches to phobic processing and its relationship to treatment outcome.

Edelbrock, C., Costello, A. J., Dulcan, M. K., Conover, N. C., & Kala, R. (1986). Parent-child agreement on child psychiatric symptoms assessed via structured interview. *Journal of Child Psychology and Psychiatry and Allied Disciplines, 27*, 181–190.

Ehlers, A. (1993). Somatic symptoms and panic attacks: a retrospective study of learning experiences. *Behaviour Research and Therapy, 31*, 269–278.

Ehlers, A. (1995). A 1-year prospective study of panic attacks: clinical course and factors associated with maintenance. *Journal of Abnormal Psychology, 104*, 164–172.

Ehlers, A., & Breuer, P. (1992). Increased cardiac awareness in panic disorder. *Journal of Abnormal Psychology, 101*, 371–382.

Ehlers, A., & Breuer, P. (1996). How good are patients with panic disorder at perceiving their heartbeats? *Biological Psychology, 42*, 165–182.

Ehlers, A., & Clark, D. M. (2000). A cognitive model of posttraumatic stress disorder. *Behaviour Research and Therapy, 38*, 319–345.

Ehlers, A., Margraf, J., Davies, S., & Roth, W. T. (1988). Selective processing of threat cues in subjects with panic attacks. *Cognition and Emotion, 2*, 201–219.

Ehlers, A., Margraf, J., Roth, W. T., Taylor, C. B., & Birbaumer, N. (1988). Anxiety induced by false heart rate feedback in patients with panic disorder. *Behaviour Research and Therapy, 26*, 1–11.

Ehlers, A., Hofmann, S. G., Herda, C. A., & Roth, W. T. (1994). Clinical characteristics of driving phobia. *Journal of Anxiety Disorders, 8*, 323–339.

Ehlers, A., Breuer, P., Dohn, D., & Fiegenbaum, W. (1995). Heartbeat perception and panic disorder: possible explanations for discrepant findings. *Behaviour Research and Therapy, 33*, 69–76.

Ehlers, A., Mayou, R. A., & Bryant, B. (1998). Psychological predictors of chronic posttraumatic stress disorder after motor vehicle accidents. *Journal of Abnormal Psychology, 107*, 508–519.

Ehlers, A., Maercker, A., & Boos, A. (2000). Posttraumatic stress disorder following political imprisonment: the role of mental defeat, alienation, and perceived permanent change. *Journal of Abnormal Psychology, 109*, 45–55.

Eich, E. (1995). Mood as a mediator of place dependent memory. *Journal of Experimental Psychology: General*, *124*, 293–308.

Eisenberg, N., Fabes, R. A., Karbon, M., Murphy, B. C., Wosinski, M., Polazzi, L., Carlos, G., & Juhnke, C. (1996a). The relations of children's dispositional prosocial behavior to emotionality, regulation, and social functioning. *Child Development*, *67*, 974–992.

Eisenberg, N., Martin, C. L., & Fabes, R. A. (1996b). Gender development and gender effects. In D. C. Berliner & R. C. Calfee (eds), *Handbook of educational psychology* (pp. 358–396). New York, NY: Macmillan Library Reference.

Eiser, C., Havermans, T., & Eiser, J. R. (1995). The emergence during adolescence of gender differences in symptom reporting. *Journal of Adolescence*, *3*, 307–316.

Ekman, P. (1973). *Darwin and facial expression: a century of research in review.* Oxford: Academic Press.

Ekman, P., Levenson, R. W., & Friesen, W. V. (1983). Autonomic nervous system activity distinguishes among emotions. *Science*, *221*, 1208–1210.

Elder, S., Gamble, T., McAfee, R. D., & Van Veen, W. J. (1979). Conditioned diastolic blood pressure. *Physiology and Behavior*, *23*, 875–880.

Eley, T. C. (2001). Contributions of behavioral genetics research: quantifying genetic, shared environmental and nonshared environmental influences. In M. W. Vasey & M. R. Dadds (eds), *The developmental psychopathology of anxiety* (pp. 45–59). New York, NY: Oxford University Press.

Eley, T. C., & Stevenson, J. (1999). Exploring the covariation between anxiety and depression symptoms: a genetic analysis of the effects of age and sex. *Journal of Child Psychology and Psychiatry and Allied Disciplines*, *40*, 1273–1282.

Elfenbein, H. A., & Ambady, N. (2002). On the universality and cultural specificity of emotion recognition: a meta-analysis. *Psychological Bulletin*, *128*, 203–235.

Elwood, S. W., Ferguson, H. B., & Thakar, J. (1986). Catecholamine response of children in a naturally occurring stressor situation. *Journal of Human Stress*, *12*, 154–161.

Emmelkamp, P. M. G., & Felten, M. (1985). The process of exposure *in vivo*: cognitive and physiological changes during treatment of acrophobia. *Behaviour Research and Therapy*, *23*, 219–223.

Emmelkamp, P. M. G., Mersch, P. P., Vissia, E., & van der Helm, M. (1985). Social phobia: a comparative evaluation of cognitive and behavioural interventions. *Behaviour Research and Therapy*, *23*, 365–369.

Enright, S. J., & Beech, A. R. (1990). Obsessional states: anxiety disorders or schizotypes? An information processing and personality assessment. *Psychological Medicine*, *20*, 621–627.

Enright, S. J., & Beech, A. R. (1993a). Further evidence of reduced inhibition in obsessive– compulsive disorder. *Personality and Individual Differences*, *14*, 387–395.

Enright, S. J., & Beech, A. R. (1993b). Reduced cognitive inhibition in obsessive–compulsive disorder. *British Journal of Clinical Psychology*, *32*, 67–74.

Enright, S. J., Beech, A. R., & Claridge, G. S. (1995). A further investigation of cognitive inhibition in obsessive–compusive disorder and other anxiety disorders. *Personality and Individual Differences*, *19*, 535–542.

Essau, C. A., Conradt, J., & Petermann, F. (1999). Frequency and comorbidity of social phobia and social fears in adolescents. *Behaviour Research and Therapy*, *37*, 831–843.

Esteves, F., Dimberg, U., & Öhman, A. (1994). Automatically elicited fear: conditioned skin conductance responses to masked facial expressions. *Cognition and Emotion*, *8*, 393–413.

Eysenck, H. J. (1967). *The biological basis of personality.* Springfield, IL: Thomas.

Eysenck, H. J., & Eysenck, S. B. G. (1976). *Psychoticism as a Dimension of Personality.* London: Hodder and Stoughton.

Eysenck, M. W. (1992). *Anxiety: the cognitive perspective*. Hillsdale, NJ: Lawrence Erlbaum.

Eysenck, M. W., & Byrne, A. (1994). Implicit memory bias, explicit memory bias, and anxiety. *Cognition and Emotion, 8*, 415–431.

Eysenck, M. W., MacLeod, C., & Mathews, A. (1987). Cognitive functioning and anxiety. *Psychological Research, 49*, 189–195.

Eysenck, M. W., Mogg, K., May, J., Richards, A., & Mathews, A. (1991). Bias in interpretation of ambiguous sentences related to threat in anxiety. *Journal of Abnormal Psychology, 100*, 144–150.

Falsetti, S. A., & Resick, P. A. (1995). Causal attributions, depression, and post-traumatic stress disorder in victims of crime. *Journal of Applied Social Psychology, 25*, 1027–1042.

Fanselow, M. S. (1994). Neural organization of the defensive behavior system responsible for fear. *Psychonomic Bulletin Review 1*, 429–438.

Fanselow, M. S., & Lester, L. S. (1988). A functional behavioristic approach to aversively motivated behavior: predatory imminence as a determinant of the topography of defensive behavior. In R. C. Bolles & M. D. Bacher (eds), *Evolution and learning* (pp. 185–212). Hillsdale, NJ: Lawrence Erlbaum.

Faravelli, C. (1985). Life events preceding the onset of panic disorder. *Journal of Affective Disorders, 9*, 103–105.

Faravelli, C., & Pallanti, S. (1989). Recent life events and panic disorder. *American Journal of Psychiatry, 146*, 622–626.

Faravelli, C., Webb, T., Ambonetti, A., Fonnesu, F., & Sessarego, A. (1985). Prevalence of traumatic early life events in 31 agoraphobic patients with panic attacks. *American Journal of Psychiatry, 142*, 1493–1494.

Faravelli, C., Pallanti, S., Biondi, F., Paterniti, S., & Scarpato, M. A. (1992). Onset of panic disorder. *American Journal of Psychiatry, 149*, 827–828.

Febbraro, G. A. R., & Clum, G. A. (1995). A dimensional analysis of claustrophobia. *Journal of Psychopathology and Behavioral Assessment, 17*, 335–351.

Feigon, S. A., Waldman, I. D., Levey, F., & Hay, D. A. (2001). Genetic and environmental influences on separation anxiety disorder symptoms and their moderation by age and sex. *Behavior Genetics, 35*, 403–411.

Feingold, A. (1994). Gender differences in personality: a meta-analysis. *Psychological Bulletin, 116*, 429–456.

Ferdinand, R. F., & Verhulst, F. C. (1995). Psychopathology from adolescence into young adulthood: an 8-year follow-up study. *American Journal of Psychiatry, 152*, 1586–1594.

Ferguson, M. L., & Katkin, E. S. (1996). Visceral perception, anhedonia, and emotion. *Biological Psychology, 1–2*, 131–145.

Fergusson, D. M., & Horwood, L. J. (1987). Vulnerability to life events exposure, *Psychological Medicine, 17*, 739–749.

Fergusson, D. M., Swain-Campbell, N. R., & Horwood, L. J. (2002). Does sexual violence contribute to elevated rates of anxiety and depression in females? *Psychological Medicine, 32*, 991–996.

Field, A. P., & Davey, G. C. L. (2001). Conditioning models of childhood anxiety. In W. K. Silverman, P. D. Treffers, & D. A. Philip (eds), *Anxiety disorders in children and adolescents: research, assessment and intervention* (pp. 187–211). New York, NY: Cambridge University Press.

Field, T. M. (1984). Early interactions between infants and their postpartum depressed mothers. *Infant Behavior and Development, 7*, 517–522.

Finkel, D., & McGue, M. (1997). Sex differences and nonadditivity in heritability of the Multidimensional Personality Questionnaire Scales. *Journal of Personality and Social Psychology, 72*, 929–938.

Finlay-Jones, R., & Brown, G. W. (1981). Types of stressful life event and the onset of anxiety and depressive disorders. *Psychological Medicine, 11*, 803–815.

Flick, S. N., Roy-Byrne, P. P., Cowley, D. S., Shores, M. M., & Dunner, D. L. (1993). DSM-III-R personality disorders in a mood and anxiety disorders clinic: prevalence, comorbidity, and clinical correlates. *Journal of Affective Disorders, 27*, 71–79.

Flinn, M. V., & England, B. G. (1995). Childhood stress and family environment. *Current Anthropology, 36*, 854–866.

Flinn, M. V., Quinlan, R. J., Decker, S. A., Turner, M. T., & England, B. G. (1996). Male–female differences in effects of parental absence on glucocorticoid stress response. *Human Nature, 7*, 125–162.

Foa, E. B. (1979). Failure in treating obsessive–compulsives. *Behaviour Research and Therapy, 17*, 169–176.

Foa, E. B., & Kozak, M. J. (1986). Emotional processing of fear: exposure to corrective information. *Psychological Bulletin, 99*, 20–35.

Foa, E. B., & McNally, R. J. (1986). Sensitivity to feared stimuli in obsessive–compulsives: a dichotic listening analysis. *Cognitive Therapy and Research, 10*, 477–485.

Foa, E. B., & Riggs, D. S. (1994). Posttraumatic stress disorder and rape. In R. S. Pynoos (ed.), *Posttraumatic stress disorder: a clinical review* (pp. 133–163). Baltimore, MD: Sidran Press.

Foa, E. B., & Riggs, D. S. (1995). Posttraumatic stress disorder following assault: theoretical considerations and empirical findings. *Current Directions in Psychological Science, 4*, 61–65.

Foa, E. B., McNally, R., & Murdock, T. B. (1989). Anxious mood and memory. *Behaviour Research and Therapy, 27*, 141–147.

Foa, E. B., Zinbarg, R., & Rothbaum, B. O. (1992). Uncontrollability and unpredictability in post-traumatic stress disorder: an animal model. *Psychological Bulletin, 112*, 218–238.

Foa, E. B., Molnar, C., & Cashman, L. (1995). Change in rape narratives during exposure therapy for posttraumatic stress disorder. *Journal of Traumatic Stress, 8*, 675–690.

Foa, E. B., Franklin, M. E., Perry, K. J., & Herbert, J. D. (1996). Cognitive biases in generalized social phobia. *Journal of Abnormal Psychology, 105*, 433–439.

Forsman, L. (1980). Habitual catecholamine excretion and its relation to habitual distress. *Biological Psychology, 11*, 83–97.

Forsyth, J. P., & Eifert, G. H. (1996). The language of feeling and the feeling of anxiety: contributions of the behaviorisms toward understanding the function-altering effects of language. *Psychological Record, 46*, 607–649.

Forsyth, J. P., & Chorpita, B. F. (1997). Unearthing the nonassociative origins of fears and phobias: a reminder. *Journal of Behavioral Therapy and Experimental Psychology, 28*, 297–305.

Forsyth, J. P., & Eifert, G. H. (1998). Response intensity in content-specific fear conditioning comparing 20% versus 13% CO_2-enriched air as unconditioned stimuli. *Journal of Abnormal Psychology, 107*, 291–304.

Forsyth, J. P., Kollins, S., Palav, A., Duff, K., & Maher, S. (1999). Has behavior therapy drifted from its experimental roots? A survey of publication trends in mainstream behavioral journals. *Journal of Behavior Therapy and Experimental Psychiatry, 30*, 205–220.

Fowles, D. C. (1993). Biological variables in psychopathology: a psychobiological perspective. In P. B. Sutker & H. E. Adams (eds), *Comprehensive handbook of psychopathology* (pp. 57–82). New York, NY: Plenum Press.

Fox, E., Lester, V., Russo, R., Bowles, R. J., Pichler, A., & Dutton, K. (2000). Facial expressions of emotion: are angry faces detected more efficiently? *Cognition and Emotion, 14*, 61–92.

Fox, N. A. (1989). Psychophysiological correlates of emotional reactivity during the first year of life. *Developmental Psychology, 25*, 364–372.

Frankenhaeuser, M. (1975). Experimental approaches to the study of catecholamines and emotions. In L. Levi (ed.), *Emotions, their parameters and measurement* (pp. 209–234). New York, NY: Raven Press.

Frankenhaeuser, M. (1986). A psychobiological framework for research on human stress and coping. In M. H. Appley & R. Trumbull (eds), *Dynamics of Stress* (pp. 101–116). New York, NY: Plenum Press.

Fredrikson, M., & Georgiades, A. (1992). Personality dimensions and classical conditioning of autonomic nervous system reactions. *Personality and Individual Differences*, *13*, 1013–1020.

Fredrikson, M., Hugdahl, K., & Öhman, A. (1976). Electrodermal conditioning to potentially phobic stimuli in male and female subjects. *Biological Psychology*, *4*, 305–314.

Fredrikson, M., Wik, G., Greitz, T., Eriksson, L., Stone-Elander, S., Ericson, K., & Sedvall, G. (1993). Regional cerebral blood flow during experimental phobic fear. *Psychophysiology*, *30*, 126–130.

Fredrikson, M., Wik, G., Annas, P., Ericson, K., & Stone-Elander, S. (1995). Functional neuroanatomy of visually elicited simple phobic fear: additional data and theoretical analysis. *Psychophysiology*, *32*, 43–48.

Fredrikson, M., Fischer, H., & Wik, G. (1997). Cerebral blood flow during anxiety provocation. *Journal of Clinical Psychiatry*, *58*(suppl. 16), 16–21.

Freedman, R. R., Ianni, P., Ettedgui, E., & Puthezhath, N. (1985). Ambulatory monitoring of panic disorder. *Archives of General Psychiatry*, *42*, 244–248.

Freeston, M. H., Ladouceur, R., Thibodeau, N., & Gagnon, F. (1991). Cognitive intrusions in a non-clinical population: I. Response style, subjective experience, and appraisal. *Behaviour Research and Therapy*, *29*, 585–597.

Freeston, M. H., Ladouceur, R., Gagnoon, F., & Thibodeau, N. (1993). Beliefs about obsessional thoughts. *Journal of Psychopathology and Behavioral Assessment*, *15*, 1–21.

Freeston, M. H., Rheaume, J., Letarte, H., Dugas, M. J., & Ladouceur, R. (1994). Why do people worry? *Personality and Individual Differences*, *17*, 791–802.

Freeston, M. H., Dugas, M. J., & Ladouceur, R. (1996). Thoughts, images, worry, and anxiety. *Cognitive Therapy and Research*, *20*, 265–273.

Freeston, M. H., Dugas, M. J., Letarte, H., Rheaume, J., Blais, F., & Ladouceur, R. (1996). Physical symptoms associated with worry in a nonclinical population. *Journal of Anxiety Disorders*, *10*, 365–377.

Friedman, B. H., & Thayer, J. F. (1998a). Anxiety and automatic flexibility: a cardiovascular approach. *Biological Psychology*, *47*, 243–263.

Friedman, B. H., & Thayer, J. F. (1998b). Autonomic balance revisited: panic anxiety and heart rate variability. *Journal of Psychosomatic Research. Special Issue: Panic Disorder in General Medicine*, *44*, 133–151.

Friedman, B. H., Thayer, J. F., Borovec, T. D., Tyrrell, R. A., Johnsen, B. H., & Colombo, R. (1993). Autonomic characteristics of nonclinical panic and blood phobia. *Biological Psychiatry*, *34*, 298–310.

Frost, R. O., Lahart, C. M., Dugas, K. M., & Sher, K. J. (1988). Information among non-clinical compulsives. *Behavior Research and Therapy*, *26*, 275–277.

Fulcher, E. P., Mathews, A., Mackintosh, B., & Law, S. (2001). Evaluative learning and the allocation of attention to emotional stimuli. *Cognitive Therapy and Research*, *25*, 261–280.

Furman, J. M., Jacob, R. G., & Redfern, M. S. (1998). Clinical evidence that the vestibular system participates in autonomic control. *Journal of Vestibular Research: Equilibrium and Orientation*, *8*, 27–34.

Furst, D., Tenenbaum, G., & Weingarten, G. (1985). Test anxiety, sex, and exam type. *Psychological Reports, 56,* 663–668.

Fyer, A. J., Mannuzza, S., Gallops, M. S., & Martin, L. Y. (1990). Familial transmission of simple phobias and fears: a preliminary report. *Archives of General Psychiatry, 47*, 252–256.

Fyer, A. J., Mannuzza, S., Chapman, T. F., Liebowitz, M. R., & Klein, D. F. (1993). A direct interview family study of social phobia. *Archives of General Psychiatry, 50*, 286–293.

Fyer, A. J., Mannuzza, S., Chapman, T. F., Martin, L. Y., & Klein, D. F. (1995). Specificity in familial aggregation on phobic disorders. *Archives of General Psychiatry, 52*, 564–573.

Garcia, J., & Koelling, R. A. (1966). Relation of cue to consequence in avoidance learning. *Psychonomic Science, 4*, 123–124.

Garcia-Coll, C., Kagan, J., & Reznick, J. S. (1984). Behavioral inhibition in young children. *Child Development, 55*, 1005–1019.

Gardenswartz, C. R., & Craske, M. G. (2001). Prevention of panic. *Behavior Therapy, 32*, 725–737.

Gasper, K., & Clore, G. L. (1998). The persistent use of negative affect by anxious individuals to estimate risk. *Journal of Personality and Social Psychology, 74*, 1350–1363.

Ge, X., & Conger, R. D. (1999). Adjustment problems and emerging personality characteristics from early to late adolescence. *American Journal of Community Psychology, 27*, 429–459.

Ge, X., Conger, R. D., & Elder, G. H. (1996). Coming of age too early: pubertal influences on girls' vulnerability to psychological distress. *Child Development, 67*, 3386–3400.

Geary, D. C., & Flinn, M. V. (2002). Sex differences in behavioral and hormonal response to social threat: commentary on Taylor *et al.* (2000). *Psychological Review, 109*, 745–750.

Geer, J. H., & Maisel, E. (1972). Evaluating the effects of the prediction-control confound. *Journal of Personality and Social Psychology, 23*, 314–319.

Geracioti, T. D., Baker, D. G., Ekhator, N. N., West, S. A., Hill, K. K., Bruce, A. B., Schmidt, D., Rounds-Kugler, B., Yehuda, R., Keck, P. E., & Kasckow, J. W. (2001). CSF norepinephrine concentrations in posttraumatic stress disorder. *American Journal of Psychiatry, 158*, 1227–1230.

Gerardi, R. J., Blanchard, E. B., & Kolb, L. C. (1989). Ability of Vietnam veterans to dissimulate a psychophysiological assessment for post-traumatic stress disorder. *Behavior Therapy, 20*, 229–243.

Gerlach, A. L., Wilhelm, F. H., Gruber, K., & Roth, W. T. (2001). Blushing and physiological arousability in social phobia. *Journal of Abnormal Psychology, 110*, 247–258.

Gershuny, B. S., & Sher, K. J. (1998). The relation between personality and anxiety: findings from a 3-year prospective study. *Journal of Abnormal Psychology, 107*, 252–262.

Gerull, F. C., & Rapee, R. M. (2002). Mother knows best: the effects of maternal modelling on the acquisition of fear and avoidance behaviour in toddlers. *Behaviour Research and Therapy, 40*, 279–287.

Gilboa-Schechtman, E., & Foa, E. B. (2001). Patterns of recovery from trauma: the use of intraindividual analysis. *Journal of Abnormal Psychology, 110*, 392–400.

Gillin, J. C. (1998). Are sleep disturbances risk factors for anxiety, depressive and addictive disorders? *Acta Psychiatrica Scandinavica, Supplementum, 393*, 39–43.

Ginsburg, G. S., & Silverman, W. K. (2000). Gender role orientation and fearfulness in children with anxiety disorders. *Journal of Anxiety Disorders, 14*, 57–67.

Girodo, M., Dotzenroth, S. E., & Stein, S. J. (1981). Causal attribution bias in shy males: implications for self-esteem and self-confidence. *Cognitive Therapy and Research, 5*, 325–338.

Glaubman, H., Mikulincer, M., Porat, A., Wasserman, O., & Birger, M. (1990). Sleep of chronic post-traumatic patients. *Journal of Traumatic Stress, 3*, 255–263.

Godart, N. T., Flament, M. F., Lecrubier, Y., & Jeammet, P. (2000). Anxiety disorders in anorexia nervosa and bulimia nervosa: co-morbidity and chronology of appearance. *European Psychiatry 15*, 38–45.

Goisman, R. M., Warshaw, M. G., Peterson, L. G., Rogers, M. P., Cuneo, P., Hunt, M. F., Tomlin-Albanese, J. M., Kazim, A., Gollan, J. K., Epstein-Kaye, T., Reich, J., & Keller, M. B. (1994). Panic, agoraphobia, and panic disorder with agoraphobia: data from a multicenter anxiety disorders study. *Journal of Nervous and Mental Disease, 182*, 72–79.

Goldsmith, H. H. (1994). Parsing the emotional domain from a developmental perspective. In P. Ekman & R. J. Davidson (eds), *The nature of emotion: fundamental questions* (pp. 68–73). New York, NY: Oxford University Press.

Goldstein, A. J., & Chambless, D. L. (1978). A reanalysis of agoraphobia. *Behavior Therapy, 9*, 47–59.

Golombok, S., & Fivush, R. (eds) (1994). *Gender development.* New York, NY: Cambridge University Press.

Gomez, R., Cooper, A., & Gomez, A. (2000). Susceptibility to positive and negative mood states: test of Eysenck's, Gray's and Newman's theories. *Personality and Individual Differences, 29*, 351–365.

Goodyear, I. M., Ashby, L., Altham, P. M. E., Vize, C., & Cooper, P. J. (1993). Temperament and major depression in 11 to 16 year olds. *Journal of Child Psychology and Psychiatry, 34*, 1409–1423.

Gorman, J. M., Papp, L. A., Coplan, J. D., Martinez, J. M., Lennon, S., Goetz, R. R., Ross, D., & Klein, D. F. (1994). Anxiogenic effects of CO_2 and hyperventilation in patients with panic disorder. *American Journal of Psychiatry, 151*, 547–553.

Gottman, J. M. (1994). *What predicts divorce? The relationship between marital processes and marital outcomes.* Hillsdale, NJ: Lawrence Erlbaum.

Gottman, J. M., & Levenson, R. W. (1992). Marital processes predictive of later dissolution: behavior, physiology, and health. *Journal of Personality and Social Psychology, 63*, 221–233.

Graf, P., & Mandler, G. (1984). Activation makes words more accessible, but not necessarily more retrievable. *Journal of Verbal Learning and Verbal Behavior, 23*, 553–568.

Graf, P., & Masson, M. E. J. (1993). *Implicit memory: new directions in cognition, development, and neuropsychology.* Hillsdale, NJ: Lawrence Erlbaum.

Graham, L. A., Cohen, S. I., & Shmavonian, R. M. (1966). Sex differences in autonomic responses during instrumental conditioning. *Psychosomatic Medicine, 28*, 264–271.

Gray, J. A. (1970). The psychophysiological basis of introversion–extraversion. *Behaviour Research and Therapy, 8*, 249–266.

Gray, J. A. (1982a). *The neuropsychology of anxiety: an enquiry into the functions of the septo-hippocampal system.* New York, NY: Oxford University Press.

Gray, J. A. (1982b). Precis of "The neuropsychology of anxiety: an enquiry into the functions of the septo-hippocampal system". *Behavioural and Brain Sciences, 5*, 469–534.

Gray, J. A. (1987). *The psychology of fear and stress.* New York, NY: Cambridge University Press.

Gray, J. A. (1997). Personality, punishment, and procedural learning: a test of J. A. Gray's anxiety theory. *Journal of Personality and Social Psychology, 73*, 337–344.

Gray, J. A., & Lalljee, B. (1974). Sex differences in emotional behaviour in the rat: correlation between open-field defecation and active avoidance. *Animal Behaviour, 22*, 856–861.

Gray, J. A., & McNaughton, N. (1996). The neuropsychology of anxiety: reprise. In D. A. Hope (ed.), *Perspectives on anxiety, panic, and fear: current theory and research in motivation* (pp. 61–134). Lincoln, NE: Nebraska Press.

Grey, S. J., Sartory, G., & Rachman, S. (1979). Synchronous and desynchronous changes during fear reduction. *Behaviour Research and Therapy, 17*, 137–147.

Grey, S. J., Rachman, S., & Sartory, G. (1981). Return of fear: the role of inhibition. *Behaviour Research and Therapy, 19*, 135–143.

Grillon, C. (2002a). Startle reactivity and anxiety disorders: aversive conditioning, context, and neurobiology. *Biological Psychiatry, 51*, 958–975.

Grillon, C. (2002b). Associative learning deficits increase symptoms of anxiety in humans. *Biological Psychiatry, 51*, 851–858.

Grillon, C., & Davis, M. (1997). Effects of stress and shock anticipation on prepulse inhibition of the startle reflex. *Psychophysiology, 34*, 511–517.

Grillon, C., & Morgan III, C. A. (1999). Fear-potentiated startle conditioning to explicit and contextual cues in gulf war veterans with posttraumatic stress disorder. *Journal of Abnormal Psychology, 108*, 134–142.

Grillon. C., Ameli, R., Woods, S. W., Merikangas, K., & Davis, M. (1991). Fear-potentiated startle in humans: effects of anticipatory anxiety on the acoustic blink reflex. *Psychophysiology, 28*, 588–595.

Grillon, C., Ameli, R., Merikangas, K., Woods, S. W., & Davis, M. (1993). Measuring the time course of anticipatory anxiety using the fear-potentiated startle reflex. *Psychophysiology, 30*, 340–346.

Grillon, C., Ameli, R., Goddard, A., Woods, S. W., & Davis M. (1994). Baseline and fear-potentiated startle in panic disorder patients. *Biological Psychiatry, 35*, 431–439.

Grillon, C., Dierker, L., & Merikangas, K. R. (1997). Startle modulation in children at risk for anxiety disorders and/or alcoholism. *Journal of the American Academy of Child and Adolescent Psychiatry, 36*, 925–932.

Grillon, C., Dierker, L., & Merikangas, K. R. (1998a). Fear-potentiated startle in adolescent offspring of parents with anxiety disorders. *Biological Psychiatry, 44*, 990–997.

Grillon, C., Morgan, C. A., Davis, M., & Southwick, S. M. (1998b). Effects of experimental context and explicit threat cues on acoustic startle in Vietnam veterans with posttraumatic stress disorders. *Biological Psychiatry, 44*, 1027–1036.

Gross, J. J., & Levenson, R. W. (1993). Emotional suppression: physiology, self-report, and expressive behavior. *Journal of Personality and Social Psychology, 64*, 970–986.

Groves, P. M., & Thompson, R. F. (1970). Habituation: a dual-process theory. *Psychological Review, 77*, 419–450.

Guimarães, F. S., Hellewell, J., Hensman, R. Wang, M., & Deakin, J. F. W. (1991). Characterization of a psychophysiological model of classical fear conditioning in healthy volunteers: influence of gender, instruction, personality and placebo *Psychopharmacology, 104*, 231–236.

Gullone, E., & King, N. J. (1993). The fears of youth in the 1990's: contemporary normative data. *Journal of Genetic Psychology, 154*, 137–153.

Gullone, E., & King, N. J. (1997). Three-year-follow-up of normal fear in children and adolescents aged 7 to 18 years. *British Journal of Developmental Psychology, 15*(Pt 1), 97–111.

Gunnar, M. R. (2001). The role of glucocorticoids in anxiety disorders: a critical analysis. In M. W. Vasey & M. R. Dadds (eds), *The developmental psychopathology of anxiety* (pp. 143–159). London: Oxford University Press.

Gunnar, M. R., Larson, M. C., Hertsgaard, L., Harris, M. L., & Brodersen, L. (1992). The stressfulness of separation among nine-month-old infants: effects of social context variables and infant temperament. *Child Development, 63*, 290–303.

Hackmann, A., Surawy, C., & Clark, D. M. (1998). Seeing yourself through others' eyes: a study of spontaneously occurring images in social phobia. *Behavioural and Cognitive Psychotherapy, 26*, 3–12.

Hadwin, J., Frost, S., French, C. C., & Richards, A. (1997). Cognitive processing and trait anxiety in typically developing children: evidence for an interpretation bias. *Journal of Abnormal Psychology, 106*, 486–490.

Hamm, A. O., Vaitl, D., & Lang, P. J. (1989). Fear conditioning, meaning, and belongingness: a selective association analysis. *Journal of Abnormal Psychology, 98*, 395–406.

Hankin, B. L., & Abramson, L. Y. (2001). Development of gender differences in depression: an elaborated cognitive vulnerability–transactional stress theory. *Psychological Bulletin, 127,* 773–796.

Hansen, C. H., & Hansen, R. D. (1988). Finding the face in the crowd: an anger superiority effect. *Journal of Personality and Social Psychology, 54,* 917–924.

Hansen, C. H., & Hansen, R. D. (1994). Automatic emotion: attention and facial efference. In P. M. Niedenthal & R. D. Hansen (eds), *The heart's eye: emotional influences in perception and attention* (pp. 217–243). San Diego, CA: Academic Press.

Hare, R. D. (1972). Psychopathy and physiological responses to adrenalin. *Journal of Abnormal Psychology, 79,* 138–147.

Harris, E. L., Noyes, R., Crowe, R. R., & Chaudhry, D. R. (1983). Family study of agoraphobia. *Archives of General Psychiatry, 40,* 1061–1064.

Harver, A., Katkin, E. S., & Bloch, E. (1993). Signal-detection outcomes on heartbeat and respiratory resistance detection tasks in male and female subjects. *Psychophysiology, 3,* 223–230.

Harvey, A. G., & Bryant, R. A. (1998). The role of valence in attempted thought suppression. *Behaviour Research and Therapy, 36,* 757–763.

Haskins, V. L. (1982). Individual and gender differences in the orienting and defensive responses (doctoral dissertation, University of Wisconsin, Madison, 1981). *Dissertation Abstracts International, 42*(8-A), 3509–3510.

Hayes, S. C., Strosahl, K. D., & Wilson, K. G. (1999). *Acceptance and commitment therapy: an experiemental approach to behavior change.* New York, NY: Guilford Press.

Hayward, C., Killen, J. D., & Taylor, C. B. (1989). Panic attacks in young adolescents. *American Journal of Psychiatry, 146,* 1061–1062.

Hayward, C., Killen, J. D., Hammer, L. D., Litt, I. F., Wilson, D. M., Simmonds, B., & Taylor, C. B. (1992). Pubertal stage and panic attack history in sixth- and seventh-grade girls. *American Journal of Psychiatry, 149,* 1239–1243.

Hayward, C., Killen, J. D., Kraemer, H. C., & Taylor, C. B. (1998). Linking self-reported childhood behavioral inhibition to adolescent social phobia. *Journal of the American Academy of Child and Adolescent Psychiatry, 37,* 1308–1316.

Hayward, C., Killen, J. D., Kraemer, H. C., & Taylor, C. B. (2000). Predictors of panic attacks in adolescents. *Journal of American Academy of Child Adolescent Psychiatry, 39,* 207–214.

Hazlett-Stevens, H., & Borkovec, T. D. (2001). Effects of worry and progressive relaxation on the reduction of fear in speech phobia: an investigation of situational exposure. *Behavior Therapy, 32,* 503–517.

Hazlett-Stevens, H., Zucker, B. G., & Craske, M. G. (2002). The relationship of thought-action fusion to pathologicial worry and generalized anxiety disorder. *Behaviour Research and Therapy, 40,* 1199–1204.

Hazlett-Stevens, H., & Craske, M. G. (2003 in press). The catastrophizing worry process in generalized anxiety disorder: a preliminary investigation of an analog population. *Behavioural and Cognitive Psychotherapy.*

Heady, B., & Wearing, A. (1989). Personality, life events, and subjective well-being: toward a dynamic equilibrium model. *Journal of Personality and Social Psychology, 57,* 731–739.

Healy, H., & Williams, M. G. (1999). Autobiographical memory. In T. Dalgleish & M. J. Power (eds), *Handbook of cognition and emotion* (pp. 229–242). Chichester: Wiley.

Hebb, D. O. (1968). Concerning imagery. *Psychological Review, 75,* 466–477.

Heduland, M. A., & Chambless, D. L. (1990.) Sex differences and menstrual cycle effects in aversive conditioning: a comparison of premenstrual and intermenstrual women with men. *Journal of Anxiety Disorders, 4,* 221–231.

Hefez, A., Metz, L., & Lavie, P. (1987). Long-term effects of extreme situational stress on sleep and dreaming. *American Journal of Psychiatry, 144*, 344–347.

Heim, C., & Nemeroff, C. B. (1999). The impact of early adverse experiences on brain systems involved in the pathophysiology of anxiety and affective disorders. *Biological Psychiatry, 46*, 1509–1522.

Heimberg, R. G., Dodge, C. S., Hope, D. A., Kennedy, C. R., Zollo, L. J., & Becker, R. E. (1990a). Cognitive-behavioural group treatment for social phobia: comparison with a credible placebo control. *Cognitive Therapy and Research, 14*, 1–23.

Heimberg, R. G., Hope, D. A., Dodge, C. S., & Becker, R. E. (1990b). DSM-III-R subtypes of social phobia: comparison of generalized social phobics and public speaking phobics. *Journal of Nervous and Mental Disease, 178*, 172–179.

Heller, W., Nitschke, J. B., Etienne, M. A., & Miller, G. A. (1997). Patterns of regional brain activity differentiate types of anxiety. *Journal of Abnormal Psychology, 106*, 376–385.

Helzer, J. E., Robins, L. N., & McEvoy, L. (1987). Post-traumatic stress disorder in the general population: findings of the Epidemiologic Catchment Area Survey. *New England Journal of Medicine, 317*, 1630–1634.

Henry, B., Moffitt, T. E., Caspi, A., Langley, J., & Silva, P. (1994). On the "remembrance of things past": a longitudinal evaluation of the retrospective method. *Psychological Assessment, 6*, 92–101.

Hettema, J. M., Prescott, C. A., & Kendler, K. S. (2001). A population-based twin study of generalized anxiety disorder in men and women. *Journal of Nervous and Mental Disease, 189*, 413–420.

Himle, J. A., McPhee, K., Cameron, O. G., & Curtis, G. C. (1989). Simple phobia: evidence for heterogeneity. *Psychiatry Research, 28*, 25–30.

Himle, J. A., Crystal, D., Curtis, G. C., & Fluent, T. E. (1991). Mode of onset of simple phobia subtypes: further evidence of heterogeneity. *Psychiatry Research, 36*, 37–43.

Hinton, J. W., & Craske, B. (1977). Differential effects of test stress on the heart rates of extraverts and introverts. *Biological Psychology, 5*, 23–28.

Hirsch, C., & Mathews, A. (1997). Interpretive inferences when reading about emotional events. *Behaviour Research and Therapy, 35*, 1123–1132.

Hirshfeld, D. R., Rosenbaum, J. F., Biederman, J., Bolduc, E. A., Faraone, S. V., Snidman, N., Reznick, J. S., & Kagan, J. (1992). Stable behavioral inhibition and its association with anxiety disorder. *Journal of the American Academy of Child and Adolescent Psychiatry, 31*, 103–111.

Hoehn-Saric, R., & Masek, B. J. (1981). Effects of naloxone on normals and chronically anxious patients. *Biological Psychiatry, 16*, 1041–1050.

Hoehn-Saric, R., & McLeod, D. R. (1988). The peripheral sympathetic nervous system: its role in normal and pathologic anxiety. *Psychiatric Clinics of North America, 11*, 375–386.

Hoehn-Saric, R., McLeod, D. R., & Zimmerli, W. D. (1989). Somatic manifestations in women with generalized anxiety disorder: psychophysiological responses to psychological stress. *Archives of General Psychiatry, 46*, 1113–1119.

Hoehn-Saric, R., McLeod, D. R., & Zimmerli, W. D. (1991). Psychophysiological response patterns in panic disorder. *Acta Psychiatrica Scandinavica, 83*, 4–11.

Hoehn-Saric, R., McLeod, D. R., & Hipsley, P. (1995). Is hyperarousal essential to obsessive–compulsive disorder? Diminished physiologic flexibility, but not hyperarousal, characterizes patients with obsessive–compulsive disorder. *Archives of General Psychiatry, 52*, 688–693.

Hofmann, S. G., Newman, M. G., Ehlers, A., & Roth, W. T. (1995). Psychophysiological differences between subgroups of social phobia. *Journal of Abnormal Psychology, 104*, 224–231.

Hollander, E., DeCaria, C., Nitescu, A., Cooper, T., Stover, B., Gully, R., Klein, D. F., & Liebowitz, M. R. (1991). Noradrenergic function in obsessive–compulsive disorder: behavioral and neuroendocrine responses to clonidine and comparison to healthy controls. *Psychiatry Research, 37*, 161–177.

Hollifield, M., Katon, W., Skipper, B., Chapman, T., Ballenger, J. C., Mannuzza, S., & Fyer, A. J. (1997). Panic disorder and quality of life: variables predictive of functional impairment. *American Journal of Psychiatry, 154*, 766–772.

Hope, D. A., Heimberg, R. G., & Klein, J. F. (1990a). Social anxiety and the recall of the interpersonal information. *Journal of Cognitive Psychotherapy, 4*, 185–195.

Hope, D. A., Rapee, R. M., Heimberg, R. G., & Dombeck, M. J. (1990b). Representations of the self in social phobia: vulnerability to social threat. *Cognitive Therapy and Research, 14*, 177–189.

Horowitz, M. (1976). *Stress response syndromes*. New York, NY: Aronson.

Horowitz, M. (1980). Psychological response to serious life events. In V. Hamilton & D. Warburton (eds), *Human stress and cognition: an information processing approach* (pp. 235–263). New York, NY: Wiley.

Horowitz, M. J., Wilner, N., & Alvarez, W. (1979). Impact of Event Scale: a measure of subjective stress. *Psychosomatic Medicine, 41*, 209–218.

Hudson, J. L., & Rapee, R. M. (2001). Parent-child interactions and anxiety disorders: an observational study. *Behaviour Research and Therapy, 39*, 1411–1427.

Hugdahl, K., & Öhman, A. (1977). Effects of instruction on acquisition and extinction of electrodermal responses to fear-relevant stimuli. *Journal of Experimental Psychology: Human Learning and Memory, 3*, 608–618.

Hugdahl, K., & Kaerker, A. C. (1981). Biological vs experiential factors in phobic conditioning. *Behaviour Research and Therapy, 19*, 109–115.

Hugdahl, K., Fredrikson, M., & Öhman, A. (1977). 'Preparedness' and 'arousability' as determinants of electrodermal conditioning. *Behaviour Research and Therapy, 15*, 345–353.

Hughes, J. W., & Stoney, C. M. (2000). Depressed mood is related to high-frequency heart rate variability during stressors. *Psychosomatic Medicine, 62*, 796–803.

Ingram, R. E. (1990a). Attentional nonspecificity in depressive and generalized anxious affective states. *Cognitive Therapy and Research, 14*, 25–35.

Ingram, R. E. (1990b). Self-focused attention in clinical disorders: review and a conceptual model. *Psychological Bulletin, 107*, 156–176.

Insel, T. R. (1992). Toward a neuroanatomy of obsessive–compulsive disorder. *Archives of General Psychiatry, 49*, 739–744.

Insel, T. R., Scanlan, J., Champoux, M., & Suomi, S. J. (1988). Rearing paradigm in nonhuman primate affects response to beta-CCE challenge. *Psychopharmacology, 96*, 81–86.

Irie, M., Maeda, M., & Nagata, S. (2001). Can conditioned histamine release occur under urethane anesthesia in guinea pigs? *Physiology and Behavior, 72*, 567–573.

Izard, C. E. (1992). Basic emotions, relations among emotions, and emotion–cognition relations. *Psychological Review, 99*, 561–565.

Izquierdo, L. A., Barros, D. M., Medina, J. H., & Izquierdo, I. (2002). Stress hormones enhance retrieval of fear conditioning acquired either one day or many months before. *Behavioural Pharmacology, 13*, 203–213.

Jackson, R. L., & Minor, T. R. (1988). Effects of signaling inescapable shock on subsequent learning: implication for theories of coping and "learned helplessness." *Journal of Experimental Psychology: Animal Behavior Processes, 14*, 390–400.

Jacob, R. G., Furman, J. M., Clark, D. B., & Durrant, J. D. (1992). Vestibular symptoms, panic, and phobia: overlap and possible relationships. *Annals of Clinical Psychiatry, 4*, 163–174.

Jacob, R. G., Furman, J. M., Durrant, J. D., & Turner, S. M. (1996). Panic, agoraphobia, and vestibular dysfunction. *American Journal of Psychiatry, 153*, 503–512.

Jacob, R. G., Furman, J. M., Durrant, J. D., & Turner, S. M. (1997). Surface dependence: a balance control strategy in panic disorder with agoraphobia. *Psychosomatic Medicine, 59,* 323–330.

Jalowiec, J. E., Calcagnetti, D. J., & Fanselow, M. S. (1989). Suppression of juvenile social behavior requires antagonism of central opioid systems. *Pharmacology, Biochemistry and Behavior, 33,* 697–700.

James, W. (1890). *The principles of psychology.* New York, NY: Holt.

Janeck, A. S., & Calamari, J. E. (1999). Thought suppression in obsessive–compulsive disorder. *Cognitive Therapy and Research, 23,* 497–509.

Janoff-Bulman, R. (1985). The aftermath of victimization: rebuilding shattered assumptions. In C. R. Figley (ed.), *Trauma and its wake* (vol. 1, pp. 15–35). New York, NY: Brunner/Mazel.

Jardine, R., Martin, N. G., & Henderson, A. S. (1984). Genetic covariation between neuroticism and the symptoms of anxiety and depression. *Genetic Epidemiology, 1,* 89–107.

Johansen, B. H. (1993). Cerebral asymmetry in autonomic conditioning to facial expressions: sex differences. *Scandinavian Journal of Psychology, 34,* 363–370.

Johnson, M. K. (1988). Discriminating the origin of information. In T. F. Oltmanns, & B. A. Maher (eds), *Delusional beliefs* (pp. 34–65). New York, NY: Wiley.

Johnson, W. M., & Davey, G. C. L. (1997). The psychological impact of negative TV news bulletins: the catastrophizing of personal worries. *British Journal of Psychology, 88,* 85–91.

Joiner Jr, T. E., Steer, R. A., Beck, A. T., Schmidt, N. B., Rudd, M. D., & Catanzaro, S. J. (1999). Physiological hyperarousal: construct validity of a central aspect of the tripartite model of depression and anxiety. *Journal of Abnormal Psychology, 108,* 290–298.

Jones, M. K., & Menzies, R. G. (1997). The cognitive mediation of obsessive–compulsive handwashing. *Behaviour Research and Therapy, 35,* 843–850.

Jones, T., & Davey, G. C. (1990). The effects of cued UCS rehearsal on the retention of differential "fear" conditioning: an experimental analogue of the "worry" process. *Behaviour Research and Therapy, 28,* 159–164.

Jordan, B. K., Schlenger, W. E., Hough, R., Kulka, R. A., Weiss, D., Fairbank, J. A., & Marmar, C. E. (1991). Lifetime and current prevalence of specific psychiatric disorders among Vietnam veterans and controls. *Archives of General Psychiatry, 48,* 207–215.

Jorm, A. F., Christensen, A., Henderson, A. S., Jacomb, P. A., Korten, A. E., & Rodgers, B. (2000). Predicting anxiety and depression from personality: is there a synergistic effect of neuroticism and extraversion? *Journal of Abnormal Psychology, 109,* 145–149.

Joseph, S., Williams, R., & Yule, W. (1995). Psychosocial perspectives on post-traumatic stress. *Clinical Psychology Review, 15,* 515–544.

Joseph, S. A., Brewin, C. R., Yule, W., & Williams, R. M. (1991). Causal attributions and psychiatric symptoms in survivors of the *Herald of Free Enterprise* disaster. *British Journal of Psychiatry, 159,* 542–546.

Joseph, S. A., Brewin, C. R., Yule, W., & Williams, R. (1993). Causal attributions and post-traumatic stress in adolescents. *Journal of Child Psychology and Psychiatry and Allied Disciplines, 34,* 247–253.

Juster, H. R., & Heimberg, R. G. (1995). Social phobia: longitudinal course and long-term outcome of cognitive–behavioral treatment. *Psychiatric Clinics of North America, 18,* 821–842.

Kagan, J. (1989). Temperamental contributions to social behavior. *American Psychologist, 44,* 668–674.

Kagan, J. (1997). Temperamental contributions to the development of social behavior. In D. Manusson (ed.), *The lifespan development of individuals: behavioral, neurological, and psychosocial perspectives: a synthesis* (pp. 376–393). New York, NY: Cambridge University Press.

Kagan, J., Reznick, J. S., Clarke, C., Snidman, N., & Garcia-Coll, C. (1984). Behavioral inhibition to the unfamiliar. *Child Development, 55*, 2212–2225.

Kagan, J., Reznick, J. S., & Snidman, N. (1987). The physiology and psychology of behavioral inhibition in children. *Child Development, 58*, 1459–1473.

Kagan, J., Reznick, J. S., & Snidman, N. (1988). The physiology and psychology of behavioral inhibition in children. *Annual Progress in Child Psychiatry and Child Development*, 102–127.

Kagan, J., Snidman, N., & Arcus, D. M. (1992). Initial reactions to unfamiliarity. *Current Directions in Psychological Science, 1*, 171–174.

Kagan, J., Arcus, D., Snidman, N., Peterson, E., Steinberg, D., & Rimm-Kaufman, S. (1995). Asymmetry of finger temperature and early behavior. *Developmental Psychobiology, 28*, 443–451.

Kaloupek, D. G., Peterson, D. A., & Levis, D. J. (1981). An investigation of the normative and factor analytic composition of six questionnaires used for subject selection. *Journal of Behavioral Assessment, 3*, 149–165.

Karno, M., & Golding, J. M. (1991). Obsessive–compulsive disorder. In L. N. Robins & D. A. Regier (eds), *Psychiatric disorders in America: the epidemiological catchment area study* (pp. 204–219). New York, NY: Free Press.

Karno, M., Golding, J. M., Sorenson, S. B., & Burnam, M. A. (1988). The epidemiology of obsessive–compulsive disorder in five US communities. *Archives of General Psychiatry, 45*, 1094–1099.

Kashani, J. H., & Orvaschel, H. (1990). A community study of anxiety in children and adolescents. *American Journal of Psychiatry, 147*, 313–318.

Katkin, E. S. (1985). Blood, sweat, and tears: individual differences in automatic self-perception. *Psychophysiology, 2*, 125–137.

Katkin, E. S., & Hoffman, L. S. (1976). Sex differences and self-report of fear: a psychophysiological assessment. *Journal of Abnormal Psychology, 85*, 607–610.

Katkin, E. S., Blascovich, J., & Goldband, S. (1981). Empirical assessment of visceral self-perception: individual and sex differences in the acquisition of heartbeat discrimination. *Journal of Personality and Social Psychology, 6*, 1095–1101.

Katkin, E. S., Wiens, S., & Öhman, A. (2001). Nonconcious fear conditioning, visceral perception, and the development of gut feelings. *Psychological Science, 12*, 366–370.

Katz, L. F., & Gottman, J. M. (1995). Vagal tone protects children from marital conflict. *Development and Psychopathology, 7*, 83–92.

Keenan, K., & Shaw, D. (1997). Developmental and social influences on young girls' early problem behavior. *Psychological Bulletin, 121*, 95–113.

Kellner, M., Yehuda, R., Arlt, J., & Wiedemann, K. (2002). Longitudinal course of salivary cortisol in post-traumatic stress disorder. *Acta Psychiatrica Scandinavica, 105*, 153–155.

Kelly, D. D. (1980). Enhancement of conditioned autonomic responses in monkeys when preshock signals occasion operant suppression. *Journal of the Experimental Analysis of Behavior, 33*, 275–284.

Kelvin, R. G., Goodyer, I. M., & Altham, P. M. E. (1996). Temperament and psychopathology amongst siblings of probands with depressive and anxiety disorders. *Journal of Child Psychology and Psychiatry and Allied Disciplines, 37*, 543–550.

Kelvin, R. G., Goodyer, I. M., Teasdale, J. D., & Brechin, D. (1999). Latent negative self-schema and high emotionality in well adolescents at risk for psychopathology. *Journal of Child Psychology and Psychiatry and Allied Disciplines, 40*, 959–968.

Kenardy, J., Oei, T. P. S., Weir, D., & Evans, L. (1993). Phobic anxiety in panic disorder: cognition, heart rate, and subjective anxiety. *Journal of Anxiety Disorders, 7*, 359–371.

Kendall, P. C., & Ingram, R. E. (1987). The future for cognitive assessment of anxiety: let's get specific. In L. Michaelson & L. M. Ascher (eds), *Anxiety and stress disorders: cognitive–behavioral assessment and treatment* (pp. 89–104). New York, NY: Guilford.

Kendall, P. C., & Hollon, S. D. (1989). Anxious self-talk: development of the Anxious Self-Statements Questionnaire (ASSQ). *Cognitive Therapy and Research, 13*, 81–93.

Kendler, K. S. (1996). Major depression and generalized anxiety disorder: same genes (partly) different environments—revisited. *British Journal of Psychiatry, 168*, 68–75.

Kendler, K. S., Heath, A., Martin, N. G., & Eaves, L. J. (1986). Symptoms of anxiety and depression in a volunteer twin population: the etiologic role of genetic and environmental factors. *Archives of General Psychiatry, 43*, 213–221.

Kendler, K. S., Heath, A. C., Martin, N. G., & Eaves, L. J (1987). Symptoms of anxiety and symptoms of depression: same genes, different environments? *Archives of General Psychiatry, 44*, 451–457.

Kendler, K. S., Kessler, R. C., Heath, A. C., Neale M. C., & Eaves, L. J. (1991). Coping: a genetic epidemiological investigation. *Psychological Medicine, 21*, 337–346.

Kendler, K. S., Neale, M. C. Kessler, R. C., & Heath, A. C. (1992). The genetic epidemiology of phobias in women: the interrelationship of agoraphobia, social phobia, situational phobia, and simple phobia. *Archives of General Psychiatry, 49*, 273–281.

Kendler, K. S., Neale, M. C., Kessler, R. C., Heath, A. C., & Eaves, L. J. (1993). Major depression and phobias: the genetic and environmental sources of comorbidity. *Psychological Medicine, 23*, 361–371.

Kendler, K. S., Walters, E. E., Neale, M. C., Kessler, R. C., Heath, A. C., & Eaves, L. J. (1995). The structure of the genetic and environmental risk factors for six major psychiatric disorders in women. *Archives of General Psychiatry, 52*, 374–383.

Kendler, K. S., Karkowski, L. M., & Prescott, C. A. (1999). Fears and phobias: reliability and heritability. *Psychological Medicine, 29*, 539–553.

Kendler, K. S., Meyers, J., Prescott, C. A., & Neale, M. C. (2001). The genetic epidemiology of irrational fears and phobias in men. *Archives of General Psychiatry, 58*, 257–265.

Kennedy, S. J., Rapee, R. M., & Mazurski, E. J. (1997). Covariation bias for phylogenetic versus ontogenetic fear-relevant stimuli. *Behaviour Research and Therapy, 35*, 415–422.

Kerig, P. K., Cowan, P. A., & Cowan, C. P. (1993). Marital quality and gender differences in parent–child interaction. *Developmental Psychology, 29*, 931–939.

Kessler, R. C. (1997). The prevalence of psychiatric comorbidity. In S. Wetzler & W. C. Sanderson (eds), *Treatment strategies for patients with psychiatric comorbidity. An Einstein psychiatry publication* (pp. 23–48). New York, NY: Wiley.

Kessler, R. C., & McLeod, J. D. (1984). Sex differences in vulnerability to undesirable life events. *American Sociological Review, 49*, 620–631.

Kessler, R. C., Kendler, K. S., Heath, A., & Neale, M. C. (1992). Social support, depressed mood, and adjustment to stress: a genetic epidemiologic investigation. *Journal of Personality and Social Psychology, 62*, 257–272.

Kessler, R. C., McGonagle, K., Zhao, S., Nelson, C., Hughes, M., Eshelman, S., Wittchen, H., & Kendler, K. (1994). Lifetime and 12-month prevalence of DSM-III-R psychiatric disorders in the United States: results from the National Comorbidity Survey. *Archives of General Psychiatry, 51*, 8–19.

Kessler, R. C., Sonnega, A., Bromet, E., Hughes, M., & Nelson, C. B. (1995). Posttraumatic stress disorder in the National Comorbidity Survey. *Archives of General Psychiatry, 52*, 1048–1060.

Kessler, R. C., Nelson, C. B., McGonagle, K. A., Liu, J., Swartz, M., & Blazer, D. G. (1996). Comorbidity of DSM-III-R major depressive disorder in the general population: results from the US National Comorbidity Survey. *British Journal of Psychiatry, 168*, 17–30.

Kessler, R. C., Davis, C. G., & Kendler, K. S. (1997). Childhood adversity and adult psychiatric disorder in the US National Comorbidity Study. *Psychological Medicine, 27*, 1101–1119.

Kessler, R. C., Stang, P. E., Wittchen, H-U., Ustun, T. B., Roy-Burne, P. P., & Walters, E. E. (1998). Lifetime panic–depression comorbidity in the National Comorbidity Survey. *Archives of General Psychiatry, 55*, 801–808.

Keyl, P. M., & Eaton, W. W. (1990). Risk factors for the onset of panic disorder and other panic attacks in a prospective, population-based study. *American Journal of Epidemiology, 131*, 301–311.

Kilpatrick, D. G., & Resnick, H. S. (1993). Posttraumatic stress disorder associated with exposure to criminal victimization in clinical and community populations. In J. R. T. Davidson & E. B. Foa (eds), *Posttraumatic stress disorder: DSM-IV and beyond* (pp. 113–143). Washington, DC: American Psychiatric Press.

Kilpatrick, D. G., Saunders, B. E., Amick-McMullan, A., Best, C. L., Veronen, L. J., & Resnick, H. S. (1989). Victim and crime factors associated with the development of crime-related posttraumatic stress disorder. *Behavior Therapy, 20*, 199–214.

Kim, J. J., & Fanselow, M. S. (1992). Modality-specific retrograde amnesia of fear. *Science, 256*, 675–677.

Kindt, M., Brosschot, J. F., & Everaerd, W. (1997a). Cognitive processing bias of children in a real life stress situation and a neutral situation. *Journal of Experimental Child Psychology, 64*, 79–97.

Kindt, M., Bierman, D., & Brosschot, J. F. (1997b). Cognitive bias in spider fear and control children: assessment of emotional interference by a card format and a single-trial format of the stroop task. *Journal of Experimental Child Psychology, 66*, 163–179.

Kindt, M., van den Hout, M., de Jong, P., & Hoekzema, B. (2000). Cognitive bias for pictorial and linguistic threat cues in children. *Journal of Psychopathology and Behavioral Assessment, 22*, 201–219.

King, D. W., King, L. A., Foy, D. W., Keane, T. M., & Fairbank, J. A. (1999). Posttraumatic stress disorder in a national sample of female and male Vietnam veterans: risk factors, war-zone stressors, and resilience-recovery variables. *Journal of Abnormal Psychology, 108*, 164–170.

King, N. J., Ollier, K., Iacuone, R., Schuster, S., Bays, K., Gullone, E., & Ollendick, T. H. (1989). Fears of children and adolescents: a cross-sectional Australian study using the Revised-Fear Survey Schedule for Children. *Journal of Child Psychology and Psychiatry and Allied Disciplines, 30*, 775–784.

King, N. J., Gullone, E., Tonge, B. J., & Ollendick, T. H. (1993). Self-reports of panic attacks and manifest anxiety in adolescents. *Behaviour Research and Therapy, 31*, 111–116.

King, N. J., Clowes-Hollins, V., & Ollendick, T. H. (1997). The etiology of childhood dog phobia. *Behaviour Research and Therapy, 35*, 77.

King, N. J., Gullone, E., & Ollendick, T. H. (1998). Etiology of childhood phobias: current status of Rachman's three pathways theory. *Behaviour Research and Therapy, 36*, 297–309.

Kirkby, K. C., Menzies, R. G., Daniels, B. A., & Smith, K. L. (1995). Aetiology of spider phobia: classificatory differences between two origins instruments. *Behaviour Research and Therapy, 33*, 955–958.

Kirkpatrick, D. P. (1984). Age, gender, and patterns of common intense fears among adults. *Behaviour Research and Therapy, 22*, 141–150.

Kirmayer, L. J., Young, A., & Hayton, B. C. (1995). The cultural context of anxiety disorder. *Cultural Psychiatry, 18*, 503–521.

Kirsch, I. (1985). Response expectancy as a determinant of experience and behavior. *American Psychologist, 40*, 1189–1202.

Kleinknecht, R. A. (1994). Acquisition of blood, injury, and needle fears and phobias. *Behaviour Research and Therapy, 32*, 817–823.

Klorman, R., Hastings, J. E., Weerts, T. C., Melamed, B. G., & Lang, P. J. (1974). Psychometric description of some specific fear questionnaires. *Behavior Therapy*, 5, 401–409.

Kochanska, G., Murray, K. T., & Harlan, E. T. (2000). Effortful control in early childhood: continuity and change, antecedents, and implications for social development. *Developmental Psychology*, 36, 220–232.

Koss, M. P., & Mukai, T. (1993). Recovering ourselves: the frequency, effects, and resolution of rape. In F. L. Denmark & M. A. Paludi (eds), *Psychology of women: a handbook of issues and theories* (pp. 477–512). Westport, CT: Greenwood Press.

Kovacs, M., Gatsonis, C., Paulauskas, S. L., & Richards, C. (1989). Depressive disorders in childhood. *Archives of General Psychiatry*, 46, 776–782.

Kozak, M. J., Foa, E. B., & Steketee, G. (1988). Process and outcome of exposure treatment with obsessive–compulsives: psychophysiological indicators of emotional processing. *Behavior Therapy*, 19, 157–169.

Kroenke, K., & Spitzer, R. L. (1998). Gender differences in the reporting of physical and somatoform symptoms. *Psychosomatic Medicine*, 2, 150–155.

Krohne, H. W., & Hock, M. (1991). Relationships between restrictive mother child interactions and anxiety of the child. *Anxiety Research*, 4, 109–124.

Krueger, R. F., Caspi, A., Moffitt, T. E., Silva, P. A., & McGee, R. (1996). Personality traits are differentially linked to mental disorders: a multitrait-multidiagnosis study of an adolescent birth cohort. *Journal of Abnormal Psychology*, 105, 299–312.

Krueger, R. F., Caspi, A., Moffitt, T. E., & Silva, P. A. (1998). The structure and stability of common mental disorders (DSM-III-R): a longitudinal-epidemiological study. *Journal of Abnormal Psychology*, 107, 216–227.

Krueger, R. F., Hicks, B. M., Patrick, C. J., Carlson, S. R., Iacono, W. G., & McGue, M. (2002). Etiological connections among substance dependence, antisocial behavior, and personality: modeling the externalizing spectrum. *Journal of Abnormal Psychology*, 111, 411–424.

Krystal, J. H., Southwick, S. M., & Charney, D. S. (1995). Posttraumatic stress disorder: psychobiological mechanisms of traumatic remembrance. In D. L. Schachter (ed.), *Memory distortion: how minds, brains, and societies reconstruct the past* (pp. 150–172). Cambridge, MA: Harvard University Press.

Kushner, M. G., Riggs, D. S., Foa, E. B., & Miller, S. M. (1993). Perceived controllability and the development of posttraumatic stress disorder (PTSD) in crime victims. *Behaviour Research and Therapy*, 31, 105–110.

LaBar, K. S., & LeDoux, J. E. (1996). Partial disruption of fear conditioning in rats with unilateral amygdale damage: correspondence with unilateral temporal lobectomy in humans. *Behavioral Neuroscience*, 110, 991–997.

LaBar, K. S., & Phelps, E. A. (1998). Arousal-mediated memory consolidation: role of the medial temporal lobe in humans. *Psychological Science*, 9, 490–493.

Lader, M. H. (1967). Palmar skin conductance measures in anxiety and phobic states. *Journal of Psychosomatic Research*, 11, 271–281.

Lader, M. H., & Wing, L. (1964). Habituation of the psycho-galvanic reflex in patients with anxiety states and in normal subjects. *Journal of Neurology, Neurosurgery and Psychiatry*, 27, 210–218.

Lader, M., & Wing, L. (eds) (1966). *Physiological measures, sedative drugs, and morbid anxiety.* London: Oxford University Press.

Ladouceur, R., Rheaume, J., Freeston, M. H., Aublet, F., Jean, K., Lachance, S., Langlois, F., & De Pokomandy-Morin, K. (1995). Experimental manipulations of responsibility: an analogue test for models of obsessive–compulsive disorder. *Behaviour Research and Therapy*, 33, 937–946.

Ladouceur, R., Blais, F., Freeston, M. H., & Dugas, M. J. (1998). Problem solving and problem orientation in generalized anxiety disorder. *Journal of Anxiety Disorders*, *12*, 139–152.

Ladouceur, R., Freeston, M. H., Rheaume, J., Dugas, M. J., Gagnon, F., Thibodeau, N., & Fournier, S. (2000). Strategies used with intrusive thoughts: a comparison of OCD patients with anxious and community controls. *Journal of Abnormal Psychology*, *109*, 179–187.

Lake, R. I. E., Eaves, L. J., Maes, H. H. M., Heath, A. C., & Martin, N. G. (2000). Further evidence against the environmental transmission of individual differences in neuroticism from a collaborative study of 45,850 twins and relatives on two continents. *Behavior Genetics*, *30*, 223–233.

Lang, A. J., Craske, M. G., Brown, M., & Ghaneian, A. (2001). Fear-related state dependent memory. *Cognition and Emotion*, *15*, 695–703.

Lang, P. J. (1979). A bio-informational theory of emotional imagery. *Psychophysiology*, *16*, 495–512.

Lang, P. J. (1985). The cognitive psychophysiology of emotion: fear and anxiety. In A. H. Tuma & J. D. Maser (eds), *Anxiety and the anxiety disorders* (pp. 131–170). Hillsdale, NJ: Lawrence Erlbaum.

Lang, P. J., Bradley, M. M., & Cuthbert, B. N. (1998). Emotion, motivation, and anxiety: brain mechanisms and psychophysiology. *Biological Psychiatry*, *44*, 1248–1263.

Langlois, F., Freeston, M. H., & Ladouceur, R. (2000). Differences and similarities between obsessive intrusive thoughts and worry in a non-clinical population: study II. *Behavioural Research and Therapy*, *38*, 175–189.

Last, C. G., Barlow, D. H., & O'Brien, G. T. (1985). Assessing cognitive aspects of anxiety. *Behavior Modification*, *9*, 72–93.

Last, C. G., Strauss, C. C., & Francis, G. (1987). Comorbidity among childhood anxiety disorders. *Journal of Nervous and Mental Disease*, *175*, 726–730.

Last, C. G., Perrin, S., Hersen, M., & Kazdin, A. E. (1992). DSM-III-R anxiety disorders in children: sociodemographic and clinical characteristics. *Journal of the American Academy of Child and Adolescent Psychiatry*, *31*, 1070–1076.

Last, C. G., Perrin, S., Hersen, M., & Kazdin, A. E. (1996). A prospective study of childhood anxiety disorders. *Journal of the American Academy of Child Adolescent Psychiatry*, *35*, 1502–1510.

Lautch, H. (1971). Dental phobia. *British Journal of Psychiatry*, *119*, 151–158.

Lavie, P., Hefez, A., Halperin, G., & Enoch, D. (1979). Long-term effects of traumatic war-related events on sleep. *American Journal of Psychiatry*, *136*, 175–178.

LeDoux, J. E. (1987). Emotion. In V. F. Plum (ed.), *Handbook of physiology — the nervous system* (pp. 419–459). Washington, DC: American Physiological Society.

LeDoux, J. E. (1996). *The emotional brain: the mysterious underpinnings of emotional life.* New York, NY: Simon & Schuster.

LeDoux, J. E. (1998). Fear and the brain: where have we been, and where are we going? *Biological Psychiatry*, *44*, 1229–1238.

Lelliott, P., Marks, I., McNamee, G., & Tobena, A. (1989). Onset of panic disorder with agoraphobia: toward an integrated model. *Archives of General Psychiatry*, *46*, 1000–1004.

Lennartz, R. C., & Weinberger, N. M. (1992). Analysis of response systems in Pavlovian conditioning reveals rapidly versus slowly acquired conditioned responses: support for two factors, implications for behavior and neurobiology. *Psychobiology*, *20*, 93–119.

Leonard, H., L., Swedo, S. E., Lenane, M. C., Rettew, D. C., Hamburger, S. D., Bartko, J. J., & Rapoport, J. L. (1993). A 2- to 7-year follow-up study of 54 obsessive–compulsive children and adolescents. *Archives of General Psychiatry*, *50*, 429–439.

Lesch, K., Bengel, D., Heils, A., Sabol, S. Z., Greenberg, B. D., Petri, S., Benjamin, J., Muller, C. R., Hamer D. H., & Murphy, D. L. (1996). Association of anxiety-related traits with a polymorphism in the serotonin transporter gene regulatory region. *Science*, *274*, 1527–153.

Leung, A. W., & Heimberg, R. G. (1996). Homework compliance, perceptions of control, and outcome of cognitive–behavioral treatment of social phobia. *Behaviour Research and Therapy, 34*, 423–432.

Levenson, M. R., Aldwin, C. M., Bosse, R., Spiro III, A. (1988). Emotionality and mental health: longitudinal findings from the normative aging study. *Journal of Abnormal Psychology, 97*, 94–96.

Levin, D. N., Cook, E. W., & Lang, P. J. (1982). Fear imagery and fear behavior: psychophysiological analysis of clients receiving treatment for anxiety disorders. *Psychophysiology, 19*, 571–572.

Levin, D. N., Hops, H., Roberts, R. E., Seeley, J. R., & Andrews, J. A. (1993). Adolescent psychopathology: I. Prevalence and incidence of depression and other DSM-III-R disorders in high school students. *Journal of Abnormal Psychology, 102*, 133–144.

Li, R. C., Chen, M., Yang, Y., Chang, H., Liu, C., Shen, S., & Chen, C. (2000). Perceptual alteration in obsessive compulsive disorder: implications for a role of the cortico-striatal circuitry in mediating awareness. *Behavioural Brain Research, 111*, 61–69.

Likierman, H., & Rachman, S. J. (1980). Spontaneous decay of compulsive urges: cumulative effects. *Behaviour Research and Therapy, 18*, 387–394.

Lilienfeld, S. O., Jacob, R. G., & Turner, S. M. (1989). Comment on Holloway and McNally's (1987) Effects of anxiety sensitivity on the response to hyperventilation. *Journal of Abnormal Psychology, 98*, 100–102.

Lipp, O. V., Waters, A. M., Logies, S., & Derakshan, N. (2003 in press). Snakes in the flowerbed — do they pop out?

Litz, B. T., King, L. A., King, D. W., Orsillo, S. M., & Friedman, M. J. (1997). Warriors as peacekeepers: features of the Somalia experience and PTSD. *Journal of Consulting and Clinical Psychology, 65*, 1001–1010.

Logan, A. C., & Goetsch, V. L. (1993). Attention to external threat cues in anxiety states. *Clinical Psychology Review, 13*, 541–559.

Lonigan, C. F., Kistner, J. A., Hooe, E. S., & David, C. (1997, November). *An affective model of anxiety and depression in children: evidence from a longitudinal study.* Poster session presented at the annual convention of the Association for the Advancement of Behavior Therapy, Miami, FL.

Lonigan, C. J., & Phillips, B. M. (2001). Temperamental influences on the development of anxiety disorders. In M. W. Vasey & M. R. Dadds (eds), *The developmental psychopathology of anxiety* (pp. 60–91). New York, NY: Oxford University Press.

Lopatka, C., & Rachman, S. (1995). Perceived responsibility and compulsive checking: an experimental analysis. *Behaviour Research and Therapy, 33*, 673–684.

Lovibond, P. F., & Chan, C. K. Y. (1990). Threat appraisal and trait anxiety. In N. McNaughton & G. Andrews (eds), *Anxiety* (pp. 160–168). Dunedin: University of Otago Press.

Lovibond, P. F., & Shanks, D. R. (2002). The role of awareness in Pavlovian conditioning: empirical evidence and theoretical implications. *Journal of Experimental Psychology: Animal Behavior Processes, 28*, 3–26.

Lowinger, S. (1999). Infant irritability and early mother-infant reciprocity patterns. *Infant and Child Development, 8*, 71–84.

Lucock, M. P., & Salkovskis, P. M. (1988). Cognitive factors in social anxiety and its treatment. *Behaviour Research and Therapy, 26*, 297–302.

Lumley, M. A., & Melamed, B. G. (1992). Blood phobics and nonphobics: psychological differences and affect during exposure. *Behaviour Research and Therapy, 30*, 425–434.

Lundh, L., & Öst, L. (1996). Stroop interference, self-focus and perfectionism in social phobics. *Personality and Individual Differences, 20*, 725–731.

Lundh, L., Czyzykow, S., & Öst, L. (1997). Explicit and implicit memory bias in panic disorder with agoraphobia. *Behaviour Research and Therapy, 35*, 1003–1014.

Luu, P., Tucker, D. M., & Derryberry, D. (1998). Anxiety and the motivational basis of working memory. *Cognitive Therapy and Research, 22,* 577–594.

Lykken, D. T. (1975). Psychology and the lie detector industry: reply. *American Psychologist, 30,* 711–712.

Lynn, R., & Martin, T. (1997). Gender differences in extraversion, neuroticism, and psychoticism in 37 nations. *Journal of Social Psychology, 137,* 369–373.

Lyonfields, J. D. (1991, November). *An examination of image and thought processes in generalized anxiety.* Paper presented at the annual convention of the Association for the Advancement of Behavior Therapy, New York, NY.

Lyonfields, J. D., Borkovec, T. D., & Thayer, J. F. (1995). Vagal tone in generalized anxiety disorder and the effects of aversive imagery and worrisome thinking. *Behavior Therapy, 26,* 457–466.

Maccoby, E. E., & Jacklin, C. N. (1974). Myth, reality and shades of gray: what we know and don't know about sex differences. *Psychology Today, 8,* 109–112.

Mackinnon, A. J., Henderson, A. S., & Andrews, G. (1990). Genetic and environmental determinants of the lability of trait neuroticism and the symptoms of anxiety and depression. *Psychological Medicine, 20,* 581–591.

Mackintosh, N. J. (1974). *The psychology of animal learning* (pp. 730). Oxford: Academic Press.

Mackintosh, N. J. (1983). *Conditioning and associative learning.* New York, NY: Oxford University Press.

MacLeod, A. K., Williams, J. M. G., & Bekerian, D. A. (1991). Worry is reasonable: the role of explanations in pessimism about future personal events. *Journal of Abnormal Psychology, 100,* 478–486.

MacLeod, C. (1999). Anxiety and anxiety disorders. In T. Dalgleish & M. J. Power (eds), *Handbook of cognition and emotion* (pp. 447–477). New York, NY: Wiley.

MacLeod, C., & Mathews, A. (1988). Anxiety and the allocation of attention to threat. *Quarterly Journal of Experimental Psychology: Human Experimental Psychology, 40*(4-A), 653–670.

MacLeod, C., & Mathews, A. M. (1991). Cognitive–experimental approaches to the emotional disorders. In P. R. Martin (ed.), *Handbook of behavior therapy and psychological science: an integrative approach* (pp. 116–150). Elmsford, NY: Pergamon.

MacLeod, C., & Hagan, R. (1992). Individual differences in the selective processing of threatening information, and emotional responses to a stressful life event. *Behaviour Research and Therapy, 30,* 151–161.

MacLeod, C., & Rutherford, E. M. (1992). Anxiety and the selective processing of emotional information: mediating roles of awareness, trait and state variables, and personal relevance of stimulus materials. *Behaviour Research and Therapy, 30,* 479–491.

MacLeod, C., & Cohen, I. L. (1993). Anxiety and the interpretation of ambiguity: a text comprehension study. *Journal of Abnormal Psychology, 102,* 238–247.

MacLeod, C., & McLaughlin, K. (1995). Implicit and explicit memory bias in anxiety: a conceptual replication. *Behaviour Research and Therapy, 33,* 1–14.

MacLeod, C., Mathews, A., & Tata, P. (1986). Attentional bias in emotional disorders. *Journal of Abnormal Psychology, 95,* 15–20.

MacLeod, C., Rutherford, E., Campbell, L., Ebsworthy, G., & Holker, L. (2002). Selective attention and emotional vulnerability: assessing the causal basis of their association through the experimental manipulation of attentional bias. *Journal of Abnormal Psychology, 111,* 107–123.

Maes, M., Mylle, J., Delmeire, L., & Altamura, C. (2000). Psychiatric morbidity and comorbidity following accidental man-made traumatic events: incidence and risk factors. *European Archives of Psychiatry and Clinical Neruoscience, 250,* 156–162.

Magnus, K., Diener, E., Fujita, F., & Payot, W. (1993). Extraversion and neuroticism as predictors for objective life events: a longtitudinal analysis. *Journal of Personality and Social Psychology, 65,* 1046–1053.

Maidenberg, E., Chen, E., Craske, M., Bohn, P., & Bystristsky, A. (1996). Specificity of attentional bias in panic disorder and social phobia. *Journal of Anxiety Disorders, 10,* 529–541.

Maier, S. F., & Seligman, M. E. (1976). Learned helplessness: theory and evidence. *Journal of experimental psychology: General, 105,* 3–46.

Maier, S. F., Laudenslager, M. L., & Ryan, S. M. (1985). Stressor controllability, immune function and endogenous opiates. In F. R. Brush & J. B. Overmeier (eds), *Affect, conditioning and cognition: essays on the determinants of behavior* (pp. 183–201). Hillsdale, NJ: Lawrence Erlbaum.

Malatesta, C. Z., & Haviland, J. M. (1982). Learning display rules: the socialization of emotion expression in infancy. *Child Development, 53,* 991–1003.

Maller, R. G., & Reiss, S. (1992). Anxiety sensitivity in 1984 and panic attacks in 1987. *Journal of Anxiety Disorders, 6,* 241–247.

Malloy, P. F., Fairbank, J. A., & Keane, T. M. (1983). Validation of a multimethod assessment of posttraumatic stress disorders in Vietnam veterans. *Journal of Consulting and Clinical Psychology, 51,* 488–494.

Maltzman, I., Gould, J., Barnett, O. J., Raskin, D. C., & Wolff, C. (1979). Habituation of the GSR and digital vasomotor components of the orienting reflex as a consequence of task instructions and sex differences. *Physiological Psychology, 7,* 213–220.

Mancini, C., Van Ameringen, M., Szatmari, P., Fugere, C., & Boyle, M. H. (1996). A high-risk pilot study of the children of adults with social phobia. *Journal of the American Academy of Child and Adolescent Psychiatry, 35,* 1511–1517.

Maren, S., De Oca, B., & Fanselow, M. S. (1994). Sex differences in hippocampal long-term potentiation (LTP) and Pavlovian fear conditioning in rats: positive correlation between LTP and contextual learning. *Brain Research, 661,* 25–34.

Margraf, J., Ehlers, A., & Roth, W. T. (1986). Sodium lactate infusions and panic attacks: a review and critique. *Psychosomatic Medicine, 48,* 23–51.

Margraf, J., Ehlers, A., & Roth, W. T. (1989). Expectancy effects and hyperventilation as laboratory stressors. In H. Weiner, I. Florin, R. Murrison, & D. Hellhammer (eds), *Frontiers of stress research. Neuronal control of bodily function: basic and clinical aspects* (pp. 395–400). Kirkland, WA: Hans Huber.

Marshall, G. N., & Schell, T. L. (2002). Reappraising the link between peritraumatic dissociation and PTSD symptom severity: evidence from a longitudinal study of community violence survivors. *Journal of Abnormal Psychology, 111,* 626–636.

Marshall, W. L., Bristol, D., & Barbaree, H. E. (1992). Cognitions and courage in the avoidance behavior of acrophobics. *Behaviour Research and Therapy, 30,* 463–470.

Martin, C. L., Ruble, D. N., & Szkrybalo, J. (2002). Cognitive theories of early gender development. *Psychological Bulletin, 128,* 903–933.

Martin, M., & Jones, G. V. (1995). Integral bias in the cognitive processing of emotionally linked pictures. *British Journal of Psychology, 86,* 419–435.

Martin, N. G., Jardine, R., Andrews, G., & Heath, A. C. (1988). Anxiety disorders and neuroticism: are there genetic factors specific to panic? *Acta Psychiatrica Scandinavica, 77,* 698–706.

Matchett, G., & Davey, G. C. L. (1991). A test of a disease-avoidance model of animal phobias. *Behavioural Research and Therapy, 29,* 91–94.

Matheny, A. P. (1989). Children's behavioral inhibition over age and across situations: genetic similarity for a trait during change. *Journal of Personality. Special Issue: Long-term Stability and Change in Personality, 57,* 215–235.

Mathew, R. J., Ho, B. T., Francis, D. J., Taylor, D. L., & Weinman, M. L. (1982). Catecholamines and anxiety. *Acta Psychiatrica Scandinavica, 65,* 142–147.

Mathew, R. J., Weinman, M. L., & Barr, D. L. (1984). Personality and regional cerebral blood flow. *British Journal of Psychiatry, 144,* 529–532.

Mathews, A. (1990). Why worry? The cognitive function of anxiety. *Behaviour Research and Therapy, 28,* 455–468.

Mathews, A., & MacLeod, C. (1985). Selective processing of threat cues in anxiety states. *Behaviour Research and Therapy, 23,* 563–569.

Mathews, A., & MacLeod, C. (1986). Discrimination of threat cues without awareness in anxiety states. *Journal of Abnormal Psychology, 95,* 131–138.

Mathews, A., & Sebastian, S. (1993). Suppression of emotional Stroop effects by fear arousal. *Cognition and Emotion, 7,* 517–530.

Mathews, A., & MacLeod, C. (1994). Cognitive approaches to emotion and emotional disorders. *Annual Review of Psychology, 45,* 25–50.

Mathews, A., & Mackintosh, B. (2000). Induced emotional interpretation bias and anxiety. *Journal of Abnormal Psychology, 109,* 602–615.

Mathews, A., & MacLeod, C. (2002). Induced processing biases have causal effects on anxiety. *Cognition and Emotion, 16,* 331–354.

Mathews, A., Mogg, K., May, J., & Eysenck, M. (1989a). Implicit and explicit memory bias in anxiety. *Journal of Abnormal Psychology, 98,* 236–240.

Mathews, A., Richards, A., & Eysenck, M. (1989b). Interpretation of homophones related to threat in anxiety states. *Journal of Abnormal Psychology, 98,* 31–34.

Mathews, A., Mogg, K., Kentish, J., & Eysenck, M. (1995). Effect of psychological treatment on cognitive bias in generalized anxiety disorder. *Behaviour Research and Therapy, 33,* 293–303.

Matt, G. E., Vazquez, C., & Campbell, W. K. (1992). Mood-congruent recall of affectively toned stimuli: a meta-analytic review. *Clinical Psychology Review, 12,* 227–255.

Mattia, J. I., Heimberg, R. G., & Hope, D. A. (1993). The revised Stroop color-naming task in social phobics. *Behaviour Research and Therapy, 31,* 305–313.

Mayes, L. C., & Carter, A. S. (1990). Emerging social regulatory capacities as seen in the still-face situation. *Child Development, 61,* 754–763.

Mayou, R., Bryant, B., & Duthie, R. (1993). Psychiatric consequences of road traffic accidents. *British Medical Journal, 307,* 647–651.

Mazurski, E. J., Bond, N. W., Siddle, D. A. T., & Lovibond, P. F. (1996). Conditioning with facial expressions of emotion: effects of CS sex and age. *Psychophysiology, 33,* 416–425.

McAllister, W. R., McAllister, D. E., Scoles, M. T., & Hampton, S. R. (1986). Persistence of fear-reducing behavior: relevance for the conditioning theory of neurosis. *Journal of Abnormal Psychology, 95,* 365–372.

McCathie, H., & Spence, S. H. (1991). What is the Revised Fear Survey Schedule for Children measuring? *Behaviour Research and Therapy, 29,* 495–502.

McClure, E. B. (2000). A meta-analytic review of sex differences in facial expression processing and their development in infants, children, and adolescents. *Psychological Bulletin, 3,* 424–453.

McCrae, R. R., & Costa, P. T. (1987). Validation of the five-factor model of personality across instruments and observers. *Journal of Personality and Social Psychology, 52,* 81–90.

McCrae, R. R., Costa, P. T., Terracciano, A., Parker, W. D., Mills, C. J., De Fruyt, F., & Mervielde, I. (2002). Personality trait development from age 12 to 18: longitudinal, cross-sectional and cross-cultural analyses. *Journal of Personality and Social Psychology, 83,* 1456–1468.

McGee, R., Feehan, M., Williams, S., Partridge, F., Silva, P. A., & Kelly, J. (1990). DSM-III disorders in a large sample of adolescents. *Journal of the American Academy of Child and Adolescent Psychiatry, 29,* 611–619.

McGee, R., Feehan, M., Williams, S., & Anderson, J. (1992). DSM-III disorders from age 11 to age 15 years. *Journal of the American Academy of Child and Adolescent Psychiatry, 31*, 50–59.

McIntosh, J., Anisman, H., & Merali, Z. (1999). Short- and long-periods of neonatal maternal separation differentially affect anxiety and feeding in adult rats: gender-dependent effects. *Developmental Brain Research, 113*, 97–106.

McLeer, S. V., Deblinger, E., Atkins, M. S., Foa, E. B., & Ralphe, D. L. (1988). Post-traumatic stress disorder in sexually abused children. *Journal of the American Academy of Child and Adolescent Psychiatry, 27*, 650–654.

McManis, M. H., Bradley, M. M., Berg, W. K., Cuthbert, B. N., & Lang, P. J. (2001). Emotional reactions in children: verbal, physiological, and behavioral responses to affective pictures. *Psychophysiology, 38*, 222–231.

McManis, M. H., Kagan, J., Snidman, N. C., & Woodward, S. A. (2002). EEG asymmetry, power, and temperament in children. *Developmental Psychobiology, 41*, 169–167.

McNally, R. J., & Steketee, G. S. (1985). The etiology and maintenance of severe animal phobias. *Behaviour Research and Therapy, 23*, 430–435.

McNally, R. J., & Lorenz, M. (1987). Anxiety sensitivity in agoraphobics. *Journal of Behavior Therapy and Experimental Psychiatry, 18*, 3–11.

McNally, R. J., & Heatherton, T. F. (1993). Are covariation biases attributable to a priori expectancy biases? *Behaviour Research and Therapy, 31*, 653–658.

McNally, R. J., & Kohlbeck, P. A. (1993). Reality monitoring in obsessive–compulsive disorder. *Behaviour Research and Therapy, 31*, 249–253.

McNally, R. J., & Ricciardi, J. N. (1996). Suppression of negative and neutral thoughts. *Behavioural and Cognitive psychotherapy, 24*, 17–25.

McNally, R. J., Foa, E. B., & Donnell, C. D. (1989). Memory bias for anxiety information in patients with panic disorder. *Cognition and Emotion, 3*, 27–44.

McNally, R. J., Riemann, B. C., Louro, C. E., Lukach, B. M., & Kim, E. (1992). Cognitive processing of emotional information in panic disorder. *Behaviour Research and Therapy, 30*, 143–149.

McNally, R. J., Metzger, L. J., Lasko, N. B., Clancy, S. A., & Pitman, R. K. (1998). Directed forgetting of trauma cues in adult survivors of childhood sexual abuse with and without posttraumatic stress disorder. *Journal of Abnormal Psychology, 107*, 596–601.

McNally, R. J., Otto, M. W., Yap, L., Pollack, M. H., & Hornig, C. D. (1999). Is panic disorder linked to cognitive avoidance of threatening information? *Journal of Anxiety Disorders, 13*, 335–348.

McNeil, D. W., Vrana, S. R., Melamed, B. G., Cuthbert, B. N., & Lang, P. J. (1993). Emotional imagery in simple and social phobia: fear versus anxiety. *Journal of Abnormal Psychology, 102*, 212–225.

Meaney, M. J., Diorio, J., Francis, D., Widdowson, J., LaPlante, P., Caldji, C., Sharma, S., Seckl, J. R., & Plotsky, P. M. (1996). Early environmental regulation of forebrain glucocorticoid receptor gene expression: implications for adrenoncortical responses to stress. *Development Neuroscience, 18*, 49–72.

Mellman, T. A., Kulick-Bell, R., Ashlock, L. E., & Nolan, B. (1995). Sleep events among veterans with combat-related posttraumatic stress disorder. *American Journal of Psychiatry, 152*, 110–115.

Menzies, R. G. (1996). The origins of specific phobias in a mixed clinical sample: classificatory differences between two origins instruments. *Journal of Anxiety Disorders, 10*, 347–354.

Menzies, R. G., & Clarke, J. C. (1993). The etiology of childhood water phobia. *Behaviour Research & Therapy, 31*, 499–501.

Menzies, R. G., & Clarke, J. C. (1995a). Danger expectancies and insight in acrophobia. *Behaviour Research and Therapy, 33*, 215–221.

Menzies, R. G., & Clarke, J. C. (1995b). The etiology of phobias: a nonassociative account. *Clinical Psychology Review, 15*, 23–48.

Menzies, R. G., & Parker, L. (2001). The origins of height fear: an evaluation of neoconditioning explanations. *Behaviour Research and Therapy, 39*, 185–199.

Merckelbach, H., van den Hout, M. A., & van der Molen, G. M. (1987). Preparedness and phobias: a critical overview of the literature. *Nederlands Tijdschrift loor de Psychologie en haar Grensgebieden, 42*, 115–124.

Merckelbach, H., Arntz, A., & de Jong, P. (1991a). Conditioning experiences in spider phobics. *Behaviour Research and Therapy, 29*, 333–335.

Merckelbach, H., Muris, P., van den Hout, M., & de Jong, P. (1991b). Rebound effects of thought suppression: instruction dependent? *Behavioural Psychotherapy, 19*, 225–238.

Merckelbach, H., Arntz, A., Arrindell, W. A., & de Jong, P. J. (1992). Pathways to spider phobia. *Behaviour Research and Therapy, 30*, 543–546.

Merikangas, K. R., Dierker, L. C., & Szatmari, P. (1998). Psychopathology among offspring of parents with substance abuse and/or anxiety disorders: a high-risk study. *Journal of Child Psychology and Psychiatry, 39*, 711–720.

Merikangas, K. R., Avenevoli, S., Dierker, L., & Grillon, C. (1999). Vulnerability factors among children at risk for anxiety disorders. *Society of Biological Psychiatry, 99*, 172–179.

Messenger, C., & Shean, G. (1998). The effects of anxiety sensitivity and history of panic on reactions to stressors in a non-clinical sample. *Journal of Behavior Therapy, 29*, 279–288.

Messer, S. C., & Beidel, D. C. (1994). Psychosocial correlates of childhood anxiety disorders. *Journal of the American Academy of Child and Adolescent Psychiatry, 33*, 975–983.

Metzger, R. L., Miller, M. L., Cohen, M., Sofka, M., & Borkovec, T. D. (1990). Worry changes decision making: the effect of negative thoughts on cognitive processing. *Journal of Clinical Psychology, 46*, 78–88.

Meyer, T. J., Miller, M. L., Metzger, R. L., & Borkovec, T. D. (1990). Development and validation of the Penn State Worry Questionnaire. *Behaviour Research and Therapy, 28*, 487–495.

Mezzacappa, E. S., Katkin, E. S., & Palmer, S. N. (1999). Epinephrine, arousal, and emotion: a new look at two-factor theory. *Cognition and Emotion, 2*, 181–199.

Middleton, H. C., & Ashby, M. (1995). Clinical recovery from panic disorder is associated with evidence of changes in cardiovascular regulation. *Acta Psychiatrica Scandinavica, 91*, 108–113.

Mikulincer, M., & Solomon, Z. (1988). Attributional style and combat-related posttraumatic stress disorder. *Journal of Abnormal Psychology, 97*, 308–313.

Miller, L. C., Barrett, C. L., & Hampe, E. (1974). Phobias of childhood in a prescientific era. In A. Davids (ed.), *Child personality and psychopathology: current topics.* Oxford: Wiley.

Miller, R. R., Greco, C., Vigorito, M., & Marlin, N. A. (1983). Signaled tailshock is perceived as similar to a stronger unsignaled tailshock: implications for a functional analysis of classical conditioning. *Journal of Experimental Psychology: Animal Behavior Processes, 9*, 105–131.

Mineka, S., & Kihlstrom, J. F. (1978). Unpredictable and uncontrollable events: a new perspective on experimental neurosis. *Journal of Abnormal Psychology, 87*, 256–271.

Mineka, S., & Henderson, R. W. (1985). Controllability and predictability in acquired motivation. *Annual Review of Psychology, 36*, 495–529.

Mineka, S., & Cook, M. (1986). Immunization against the observational conditioning of snake fear in rhesus monkeys. *Journal of Abnormal Psychology, 95*, 307–318.

Mineka, S., & Kelly, K. A. (1989). The relationship between anxiety, lack of control and loss of control. In A. Steptoe & A. Appels (eds), *Stress, personal control, and worker health* (pp. 163–191). Brussels: Wiley.

Mineka, S., & Sutton, S. K. (1992). Cognitive biases and the emotional disorders. *Psychological Science*, *3*, 65–69.

Mineka, S., & Cook, M. (1993). Mechanisms involved in the observational conditioning of fear. *Journal of Experimental Psychology: General*, *122*, 23–38.

Mineka, S., & Nugent, K. (1995). Mood-congruent memory biases in anxiety and depression. In D. L. Schachter (ed.), *Memory distortions: how minds, brains, and societies reconstruct the past* (pp. 173–193). Cambridge, MA: Harvard University Press.

Mineka, S., & Zinbarg, R. (1995). Conditioning and ethological models of social phobia. In R. G. Heimberg & M. R. Liebowitz (eds), *Social phobia: diagnosis, assessment, and treatment* (pp. 134–162). New York, NY: Guilford Press.

Mineka, S., & Öhman, A. (2002). Born to fear: non-associative vs associative factors in the etiology of phobias. *Behaviour Research and Therapy*, *40*, 173–184.

Mineka, S., Suomi, S. J., & Delizio, R. (1981). Multiple peer separations in adolescent monkeys: an opponent process interpretation. *Journal of Experimental Psychology: General*, *110*, 56–85.

Mineka, S., Cook, M., & Miller, S. (1984a). Fear conditioned with escapable and inescapable shock: effects of a feedback stimulus. *Journal of Experimental Psychology: Animal Behavior Processes*, *10*, 307–323.

Mineka, S., Davidson, M., Cook, M., & Keir, R. (1984b). Observational conditioning of snake fear in rhesus monkeys. *Journal of Abnormal Psychology*, *93*, 355–372.

Mineka, S., Gunnar, M., & Champoux, M. (1986). Control and early socioemotional development: infant rhesus monkeys reared in controllable versus uncontrollable environments. *Child Development*, *57*, 1241–1256.

Mineka, S., Watson, D., & Clark, L. A. (1998). Comorbidity of anxiety and unipolar mood disorders. *Annual Review of Psychology*, *49*, 377–412.

Minor, T. R., Trauner, M. A., Lee, C., & Dess, N. K. (1990). Modeling signal features of escape response: effects of cessation conditioning in "learned helplessness" paradigm. *Journal of Experimental Psychology: Animal Behavior Processes*, *16*, 123–136.

Minor, T. R., Dess, N. K., & Overmier, J. B. (1991). Inverting the traditional view of "learned helplessness". In M. R. Denny (ed.), *Fear, avoidance, and phobias: a fundamental analysis* (pp. 87–133). Hillsdale, NJ: Lawrence Erlbaum.

Mogg, K., & Mathews, A. (1990). Is there a self-referent mood-congruent recall bias in anxiety? *Behaviour Research and Therapy*, *28*, 91–92.

Mogg. K., & Bradley, B. P. (1998). A cognitive-motivational analysis of anxiety. *Behaviour Research and Therapy*, *36*, 809–848.

Mogg, K., & Bradley, B. P. (1999). Orienting of attention to threatening facial expressions presented under conditions of restricted awareness. *Cognition and Emotion*, *6*, 713–740.

Mogg, K., & Bradley, B. P. (2002). Selective orienting of attention to masked threat faces in social anxiety. *Behaviour Research and Therapy*, *40*, 1403–1414.

Mogg, K., Mathews, A., & Weinman, J. (1987). Memory bias in clinical anxiety. *Journal of Abnormal Psychology*, *96*, 94–98.

Mogg, K., Mathews, A., & Weinman, J. (1989). Selective processing of threat cues in anxiety states: a replication. *Behaviour Research and Therapy*, *27*, 317–323.

Mogg, K., Gardiner, J. M., Stavrou, A., & Golombok, S. (1992). Recollective experience and recognition memory for threat in clinical anxiety states. *Bulletin of the Psychonomic Society*, *30*, 109–112.

Mogg, K., Mathews, A., & Eysenck, M. (1992). Attentional bias to threat in clinical anxiety states. *Cognition and Emotion*, *6*, 149–159.

Mogg, K., Bradley, B. P., Williams, R., & Mathews, A. (1993a). Subliminal processing of emotional information in anxiety and depression. *Journal of Abnormal Psychology*, *102*, 304–311.

Mogg, K., Kentish, J., & Bradley, B. P. (1993b). Effects of anxiety and awareness on colour-identification latencies for emotional words. *Behaviour Research and Therapy, 31*, 559–567.

Mogg, K., Bradley, B. P., & Williams, R. (1995). Attentional bias in anxiety and depression: the role of awareness. *British Journal of Clinical Psychology, 34*, 17–36.

Mogg, K., Bradley, B. P., Dixon, C., Fisher, S., Twelftree, H., & McWilliams, A. (2000a). Trait anxiety, defensiveness and selective processing of threat: an investigation using two measures of attentional bias. *Personality and Individual Differences, 28*, 1063–1077.

Mogg, K., McNamara, J., Powys, M., Rawlinson, H., Seiffer, A., & Bradley, B. P. (2000b). Selective attention to threat: a test of two cognitive models of anxiety. *Cognition and Emotion, 14*, 375–399.

Mondschein, E. R., Adolph, K. E., & Tamis-LeMonda, C. S. (2000). Gender bias in mothers' expectations about infant crawling. *Journal of Experimental Child Psychology, 77*, 304–316.

Monroe, S. M., Imhoff, D. F., Wise, B. D., Harris, J. E. (1983). Prediction of psychological symptoms under high-risk psychosocial circumstances: life events, social support, and symptom. *Journal of Abnormal Psychology, 92*, 338–350.

Montgomery, W. A., & Jones, G. E. (1984). Laterality, emotionality, and heartbeat perception. *Psychophysiology, 21*, 459–465.

Moore, R., Brodsgaard, I., & Birn, H. (1991). Manifestations, acquisition and diagnostic categories of dental fear in a self-referred population. *Behaviour Research and Therapy, 29*, 51–60.

Mor, N., & Winquist, J. (2002). Self-focused attention and negative affect: a meta-analysis. *Psychological Bulletin, 128*, 638–662.

Moradi, A. R., Neshat-Doost, H. T., Taghavi, R, Yule, W., & Dalgleish. T. (1999). Performance of children of adults with PTSD on the Stroop color-naming task: a preliminary study. *Journal of Traumatic Stress, 12*, 663–671.

Morgan, C. A. III, Grillon, C., Southwick, S. M., Nagy, L. M., Davis, M., Krystal, J. H., & Charney, D. S. (1995). Yohimbine facilitated acoustic startle in combat veterans with post-traumatic stress disorder. *Psychopharmacology, 117*, 466–471.

Morris, J. S., Ohman, A., & Dolan, R. J. (1998). Conscious and unconscious emotional learning in the human amygdala. *Nature, 393,* 467–470.

Morris, J. S., Öhman, A., & Dolan, R. J. (1999). A subcortical pathway to the right amygdale mediating "unseen" fear. *Proceedings of the National Academy of Sciences of the USA, 96*, 1680–1685.

Morris, W. N. (1999). The mood system. In D. Kahneman & E. Diener (eds), *Well-being: the foundations of hedonic psychology* (pp. 169–189). New York, NY: Russel Sage Foundation.

Morrow, J., & Nolen-Hoeksema, S. (1990). Effects of responses to depression on the remediation of depressive affect. *Journal of Personality and Social Psychology, 58,* 519–527.

Moser, M., Lehofer, M., Hoehn-Saric, R., McLeod, D. R., Hildebrandt, G., Steinbrenner, B., Voica, M., Liebmann, P., & Zapotoczky, H. G. (1998). Increased heart rate in depressed subjects in spite of unchanged autonomic balance? *Journal of Affective Disorders, 48*, 115–124.

Mowrer, O. H. (1939). Anxiety and learning. *Psychological Bulletin, 36*, 517–518.

Mumme, D. L., & Fernald, A. (1996). Infant's responses to facial and vocational emotional signals in a social referencing paradigm. *Child Development, 67*, 3219–3237.

Munjack, D. (1984). The onset of driving phobias. *Journal of Behavior Therapy and Experimental Psychiatry, 15*, 305–308.

Muris, P., Merckelbach, H., & Horselenberg, R. (1996). Individual differences in thought suppression. The with bear suppression inventory: factor structure, reliability, validity and correlates. *Behaviour Research and Therapy, 34*, 501–513.

Muris, P., Steerneman, P., Merckelbach, H., & Meesters, C. (1996a). Parental modeling and fearfulness in middle childhood. *Behaviour Research and Therapy, 28,* 263–267.

Muris, P., Steerneman, P., Merckelbach, H., & Meesters, C. (1996b). The role of parental fearfulness and modeling in children's fear. *Behaviour Research and Therapy, 34,* 265–268.

Muris, P., Merckelbach, H., & Clavan, M. (1997a). Abnormal and normal compulsions. *Behaviour Research and Therapy, 35,* 249–252.

Muris, P., Merckelbach, H., & Collaris, R. (1997b). Common childhood fears and their origins. *Behaviour Research and Therapy, 35,* 929–937.

Muris, P., Merckelbach, H., Gadel, B., & Moulaert, V. (2000). Fears, worries, and scary dreams in 4- to 12-year-old children: their content, developmental pattern, and origins. *Journal of Clinical Child Psychology, 29,* 43–52.

Muris, P., Meesters, C., Rassin, E., Merckelbach, H., & Campbell, J. (2001). Thought–action fusion and anxiety disorders symptoms in normal adolescents. *Behaviour Research and Therapy, 39,* 843–852.

Murphy, J. M., Sobol, A. M., Olivier, D. C., Monson, R. R., Leighton, A. H., & Pratt, L. A. (1989). Prodromes of depression and anxiety: the Sterling County Study. *British Journal of Psychiatry, 155,* 490–495.

Myers, J. K., Weissman, M. M., Tischler, G. L., Holzer, C. E., Leaf, P. J., Orvaschel, H., Anthony, J. C., Boyd, J. H., Burke Jr, J. D., Kramer, M., & Stoltzman, R. (1984). Six-month prevalence of psychiatric disorders in three communities. *Archives of General Psychiatry, 41,* 959–967.

Neale, M. C., Walters, E. E., Eaves, L. J., Kessler, R. C., Heath, A. C., & Kendler, K. S. (1994). Genetics of blood-injury fears and phobias: a population-based twin study. *American Journal of Medical Genetics, 15,* 326–334.

Nelles, W. B., & Barlow, D. H. (1988). Do children panic? *Clinical Psychology Review, 8,* 359–372.

Newman, D. L., Moffitt, T. E., Caspi, A., Magdol, L., Silva, P. A., & Stanton, W. R. (1996). Psychiatric disorder in a birth cohort of young adults: prevalence, comorbidity, clinical significance, and new case incidence from ages 11–21. *Journal of Consulting and Clinical Psychology, 64,* 552–562.

Neshat-Doost H. T., Moradi, A. R., Taghavi, S. M., Yule, W., & Dalgleish, T. (1997). The performance of clinically depressed children and adolescents on the modified Stroop paradigm. *Personality and Individual Differences, 23,* 753–759.

Nesse, R. M., Cameron, O. G., Curtis, G. C., McCann, D. S., & Huber-Smith, M. J. (1984). Adrenergic function in patients with panic anxiety. *Archives of General Psychiatry, 41,* 771–776.

Niedenthal, P. M., & Beike, D. R. (1997). Interrelated and isolated self-concepts. *Personality and Social Psychology Review, 1,* 106–128.

Nolen-Hoeksema, S. (1991). Responses to depression and their effects on the duration of depressive episodes. *Journal of Abnormal Psychology, 100,* 569–582.

Nolen-Hoeksema, S., Morrow, J., & Fredrickson, B. L. (1993). Response styles and the duration of episodes of depressed mood. *Journal of Abnormal Psychology, 102,* 20–28.

Norton, G. R., Cox, B. J., & Malan, J. (1992). Nonclinical panickers: a critical review. *Clinical Psychology Review, 12,* 121–139.

Noyes, R., Clancy, J., Garvey, M. J., & Anderson, D. J. (1987). Is agoraphobia a variant of panic disorder or a separate illness? *Journal of Anxiety Disorders, 1,* 3–13.

Oakley-Browne, M. A., Joyce, P. R., Wells, J. E., Bushnell, J. A., & Hornblow, A. R. (1995). Adverse parenting and other childhood experience as risk factors for depression in women aged 18–44 years. *Journal of Affective Disorders, 34,* 13–23.

O'Banion, K., & Arkowitz, H. (1977). Social anxiety and selective memory for affective information about the self. *Journal of Consulting and Clinical Psychology, 45,* 217–218.

Ochoa, L., Beck, A. T., & Steer, R. A. (1992). Gender differences in comorbid anxiety and mood disorders. *American Journal of Psychiatry, 149*, 1409–1410.

Oei, T. P., Wanstall, K., & Evans, L. (1990). Sex differences in panic disorder with agoraphobia. *Journal of Anxiety Disorders, 4*, 317–324.

Offord, D. R., Boyle, M. H., Szatmari, P., Rae Grant, N. I., Links, P. S., Cadman, D. T., Byles, J. A., Crawford, J. W., Munroe Blum, H., Byrne, C., Thomas, H., & Woodward, C. A. (1987). Ontario Child Health Study: II. Six-month prevalence of disorder and rates of service utilization. *Archives of General Psychiatry, 44*, 832–836.

Offord, D. R., Boyle, M. H., Racine, Y. A., Fleming, J. E., Cadman, D. T., Blum, H. M., Byrne, C., Links, P.l S., Lipman, E. L., MacMillan, H. L., Grant, N. I. R., Sanford, M. N., Szatmari, P., Thomas, H., & Woodward, C. A. (1992). Outcome, prognosis, and risk in a longitudinal follow-up study. *American Academy of Child and Adolescent Psychiatry, 31*, 916–923.

Offord, D. R., Boyle, M. H., Campbell, D., Goering, P., Lin, E., Wong, M., & Racine, Y. A. (1996). One-year prevalence of psychiatric disorder Ontarians 15 to 16 years of age. *Canadian Journal of Psychiatry, 41*, 559–563.

Ohannessian, C. M., Lerner, R. M., Lerner, J. V., & Eye, A. (1999). Does self-competence predict gender differences in adolescent depression and anxiety? *Journal of Adolescence, 22*, 397–411.

Ohara, K., Suzuki, Y., Ochiai, M., Yoshida, K., & Ohara, K. (1999). Age of onset anticipation in anxiety disorders. *Psychiatry Research, 89*, 215–221.

Öhman, A. (1986). Face the beast and fear the face: animal and social fears as prototypes for evolutionary analyses of emotion. *Psychophysiology, 23*, 123–145.

Öhman, A. (1993). Fear and anxiety as emotional phenomena: clinical phenomenology, evolutionary perspectives, and information-processing mechanisms. In M. Lewis & Haviland, J. M. (eds), *Handbook of emotions* (pp. 511–536). New York, NY: Guilford Press.

Öhamn, A. (1997). As fast as the blink of an eye: evolutionary preparedness for preattentive processing of threat. In P. J. Lang, R. F. Simons, & M. T. Balaban (eds), *Attention and orienting: sensory and motivational processes* (pp. 165–184). Mahwah, NJ: Lawrence Erlbaum.

Öhman, A., & Bohlin, G. (1973). The relationship between spontaneous and stimulus-correlated electrodermal responses in simple and discriminative conditioning paradigms. *Psychophysiology, 10*, 589–600.

Öhman, A., & Dimberg, U. (1978). Facial expressions as conditioned stimuli for electrodermal responses: a case of "preparedness"? *Journal of Personality and Social Psychology, 36*, 1251–1258.

Öhman, A., & Mineka, S. (2001). Fears, phobias, and preparedness: toward an evolved module of fear and fear learning. *Psychological Review, 108*, 483–522.

Öhman, A., & Soares, J. J. (1993). On the automatic nature of phobic fear: conditioned electrodermal responses to masked fear-relevant stimuli. *Journal of Abnormal Psychology, 102*, 121–132.

Öhman, A., & Soares, J. J. (1998). Emotional conditioning to masked stimuli: expectancies for aversive outcomes following nonrecognized fear-relevant stimuli. *Journal of Experimental Psychology: General, 127*, 69–82.

Öhman, A., Fredrikson, M., Hugdahl, K., & Rimmo, P. A. (1976). The premise of equipotentiality in human classical conditioning: conditioned electrodermal responses to potentially phobic stimuli. *Journal of Experimental Psychology: General, 105*, 313–337.

Öhman, A., Fredrikson, M., & Hugdahl, K. (1978). Orienting and defensive responding in the electrodermal system: palmar-dorsal differences and recovery-rate during conditioning to potentially phobic stimuli. *Psychophysiology, 15*, 93–101.

Öhman, A., Flykt, A., & Esteves, F. (2001). Emotion drives attention: detecting the snake in the grass. *Journal of Experimental Psychology, 130*, 466–478.

Ollendick, T. H. (1979). Fear reduction techniques with children. In M. Hersen, R. M. Eisler, & P. M. Miller (eds), *Progress in behavior modification* (pp. 127–168). New York, NY: Academic Press.

Ollendick, T. H. (1983). Reliability and validity of the Revised Fear Survey Schedule for Children (FSSC-R). *Behaviour Research and Therapy, 21*, 685–692.

Ollendick, T. H., & King, N. J. (1991). Origins of childhood fears: an evaluation of Rachman's theory of fear acquisition. *Behaviour Research and Therapy, 29*, 117–123.

Ollendick, T. H., & King, N. J. (1994). Diagnosis, assessment, and treatment of internalizing problems in children: the role of longitudinal data. *Journal of Consulting and Clinical Psychology, 62*, 918–927.

Ollendick, T. H., Yule, W., & Ollier, K. (1991). Fears in British children and their relationship to manifest anxiety and depression. *Journal of Child Psychology and Psychiatry and Allied Disciplines, 32*, 321–331.

Orozco, S., & Ehlers, C. L. (1998). Gender differences in electrophysiological responses to facial stimuli. *Biological Psychiatry, 44*, 281–289.

Orr, S. P., Metzger, L. J., Lasko, N. B., Macklin, M. L., Peri, T., & Pitman, R. K. (2000). *De novo* conditioning in trauma-exposed individuals with and without posttraumatic stress disorder. *Journal of Abnormal Psychology, 109*, 290–298.

Os, J. V., & Jones, P. B. (1999). Early risk factors and adult person-environment relationships in affective disorder. *Psychological Medicine, 29*, 1055–1067.

Öst, L.-G. (1885). Ways of acquiring phobias and outcome of behavioural treatment. *Behaviour Research and Therapy, 23*, 683–689.

Öst, L.-G. (1987). Age of onset in different phobias. *Journal of Abnormal Psychology, 96*, 223–229.

Öst, L.-G. (1991). Acquisition of blood and injection phobia and anxiety response patterns in clinical patients. *Behaviour Research and Therapy, 29*, 323–332.

Öst, L.-G., & Hugdahl, K. (1981). Acquisition of phobias and anxiety response patterns in clinical patients. *Behavour Research and Therapy, 19*, 439–447.

Öst, L.-G., & Hugdahl, K. (1983). Acquisition of agoraphobia, mode of onset and anxiety response patterns. *Behaviour Research and Therapy, 21*, 623–631.

Öst, L.-G., & Hugdahl, K. (1985). Acquisition of blood and dental phobia and anxiety response patterns in clinical patients. *Behaviour Research and Therapy, 23*, 27–34.

Öst, L.-G., & Treffers, P. D. A. (2001). Onset, course, and outcome for anxiety disorders in children. In W. K. Silverman & P. D. A. Treffers (eds), *Anxiety disorders in children and adolescents: research, assessment and intervention* (pp. 293–312). Cambridge: Cambridge University Press.

Öst, L.-G., Sterner, U., & Lindahl, I. L. (1984). Physiological responses in blood phobics. *Behaviour Research and Therapy, 22*, 109–117.

Overmier, J. B., & Murison, R. (1989). Poststress effects of danger and safety signals on gastric ulceration in rats. *Behavioral Neuroscience, 103*, 1296–1301.

Ozer, E. J., Best, S. R., Lipsey, T. L., & Weiss, D. S. (2003). Predictors of posttraumatic stress disorder and symptoms in adults: a meta-analysis. *Psychological Bulletin, 129*, 52–73.

Panksepp, J. (1998). Loneliness and the social bond. In J. Panksepp (ed.), *Affective neuroscience: the foundations of human and animal emotions* (pp. 261–279). London: Oxford University Press.

Papageorgiou, C., & Wells, A. (2002). Effects of heart rate information on anxiety, perspective taking, and performance in high and low social-evaluative anxiety. *Behavior Therapy, 33*, 181–199.

Papousek, H., & Papousek, M. (1997). Fragile aspects of early social integration. In L. Murray & P. J. Cooper (eds), *Postpartum depression and child development* (pp. 35–53). New York, NY: Guilford Press.

Papousek, H., & Papousek, M. (2002). Intuitive parenting. In M. H. Bornstein (ed.), *Handbook of parenting* (2nd ed., vol. 2). *Biology and ecology of parenting* (pp. 183–203). Mahwah, NJ: Lawrence Erlbaum.

Parker, G., Tupling, H., & Brown, L. B. (1979). A parental bonding instrument. *British Journal of Medical Psychology, 52*, 1–10.

Parkinson, L., & Rachman, S. (1981a). Part II. The nature of intrusive thoughts. *Advances in Behaviour Research and Therapy, 3*, 101–110.

Parkinson, L., & Rachman, S. (1981b). Part III — Intrusive thoughts: the effects of an uncontrived stress. *Advances in Behaviour Research and Therapy, 3*, 111–118.

Parkinson, L., & Rachman, S. (1981c). Part IV — Speed of recovery from an uncontrived stress. *Advances in Behaviour Research and Therapy, 3*, 119–123.

Parra, C., Esteves, F., Flykt, A., & Öhman, A. (1997). Pavlovian conditioning to social stimuli: backward masking and the dissociation of implicit and explicit cognitive processes. *European Psychologist. Special Issue: 100 Years after Ivan P. Pavlov's The Work of the Digestive Glands, 2*, 106–117.

Patton, G. C., Carlin, J. B., Coffey, C., Wolfe, R., Hibbert, M., & Bowes, G. (1998). Depression, anxiety, and smoking initiation: a prospective study over 3 years. *American Journal of Public Health, 88*, 1518–1522.

Peasley-Miklus, C., & Vrana, S. R. (2000). Effect of worrisome and relaxing thinking on fearful emotional processing. *Behaviour Research and Therapy, 38*, 129–144.

Pennebaker, J. W. (1982). *The psychology of physical symptoms.* New York, NY: Springer-Verlag.

Pennebaker, J. W. (1992). Inhibition as the linchpin of health. In H. S. Friedman (ed.), *Hostility coping and health*. Washington, DC: American Psychological Association.

Pennebaker, J. W. (2000). Psychological factors influencing the reporting of physical symptoms. In A. A. Stone & J. S. Turkkan (eds), *The science of self-report: implications for research and practice* (pp. 299–315). Mahwah, NJ: Lawrence Erlbaum.

Pennebaker, J. W., & Roberts, T. (1992). Toward a his and hers theory of emotion: gender differences in visceral perception. *Journal of Social and Clinical Psychology, 11*, 199–212.

Perna, G., Bertani, A., Arancio, C., Ronchi, P., & Bellodi, L. (1995). Laboratory response of patients with panic and obsessive–compulsive disorders to 35% CO_2 challenges. *American Journal of Psychiatry, 152*, 85–89.

Perna, G., Bertani, A., Caldirola, D., & Bellodi, L. (1996). Family history of panic disorder and hypersensitivity to CO_2 in patients with panic disorder. *American Journal of Psychiatry, 153*, 1060–1064.

Peterson, C., Maier, S. F., & Seligman, M. E. P. (1993). *Learned helplessness: a theory for the age of personal control.* New York, NY: Oxford University Press.

Philips, H. C. (1985). Return of fear in the treatment of a fear of vomiting. *Behaviour Research and Therapy, 23*, 45–52.

Phillips, M. L., Young, A. W., Senior, C., Brammer, M., Andrews, C., Calder, A. J., Bullmore, E. T., Perrett, D. I., Rowland, D., Williams, S. C. R., Gray, J. A., & David, A. S. (1997). A specific neural substrate for pereceiving facial expressions of disgust. *Nature, 389*, 495–498.

Pigott, T. D. (1994). Methods for handling missing data in research synthesis. In H. Cooper & L. V. Hedges (eds), *The handbook of research synthesis* (pp. 163–175). New York, NY: Russell Sage Foundation.

Pine, D. S., Cohen, P., Gurley, D., Brook, J., & Ma, Y. (1998). The risk for early-adulthood anxiety and depressive disorders in adolescents with anxiety and depressive disorders. *Archives of General Psychiatry, 55,* 56–64.

Pitman, R. K., & Orr, S. P. (1986). Test of the conditioning model of neurosis: differential aversive conditioning of angry and neutral facial expressions in anxiety disorder patients. *Journal of Abnormal Psychology, 95,* 208–213.

Pitman, R. K., Orr, S. P., Forgue, D. F., de Jong, J. B., & Claiborn, J. M. (1987). Psychophysiologic assessment of posttraumatic stress disorder imagery in Vietnam combat veterans. *Archives of General Psychiatry, 44,* 970–975.

Pitman, R. K., Orr, S. P., Forgue, D. F., Altman, B., de Jong, J. B., & Herz, L. R. (1990). Psychophysiologic responses to combat imagery in Vietnam veterans with posttraumatic stress disorder versus other anxiety disorders. *Journal of Abnormal Psychology, 99,* 49–54.

Pollard, C. A., Pollard, H. J., & Corn, K. J. (1989). Panic onset and major events in the lives of agoraphobics: a test of contiguity. *Journal of Abnormal Psychology, 98,* 318–321.

Pomerantz, E. M., & Ruble, D. N. (1998). The role of maternal control in the development of sex differences in child self-evaluative factors. *Child Development, 69,* 458–478.

Porges, S. W. (1992). Autonomic regulation and attention. In B. A. Campbell & H. Hayne (eds), *Attention and information processing in infants and adults: perspectives from human and animal research* (pp. 201–223). Hillsdale, NJ: Lawrence Erlbaum.

Porges, S. W., Doussard-Roosevelt, J. A., & Maita, A. K. (1994). Vagal tone and the physiological regulation of emotion. *Monographs of the Society for Research in Child Development, 59,* 167–186, 250–283.

Posner, M. I., & Rothbart, M. K. (1998). Summary and commentary: developing attentional skills. In J. E. Richards (ed.), *Cognitive neuroscience of attention: a developmental perspective* (pp. 317–323). New Jersey, NJ: Lawrence Erlbaum.

Poulton, R., Trainor, A. J., Stanton, W. R., McGee, R., Davies, S., & Silva, P. A. (1997). The (in)stability of adolescent fears. *Behaviour Research and Therapy, 35,* 159–163.

Poulton, R., Milne, B. J., Craske, M. G., & Menzies, R. G. (2001a). A longitudinal study of the etiology of separation anxiety. *Behaviour Research and Therapy, 39,* 1395–1410.

Poulton, R., Waldie, K. E., Thomson, W. M., & Locker, D. (2001b). Determinants of early- vs late-onset dental fear in a longitudinal–epidemiological study. *Behaviour Research and Therapy, 39,* 777–785.

Power, M. J., Brewin, C. R., Stuessy, A., & Mahony, T. (1991). The emotional priming task: results from a student population. *Cognitive Therapy and Research, 15,* 21–31.

Prior, M., Smart, D., Sanson, A., & Oberklaid, F. (1993). Sex differences in psychological adjustment from infancy to 8 years. *Journal of the American Academy of Child and Adolescent Psychiatry, 32,* 291–304.

Ptacek, J. T., Smith, R. E., & Zanas, J. (1992). Gender, appraisal, and coping: a longitudinal analysis. *Journal of Personality, 60,* 747–770.

Puigcerver, A., Martinez-Selva, J. M., Garcia-Sanchez, F. A., & Gomez-Amor, J. (1989). Individual differences in psychophysiological and subjective correlates of speech anxiety. *Journal of Psychophysiology, 3,* 75–81.

Purdon, C. (2001). Appraisal of obsessional thought recurrences: impact of anxiety and mood state. *Behavior Therapy, 32,* 47–64.

Purdon, C., & Clark, D. A. (2001). Suppression of obsession-like thoughts in nonclinical individuals: impact on thought frequency, appraisal, and mood state. *Behaviour Research and Therapy, 39,* 1163–1181.

Pury, C. L. S. (2002). Information-processing predictors of emotional response to stress. *Cognition and Emotion, 16,* 667–683.

Pury, C. L. S., & Mineka, S. (1997). Covariation bias for blood-injury stimuli and aversive outcomes. *Behaviour Research and Therapy, 35*, 35–47.

Pynoos, R., Goenjian, A., Tashjian, M., Krakashian, M., Manjikian, A., Manoukian, G., Steinerg, A. M., & Fairbanks, L. A. (1993). Post-traumatic stress reactions in children after the 1988 Armenian earthquake. *British Journal of Psychiatry, 163*, 239–247.

Quas, J. A., Hong, M., Alkon, A., & Boyce, W. T. (2000). Dissociations between psychobiologic reactivity and emotional expression in children. *Developmental Psychobiology, 37*, 153–175.

Rachman, S. (1966). Studies in desensitization: III. Speed of generalization. *Behaviour Research and Therapy, 4*, 7–15.

Rachman, S. (1976). The modification of obsessions: a new formulation. *Behaviour Research and Therapy, 14*, 437–443.

Rachman, S. J. (1978). *Fear and courage*. Oxford: Freeman.

Rachman, S. (1984). Agoraphobia: a safety-signal perspective. *Behaviour Research and Therapy, 22*, 59–70.

Rachman, S. (1989). The return of fear: review and prospect. *Clinical Psychology Review, 9*, 147–168.

Rachman, S. (1990). The determinants and treatment of simple phobias. *Advances in Behaviour Research and Therapy, 12*, 1–30.

Rachman, S. (1991a). Neo-conditioning and the classical theory of fear acquisition. *Clinical Psychology Review, 11*, 155–173.

Rachman, S. (1991b). The consequences of panic. *Journal of Cognitive Psychotherapy, 5*, 187–197.

Rachman, S. (1994). The overprediction of fear: a review. *Behaviour Research and Therapy, 32*, 683–690.

Rachman, S. (1997). A cognitive theory of obsessions. *Behaviour Research and Therapy, 35*, 793–802.

Rachman, S. (1998a). A cognitive theory of obsessions. In E. Sanavio (ed.), *Behaivor and cognitive therapy today: essays in honor of Hans J. Eysenck* (pp. 209–222). Oxford: Elsevier.

Rachman, S. (1998b). A cognitive theory of obsessions: elaborations. *Behaviour Research and Therapy, 36*, 385–401.

Rachman, S., & de Silva, P. (1978). Abnormal and normal obsessions. *Behaviour Research and Therapy, 16*, 233–248.

Rachman, S., & Levitt, K. (1985). Panics and their consequences. *Behaviour Research and Therapy, 23*, 585–600.

Rachman, S., & Lopatka, C. (1986a). Do fears summate? III. *Behaviour Research & Therapy, 24*, 653–660.

Rachman, S., & Lopatka, C. (1986b). Match and mismatch in the prediction of fear: I. *Behaviour Research and Therapy, 24*, 387–393.

Rachman, S., & Lopatka, C. (1986c). Match and mismatch of fear of Gray's theory: II. *Behaviour Research and Therapy, 24*, 395–401.

Rachman, S., & Lopatka, C. (1986d). A simple method for determining the functional independence of two or more fears: IV. *Behaviour Research and Therapy, 24*, 661–664.

Rachman, S., & Levitt, K. (1988). Panic, fear reduction and habituation. *Behaviour Research and Therapy, 26*, 199–206.

Rachman, S., & Lopatka, C. (1988). Return of fear: underlearning and overlearning. *Behaviour Research and Therapy, 26*, 99–104.

Rachman, S., & Whittal, M. (1989a). Fast, slow and sudden reductions in fear. *Behaviour Research and Therapy, 27*, 613–620.

Rachman, S., & Whittal, M. (1989b). The effect of an aversive event on the return of fear. *Behaviour Research and Therapy, 27*, 513–520.

Rachman, S. & Taylor, S. (1993). Analysis of Claustrophobia. *Journal of Anxiety Disorders, 7*, 281–291.

Rachman, S., Robinson, S., & Lopatka, C. (1987). Is incomplete fear-reduction followed by a return of fear? *Behaviour Research and Therapy, 25*, 67–69.

Rachman, S., Levitt, K., & Lopatka, K. (1988). Experimental analyses of panic — III. Claustrophobic subjects. *Behaviour Research and Therapy, 26*, 41–52.

Rachman, S., Throdarson, D. S., Shafran, R., & Woody, S. R. (1995). Perceived responsibility: structure and significance. *Behaviour Research and Therapy, 33*, 779–784.

Rachman, S., Shafran, R., Mitchell, D., Trant, J., & Teachman, B. (1996). How to remain neutral: an experimental analysis of neutralization. *Behaviour Research and Therapy, 34*, 889–898.

Radomsky, A. S., & Rachman, S. (1999). Memory bias in obsessive–compulsive disorder (OCD). *Behaviour Research and Therapy, 37*, 605–618.

Radomsky, A. S., Rachman, S., & Hammond, D. (2001). Memory bias, confidence and responsibility in compulsive checking. *Behaviour Research and Therapy, 37*, 813–822.

Raine, A., Venables, P. H., & Williams, M. (1995). High autonomic arousal and electrodermal orienting at age 15 years as protective factors against criminal behavior at age 29 years. *American Journal of Psychiatry, 152*, 1595–1600.

Rapee, R. M. (1986). Differential response to hyperventilation in panic disorder and generalized anxiety disorder. *Journal of Abnormal Psychology, 95*, 24–28.

Rapee, R. M. (1993). The utilization of working memory by worry. *Behaviour Research and Therapy, 31*, 617–620.

Rapee, R. M. (1994a). Detection of somatic sensations in panic disorder. *Behaviour Research and Therapy, 32*, 825–831.

Rapee, R. M. (1994b). Failure to replicate a memory bias in panic disorder. *Journal of Anxiety Disorders, 8*, 291–300.

Rapee, R. M. (1997). Potential role of childrearing practices in the development of anxiety and depression. *Clinical Psychology Review, 17*, 47–67.

Rapee, R. M., & Murrell, E. (1988). Predictors of agoraphobic avoidance. *Journal of Anxiety Disorder, 2*, 203–217.

Rapee, R. M., & Lim, L. (1992). Discrepancy between self- and observer ratings of performance in social phobics. *Journal of Abnormal Psychology, 101*, 728–731.

Rapee, R. M., & Medoro, L. (1994). Fear of physical sensations and trait anxiety as mediators of the response to hyperventilation in nonclinical subjects. *Journal of Abnormal Psychology, 103*, 693–699.

Rapee, R. M., & Egliston, K. (2003). *Examination of parent-child interactions in anxious children.* Paper presented at European Association for Behaviour and Cognitive Therapy, Prague.

Rapee, R., Mattick, R., & Murrell, E. (1986). Cognitive mediation in the affective component of spontaneous panic attacks. *Journal of Behavior Therapy and Experimental Psychiatry, 17*, 245–253.

Rapee, R. M., Litwin, E. M., & Barlow, D. H. (1990). Impact of life events on subjects with panic disorders and on comparison subjects. *American Journal of Psychiatry, 147*, 640–644.

Rapee, R. M., Brown, T. A., Antony, M. M., & Barlow, D. H. (1992). Response to hyperventilation and inhalation of 5.5% carbon dioxide-enriched air across the DSM-III-R anxiety disorders. *Journal of Abnormal Psychology, 101*, 538–552.

Rapee, R. M., McCallum, S. L., Melville, L. F., Ravenscroft, H., & Rodney, J. M. (1994). Memory bias in social phobia. *Behaviour Research and Therapy, 32*, 89–99.

Rapoport, J. (1989). *The boy who couldn't stop washing: the experience and treatment of obsessive–compulsive disorder.* New York, NY: Penguin.

Rapoport, J. L., Swedo, S. E., & Leonard, H. L. (1992). Childhood obsessive compulsive disorder. *Journal of Clinical Psychiatry, 53*(suppl. 4), 11–16.

Rassin, E., Merckelbach, H., Muris, P., & Spaan, V. (1999). Though-action fusion as a causal factor in the development of intrusions. *Behaviour Research and Therapy, 37*, 231–237.

Rauch, S. L., Jenike, M. A., Alpert, N. M., Baer, L., Breiter, H. C. R., Savage, C. R., & Fischman, A. J. (1994). Regional cerebral blood flow measured during symptom provocation in obsessive–compulsive disorder using oxygen 15-labeled carbon dioxide and positron emission tomography. *Archives of General Psychiatry, 51,* 62–70.

Rauch, S. L., van der Kolk, B. A., Fisler, R. E., & Alpert, N. M. (1996). A symptom provocation study of posttraumatic stress disorder using positron emission tomography and script-driven imagery. *Archives of General Psychiatry, 53,* 380–387.

Rauste-Von Wright, M., Von Wright, J., & Frankenhaeuser, M. (1981). Relationships between sex-related psychological characteristics during adolescence and catecholamine excretion during a chronic stressor. *Psychophysics, 18,* 362–370.

Ray, J. C., & Sapolsky, R. M. (1992). Styles of male social behavior and their endocrine correlates among high-ranking wild baboons. *American Journal of Primatology, 28,* 231–250.

Razran, G. (1961). The observable and the inferable conscious in current Soviet psychophysiology: interoceptive conditioning, semantic conditioning, and the orienting reflex. *Psychological Review, 68,* 81–147.

Rechlin, T., Weis, M., Spitzer, A., & Kaschka, W. P. (1994). Are affective disorders associated with alterations of heart rate variability? *Journal of Affective Disorders, 32,* 271–275.

Rechlin, T., Weis, M., & Kaschka, W. P. (1995). Is diurnal variation of mood associated with parasympathetic activity? *Journal of Affective Disorders, 34,* 249–255.

Reddy, V., Hay, D., Murray, L., & Trevarthen, C. (1997). Communication in infancy: mutual regulation of affect and attention. In G. Bremner, A. Slater, & G. Butterworth (eds), *Infant development: recent advances* (pp. 247–273). London: Psychology Press.

Reich, J., Noyes, R., & Troughton, E. (1987). Dependent personality disorder associated with phobic avoidance in patients with panic disorder. *American Journal of Psychiatry, 144,* 323–326.

Reiss, S. (1991). Expectancy model of fear, anxiety and panic. *Clinical Psychology Review, 11,* 141–155.

Reiss, S., Peterson, R. A., Gursky, D. M., & McNally, R. J. (1986). Anxiety sensitivity, anxiety frequency and the predictions of fearfulness. *Behaviour Research and Therapy, 24,* 1–8.

Rescorla, R. A. (1974). Effect of inflation of the unconditioned stimulus value following conditioning. *Journal of Comparative and Physiological Psychology, 86,* 101–106.

Rescorla, R. A. (1988a). Facilitation based on inhibition. *Animal Learning and Behavior, 16,* 169–176.

Rescorla, R. A. (1988b). Pavlovian conditioning: it's not what you think it is. *American Psychologist, 43,* 151–160.

Resick, P. A., & Schnicke, M. K. (1990). Treating symptoms in adult victims of sexual assault. *Journal of Interpersonal Violence, 5,* 488–506.

Reynolds, M., & Salkovskis, P. M. (1992). Comparison of positive and negative intrusive thoughts and experimental investigation of the differential effects of mood. *Behaviour Research and Therapy, 30,* 273–281.

Reynolds, C. R., & Richmond, B. O. (1978). What I think and feel: a revised measure of children's manifest anxiety. *Journal of Abnormal Child Psychology, 6,* 271–280.

Reznick, J. S., Kagan, J., Snidman, N., Gersten, M., Baak, K., & Rosenberg, A. (1986). Inhibited and uninhibited children: a follow-up study. *Child Development, 57,* 660–680.

Rheaume, J., Freeston, M. H., Dugas, M. J., Letarte, H., & Ladouceur, R. (1995). Perfectionism, responsibility and obsessive–compulsive symptoms. *Behaviour Research and Therapy, 33,* 785–794.

Rhee, S. H., Waldman, I. D., Hay, D. A., & Levy, F. (1999). Sex differences in genetic and environmental influences on DSM-III-R attention-deficit/hyperactivity disorder. *Journal of Abnormal Psychology, 108,* 24–41.

Richards, A., & French, C. C. (1991). Effects of encoding and anxiety on implicit and explicit memory performance. *Personality and Individual Differences*, *12*, 131–139.

Richards, A., & French, C. C. (1992). An anxiety-related bias in semantic activation when processing threat/neutral homographs. *Quarterly Journal of Experimental Psychology: Human Experimental Psychology*, *45A*, 503–525.

Richards, A., French, C. C., Johnson, W., Naparstek, J., & Williams, J. (1992). Effects of mood manipulation and anxiety on performance of an emotional Stroop task. *British Journal of Psychology*, *83*, 479–491.

Richards, A., French, C. C., Calder, A. J., Web, B., Fox, R., & Young, A. W. (2002). Anxiety-related bias in the classification of emotionally ambiguous facial expressions. *Emotion*, *2*, 273–287.

Rief, W., Hiller, W., Geissner, E., & Fichter, M. M. (1995). A two-year follow-up study of patients with somatoform disorders. *Psychosomatics*, *36*, 376–386.

Riemann, B. C., & McNally, R. J. (1995). Cognitive processing of personally relevant information. *Cognition and Emotion*, *9*, 325–340.

Riggs, D. S., Rothbaum, B. O., & Foa, E. B. (1995). A prospective examination of symptoms of posttraumatic stress disorder in vicitms of nonsexual assault. *Journal of Interpersonal Violence*, *10*, 201–214.

Roberts, J. E., Gilboa, E., & Gotlib, J. H. (1998). Ruminative response style and vulnerability to episodes of dysphoria: gender, neuroticism, and episode duration. *Cognitive Therapy and Research*, *22*, 401–423.

Roberts, S. B., & Kendler, K. S. (1999). Neuroticism and self-esteem as indices of the vulnerability to major depression in women. *Psychological Medicine*, *29*, 1101–1109.

Robinson, D., Wu, H., Munne, R. A., Ashtari, M., Alvir, J. M. J., Lerner, G., Koreen, A., Cole, K., & Bogerts, B. (1995). Reduced caudate nucleus volume in obsessive–compulsive disorder. *Archives of General Psychiatry*, *52*, 393–398.

Robinson, J. L., Kagan, J., Reznick, J. S., & Corley, R. (1992). The heritability of inhibited and uninhibited behavior: a twin study. *Developmental Psychology*, *28*, 1030–1037.

Rochat, P., & Striano, T. (1999). Social-cognitive development in the first year. In P. Rochat (ed,), *Early social cognition: understanding others in the first months of life* (pp. 3–34). Mahwah, NJ: Lawrence Erlbaum.

Roemer, L., Molina, S., & Borkovec, T. D. (1997). An investigation of worry content among generally anxious individuals. *Journal of Nervous and Mental Disease*, *185*, 314–319.

Roggman, L. A. (1991). Assessing social interactions of mothers and infants through play. In C. E. Schaefer, K. Gitlin, & A. Sangrund (eds) *Play diagnosis and assessment* (pp. 427–462). New York, NY: Wiley.

Romano, E., Tremblay, R. E., Vitaro, F., Zoccolillo, M., & Pagani, L. (2001). Prevalence of psychiatric diagnosis and the role of perceived impairment: findings from an adolescent community sample. *Journal of Child Psychology and Psychiatry and Allied Disciplines*, *42*, 451–461.

Rosellini, R. A., DeCola, J. P., & Warren, D. A. (1986). The effect of feedback stimuli on contextual fear depends upon the length of the minimum intertrial interval. *Learning and Motivation*, *17*, 229–242.

Rosen, J. B., & Schulkin, J. (1998). From normal fear to pathological anxiety. *Psychological Review*, *105*, 325–350.

Rosenbaum, J. F., Biederman, J., Gersten, M., Hirshfeld, D. R., Meminger, S. R., Herman, J. B., Kagan, J., Reznick, S., & Snidman, N. (1988). Behavioral inhibition in children of parents with panic disorder and agoraphobia. *Archives of General Psychiatry*, *45*, 463–470.

Rosenbaum, J. F., Biederman, J., Hirshfeld, D. R., Bolduc, E. A., Faraone, S. V., Kagan, J., Snidman, N., & Reznick, S. J. (1991). Further evidence of an association between behavioral inhibition and anxiety disorders: results from a family study of children from a non-clinical sample. *Journal of Psychiatric Research*, *25*, 49–65.

Rosenblum, L., & Paully, G. S. (1984). The effects of varying emotional demands on maternal and infant behavior. *Child Development*, *55*, 305–314.

Ross, R. J., Ball, W. A., Dinges, D. F., Mulvaney, F. D., Kribbs, N. R., Morrison, A. R., & Silver, S. M. (1990). Motor activation during REM sleep in posttraumatic stress disorder (abstract). *Sleep Research*, *19*, 175.

Roth, W. T., Telch, M. J., Taylor, C. B., Sachitano, J. A., Gallen, C. C., Kopell, M. L., McClenahn, K. L., Agras, W. S., & Pfefferbaum, A. (1986). Autonomic characteristics of agoraphobia with panic attacks. *Biological Psychiatry*, *21*, 1133–1154.

Roth, W. T., Margraf, J., Ehlers, A., Taylor, C. B., Maddock, R. J., Davies, S., & Agras, W. S. (1992). Stress test reactivity in panic disorder. *Archives of General Psychiatry*, *49*, 301–310.

Rothbart, M. K. (1989). Temperament and development. In G. A. Kohnstamm, J. E. Bates, & M. K. Rothbart (eds), *Temperament in childhood* (pp. 187–247). Oxford: Wiley.

Rothbaum, B. O., Foa, E. B., Riggs, D. S., Murdock, T. & Walsh, W. (1992). A prospective examination of post-traumatic stress disorder in rape victims. *Journal of Traumatic Stress*, *5*, 455–475.

Roy, M., Neale, M. C., Pedersen, N. L., Mathe, A. A., & Kendler, K. S. (1995). A twin study of generalized anxiety disorder and major depression. *Psychological Medicine*, *25*, 1037–1049.

Roy-Byrne, P. P., Geraci, M., & Uhde, T. W. (1986). Life events and the onset of panic disorder. *American Journal of Psychiatry, 143*, 1424–1427.

Rozin, P., & Fallon, A. E. (1987). A perspective on disgust. *Psychological Review*, *94*, 23–41.

Ruddy, M. G., & Bornstein, M. H. (1982). Cognitive correlates of infant attention and maternal stimulation over the first year of life. *Child Development*, *53*, 183–188.

Rueter, M. A., Scaramella, L., Wallace, L. E., & Conger, R. D. (1999). First onset of depressive or anxiety disorders predicted by the longitudinal course of internalizing symptoms and parent–adolescent disagreements. *Archives of General Psychiatry*, *56*, 726–732.

Ruff, H. A., & Rothbart, M. K. (1996). *Attention in early development: themes and variations.* London: Oxford University Press.

Rutledge, P. C. (1998). Obsessionality and the attempted suppression of unpleasant personal intrusive thoughts. *Behaviour Research and Therapy, 36,* 403–416.

Sachs, A., Davison, J., & Craske, M. G. (2003 in press). Interpretation bias in generalized anxiety: a content analysis of articulated thoughts in simulated situations.

Sadowski, H., Ugarte, B., Kolvin, I., Kaplan, C., & Barnes, J. (1999). Early life family disadvantages and major depression in adulthood. *British Journal of Psychiatry*, *174*, 112–120.

Salkovskis, P. M. (1985). Obsessional–compulsive problems: a cognitive–behavioural analysis. *Behaviour Research and Therapy*, *23*, 571–583.

Salkovskis, P. M. (1989). Cognitive–behavioural factors and the persistence of intrusive thoughts in obsessional problems. *Behaviour Research and Therapy*, *27*, 677–682.

Salkovskis, P. M., & Harrison, J. (1984). Abnormal and normal obsessions: a replication. *Behaviour Research and Therapy*, *22*, 549–552.

Salkovskis, P. M., & Campbell, P. (1994). Thought suppression induces intrusion in naturally occurring negative intrusive thoughts. *Behaviour Research and Therapy*, *32*, 1–8.

Salkovskis, P. M., & Mills, I. (1994). Induced mood, phobic responding and the return of fear. *Behaviour Research and Therapy*, *32*, 439–445.

Salkovskis, P. M., Clark, D. M., & Gelder, M. G. (1996). Cognition–behaviour links in the persistence of panic. *Behaviour Research and Therapy*, *34*, 453–458.

Salkovskis, P. M., Westbrook, D., Davis, J., Jeavons, A., & Gledhill, A. (1997). Effects of neutralizing on intrusive thoughts: an experiment investigating the etiology of obsessive–compulsive disorder. *Behaviour Research and Therapy, 35*, 211–219.

Salkovskis, P., Shafran, R., Rachman, S., & Freeston, M. H. (1999). Multiple pathways to inflated responsibility beliefs in obsessional problems: possible origins and implications for therapy and research. *Behaviour Research and Therapy, 37*, 1055–1072.

Salkovskis, P. M. Thorpe, S. J., Wahl, K., Wroe, A., & Forrester, E. (2003 in press). Neutralizing increases discomfort associated with obsessional thoughts: an experimental study with obsessional patients. *Journal of Abnormal Psychology.*

Sanderson, W. C., Rapee, R. M., & Barlow, D. H. (1989). The influence of an illusion of control on panic attacks induced via inhalation of 5.5% carbon dioxide-enriched air. *Archives of General Psychiatry, 46*, 157–162.

Sartory, G., Rachman, S., & Grey, S. J. (1982). Return of fear: the role of rehearsal. *Behaviour Research and Therapy, 20*, 123–134.

Sartory, G., Roth, W. T., & Kopell, M. L. (1992). Psychophysiological assessment of driving phobia. *Journal of Psychophysiology, 6*, 311–320.

Satinder, K. P. (1977). Arousal explains difference in avoidance learning of genetically selected rat strains. *Journal of Comparative and Physiological Psychology, 91*, 1326–1336.

Savage, C. R., Keuthen, N. J., Jenike, M. A., Brown, H. D., Baer, L., Kendrick, A. D., Miguel, E. C., Rauch, S. L., & Albert, M. S. (1996). Recall and recognition memory in obsessive–compulsive disorder. *Journal of Neuropsychiatry and Clinical Neurosciences, 8*, 99–103.

Sawchuk, C. N., Lohr, J. M., Tolin, D. F., Lee, T. C., & Kleinknecht, R. A. (2000). Disgust sensitivity and contamination fears in spider and blood–injection–injury phobias. *Behavior Research and Therapy, 38*, 753–762.

Sawchuk, C. N., Lohr, J. M., Westendorf, D. H., Meunier, S. A., & Tolin, D. F. (2002). Emotional responding to fearful and disgusting stimuli in specific phobics. *Behaviour Research and Therapy, 40*, 1031–1046.

Scarpa, A., Raine, A., Venables, P. H., & Mednick, S. A. (1997). Heart rate and skin conductance in behaviorally inhibited Mauritian children. *Journal of Abnormal Psychology, 106*, 182–190.

Scarrabelotti, M. B., Duck, J. M., & Dickerson, M. M. (1995). Individual differences in obsessive–compulsive behaviour: the role of the Eysenckian dimentions and appraisals of responsibility. *Personality and Individual Differences, 18*, 413–421.

Schachter, S., & Singer, J. (1962). Cognitive, social, and physiological determinants of emotional state. *Psychological Review, 69*, 379–399.

Schandry, R. (1981). Heart beat perception and emotional experience. *Psychophysiology, 18*, 483–488.

Scheibe, G., & Albus, M. (1992). Age at onset, precipitating events, sex distribution, and co-occurrence of anxiety disorders. *Psychopathology, 25*, 11–18.

Schell, A. M., Dawson, M. E., & Marindovic, K. (1991). Effects of potentially phobic conditioned stimuli on retention, reconditioning, and extinction of the conditioned skin conductance response. *Psychophysiology, 28*, 140–153.

Scherer, M. W., & Nakamura, C. Y. (1968). A Fear Survey Schedule for Children (Fss–Fc): a factor analytic comparison with Manifest Anxiety (Cmas). *Behaviour Research and Therapy, 6*, 173–182.

Scherrer, J. F., True, W. R., Xian, H., Lyons, M. J., Eisen, S. A., Goldberg, J., Nong, L., & Tsuang, M. T. (2000). Evidence for genetic influences common and specific to symptoms of generalized anxiety and panic. *Journal of Affective Disorders, 57*, 25–35.

Schmidt, L. A., & Fox, N. A. (1998). Fear-potentiated startle responses in temperamentally different human infants. *Developmental Psychobiology, 32*, 113–120.

Schmidt, N. B., Jacquin, K., & Telch, M. J. (1994). The overprediction of fear and panic in panic disorder. *Behaviour Research and Therapy, 32*, 701–707.

Schmidt, N. B., Lerew, D. R., & Jackson, R. J. (1997). The role of anxiety sensitivity in the pathogenesis of panic: prospective evaluation of spontaneous panic attacks during acute stress. *Journal of Abnormal Psychology, 106*, 355–364.

Schmidt, N. B., Trakowski, J. H., & Staab, J. P. (1997). Extinction of panicogenic effects of a 35% CO_2 challenge in patients with panic disorder. *Journal of Abnormal Psychology, 106*, 630–638.

Schmidt, N. B., Lerew, D. R., & Jackson, R. J. (1999). Prospective evaluation of anxiety sensitivity in the pathogenesis of panic: replication and extension. *Journal of Abnormal Psychology, 108*, 532–537.

Schmidt, N. B., Storey, J., Greenberg, B. D., Santiago, H. T., Li, Q., & Murphy, D. L. (2000). Evaluating gene × psychological risk factor effects in the pathogenesis of anxiety: a new model approach. *Journal of Abnormal Psychology, 109*, 308–320.

Schore, A. N. (2001). Effects of a secure attachment relationship on right brain development, affect regulation, and infant mental health. *Infant Mental Health Journal. Special Issue: Contributions from the Decade of the Brain to Infant Mental Health, 22*, 7–66.

Schwartz, J. M., Stoessel, P. W., Baxter, L. R., Martin, K. M., & Phelps, M. E. (1996). Systematic changes in cerebral glucose metabolic rate after successful behavior modification treatment of obsessive–compulsive disorder. *Archives of General Psychology, 53*, 109–113.

Segerstrom, S. C., Glover, D. A., Craske, M. G., & Fahey, J. L. (1999). Worry affects the immune response to phobic fear. *Brain, Behavior, and Immunity, 13*, 80–92.

Segerstrom, S. C., Tsao, J. C. I, Alden, L. E., & Craske, M. G. (2000). Worry and rumination: repetitive thought as a concomitant and predictor of negative mood. *Cognitive Therapy and Research, 24*, 671–688.

Seligman, M. E. P. (1968). Chronic fear produced by unpredictable electric shock. *Journal of Comparative and Physiological Psychology, 66*, 402–411.

Seligman, M. E. P. (1970). On the generality of the laws of learning. *Psychological Review, 77*, 406–418.

Seligman, M. E. P., & Hager, J. L. (1972). *Biological boundaries of learning.* East Norwalk, CT: Appleton-Century-Crofts.

Seligman, M. E. P., & Binik, Y. (1977). The safety signal hypothesis. In H. Davis & H. M. B. Hurwitz (eds), *Operant Pavlovian interactions* (pp. 165–188). Hillsdale, NJ: Lawrence Erlbaum.

Shafran, R., Booth, R., & Rachman, S. (1993). The reduction of claustrophobia: II. Cognitive analyses. *Behaviour Research and Therapy, 31*, 75–85.

Shafran, R., Thordarson, D. S., & Rachman, S. (1996). Thought-action fusion in obsessive compulsive disorder. *Journal of Anxiety Disorders, 10*, 379–391.

Shaywitz, B. A., Shaywitz, S. E., Pugh, K. R., Constable, R. T., Skudlarski, P., Bronen, R. T., Fulbright, R. K., Fletcher, J. M., Shankweiler, D. P., Katz, L., & Gore, J. C. (1995). Sex differences in the functional organization of the brain for language. *Nature, 373*, 607–609.

Shear, M. K., Polan J. J., Harshfield, G., Pickering T., Mann, J. J., Frances, A., & James, G. (1992). Ambulatory monitoring of blood pressure and heart rate in panic patients. *Journal of Anxiety Disorders, 6*, 213–221.

Sheilds, S. A. (1984). Reports of bodily change in anxiety, sadness, and anger. *Motivation and Emotion, 1*, 1–21.

Shibuki, K., Hamamura, M., Yagi, K. (1984). Conditioned heart rate response: testing under anaesthesia in rats. *Neuroscience Research, 1*, 373–378.

Shipherd, J. C., & Beck, J. G. (1999). The effects of suppressing trauma-related thoughts on women with rape-related posttraumatic stress disorder. *Behaviour Research and Therapy, 37*, 99–112.

Shore, J. H., Tatum, E. L., & Vollmer, W. M. (1986). Psychiatric reactions to disaster: the Mount St. Helens experience. *American Journal of Psychiatry*, *143*, 590–595.

Shulman, I. D., Cox, B. J., Swinson, R. P., Kuch, K., & Reichman, J. T. (1994). Precipitating events, locations and reactions associated with initial unexpected panic attacks. *Behaviour Research and Therapy*, *32*, 17–20.

Sica, C., Novara, C., & Sanavio, E. (2002). Religiousness and obsessive–compulsive cognitions and symptoms in an Italian population. *Behaviour Research and Therapy*, *40*, 813–823.

Siddle, D. A., & Bond, N. W. (1988). Avoidance learning, Pavlovian conditioning, and the development of phobias. *Biological Psychology*, *27*, 167–183.

Silove, D., Parker, G., Hadzi-Pavlovic, D., Manicavasagar, V., & Blaszczynski, A. (1991). Parental representations of patients with panic disorder and generalized anxiety disorder. *British Journal of Psychiatry*, *159*, 835–841.

Silverman, W. K., Cerny, J. A., Nelles, W. B., & Burke, A. E. (1988). Behavior problems in children of parents with anxiety disorders. *Journal of American Academy of Child and Adolescent Psychiatry, 27,* 779–784.

Silverman, W. K., & Rabian, B. (1994). Specific phobia. In T. H. Ollendick, N. J. Neville, & W. Yule (eds), *International handbook of phobic and anxiety disorders in children and adolescents. Issues in clinical child psychology* (pp. 87–109). New York, NY: Plenum Press.

Simpson, A. E., & Stevenson-Hinde, J. (1985). Temperamental characteristics of three- to four-year-old boys and girls and child-family interactions. *Journal of Child Psychology and Psychiatry and Allied Disciplines*, *26*, 43–53.

Siqueland, L., Kendall, P. C., & Steinberg, L. (1996). Anxiety in children: perceived family environments and observed family interaction. *Journal of Clinical Child Psychology*, *25*, 225–237.

Skoe, E. E. A., Cumberland, A., Eisenberg, N., Hansen, K., & Perry, J. (2002). The influences of sex and gender-role identity on moral cognition and prosocial personality traits. *Sex Roles*, *46*, 295–309.

Smari, J., Birgisdottir, A. B., & Brynjolfsdottir, B. (1995). Obsessive–compulsive symptoms and suppression of personally relevant unwanted thoughts. *Behaviour Research and Therapy*, *18*, 621–625.

Smith, B. D., & Wigglesworth, M. J. (1978). Extraversion and neuroticism in orienting reflex dishabituation. *Journal of Research in Personality*, *12*, 284–296.

Smith, T. W., & Allred, K. D. (1989). Major life events in anxiety and depression. In P. C. Kendall, & D. Watson (eds), *Anxiety and depression: distinction and overlapping features* (pp. 205–223). San Diego, CA: Academic Press.

Snidman, N., Kagan, J., Riordan, L., & Shannon, D. C. (1995). Cardiac function and behavioral reactivity during infancy. *Psychophysiology*, *32*, 199–207.

Snodgrass, S. E. (1985). Women's intuition: the effect of subordinate role on interpersonal sensitivity. *Journal of Personality and Social Psychology*, *49*, 146–155.

Soares, J. J. F., & Öhman, A. (1993a). Backward masking and skin conductance responses after conditioning to non-feared but fear-relevant stimuli in fearful subjects. *Psychophysiology*, *30*, 460–466.

Soares, J. J. F., & Öhman, A. (1993b). Preattentive processing, preparedness and phobias: effects of instruction on conditioned electrodermal responses to masked and non-masked fear-relevant stimuli. *Behaviour Research and Therapy*, *31*, 87–95.

Sokolowska, M., Siegal, S., & Kim, J. (2002) Intraadministration associations: conditional hyperalgesia elicited by morphine onset cues. *Journal of Experimental Psychology: Animal Behavior Processes*, *28*, 309–320.

Solomon, Z., Mikulincer, M., & Benbenishty, R. (1989). Locus of control and combat-related post-traumatic stress disorder: the intervening role of battle intensity, threat appraisal and coping. *British Journal of Clinical Psychology, 28,* 131–144.

Sorce, J. F., Emde, R. N., Campos, J. J., & Klinnert, M. D. (1985). Maternal emotional signaling: its effect on the visual cliff behavior of 1-year-olds. *Developmental Psychology, 21,* 195–200.

Southwick, S. M., Krystal, J. H., Morgan, A., Johnson, D., Nagy, L. M., Nicolaou, A., Heninger, G. R., & Charney, D. S. (1993). Abnormal noradrenergic function in posttraumatic stress disorder. *Archives of General Psychiatry, 50,* 266–274.

Speltz, M. L., & Bernstein, D. A. (1976). Sex differences in fearfulness: verbal report, overt avoidance and demand characteristics. *Journal of Behavior Therapy and Experimental Psychiatry, 7,* 117–122.

Spence, K. W., & Spence, J. T. (1966). Sex and anxiety differences in eyelid conditioning. *Psychological Bulletin, 65,* 137–142.

Spence, S. (1992). *The role of the right hemisphere in cognitive and physiological components of emotional processing.* Unpublished doctoral dissertation, University of California, Los Angeles.

Spence, S. H., Donovan, C., & Brechman-Toussaint, M. (1999). Social skills, social outcomes, and cognitive features of childhood social phobia. *Journal of Abnormal Psychology, 108,* 211–221.

Stamps, L. E., & Porges, S. W. (1975). Heart rate conditioning in newborn infants: relationships among conditionability, heart rate variability, and sex. *Developmental Psychology, 11,* 424–431.

Startup, H. M., & Davey, G. C. L. (2001). Mood as input and catastrophic worrying. *Behaviour Research and Therapy, 110,* 83–96.

Stein, D. J., Shoulberg, N., Helton, K., & Hollander, E. (1992). The neuroethological approach to obsessive–compulsive disorder. *Comprehensive Psychiatry, 33,* 274–281.

Stein, D. J., Hollander, E., Chan, S., DeCaria, C. M., Hilal, S., Liebowitz, M. R., & Klein, D. F. (1993). Computed tomography and neurological soft signs in obsessive–compulsive disorder. *Psychiatry Research: Neuroimaging, 50,* 143–150.

Stein, M. B., Walker, J. R., & Forde, D. R. (1996). Public-speaking fears in a community sample. Prevalence, impact on functioning, and diagnostic classification. *Archives of General Psychiatry, 53,* 169–174.

Stein, M. B., Jang, K. L., & Livesley, W. J. (1999). Heritability of anxiety sensitivity: a twin study. *American Journal of Psychiatry, 156,* 246–251.

Stein, M. B., Fuetsch, M., Muller, N., Hofler, M., Lieb, R., Wittchen, H. U. (2001). Social anxiety disorder and the risk of depression: a prospective community study of adolescents and young adults. *Archives of General Psychiatry, 58,* 251–256.

Stelmack, R. M., & Mandelzys, N. (1975). Extraversion and pupillary response to affective and taboo words. *Psychophysiology, 12,* 536–540.

Stemberger, R. T., Turner, S. M., Beidel, D. C., & Calhoun, K. S. (1995). Social phobia: an analysis of possible developmental factors. *Journal of Abnormal Psychology, 104,* 526–531.

Stevenson, J., Batten, N., Cherner, M. (1992). Fears and fearfulness in children and adolescents: a genetic analysis of twin data. *Journal of Clinical Psychology and Psychiatry and Allied Disciplines, 33,* 977–985.

Stevenson-Hinde, J., & Shouldice, A. (1993). Wariness to strangers: a behavior systems perspective revisited. In K. H. Rubin & J. B. Asendorpf (eds), *Social withdrawal, inhibition, and shyness in childhood* (pp. 101–116). Hillsdale, NJ: Lawrence Erlbaum.

Stober, J., Tepperwien, S., & Staak, M. (2000). Worrying leads to reduced concreteness of problem elaborations: evidence for the avoidance theory of worry. *Anxiety, Stress, and Coping, 13,* 217–227.

Stopa, L., & Clark, D. M. (1993). Cognitive processes in social phobia. *Behaviour Research and Therapy, 31,* 255–267.

Strauss, C. C., & Last, C. G. (1993). Social and simple phobias in children. *Journal of Anxiety Disorders*, 7, 141–152.

Sturges, L. V., Goetsch, V. L., Ridley, J., & Whittal, M. (1998). Anxiety sensitivity and response to hyperventilation challenge: physiologic arousal, interoceptive acuity, and subjective distress. *Journal of Anxiety Disorders*, 12, 103–115.

Suarez, L., & Bell-Dolan, D. (2001). The relationship of child worry to cognitive biases: threat interpretation and likelihood of event occurrence. *Behavior Therapy*, 32, 425–442.

Sullivan, G. M., Coplan, J. D., & Gorman, J. M. (1998). Psychoneuroendocrinology of anxiety disorders. *Psychiatric Clinics of North America*, 21, 397–412.

Sullivan, G. M., Coplan, J. D., Kent, J. M., & Gorman, J. M. (1999). The noradrenergic system in pathological anxiety: a focus on panic with relevance to generalized anxiety and phobias. *Biological Psychiatry*, 46, 1205–1218.

Suomi, S. J. (1987). Genetic and maternal contributions to individual differences in rhesus monkey biobehavioral development. In N. A. Krasnegor & E. M. Elliot (eds), *Perinatal development: a psychobiological perspective. Behavioral biology* (pp. 397–419). San Diego, CA: Academic Press.

Suomi, S. J., Kraemer, G. W., Baysinger, C. M., & DeLizio, R. D. (1981). Inherited and experiential factors associated with individual differences in anxious behavior displayed by rhesus monkeys. In D. F. Klein & J. Rabkin (eds), *Anxiety: new research and changing concepts* (pp. 179–200). New York, NY: Raven Press.

Swedo, S. E., Pietrini, P., Leonard, H. L., Schapiro, M. B., Rettew, D. C., Goldberger, E. L., Rapoport, S. I., Rappoport, J. L., & Grady, C. L. (1992). Cerebral glucose metabolism in childhood-onset obsessive–compulsive disorder: revisualization during pharmacotherapy. *Archives of General Psychiatry*, 49, 690–694.

Swendsen, J. D., Merikangas, K. R., Canino, G. J., Kessler, R. C., Rubio-Stipec, M., & Angst, J. (1998). The comorbidity of alcoholism with anxiety and depressive disorders in four geographic communities. *Comprehensive Psychiatry*, 39, 176–184.

Szollos, S., Eshelman, E., & Keffer, M. (1990, November). *Worry vs. focal phobia: may worry decrease physiological arousal?* Paper presented at the annual convention of the Association for the Advancement of Behavior Therapy, San Francisco, CA.

Taghavi, M. R., Neshat-Doost, H. T., Moradi, A. R., Yule, W., & Dalgleish, T. (1999). Biases in visual attention in children and adolescents with clinical anxiety and mixed anxiety–depression. *Journal of Abnormal Child Psychology*, 27, 215–223.

Taghavi, M. R., Moradi, A. R., Neshat-Doost, H. T., Yule, W., & Dalgleish, T. (2000). Interpretation of ambiguous emotional information in clinically anxious children and adolescents. *Cognition and Emotion*, 14, 809–822.

Tallis, F., Eysenck, M., & Mathews, A. (1991). Elevated evidence requirements and worry. *Personality and Individual Differences*, 12, 21–27.

Tallis, F., Davey, G. C. L., & Capuzzo, N. (1994). The phenomenology of non-pathological worry: a preliminary investigation. In G. C. L. Davey & F. Tallis (eds), *Worrying: perspectives on theory, assessment and treatment* (pp. 61–89). New York, NY: Wiley.

Tata, P. R., Leibowitz, J. A., Prunty, M. J., Cameron, M., & Pickering, A. D. (1996). Attentional bias in obsessional compulsive disorder. *Behaviour Research and Therapy*, 34, 53–60.

Taylor, J. E., Deane, E. P., & Podd, J. V. (1999). Stability of driving fear acquisition pathways over one year. *Behaviour Research and Therapy*, 37, 927–939.

Taylor, S. (1983). Adjustment to threatening events: a theory of cognitive adaptation. *American Psychologist*, 38, 1161–1173.

Taylor, S., & Rachman, S. J. (1994). Stimulus estimation and the overprediction of fear. *British Journal of Clinical Psychology*, 33, 173–181.

Taylor, S., Koch, W. J., & McNally, R. J. (1992). How does anxiety sensitivity vary across the anxiety disorders? *Journal of Anxiety Disorders, 6,* 249–259.

Taylor, S. E. (1999). *Health psychology* (4th ed.). New York, NY: McGraw-Hill.

Taylor, S. E., Klein, L. C., Lewis, B. P., Gruenewald, T. L., Gurung, R. A. R., & Updegraff, J. A. (2000). Biobehavioral responses to stress in females: tend-and-befriend, not fight-or-flight. *Psychological Review, 107,* 411–429.

Tazi, A., Dantzer, R., & Le Moal, M. (1987). Prediction and control of food rewards modulate endogenous pain inhibitory systems. *Behavioral Brain Research, 23,* 197–204.

Teasdale, J. D. (1993). Emotion and two kinds of meaning: cognitive therapy and applied cognitive science. *Behaviour Research and Therapy, 31,* 339–354.

Telch, M. J., Lucas, J. A., & Nelson, P. (1989a). Non-clinical panic in college students: an investigation of prevalence and symptomatology. *Journal of Abnormal Psychology, 98,* 300–306.

Telch, M. J., Brouilard, M., Telch, C. F., Agras, W. S., & Taylor, C. B. (1989b). Role of cognitive appraisal in panic-related avoidance. *Behaviour Research and Therapy, 27,* 373–383.

Telch, M. J., Ilai, D., Valentiner, D., & Craske, M. G. (1994). Match-mismatch of fear, panic and performance. *Behaviour Research and Therapy, 32,* 691–700.

Telch, M. J., Valentiner, D., & Bolte, M. (1994). Proximity to safety and its effects on fear prediction bias. *Behaviour Research and Therapy, 32,* 747–751.

Tellegen, A. (1982). Brief manual for the Multidimensional Personality Questionnaire. Unpublished manuscript. University of Minnesota at Minneapolis.

Thayer, J. F., & Johnsen, B. H. (2000). Sex differences in judgement of facial affect: a multivariate analy of recognition errors. *Scandinavian Journal of Psychology, 41,* 243–246.

Thayer, J. F., Friedman, B. H., & Borkovec, T. D. (1996). Autonomic characteristics of generalized anxiety disorder and worry. *Biological Psychiatry, 39,* 255–266.

Thayer, J. F., Smith, M., Rossy, L. A., Sollers, J. J., & Friedman, B. H. (1998). Heart period variability and depressive symptoms: gender differences. *Biological Psychiatry, 44,* 304–306.

Thayer, J. F., Friedman, B. H., Borkovec, T. D., Johnsen, B. H., & Molina, S. (2000). Phasic heart period reactions to cued threat and nonthreat stimuli in generalized anxiety disorder. *Psychophysiology, 37,* 361–368.

Thoits, P. A. (1987). Gender and marital status differences in control and distress: common stress versus unique stress explanation. *Journal of Health and Social Behavior, 28,* 7–22.

Thomas, K. M., Drevets, W. C., Whalen, P. J., Eccard, C. H., Dahl, R. E., Ryan, N. D., & Case, B. J. (2001). Amygdala response to facial expressions in children and adults. *Society of Biological Pyschiatry, 49,* 309–316.

Thompson, R. A. (2001). Childhood anxiety disorders from the perspective of emotion regulation and attachment. In M. W. Vasey & M. R. Dadds (eds), *The developmental psychopathology of anxiety* (pp. 160–182). London: Oxford University Press.

Thorpe, S. J., & Salkovskis, P. M. (1995). Phobic beliefs: do cognitive factors play a role in specific phobias? *Behaviour Research and Therapy, 33,* 805–816.

Thorpe, S. J., & Salkovskis, P. M. (1998). Studies on the role of disgust in the acquisition and maintenance of specific phobias. *Behaviour Research and Therapy, 36,* 877–893.

Thyer, B. A., Himle, J., Curtis, G. C., Cameron, O. G., & Nesse, R. M. (1985). A comparison of panic disorder and agoraphobia with panic attacks. *Comprehensive Psychiatry, 26,* 208–214.

Tillfors, M., Furmark, T., Ekselius, L., & Fredrickson, M. (2001). Social phobia and avoidant personality disorder as related to parental history of social anxiety: a general population study. *Behaviour Research and Therapy, 39,* 289–298.

Tolin, D. F., Abramowitz, J. S., Przeworski, A., & Foa, E. B. (2002). Thought suppression in obsessive–compulsive disorder. *Behaviour Research and Therapy, 40,* 1255–1274.

Tomarken, A. J., Mineka, S., & Cook, M. (1989). Fear-relevant selective associations and covariation bias. *Journal of Abnormal Psychology, 98*, 381–394.

Tomarken, A. J., Sutton, S. K., & Mineka, S. (1995). Fear-relevant illusory correlations: what types of associations promote judgmental bias? *Journal of Abnormal Psychology, 104*, 312–326.

Topolski, T. D., Hewitt, J. K., Eaves, L. J., Silberg, J. L., Meyer, J. M., Rutter, M. L., Pickles, A., & Simonoff, E. (1997). Genetic and environmental influences on child reports of manifest anxiety and symptoms of separation anxiety and overanxious disorders: a community-based twin study. *Behavior Genetics, 27*, 15–28.

Tracy, J. A., Ghose, S. S., Stecher, T., McFall, R. M., & Steinmetz, J. E. (1999). Classical conditioning in a nonclinical obsessive–compulsive population. *Psychological Science, 10*, 9–13.

Tran, G. Q., & Chambless, D. L. (1995). Psychopathology of social phobia: effects of subtype and of avoidant personality disorder. *Journal of Anxiety Disorders, 9*, 489–501.

Treisman, A., & Souther, J. (1985). Search asymmetry: a diagnostic for preattentive processing of separable features. *Journal of Experimental Psychology: General, 114*, 285–310.

Trinder, H., & Salkovskis, P. M. (1994). Personally relevant intrusions outside the laboratory: long-term suppression increases intrusion. *Behaviour Research and Therapy, 32*, 833–842.

Tronick, E. Z. (1989). Emotions and emotional communication in infants. *American Psychologist, 44*, 112–119.

Tronick, E. Z., & Cohn, J. F. (1989). Infant-mother face-to-face interaction: age and gender differences in coordination and the occurrence of miscoordination. *Child Development, 60*, 85–92.

Trower, P., Yardley, K., Bryant, B. M., & Shaw, P. (1978). The treatment of social failure: a comparison of anxiety-reduction and skills-acquisition procedures on two social problems. *Behavior Modification, 2*, 41–60.

True, W. R., Rice, J., Eisen, S. A., Heath, A. C., Goldberg, J., Lyons, M. J., & Nowak, J. (1993). A twin study of genetic and environmental contributions to liability for posttraumatic stress symptoms. *Archives of General Psychiatry, 50*, 257–264.

Trullas, R., & Skolnick, P. (1993). Differences in fear motivated behaviors among inbred mouse strains. *Psychopharmacology, 111*, 323–331.

Tsao, J. C. I., Glover, D. A., Bursch, B., Ifekwunigwe, M., & Zeltzer, L. K. (2002). Laboratory pain reactivity and gender: relationship to school nurse visits and school absences. *Journal of Developmental and Behavioral Pediatrics, 23*, 217–224.

Tucker, M., & Bond, N. W. (1997). The roles of gender, sex role, and disgust in fear of animals. *Personality and Individual Differences, 22*, 135–138.

Turner, S. M., Beidel, D. C., & Costello, A. (1987). Psychopathology in the offspring of anxiety disorders patients. *Journal of Consulting and Clinical Psychology, 55*, 229–235.

Turner, S. M., Beidel, D. C., & Wolff, P. L. (1996). Is behavioral inhibition related to the anxiety disorders? *Clinical Psychology Review, 16*, 157–172.

Tversky, A., & Kahneman, D. (1974). Judgment under uncertainty: heuristics and biases in judgments reveal some heuristics of thinking under uncertainty. *Science, 185*, 1124–1131.

Tyrer, P., Alexander, J., Remington, M., & Riley, P. (1987). Relationship between neurotic symptoms and neurotic diagnosis: a longitudinal study. *Journal of Affective Disorders, 13*, 13–21.

Uhlenhuth, E. H., & Paykel, E. S. (1973). Symptom configuration and life events. *Archives of General Psychiatry, 28*, 744–748.

Uno, T. (1970). The effects of awareness and successive inhibition on interoceptive and exteroceptive conditioning of the galvanic skin response. *Psychophysiology, 7*, 27–43.

Valentiner, D. P., Foa, E. B., Riggs, D. S., & Gershuny, B. S. (1996). Coping strategies and posttraumatic stress disorder in female victims of sexual and nonsexual assault. *Journal of Abnormal Psychology, 105*, 455–458.

Valleni-Basile, L. A., Garrison, C. Z., Waller, J. L., Addy, C. L., McKeown, R. E., Jackson, K. L., & Cuffs, S. P. (1996). Incidence of obsessive–compulsive disorder in a community sample of young adolescents. *Journal of the American Academy of Child and Adolescent Psychiatry, 35,* 898–906.

van Hout, W. J. P. J., & Emmelkamp, P. M. G. (1994). Overprediction of fear in panic disorder patients with agoraphobia: does the (mis)match model generalize to exposure *in vivo* therapy. *Behaviour Research and Therapy, 32,* 723–734.

van Os, J., & Jones, P. B. (1999). Early risk factors and adult person–environment relationships in affective disorder. *Psychological Medicine, 29,* 1055–1067.

Vasey, M. W., & Borkovec, T. D. (1992). A catastrophizing assessment of worrisome thoughts. *Cognitive Therapy and Research, 16,* 505–520.

Vasey, M. W., Deleiden, E., & Williams, L. L. (1992, November). Coping with worrisome thoughts: strategies of anxiety-disordered and normal children. Poster presented at the annual convention of the Association for the Advancement of Behavior Therapy, Boston.

Vasey, M. W., Daleiden, E. L., Williams, L. L., & Brown, L. M. (1995). Biased attention in childhood anxiety disorders: a preliminary study. *Journal of Abnormal Child Psychology, 23,* 267–279.

Vasey, M. W., El-Hag, N., & Daleiden, E. L. (1996). Anxiety and the processing of emotionally threatening stimuli: distinctive patterns of selective attention among high- and low-test-anxious children. *Child Development, 67,* 1173–1185.

Velez, C. N., Johnson, J., & Cohen, P. (1989). A longitudinal analysis of selected risk factors for childhood psychopathology. *Journal of the American Academy of Child and Adolescent Psychiatry, 28,* 861–864.

Veltman, D. J., van Zijderveld, G., Tilders, F. J. H., & van Dyck, R. (1996). Epinephrine and fear of bodily sensations in panic disorder and social phobia. *Journal of Psychopharmacology, 10,* 259–265.

Veltman, D. J., van Zijderveld, G. A., van Dyck, R., & Bakker, A. (1998). Predictability, controllability, and fear of symptoms of anxiety in epinephrine-induced panic. *Biological Psychiatry, 44,* 1017–1026.

Verburg, K., Griez, E., & Meijer, J. (1994). A 35% carbon dioxide challenge in simple phobias. *Acta Psychiatrica Scandinavica, 90,* 420–423.

Verburg, K., Griez, E., Meijer, J., & Pols, H. (1995). Respiratory disorders as a possible predisposing factor for disorder. *Journal of Affective Disorders, 33,* 129–134.

Vogel, J. M., & Vernberg, Eric M. (1993). Psychological responses of children to natural and human-made disasters: I. Children's psychological responses to disasters. *Journal of Clinical Child Psychology, 22,* 464–484.

Vrana, S. R., & Rollock, D. (2002). The role of ethnicity, gender, emotional content, and contextual differences in physiological, expressive, and self-reported emotional responses to imagery. *Cognition and Emotion, 16,* 165–192.

Vrana, S. R., Cuthbert, B. N., & Lang, P. J. (1986). Fear imagery and text processing. *Psychophysiology, 23,* 247–253.

Vrana, S. R., Cuthbert, B. N., & Lang, P. J. (1989). Processing fearful and neutral sentences: memory and heart rate change. *Cognition and Emotion, 3,* 179–195.

Warner, V., Mufson, L., & Weissman, M. M. (1995). Offspring at high and low risk for depression and anxiety: mechanisms of psychiatric disorder. *Journal of the American Academy of Child and Adolescent Psychiatry, 34,* 786–797.

Waters, A. M., Lipp, O. V., & Spence, S. H. (2003 in press). Differences in selective processing of emotional information: an investigation with adults and children and those with anxiety disorders.

Watkins, E., & Teasdale, J. D. (2001). Rumination and overgeneral memory in depression: effects of self-focus and analytic thinking. *Journal of Abnormal Psychology, 110*, 353–357.

Watson, D., & Clark, L. A. (1984). Negative affectivity: the disposition to experience aversive emotional states. *Psychological Bulletin, 96*, 465–490.

Watson, D., & Tellegen, A. (1985). Toward a consensual structure of mood. *Psychological Bulletin, 98*, 219–235.

Watson, D., Clark, L. A., & Carey, G. (1988). Positive and negative affectivity and their relation to anxiety and depressive disorders. *Journal of Abnormal Psychology, 97*, 346–353.

Watson, D., Clark, L. A., & Tellegen, A. (1988). Development and validation of brief measures of positive and negative affect: the PANAS scales. *Journal of Personality and Social Psychology, 54*, 1063–1070.

Watt, M. C., & Stewart, S. H. (2000). Anxiety sensitivity mediates the relationships between childhood learning experiences and elevated hypochondriacal concerns in young adulthood. *Journal of Psychosomatic Research, 49*, 107–118.

Watt, M. C., Stewart, S. H., & Cox, B. J. (1998). A retrospective study of the learning history origins of anxiety sensitivity. *Behaviour Research and Therapy, 36*, 505–525.

Watts, F. N., & Dalgleish, T. (1991). Memory for phobia-related words in spider phobics. *Cognition and Emotion, 5*, 313–329.

Watts, F. N., Trezise, L., & Sharrock, R. (1986). Processing of phobic stimuli. *British Journal of Clinical Psychology, 25*, 253–259.

Webb, K., & Davey, G. C. L. (1992). Disgust sensitivity and fear of animals: effect of exposure to violent of repulsive material. *Anxiety, Stress and Coping: An International Journal, 5*, 329–335.

Weems, C. F., Hayward, C., Killen, J., & Taylor, C. B. (2002). A longitudinal investigation of anxiety sensitivity in adolescence. *Journal of Abnormal Psychology, 111*, 471–477.

Wegner, D. M., & Guiliano, T. (1980). Arousal-induced attention to self. *Journal of Personality and Social Psychology, 38*, 719–726.

Wegner, D. M., & Zanakos, S. (1994). Chronic thought suppression. *Journal of Personality, 62*, 615–640.

Wegner, D. M., & Smart, L. (1997). Deep cognitive activation: a new approach to the unconscious. *Journal of Consulting and Clinical Psychology, 65*, 984–995.

Weinberg, J., & Levine, S. (1980). Psychobiology of coping in animals: the effect of predictability. In S. Levine & H. Ursin (eds), *Coping and health* (pp. 39–59). New York, NY: Plenum Press.

Weinberg, M. K., Tronick, E. Z., Cohn, J. F., & Olson, K. L. (1999). Gender differences in emotional expressivity and self-regulation during early infancy. *Developmental Psychology, 35*, 175–188.

Weiss, D. D., & Last, C. G. (2001). Developmental variations in the prevalence and manifestations of anxiety disorders. In M. W. Vasey & M. R. Dadds (eds), *The developmental psychopathology of anxiety* (pp. 27–42). New York, NY: Oxford University Press.

Weiss, J. M. (1970). Somatic effects of predictable and unpredictable shock. *Psychosomatic Medicine, 32*, 397–408.

Weiss, J. M. (1971a). Effects of coping behavior in different warning signal conditions on stress pathology in rats. *Journal of Comparative and Physiological Psychology, 77*, 1–13.

Weiss, J. M. (1971b). Effects of punishing the coping response (conflict) on stress pathology in rats. *Journal of Comparative and Physiological Psychology, 77*, 14–21.

Weiss, J. M. (1971c). Effects of coping behavior with and without feedback signal on stress pathology in the rat. *Journal of Comparative and Physiological Psychology, 77*, 22–30.

Weissman, M. M., & Merikangas, K. R. (1986). The epidemiology of anxiety and panic disorders: an update. *Journal of Clinical Psychiatry, 47*, 11–17.

Weissman, M. M., Wickramaratne, P., Warner, V., John, K., Prusoff, B. A., Merikangas, K. R., & Gammon, D. (1987). Assessing psychiatric disorders in children: discrepancies between mothers' and children's reports. *Archives of General Psychiatry, 44*, 747–753.

Weissman, M. M., Bland, R., Canino, G., Greenwald, S., Hwu, H., Lee, C. K., Newman, S., Oakley-Browne, M. A., Rubio-Stipec, M., Wickramaratne, P., Wittchen, H., & Yeh, E. (1994). The cross national epidemiology of obsessive compulsive disorder: the Cross National Collaborative Group. *Journal of Clinical Psychiatry, 55*(suppl. 3), 5–10.

Wells, A. (1994). Attention and the control of worry, In G. C. L. Davey & F. Tallis (eds), *Worrying: perspectives on theory, assessment and treatment* (pp. 91–114). Chichester: Wiley.

Wells, A. (1995). Meta-cognition and worry: a cognitive model of generalized anxiety disorder. *Behavioural and Cognitive Psychotherapy, 23*, 301–320.

Wells, A. (1997). *Cognitive therapy of anxiety disorders: a practice manual and conceptual guide.* New York, NY: Wiley.

Wells, A., & Matthews, G. (1994). *Attention and emotion: a clinical perspective.* Hove: Lawrence Erlbaum.

Wells, A., & Morrison, A. P. (1994). Qualitative dimensions of worry and normal obsessions: a comparative study. *Behaviour Research and Therapy, 32*, 867–870.

Wells, A., & Papageorgiou, C. (1995). Worry and the incubation of intrusive images following stress. *Behaviour Research and Therapy, 33*, 579–583.

Wells, A., & Clark, D. M. (1997). Social phobia: a cognitive approach. In G. C. L. Davey (ed.), *Phobias — a handbook of theory, research and treatment* (pp. 3–26). New York, NY: Wiley.

Wells, A., & Papageorgiou, C. (1998). Social phobia: effects of external attention on anxiety, negative beliefs, and perspective taking. *Behavior Therapy, 29*, 357–370.

Wells, A., & Carter, K. (1999). Preliminary test of a cognitive model of generalized anxiety disorder. *Behaviour Research and Therapy, 37*, 585–594.

Wells, A., & Papageorgiou, C. (1999). The observer perspective: biased imagery in social phobia, agoraphobia, and blood/injury phobia. *Behaviour Research and Therapy, 37*, 653–658.

Wells, A., & Carter, K. (2001). Further tests of cognitive model of generalized anxiety disorder: metacognitions and worry in GAD, panic disorder, social phobia, depression, and nonpatients. *Behavior Therapy, 32*, 85–102.

Wells, A., Clark, D. M., & Ahmad, S. (1998). How do I look with my minds eye: perspective taking in social phobic imagery. *Behaviour Research and Therapy, 36*, 631–634.

Wenzlaff, R. M., & Wegner, D. M. (2000). Thought suppression. *Annual Review of Pscyhology, 51*, 59–91.

Werry, J. S. (1991). Overanxious disorder: a review of its taxonomic properties. *Journal of the American Academy of Child and Adolescent Psychiatry, 30*, 533–544.

Westermeyer, J., Tucker, P., & Nugent, S. (1995). Comorbid anxiety disorder among patients with substance abuse disorders. *American Journal on Addictions, 4*, 97–106.

Wethington, E., McLeod, J., & Kessler, R. C. (1987). The importance of life events for explaining sex differences in psychological distress. In R. C. Barnett & L. Biener (eds), *Gender and stress* (pp. 144–154). New York, NY: Free Press.

Whalen, P. J., Rauch, S. L., Etcoff, N. L., McInerney, S. C., Lee, M. B., & Jenike, M. A. (1998). Masked presentations of emotional facial expressions modulate amygdala activity without explicit knowledge. *Journal of Neuroscience, 18*, 411–418.

Whaley, S. E., Pinto, A., & Sigman, M. (1999). Characterizing interactions between anxious mothers and their children. *Journal of Consulting and Clinical Psychology, 67*, 826–836.

White, M. (1995). Preattentive analysis of facial expressions of emotion. *Cognitive and Emotion, 9*, 439–460.

Wieland, S., Boren, J. L., Consroe, P. F., & Martin, A. (1986). Stock differences in the susceptibility of rats to learned helplessness training. *Life Sciences*, *39*, 937–944.

Wigglesworth, M. J., & Smith, B. D. (1976). Habituation and dishabituation of the electrodermal orienting reflex in relation to extraversion and neuroticism. *Journal of Research in Personality*, *10*, 437–445.

Wilhelm, S., McNally, R. J., Baer, L., & Florin, I. (1996). Directed forgetting in obsessive–compulsive disorder. *Behaviour Research and Therapy*, *34*, 633–641.

Williams, J. M. G., Watts, F. N., Macleod, C., & Mathews, A. (1988). *Cognitive psychology and emotional disorders*. Oxford: Wiley.

Williams, S. L. (1992). Perceived self-efficacy and phobic disability. In R. Schwarzer (ed.), *Self-efficacy: thought control of action* (pp. 149–176). Washington, DC: Hemisphere.

Williams, S. L., & Rappoport, A. (1983). Cognitive treatment in the natural environment for agoraphobia. *Behavior Therapy*, *14*, 299–313.

Williams, S. L., & Watson, N. (1985). Perceived danger and perceived self-efficacy as cognitive determinants of acrophobic behavior. *Behavior Therapy*, *16*, 136–146.

Williams, S. L., Dooseman, G., & Kleifield, E. (1984). Comparative effectiveness of guided mastery and exposure treatments for intractable phobics. *Journal of Consulting and Clinical Psychology*, *52*, 505–518.

Williams, S. L., Turner, S. M., & Peer, D. F. (1985). Guided mastery and performance desensitization treatments for severe acrophobia. *Journal of Consulting and Clinical Psychology*, *53*, 237–247.

Williams, S. L., Kinney, P. J., & Farbo, J. (1989). Generalization of therapeutic changes in agoraphobia: the role of perceived self-efficacy. *Journal of Consulting and Clinical Psychology*, *57*, 436–442.

Williams, S. L., Kinney, P. J., Harap, S. T., & Liebmann, M. (1997). Thoughts of agoraphobic people during scary tasks. *Journal of Abnormal Psychology*, *106*, 511–520.

Wilson, B. J., & Gottman, J. M. (1996). Attention — the shuttle between emotion and cognition: risk, resiliency, and physiological bases. In E. M. Hetherington & E. A. Blechman (eds), *Stress, coping, and resiliency in children and families* (pp. 189–228) Hillsdale, NJ: Lawrence Erlbaum.

Wilson, G. D., Kumari, V., Gray, J. A., & Corr, P. J. (2000). The role of neuroticism in startle reactions to fearful and disgusting stimuli. *Personality and Individual Differences*, *29*, 1077–1082.

Wittchen, H. U. (1988). Natural course and spontaneous remissions of untreated anxiety disorder: results of the Munich Follow-up Study (MFS). In H. Hand & H. Wittchen (eds), *Panic and phobias: treatments and variables affecting course and outcome* (pp. 3–17). Berlin: Springer-Verlag.

Wong, P. S., Shevrin, H., & Williams, W. J. (1994). Conscious and nonconscious processes: an ERP index of an anticipatory response in a conditioning paradigm using visually masked stimuli. *Psychophysiology*, *31*, 87–101.

Wood, J. V., Saltzberg, J. A., & Goldsamt, L. A. (1990). Does affect induce self-focused attention? *Journal of Personality and Social Psychology*, *58*, 899–908.

Wood, W., & Eagly, A. H. (2002). A cross-cultural analysis of the behavior of women and men: implications for the origins of sex differences. *Psychological Bulletin*, *128*, 699–727.

Woodruff-Borden, J., Brothers, A. J., & Lister, S. C. (2001). Self-focused attention: commonalities across psychopathologies and predictors. *Behavioural and Cognitive Psychotherapy*, *29*, 169–178.

Woodward, S. A., McManis, M. H., Kagan, J., Deldin, P., Snidman, N., Lewis, M., & Kahn, V. (2001). Infant temperament and the brainstem auditory evoked response in later childhood. *Developmental Psychology*, *37*, 533–538.

Woody, S. R. (1996). Effects of attention on anxiety levels on social performance of individuals with social phobia. *Journal of Abnormal Psychology*, *105*, 61–69.

Yarrow, L. J., MacTurk, R. H., Vietze, P. M., McCarthy, M. E., Klein, R. P., & McQuiston, S. (1984). Developmental course of parental stimulation and its relationship to mastery motivation during infancy. *Developmental Psychology, 20*, 492–503.

Yehuda, R. (1999). Parental PTSD as a risk factor for PTSD. In R. Yehuda (ed), *Risk factors for posttraumatic stress disorder*. Washington, DC: American Psychiatric Association.

Yehuda, R. (2001). Biology of posttraumatic stress disorder. *Journal of Clinical Psychiatry. Special Issue: Understanding Posttraumatic Stress Disorder, 62*, 41–46.

Yehuda, R., Southwick, S. M., Giller, E. L., Ma, X., & Mason, J. W. (1992). Urinary catecholamine excretion and severity of PTSD symptoms in Vietnam combat veterans. *Journal of Nervous and Mental Disease, 180*, 321–325.

Yehuda, R., Kahana, B., Binder-Brynes, K., Southwick, S., Zemelman, S., Mason, M., & Giller, E. L. (1995a). Low urinary cortisol excretion in Holocaust survivors with posttraumatic stress disorder. *American Journal of Psychiatry, 152*, 7.

Yehuda, R., Boisoneau, D., Lowy, M. T., & Giller, E. L. (1995b). Dose–response changes in plasma cortisol and lymphocyte glucocorticoid receptors following dexamethasone administration in combat veterans with and without posttraumatic stress disorder. *Archives of General Psychiatry, 52*, 583–593.

Yeragani, V. K., Balon, R., Pohl, R., Ramesh, C., Glitz, D., Weinberg, P., & Merlos, B. (1990). Decreased R-R variance in panic disorder patients. *Acta Psychiatrica Scandinavica, 81*, 554–559.

Yeragani, V. K., Sobolewski, E., Igel, G., Johnson, C., Jampala, V. C., Kay, J., Hillman, N., Yeragani, S., & Vempati, S. (1998). Decreased heart-period variability in patients with panic disorder: a study of Holter ECG records. *Psychiatry Research, 78*, 89–99.

Yonkers, K. A., Warshaw, M. G., Massion, A. O., & Keller, M. B. (1996). Phenomenology and course of generalized anxiety disorder. *British Journal of Psychiatry, 168*, 308–313.

Yonkers, K. A., Zlotnick, C., Allsworth, J., Warshaw, M., Shea, T., & Keller, M. B. (1998). Is the course of panic disorder the same in women and men? *American Journal of Psychiatry, 155*, 596–602.

Yonkers, K. A., Dyck, I. R., & Keller, M. B. (2001). An eight-year longitudinal comparison of clinical course and characteristics of social phobia among men and women. *Psychiatric Services, 52*, 637–643.

Yovel, I., & Mineka, S. (2000, November). *Levels of awareness in the emotional Stroop: the hierarchical model perspective*. Poster presented at the annual meeting of Society for Research in Psychopathology. Boulder, CO.

Zahn-Waxler, C., Robinson, J. L., & Emde, R. N. (1992). The development of empathy in twins. *Developmental Psychology, 28*, 1038–1047.

Zahn, T. P., Leonard, H. L., Swedo, S. E., & Rapoport, J. L. (1996). Autonomic activity in children and adolescents with obsessive–compulsive disorder. *Psychiatry Research, 60*, 67–76.

Zarate, R., Rapee, R. M., Craske, M. G., & Barlow, D. H. (1988, November). *Response-norms for symptom induction procedures*. Poster presented at the annual convention of the Association for the Advancement of Behavior Therapy, New York, NY.

Zinbarg, R. E. (1998). Concordance and synchrony in measures of anxiety and panic reconsidered: a hierarchical model of anxiety and panic. *Behavior Therapy, 29*, 301–323.

Zinbarg, R. E., & Barlow, D. H. (1996). Structure of anxiety and the anxiety disorders: a hierarchical model. *Journal of Abnormal Psychology, 105*, 184–193.

Zinbarg, R. E., & Mohlman, J. (1998). Individual differences in the acquisition of affectively valenced associations. *Journal of Personality and Social Psychology, 74*, 1024–1040.

Zinbarg, R., Barlow, D. H., & Brown, T. (1997). The hierarchical structure and general factor saturation of the Anxiety Sensitivity Index: evidence and implications. *Psychological Assessment, 9*, 277–284.

Zinbarg, R., Mohlman, J., & Hong, N. (1999). Dimensions of anxiety sensitivity. In S. Taylor (ed.), *Anxiety sensitivity: theory, research, and treatment of the fear of anxiety.* Hillsdale, NJ: Lawrence Erlbaum.

Zoellner, L. A., & Craske, M. G. (1999). Interoceptive accuracy and panic. *Behaviour Research and Therapy, 37,* 1141–1158.

Zucker, B. G., Craske, M. G., Barrios, V., & Holguin, M. (2002). Thought action fusion: can it be corrected? *Behaviour Research and Therapy,* 40, 652–664.

Zvolensy, M. J., Eifert, G. H., Lejuez, C. W., & McNeil, D. W. (1999). The effects of offset control over 205 carbon-dioxide-enriched air on anxious responding. *Journal of Abnormal Psychology, 108,* 624–632.

Author Index

Plomin, R. 37
Plotkin, D. 37, 49, 88, 121
Plotsky, P. M. 47
Podd, J. V. 100
Pohl, R. 25, 55, 86, 169
Polan, J. J. 87
Polazzi, L. 55, 183
Pollack, M. H. 85
Pollard, C. A. 13, 96
Pollard, H. J. 13, 96
Pols, H. 121
Pomerantz, E. M. 184
Pontillo, D. 29
Porat, A. 143
Porges, S. W. 53, 54, 176
Posner, M. I. 73
Poulton, R. 6, 14, 37, 49, 88, 100, 114, 121
Power, M. J. 51, 191
Powers, J. L. 179
Powers, M. 29
Powys, M. 74, 163
Pratt, L. A. 11
Prescott, C. A.42, 43, 44, 179
Prior, M. 176
Prunty, M. J. 71
Prusoff, B. A. 15
Przeworski, A. 149
Ptacek, J. T. 197
Pugh, K. R. 192
Puigcerver, A. 131
Purdon, C. 144, 152, 153
Pury, C. L. S. 78, 81, 108
Puthezhath, N. 87
Pynoos, R. 13

Quas, J. A. 55, 186
Quinlan, R. J. 194

Rabavilas, A. D. 147
Rabian, B. 4
Rachman, S. 11, 64, 93, 94, 99, 100, 106, 107,
    110, 111, 112, 126, 144, 145, 146, 147,
    148, 150, 151, 152, 153, 154, 155, 156, 157
Rachman, S. J. 93, 110, 111, 112
Racine, Y. A. 6, 7, 12, 15
Radomsky, A. S. 148
Rae, D. S. 9, 12, 13, 123
Rae Grant, N. I. 14
Raine, A. 90, 91

Ralphe, D. L. 139
Ramesh, C. 25, 55, 86, 169
Rapee, R. 127
Rapee, R. M. 13, 25, 43, 61, 62, 64, 65, 82, 85,
    92, 96, 101, 106, 109, 120, 121, 127, 129,
    133, 134, 164, 168, 186, 188, 196
Rapoport, J. 150
Rapoport, J. L. 4, 7, 11, 148, 151
Rapoport, S. I. 149
Rappoport, A. 160
Rappoport, J. L. 149
Rashes, R. 104, 105
Raskin, D. C. 195
Rassin, E. 146
Rauch, S. L. 28, 148, 149
Rauste-Von Wright, M. 195
Ravenscroft, H. 85
Rawlinson, H. 74, 163
Ray, J. C. 88
Razran, G. 110, 123
Rechlin, T. 26, 169
Reddy, V. 57
Redfern, M. S. 122
Reed, M. A. 52, 71, 72, 74, 77
Reese, L. 160
Regier, D. A. 123
Reich, J. 16, 129
Reichman, J. T. 16, 17, 122
Reiss, S. 93, 119, 120
Remington, M. 8, 93
Rescorla, R. A. 63, 106, 110
Resick, P. A. 138, 142
Resnick, H. S. 136
Rettew, D. C. 7, 149
Reynolds, C. A. 46
Reynolds, C. R. 13
Reynolds, M. 151
Reznick, J. S. 10, 38, 39, 40, 42, 49, 90, 176,
    177
Reznick, S. 39, 40
Reznick, S. J. 39, 40
Rheaume, J. 25, 94, 95, 145, 146, 165, 170
Rhee, S. H. 178, 179
Ricciardi, J. N. 153
Rice, J. 137
Richards, A. 78, 82, 85, 134, 163
Richards, C. 8
Richards, J. C. 148
Richmond, B. O. 13

Subject Index

uncontrollability 128
unpredictability, consequences of 68, 128

vagal tone, cardiac
    emotion distress and 54–6, 68, 91–2, 97
    worry and 168–9
verbal recognition of conditioned–
        unconditioned stimulus 54–5
vestibular dysfunction 122
vicarious observation 100–1
vigilance avoidance 73, 207

worry 11
    autonomic symptoms 25, 168, 169–70, 205

avoidance 168
chronic 167–8
sex differences 13, 188–9, 201
personal incompetence and 165–6
reasoning and 168
responses and function 24–6
as a verbal state 25, 168
about worry 163–5

youth anxiety disorders
    continuity of anxiety disorders 6–8
    diagnostic issues 3–5
    impact 8–9
    prevalence and co-occurring distress 5–6